University of Wyoming

# ES 1060

Introduction to Engineering

Problem Solving

**Pearson Custom Publishing**

New York   Boston   San Francisco
London   Toronto   Sydney   Tokyo   Singapore   Madrid
Mexico City   Munich   Paris   Cape Town   Hong Kong   Montreal

**Pearson Prentice Hall**

*Editorial Director, ECS:* Marcia J. Horton
*Senior Editor:* Holly Stark
*Associate Editor:* Dee Bernhard
*Senior Marketing Manager:* Tim Galligan
*Managing Editor:* Scott Disanno
*Art Director:* Greg Dulles
*Manufacturing Buyer:* Lisa McDowell

**Pearson Custom Publishing**

*Senior Vice President, Editorial and Marketing:* Patrick F. Boles
*Executive Marketing Manager:* Nathan L. Wilbur
*Sponsoring Editor:* Debbie Coniglio
*Operations Manager:* Eric M. Kenney
*Development Editor:* Amy Galvin
*Database Product Manager:* Jennifer Berry

This special edition published in cooperation with Pearson Custom Publishing.

Printed in the United States of America.

Please visit our web site at *www.prenhall.com/esource*

Attention bookstores: For permission to return any unsold stock, contact us at *pe-uscustomreturns@pearson.com*.

**Pearson**
**Custom Publishing**
is a division of

www.pearsonhighered.com

ISBN 10: 0558271200
ISBN 13: 9780558271206

# About ESource

### ESource—The Prentice Hall Engineering Source—
### www.prenhall.com/esource

ESource—The Prentice Hall Engineering Source gives professors the power to harness the full potential of their text and their first-year engineering course. More than just a collection of books, ESource is a unique publishing system revolving around the ESource website—www.prenhall.com/esource. ESource enables you to put your stamp on your book just as you do your course. It lets you:

*Control*    You choose exactly what chapters are in your book and in what order they appear. Of course, you can choose the entire book if you'd like and stay with the authors' original order.

*Optimize*    Get the most from your book and your course. ESource lets you produce the optimal text for your students needs.

*Customize*    You can add your own material anywhere in your text's presentation, and your final product will arrive at your bookstore as a professionally formatted text. Of course, all titles in this series are available as stand-alone texts, or as bundles of two or more books sold at a discount. Contact your PH sales rep for discount information.

### ESource ACCESS

Professors who choose to bundle two or more texts from the ESource series for their class, or use an ESource custom book will be providing their students with an on-line library of intro engineering content—ESource Access. We've designed ESource ACCESS to provide students a flexible, searchable, on-line resource. Free access codes come in bundles and custom books are valid for one year after initial log-on. Contact your PH sales rep for more information.

### ESource Content

All the content in ESource was written by educators specifically for freshman/first-year students. Authors tried to strike a balanced level of presentation, an approach that was neither formulaic nor trivial, and one that did not focus too heavily on advanced topics that most introductory students do not encounter until later classes. Because many professors do not have extensive time to cover these topics in the classroom, authors prepared each text with the idea that many students would use it for self-instruction and independent study. Students should be able to use this content to learn the software tool or subject on their own.

While authors had the freedom to write texts in a style appropriate to their particular subject, all followed certain guidelines created to promote a consistency that makes students comfortable. Namely, every chapter opens with a clear set of **Objectives**, includes **Practice Boxes** throughout the chapter, and ends with a number of **Problems**, and a list of **Key Terms**. **Applications Boxes** are spread throughout the book with the intent of giving students a real-world perspective of engineering. **Success Boxes** provide the student with advice about college study skills, and help students avoid the common pitfalls of first-year students. In addition, this series contains an entire book titled ***Engineering Success*** by Peter Schiavone of the University of Alberta intended to expose students quickly to what it takes to be an engineering student.

### Creating Your Book

Using ESource is simple. You preview the content either on-line or through examination copies of the books you can request on-line, from your PH sales rep, or by calling 1-800-526-0485. Create an on-line outline of the content you want, in the order you want, using ESource's simple interface. Insert your own material into the text flow. If you are not ready to order, ESource will save your work. You can come back at any time and change, re-arrange, or add more material to your creation. Once you're finished you'll automatically receive an ISBN. Give it to your bookstore and your book will arrive on their shelves four to six weeks after they order. Your custom desk copies with their instructor supplements will arrive at your address at the same time.

To learn more about this new system for creating the perfect textbook, go to www.prenhall.com/esource. You can either go through the on-line walkthrough of how to create a book, or experiment yourself.

### Supplements

Adopters of ESource receive an instructor's CD that contains professor and student code from the books in the series, as well as other instruction aides provided by authors. The website also holds approximately **350 PowerPoint transparencies** created by Jack Leifer of University of Kentucky–Paducah. Professors can either follow these transparencies as pre-prepared lectures or use them as the basis for their own custom presentations.

http://www.prenhall.com/esource

# Titles in the ESource Series

**Design Concepts for Engineers, 2/e**
*0-13-093430-5*
*Mark Horenstein*

**Engineering Success, 2/e**
*0-13-041827-7*
*Peter Schiavone*

**Engineering Design and Problem Solving, 2E**
*ISBN 0-13-093399-6*
*Steven K. Howell*

**Exploring Engineering**
*ISBN 0-13-093442-9*
*Joe King*

**Engineering Ethics**
*0-13-784224-4*
*Charles B. Fleddermann*

**Introduction to Engineering Analysis**
*0-13-016733-9*
*Kirk D. Hagen*

**Introduction to Engineering Experimentation**
*0-13-032835-9*
*Ronald W. Larsen, John T. Sears, and Royce Wilkinson*

**Introduction to Mechanical Engineering**
*0-13-019640-1*
*Robert Rizza*

**Introduction to Electrical and Computer Engineering**
*0-13-033363-8*
*Charles B. Fleddermann and Martin Bradshaw*

**Introduction to MATLAB 6—Update**
*0-13-140918-2*
*Delores Etter and David C. Kuncicky, with Douglas W. Hull*

**MATLAB Programming**
*0-13-035127-X*
*David C. Kuncicky*

**Introduction to MATLAB**
*0-13-013149-0*
*Delores Etter with David C. Kuncicky*

**Introduction to Mathcad 2000**
*0-13-020007-7*
*Ronald W. Larsen*

**Introduction to Mathcad 11**
*0-13-008177-9*
*David W. Larsen*

**Introduction to Maple 8**
*0-13-032844-8*
*David I. Schwartz*

**Mathematics Review**
*0-13-011501-0*
*Peter Schiavone*

**Power Programming with VBA/Excel**
*0-13-047377-4*
*Steven C. Chapra*

**Introduction to Excel 2002**
*0-13-008175-2*
*David C. Kuncicky*

http://www.prenhall.com/esource

# About the Authors

No project could ever come to pass without a group of authors who have the vision and the courage to turn a stack of blank paper into a book. The authors in this series, who worked diligently to produce their books, provide the building blocks of the series.

**Martin D. Bradshaw** was born in Pittsburg, KS in 1936, grew up in Kansas and the surrounding states of Arkansas and Missouri, graduating from Newton High School, Newton, KS in 1954. He received the B.S.E.E. and M.S.E.E. degrees from the University of Wichita in 1958 and 1961, respectively. A Ford Foundation fellowship at Carnegie Institute of Technology followed from 1961 to 1963 and he received the Ph.D. degree in electrical engineering in 1964. He spent his entire academic career with the Department of Electrical and Computer Engineering at the University of New Mexico (1961-1963 and 1991-1996). He served as the Assistant Dean for Special Programs with the UNM College of Engineering from 1974 to 1976 and as the Associate Chairman for the EECE Department from 1993 to 1996. During the period 1987-1991 he was a consultant with his own company, EE Problem Solvers. During 1978 he spent a sabbatical year with the State Electricity Commission of Victoria, Melbourne, Australia. From 1979 to 1981 he served an IPA assignment as a Project Officer at the U.S. Air Force Weapons Laboratory, Kirkland AFB, Albuquerque, NM. He has won numerous local, regional, and national teaching awards, including the George Westinghouse Award from the ASEE in 1973. He was awarded the IEEE Centennial Medal in 2000.

*Acknowledgments:* Dr. Bradshaw would like to acknowledge his late mother, who gave him a great love of reading and learning, and his father, who taught him to persist until the job is finished. The encouragement of his wife, Jo, and his six children is a never-ending inspiration.

**Stephen J. Chapman** received a B.S. degree in Electrical Engineering from Louisiana State University (1975), the M.S.E. degree in Electrical Engineering from the University of Central Florida (1979), and pursued further graduate studies at Rice University.

Mr. Chapman is currently Manager of Technical Systems for British Aerospace Australia, in Melbourne, Australia. In this position, he provides technical direction and design authority for the work of younger engineers within the company. He also continues to teach at local universities on a part-time basis.

Mr. Chapman is a Senior Member of the Institute of Electrical and Electronics Engineers (and several of its component societies). He is also a member of the Association for Computing Machinery and the Institution of Engineers (Australia).

**Steven C. Chapra** presently holds the Louis Berger Chair for Computing and Engineering in the Civil and Environmental Engineering Department at Tufts University. Dr. Chapra received engineering degrees from Manhattan College and the University of Michigan. Before joining the faculty at Tufts, he taught at Texas A&M University, the University of Colorado, and Imperial College, London. His research interests focus on surface water-quality modeling and advanced computer applications in environmental engineering. He has published over 50 refereed journal articles, 20 software packages and 6 books. He has received a number of awards including the 1987 ASEE Merriam/Wiley Distinguished Author Award, the 1993 Rudolph Hering Medal, and teaching awards from Texas A&M, the University of Colorado, and the Association of Environmental Engineering and Science Professors.

*Acknowledgments:* To the Berger Family for their many contributions to engineering education. I would also like to thank David Clough for his friendship and insights, John Walkenbach for his wonderful books, and my colleague Lee Minardi and my students Kenny William, Robert Viesca and Jennifer Edelmann for their suggestions.

**Mark Dix** began working with AutoCAD in 1985 as a programmer for CAD Support Associates, Inc. He helped design a system for creating estimates and bills of material directly from AutoCAD drawing databases for use in the automated conveyor industry. This system became the basis for systems still widely in use today. In 1986 he began collaborating with Paul Riley to create AutoCAD training materials, combining Riley's background in industrial design and training with Dix's background in writing, curriculum development, and programming. Mr. Dix received the M.S. degree in education from the University of Massachusetts. He is currently the Director of Dearborn Academy High School in Arlington, Massachusetts.

**Delores M. Etter** is a Professor of Electrical and Computer Engineering at the University of Colorado. Dr. Etter was a faculty member at the University of New Mexico and also a Visiting Professor at Stanford University. Dr. Etter was responsible for the Freshman Engineering Program at the University of New Mexico and is active in the Integrated Teaching Laboratory at the University of Colorado. She was elected a Fellow of the Institute of Electrical and Electronics Engineers for her contributions to education and for her technical leadership in digital signal processing.

**Charles B. Fleddermann** is a professor in the Department of Electrical and Computer Engineering at the University of New Mexico in Albuquerque, New Mexico. All of his degrees are in electrical engineering: his Bachelor's degree from the University of Notre Dame, and the Master's and Ph.D. from the University of Illinois at Urbana-Champaign. Prof. Fleddermann developed an engineering ethics course for his department in response to the ABET requirement to incorporate ethics topics into the undergraduate engineering curriculum. *Engineering Ethics* was written as a vehicle for presenting ethical

theory, analysis, and problem solving to engineering undergraduates in a concise and readily accessible way.

*Acknowledgments:* I would like to thank Profs. Charles Harris and Michael Rabins of Texas A & M University whose NSF sponsored workshops on engineering ethics got me started thinking in this field. Special thanks to my wife Liz, who proofread the manuscript for this book, provided many useful suggestions, and who helped me learn how to teach "soft" topics to engineers.

**Kirk D. Hagen** is a professor at Weber State University in Ogden, Utah. He has taught introductory-level engineering courses and upper-division thermal science courses at WSU since 1993. He received his B.S. degree in physics from Weber State College and his M.S. degree in mechanical engineering from Utah State University, after which he worked as a thermal designer/analyst in the aerospace and electronics industries. After several years of engineering practice, he resumed his formal education, earning his Ph.D. in mechanical engineering at the University of Utah. Hagen is the author of an undergraduate heat transfer text.

**Mark N. Horenstein** is a Professor in the Department of Electrical and Computer Engineering at Boston University. He has degrees in Electrical Engineering from M.I.T. and U.C. Berkeley and has been involved in teaching engineering design for the greater part of his academic career. He devised and developed the senior design project class taken by all electrical and computer engineering students at Boston University. In this class, the students work for a virtual engineering company developing products and systems for real-world engineering and social-service clients.

*Acknowledgments:* I would like to thank Prof. James Bethune, the architect of the Peak Performance event at Boston University, for his permission to highlight the competition in my text. Several of the ideas relating to brainstorming and teamwork were derived from a

http://www.prenhall.com/esource

workshop on engineering design offered by Prof. Charles Lovas of Southern Methodist University. The principles of estimation were derived in part from a freshman engineering problem posed by Prof. Thomas Kincaid of Boston University.

**Steven Howell** is the Chairman and a Professor of Mechanical Engineering at Lawrence Technological University. Prior to joining LTU in 2001, Dr. Howell led a knowledge-based engineering project for Visteon Automotive Systems and taught computer-aided design classes for Ford Motor Company engineers. Dr. Howell also has a total of 15 years experience as an engineering faculty member at Northern Arizona University, the University of the Pacific, and the University of Zimbabwe. While at Northern Arizona University, he helped develop and implement an award-winning interdisciplinary series of design courses simulating a corporate engineering-design environment.

**Douglas W. Hull** is a graduate student in the Department of Mechanical Engineering at Carnegie Mellon University in Pittsburgh, Pennsylvania. He is the author of *Mastering Mechanics I Using Matlab 5*, and contributed to *Mechanics of Materials* by Bedford and Liechti. His research in the Sensor Based Planning lab involves motion planning for hyper-redundant manipulators, also known as serpentine robots.

**Scott D. James** is a staff lecturer at Kettering University (formerly GMI Engineering & Management Institute) in Flint, Michigan. He is currently pursuing a Ph.D. in Systems Engineering with an emphasis on software engineering and computer-integrated manufacturing. He chose teaching as a profession after several years in the computer industry. "I thought that it was really important to know what it was like outside of academia. I wanted to provide students with classes that  were up to date and provide the information that is really used and needed."

*Acknowledgments:* Scott would like to acknowledge his family for the time to work on the text and his students and peers at Kettering who offered helpful critiques of the materials that eventually became the book.

**Joe King** received the B.S. and M.S. degrees from the University of California at Davis. He is a Professor of Computer Engineering at the University of the Pacific, Stockton, CA, where he teaches courses in digital design, computer design, artificial intelligence, and computer networking. Since joining the UOP faculty, Professor King has spent yearlong sabbaticals teaching in Zimbabwe, Singapore, and Finland. A licensed engineer in the state of California, King's industrial experience includes major design projects with Lawrence Livermore National Laboratory, as well as independent consulting projects. Prof. King has had a number of books published with titles including MATLAB, MathCAD, Exploring Engineering, and Engineering and Society.

**David C. Kuncicky** is a native Floridian. He earned his Baccalaureate in psychology, Master's in computer science, and Ph.D. in computer science from Florida State University. He has served as a faculty member in the Department of Electrical Engineering at the FAMU–FSU College of Engineering and the Department of Computer Science at Florida State University. He has taught computer science and computer engineering courses for over 15 years. He has published research in the areas of intelligent hybrid systems and neural networks. He is currently the Director of Engineering at Bioreason, Inc. in Sante Fe, New Mexico.

*Acknowledgments:* Thanks to Steffie and Helen for putting up with my late nights and long weekends at the computer. Finally, thanks to Susan Bassett for having faith in my abilities, and for providing continued tutelage and support.

**Ron Larsen** is a Professor of Chemical Engineering at Montana State University, and received his Ph.D. from the Pennsylvania State University. He was initially attracted to engineering by the challenges the profession offers, but also appreciates that engineering is a serving profession. Some of the greatest challenges he has faced while teaching have involved non-traditional teaching methods, including evening courses for practicing engineers and teaching through an interpreter at the Mongolian National University. These experiences have provided tremendous opportunities to learn new ways to communicate technical material. Dr. Larsen views modern software as one of the new tools that will radically alter the way engineers work, and his book *Introduction to Math-CAD* was written to help young engineers prepare to meet the challenges of an ever-changing workplace.

Acknowledgments: To my students at Montana State University who have endured the rough drafts and typos, and who still allow me to experiment with their classes—my sincere thanks.

**Sanford Leestma** is a Professor of Mathematics and Computer Science at Calvin College, and received his Ph.D. from New Mexico State University. He has been the long-time co-author of successful textbooks on Fortran, Pascal, and data structures in Pascal. His current research interest are in the areas of algorithms and numerical computation.

**Jack Leifer** is an Assistant Professor in the Department of Mechanical Engineering at the University of Kentucky Extended Campus Program in Paducah, and was previously with the Department of Mathematical Sciences and Engineering at the University of South Carolina–Aiken. He received his Ph.D. in Mechanical Engineering from the University of Texas at Austin in December 1995. His current research interests include the analysis of ultra-light and inflatable (Gossamer) space structures.

*Acknowledgments:* I'd like to thank my colleagues at USC–Aiken, especially Professors Mike May and Laurene Fausett, for their encouragement and feedback; and my parents, Felice and Morton Leifer, for being there and providing support (as always) as I completed this book.

**Richard M. Lueptow** is the Charles Deering McCormick Professor of Teaching Excellence and Associate Professor of Mechanical Engineering at Northwestern University. He is a native of Wisconsin and received his doctorate from the Massachusetts Institute of Technology in 1986. He teaches design, fluid mechanics, an spectral analysis techniques. Rich has an active research program on rotating filtration, Taylor Couette flow, granular flow, fire suppression, and acoustics. He has five patents and over 40 refereed journal and proceedings papers along with many other articles, abstracts, and presentations.

*Acknowledgments:* Thanks to my talented and hard-working co-authors as well as the many colleagues and students who took the tutorial for a "test drive." Special thanks to Mike Minbiole for his major contributions to Graphics Concepts with SolidWorks. Thanks also to Northwestern University for the time to work on a book. Most of all, thanks to my loving wife, Maiya, and my children, Hannah and Kyle, for supporting me in this endeavor. (Photo courtesy of Evanston Photographic Studios, Inc.)

**Larry Nyhoff** is a Professor of Mathematics and Computer Science at Calvin College. After doing bachelor's work at Calvin, and Master's work at Michigan, he received a Ph.D. from Michigan State and also did graduate work in computer science at Western Michigan. Dr. Nyhoff has taught at Calvin for the past 34 years—mathematics at first and computer science for the past several years.

*Acknowledgments:* We thank our families—Shar, Jeff, Dawn, Rebecca, Megan, Sara, Greg, Julie, Joshua, Derek, Tom, Joan; Marge, Michelle, Sandy, Lory, Michael—for being patient and understanding. We thank God for allowing us to write this text.

**Paul Riley** is an author, instructor, and designer specializing in graphics and design for multimedia. He is a founding partner of CAD Support Associates, a contract service and professional training organization for computer-aided design. His 15 years of business experience and 20 years of teaching experience are supported by degrees in education and computer science. Paul has taught AutoCAD at the University of Massachusetts at Lowell and is presently teaching AutoCAD at Mt. Ida College in Newton, Massachusetts. He has developed a program, Computer-aided Design for Professionals that is highly regarded by corporate clients and has been an ongoing success since 1982.

**Robert Rizza** is an Assistant Professor of Mechanical Engineering at North Dakota State University, where he teaches courses in mechanics and computer-aided design. A native of Chicago, he received the Ph.D. degree from the Illinois Institute of Technology. He is also the author of *Getting Started with Pro/ENGINEER*. Dr. Rizza has worked on a diverse range of engineering projects including projects from the railroad, bioengineering, and aerospace industries. His current research interests include the fracture of composite materials, repair of cracked aircraft components, and loosening of prostheses.

**Peter Schiavone** is a professor and student advisor in the Department of Mechanical Engineering at the University of Alberta, Canada. He received his Ph.D. from the University of Strathclyde, U.K. in 1988. He has authored several books in the area of student academic success as well as numerous papers in international scientific research journals. Dr. Schiavone has worked in private industry in several different areas of engineering including aerospace and systems engineering. He founded the first Mathematics Resource Center at the University of Alberta, a unit designed specifically

to teach new students the necessary survival skills in mathematics and the physical sciences required for success in first-year engineering. This led to the Students' Union Gold Key Award for outstanding contributions to the university. Dr. Schiavone lectures regularly to freshman engineering students and to new engineering professors on engineering success, in particular about maximizing students' academic performance.

*Acknowledgements:* Thanks to Richard Felder for being such an inspiration; to my wife Linda for sharing my dreams and believing in me; and to Francesca and Antonio for putting up with Dad when working on the text.

**David I. Schneider** holds an A.B. degree from Oberlin College and a Ph.D. degree in Mathematics from MIT. He has taught for 34 years, primarily at the University of Maryland. Dr. Schneider has authored 28 books, with one-half of them computer programming books. He has developed three customized software packages that are supplied as supplements to over 55 mathematics textbooks. His involvement with computers dates back to 1962, when he programmed a special purpose computer at MIT's Lincoln Laboratory to correct errors in a communications system.

**David I. Schwartz** is an Assistant Professor in the Computer Science Department at Cornell University and earned his B.S., M.S., and Ph.D. degrees in Civil Engineering from State University of New York at Buffalo. Throughout his graduate studies, Schwartz combined principles of computer science to applications of civil engineering. He became interested in helping students learn how to apply software tools for solving a variety of engineering problems. He teaches his students to learn incrementally and practice frequently to gain the maturity to tackle other subjects. In his spare time, Schwartz plays drums in a variety of bands.

*Acknowledgments:* I dedicate my books to my family, friends, and students who all helped in so many ways.

Many thanks go to the schools of Civil Engineering and Engineering & Applied Science at State University of New York at Buffalo where I originally developed and tested my UNIX and Maple books. I greatly appreciate the opportunity to explore my goals and all the help from everyone at the Computer Science Department at Cornell.

 **John T. Sears** received the Ph.D. degree from Princeton University. Currently, he is a Professor and the head of the Department of Chemical Engineering at Montana State University. After leaving Princeton he worked in research at Brookhaven National Laboratory and Esso Research and Engineering, until he took a position at West Virginia University. He came to MSU in 1982, where he has served as the Director of the College of Engineering Minority Program and Interim Director for BioFilm Engineering. Prof. Sears has written a book on air pollution and economic development, and over 45 articles in engineering and engineering education.

 **Michael T. Snyder** is President of Internet startup Appointments123.com. He is a native of Chicago, and he received his Bachelor of Science degree in Mechanical Engineering from the University of Notre Dame. Mike also graduated with honors from Northwestern University's Kellogg Graduate School of Management in 1999 with his Masters of Management degree. Before Appointments123.com, Mike was a mechanical engineer in new product development for Motorola Cellular and Acco Office Products. He has received four patents for his mechanical design work. "Pro/ENGINEER was an invaluable design tool for me,

and I am glad to help students learn the basics of Pro/ENGINEER."

*Acknowledgments:* Thanks to Rich Lueptow and Jim Steger for inviting me to be a part of this great project. Of course, thanks to my wife Gretchen for her support in my various projects.

 **Jim Steger** is currently Chief Technical Officer and cofounder of an Internet applications company. He graduated with a Bachelor of Science degree in Mechanical Engineering from Northwestern University. His prior work included mechanical engineering assignments at Motorola and Acco Brands. At Motorola, Jim worked on part design for two-way radios and was one of the lead mechanical engineers on a cellular phone product line. At Acco Brands, Jim was the sole engineer on numerous office product designs. His Worx stapler has won design awards in the United States and in Europe. Jim has been a Pro/ENGINEER user for over six years.

*Acknowledgments:* Many thanks to my co-authors, especially Rich Lueptow for his leadership on this project. I would also like to thank my family for their continuous support.

 **Royce Wilkinson** received his undergraduate degree in chemistry from Rose-Hulman Institute of Technology in 1991 and the Ph.D. degree in chemistry from Montana State University in 1998 with research in natural product isolation from fungi. He currently resides in Bozeman, MT and is involved in HIV drug research. His research interests center on biological molecules and their interactions in the search for pharmaceutical advances.

http://www.prenhall.com/esource

# Reviewers

We would like to thank everyone who has reviewed texts in this series.

## ESource Reviewers

Christopher Rowe, *Vanderbilt University*
Steve Yurgartis, *Clarkson University*
Heidi A. Diefes-Dux, *Purdue University*
Howard Silver, *Fairleigh Dickenson University*
Jean C. Malzahn Kampe, *Virginia Polytechnic Institute and State University*
Malcolm Heimer, *Florida International University*
Stanley Reeves, *Auburn University*
John Demel, *Ohio State University*
Shahnam Navee, *Georgia Southern University*
Heshem Shaalem, *Georgia Southern University*
Terry L. Kohutek, *Texas A & M University*
Liz Rozell, *Bakersfield College*
Mary C. Lynch, *University of Florida*
Ted Pawlicki, *University of Rochester*
James N. Jensen, *SUNY at Buffalo*
Tom Horton, *University of Virginia*
Eileen Young, *Bristol Community College*
James D. Nelson, *Louisiana Tech University*
Jerry Dunn, *Texas Tech University*
Howard M. Fulmer, *Villanova UniversityBerkeley*
Naeem Abdurrahman *University of Texas, Austin*
Stephen Allan *Utah State University*
Anil Bajaj *Purdue University*
Grant Baker *University of Alaska–Anchorage*
William Beckwith *Clemson University*
Haym Benaroya *Rutgers University*
John Biddle *California State Polytechnic University*
Tom Bledsaw *ITT Technical Institute*
Fred Boadu *Duke University*
Tom Bryson *University of Missouri, Rolla*
Ramzi Bualuan *University of Notre Dame*
Dan Budny *Purdue University*
Betty Burr *University of Houston*
Dale Calkins *University of Washington*
Harish Cherukuri *University of North Carolina –Charlotte*
Arthur Clausing *University of Illinois*

Barry Crittendon *Virginia Polytechnic and State University*
James Devine *University of South Florida*
Ron Eaglin *University of Central Florida*
Dale Elifrits *University of Missouri, Rolla*
Patrick Fitzhorn *Colorado State University*
Susan Freeman *Northeastern University*
Frank Gerlitz *Washtenaw College*
Frank Gerlitz *Washtenaw Community College*
John Glover *University of Houston*
John Graham *University of North Carolina–Charlotte*
Ashish Gupta *SUNY at Buffalo*
Otto Gygax *Oregon State University*
Malcom Heimer *Florida International University*
Donald Herling *Oregon State University*
Thomas Hill *SUNY at Buffalo*
A.S. Hodel *Auburn University*
James N. Jensen *SUNY at Buffalo*
Vern Johnson *University of Arizona*
Autar Kaw *University of South Florida*
Kathleen Kitto *Western Washington University*
Kenneth Klika *University of Akron*
Terry L. Kohutek *Texas A&M University*
Melvin J. Maron *University of Louisville*
Robert Montgomery *Purdue University*
Mark Nagurka *Marquette University*
Romarathnam Narasimhan *University of Miami*
Soronadi Nnaji *Florida A&M University*
Sheila O'Connor *Wichita State University*
Michael Peshkin *Northwestern University*
Dr. John Ray *University of Memphis*
Larry Richards *University of Virginia*
Marc H. Richman *Brown University*
Randy Shih *Oregon Institute of Technology*
Avi Singhal *Arizona State University*
Tim Sykes *Houston Community College*
Neil R. Thompson *University of Waterloo*
Dr. Raman Menon Unnikrishnan *Rochester Institute of Technology*
Michael S. Wells *Tennessee Tech University*
Joseph Wujek *University of California, Berkeley*
Edward Young *University of South Carolina*
Garry Young *Oklahoma State University*
Mandochehr Zoghi *University of Dayton*

# Contents

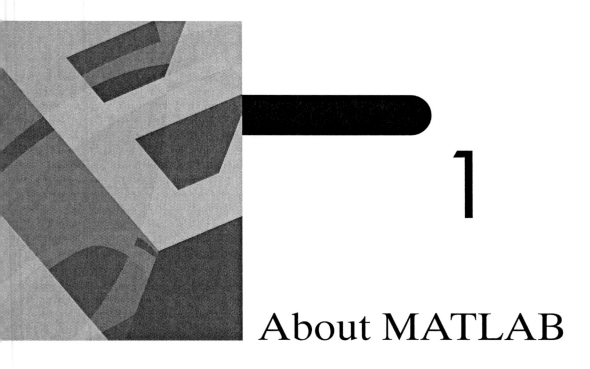

# 1

# About MATLAB

## Objectives

After reading this chapter, you should be able to

- understand what MATLAB is and why it is widely used in engineering and science
- understand the advantages and limitations of the student edition of MATLAB
- formulate problems by using a structured problem-solving approach

## 1 WHAT IS MATLAB?

MATLAB is one of a number of commercially available, sophisticated mathematical computation tools, which also include Maple, Mathematica, and Math-Cad. Despite what proponents may claim, no single one of these tools is "the best." Each has strengths and weaknesses. Each allows you to perform basic mathematical computations. They differ in the way they handle symbolic calculations and more complicated mathematical processes, such as matrix manipulation. For example, MATLAB (short for **Mat**rix **Lab**oratory) excels at computations involving matrices, whereas Maple excels at symbolic calculations. At a fundamental level, you can think of these programs as sophisticated computer-based calculators. They can perform the same functions as your scientific calculator—and **many more**. If you have a computer on your desk, you may find yourself using MATLAB instead of your calculator for even the simplest mathematical applications—for example, balancing your checkbook. In many engineering classes, the use of programs such as MATLAB to perform computations is replacing more traditional computer programming. Although programs such as MATLAB have become a standard tool for engineers and scientists this doesn't mean that you shouldn't learn a high-level language such as C++ or FORTRAN.

Because MATLAB is so easy to use, you can perform many programming tasks with it, but it isn't always the best tool for a programming task. It excels at numerical calculations—especially matrix calculations—and graphics, but you wouldn't want to use it to write a word-processing program. For large applications, such as operating systems or design software, C++ and FORTRAN would be the programs of choice. (In fact, MATLAB, which *is* a large application program, was originally written in FORTRAN and later rewritten in C, a precursor of C++.) Usually, high-level programs do not offer easy access to graphing—an application at which MATLAB excels. The primary area of overlap between MATLAB and high-level programs is "number crunching"—repetitive calculations or the processing of large quantities of data. Both MATLAB and high-level programs are good at processing numbers.

A "number-crunching" program is generally easier to write in MATLAB, but usually it will execute faster in C++ or FORTRAN. The one exception to this rule is calculations involving matrices. MATLAB is optimized for matrices. Thus, if a problem can be formulated with a matrix solution, MATLAB executes substantially faster than a similar program in a high-level language.

MATLAB is available in both a professional and a student version. The professional version is probably installed in your college or university computer laboratory, but you may enjoy having the student version at home. MATLAB is updated regularly; this textbook is based on MATLAB 7.5. If you are using MATLAB 6, you may notice some minor differences between it and MATLAB 7.5. There are substantial differences in versions that predate MATLAB 5.5.

The standard installation of the professional version of MATLAB is capable of solving a wide variety of technical problems. Additional capability is available in the form of function toolboxes. These toolboxes are purchased separately, and they may or may not be available to you. You can find a complete list of the MATLAB product family at The MathWorks web site, www.mathworks.com.

## 2  STUDENT EDITION OF MATLAB

The professional and student editions of MATLAB are very similar. Beginning students probably won't be able to tell the difference. Student editions are available for Microsoft Windows, Mac OSX, and Linux operating systems and can be purchased from college bookstores or online from The MathWorks at www.mathworks.com.

The MathWorks packages its software in groups called *releases*, and MATLAB 7.5 is featured, along with other products, such as Simulink 7.1, in Release R2007b. New versions are released every six months. The release number is the same for both the student and professional edition, but the student version may lag the professional version by several months. The student edition of R2007b includes the following features:

- Full MATLAB
- Simulink, with the ability to build models with up to 1000 blocks (the professional version allows an unlimited number of blocks)
- Major portions of the Symbolic Math Toolbox
- Control System Toolbox     `
- Signal Processing Toolbox
- Signal Processing Blockset
- Statistics Toolbox
- Optimization Toolbox
- Image Processing Toolbox
- Software manuals for both MATLAB 7 and Simulink
- A CD containing the full electronic documentation
- A single-user license, limited to students for use in their classwork (the professional version is licensed either singly or to a group)

Toolboxes other than those included with the student edition may be purchased separately.

The biggest difference you should notice between the professional and student editions is the command prompt, which is

>>

in the professional version and

`EDU>>`

in the student edition.

## 3 HOW IS MATLAB USED IN INDUSTRY?

The ability to use tools such as MATLAB is quickly becoming a requirement for many engineering positions. A recent job search on Monster.com found the following advertisement:

> ... is looking for a System Test Engineer with Avionics experience.... Responsibilities include modification of MATLAB scripts, execution of Simulink simulations, and analysis of the results data. Candidate MUST be very familiar with MATLAB, Simulink, and C++....

This ad isn't unusual. The same search turned up 75 different companies that specifically required MATLAB skills for entry-level engineers. Widely used in all engineering and science fields, MATLAB is particularly popular for electrical engineering applications. The sections that follow outline a few of the many applications currently using MATLAB.

KEY IDEA: MATLAB is widely used in engineering

### 3.1 Electrical Engineering

MATLAB is used extensively in electrical engineering for signal-processing applications. For example, Figure 1 includes several images created during a research program at the University of Utah to simulate collision-detection algorithms used by the housefly (and adapted to silicon sensors in the laboratory). The research resulted in the design and manufacture of a computer chip that detects imminent collisions. This has potential use in the design of autonomous robots using vision for navigation and especially in automobile safety applications.

### 3.2 Biomedical Engineering

Medical images are usually saved as dicom files (the Digital Imaging and Communications in Medicine standard). Dicom files use the file extension .dcm. The Math-Works offers an Image Processing Toolbox that can read these files, making their data available to MATLAB. (The Image Processing Toolbox is included with the student edition and is optional with the professional edition.) The Image Processing Toolbox also includes a wide range of functions, many of them especially appropriate for medical imaging. A limited MRI data set that has already been converted to a format compatible with MATLAB ships with the standard MATLAB program.

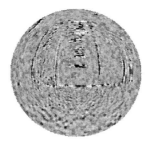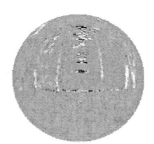

**Figure 1**
Image processing using a fisheye leans camera to simulate the visual system of a housefly's brain.
(Used by permission of Dr. Reid Harrison, University of Utah.)

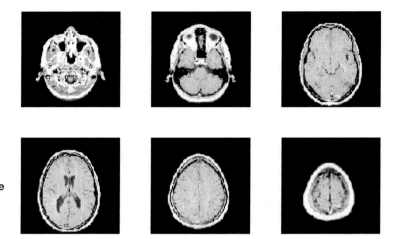

**Figure 2**
Horizontal slices through the brain, based on the sample data file included with MATLAB.

This data set allows you to try out some of the imaging functions available both with the standard MATLAB installation and with the expanded imaging toolbox, if you have it installed on your computer. Figure 2 shows six images of horizontal slices through the brain based on the MRI data set.

The same data set can be used to construct a three-dimensional image, such as either of those shown in Figure 3. Detailed instructions on how to create these images are included in the MATLAB **help** tutorial.

### 3.3 Fluid Dynamics

Calculations describing fluid velocities (speeds and directions) are important in a number of different fields. Aerospace engineers in particular are interested in the behavior of gases, both outside an aircraft or space vehicle and inside the combustion chambers. Visualizing the three-dimensional behavior of fluids is tricky, but MATLAB offers a number of tools that make it easier. In Figure 4, the flow-field calculation results for a thrust-vector control device are represented as a quiver plot. Thrust-vector control is the process of changing the direction in which a nozzle points (and hence the direction a rocket travels) by pushing on an actuator (a piston-cylinder device). The model in the figure represents a high-pressure reservoir of gas (a plenum) that eventually feeds into the piston and thus controls the length of the actuator.

**Figure 3**
Three-dimensional visualization of MRI data, based on the sample data set included with MATLAB.

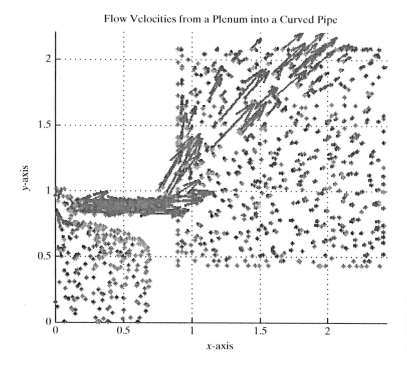

**Figure 4**
Quiver plot of gas behavior in a thrust vector control device.

## 4 PROBLEM SOLVING IN ENGINEERING AND SCIENCE

A consistent approach to solving technical problems is important throughout engineering, science, and computer programming disciplines. The approach we outline here is useful in courses as diverse as chemistry, physics, thermodynamics, and engineering design. It also applies to the social sciences, such as economics and sociology. Different authors may formulate their problem-solving schemes differently, but they all have the same basic format:

KEY IDEA: Always use a systematic problem-solving strategy

- **State the problem.**
  - Drawing a picture is often helpful in this step.
  - If you do not have a clear understanding of the problem, you are not likely to be able to solve it.
- **Describe the input** values (knowns) **and** the required **outputs** (unknowns).
  - Be careful to include units as you describe the input and output values. Sloppy handling of units often leads to wrong answers.
  - Identify constants you may need in the calculation, such as the ideal-gas constant and the acceleration due to gravity.
  - If appropriate, label a sketch with the values you have identified, or group them into a table.
- Develop an algorithm to solve the problem. In computer applications, this can often be accomplished with a **hand example**. You'll need to
  - Identify any equations relating the knowns and unknowns.
  - Work through a simplified version of the problem by hand or with a calculator.
- **Solve** the problem. In this selection, this step involves creating a **MATLAB solution.**
- **Test the solution.**
  - Do your results make sense physically?

○ Do they match your sample calculations?

○ Is your answer really what was asked for?

○ Graphs are often useful ways to check your calculations for reasonableness.

If you consistently use a structured problem-solving approach, such as the one just outlined, you'll find that "story" problems become much easier to solve. Example 1 illustrates this problem-solving strategy.

---

### EXAMPLE 1

## The Conversion of Matter to Energy

Albert Einstein (see Figure 5) is arguably the most famous physicist of the 20th century. Einstein was born in Germany in 1879 and attended school in both Germany and Switzerland. While working as a patent clerk in Bern, he developed his famous theory of relativity. Perhaps the best-known physics equation today is his:

$$E = mc^2$$

This astonishingly simple equation links the previously separate worlds of matter and energy and can be used to find the amount of energy released as matter is changed in form in both natural and human-made nuclear reactions.

The sun radiates $385 \times 10^{24}$ J/s of energy, all of which is generated by nuclear reactions converting matter to energy. Use MATLAB and Einstein's equation to determine how much matter must be converted to energy to produce this much radiation in one day.

1. State the Problem
   Find the amount of matter necessary to produce the amount of energy radiated by the sun every day.

**Figure 5**
Albert Einstein (Courtesy of the Library of Congress, LC-USZ62-60242).

2. Describe the Input and Output

*Input*

Energy:    $E = 385 \times 10^{24}$ J/s, which must be converted into the total energy radiated during one day

Speed of light: $c = 3.0 \times 10^8$ m/s

*Output*

Mass $m$ in kg

3. Develop a Hand Example

The energy radiated in one day is

$$385 \times 10^{24} \frac{J}{s} \times 3600 \frac{s}{hour} \times 24 \frac{hours}{day} \times 1 \text{ day} = 3.33 \times 10^{31} \text{ J}$$

The equation $E = mc^2$ must be solved for $m$ and the values for $E$ and $c$ substituted. We have

$$m = \frac{E}{c^2}$$

$$m = \frac{3.33 \times 10^{31} \text{ J}}{(3.0 \times 10^8 \text{ m/s})^2}$$

$$= 3.7 \times 10^{14} \frac{J}{m^2/s^2}$$

We can see from the output criteria that we want the mass in kg, so what went wrong? We need to do one more unit conversion:

$$1 \text{ J} = 1 \text{ kg m}^2/s^2$$

$$= 3.7 \times 10^{14} \frac{\text{kg m}^2/s^2}{m^2/s^2} = 3.7 \times 10^{14} \text{ kg}$$

4. Develop a MATLAB Solution

At this point, you have not learned how to create MATLAB code. However, you should be able to see from the following sample code that MATLAB syntax is similar to that used in most algebraic scientific calculators. MATLAB commands are entered at the prompt (>>), and the results are reported on the next line. The code is as follows:

```
>> E=385e24
E =
   3.8500e+026
>> E=E*3600*24
E =
   3.3264e+031
>> c=3e8
c =
   300000000
>> m=E/c^2
m =
   3.6960e+014
```

From this point on, we will not show the prompt when describing interactions in the command window.

5. Test the Solution

The MATLAB solution matches the hand calculation, but do the numbers make sense? Anything times $10^{14}$ is a really large number. Consider, however, that the mass of the sun is $2 \times 10^{30}$ kg. We can calculate how long it would take to consume the mass of the sun completely at a rate of $3.7 \times 10^{14}$ kg/day. We have

$$\text{time} = (\text{mass of the sun})/(\text{rate of consumption})$$

$$\text{time} = \frac{2 \times 10^{30} \text{ kg}}{3.7 \times 10^{14} \text{ kg/day}} \times \frac{\text{year}}{365 \text{ days}} = 1.5 \times 10^{13} \text{ years}$$

That's 15 trillion years! We don't need to worry about the sun running out of matter to convert to energy in our lifetimes.

# 2

# MATLAB Environment

## Objectives

After reading this chapter, you should be able to

- start the MATLAB program and solve simple problems in the command window
- understand MATLAB's use of matrices
- identify and use the various MATLAB windows
- define and use simple matrices
- name and use variables
- understand the order of operations in MATLAB
- understand the difference between scalar, array, and matrix calculations in MATLAB
- express numbers in either floating-point or scientific notation
- adjust the format used to display numbers in the command window
- save the value of variables used in a MATLAB session
- save a series of commands in an M-file

## 1 GETTING STARTED

Using MATLAB for the first time is easy; mastering it can take years. In this chapter, we'll introduce you to the MATLAB environment and show you how to perform basic mathematical computations. After reading this chapter, you should be able to start using MATLAB for homework assignments or on the job.

Because the procedure for installing MATLAB depends upon your operating system and your computing environment, we'll assume that you have already installed MATLAB on your computer or that you are working in a computing laboratory with MATLAB already installed. To start MATLAB in either the Windows or Apple environment, click on the icon on the desktop, or use the start menu to find the program. In the UNIX environment, type **Matlab** at the shell prompt. No matter how you start it, once MATLAB opens, you should see the MATLAB prompt (**>>** or **EDU>>**), which tells you that MATLAB is ready for you to enter a command. When you've finished your MATLAB session, you can exit MATLAB by typing **quit** or **exit** at the MATLAB prompt. MATLAB also uses the standard Windows menu bar, so you can exit the program by choosing **EXIT MATLAB** from the File menu or by selecting the close icon (**x**) at the upper right-hand corner of the screen. The default MATLAB screen, which opens each time you start the program, is shown in Figure 1.

To start using MATLAB, you need be concerned only with the command window (on the right of the screen). You can perform calculations in the command window in a manner similar to the way you perform calculations on a scientific calculator. Even most of the syntax is the same. For example, to compute the value of 5 squared, type the command

    5^2

The following output will be displayed:

    ans =

    25

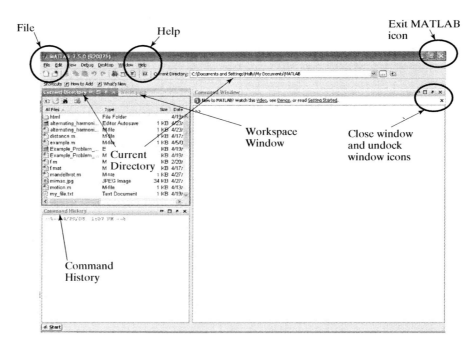

**Figure 1**
MATLAB opening window. The MATLAB environment consists of a number of windows, four of which open in the default view. Others open as needed during a MATLAB session.

Or, to find the value of cos $(\pi)$, type

```
cos(pi)
```

which results in the output

```
ans =
      -1
```

KEY IDEA: MATLAB uses the standard algebraic rules for order of operation

MATLAB uses the standard algebraic rules for order of operation, which becomes important when you chain calculations together. These rules are discussed in Section 3.2. Notice that the value of pi is built into MATLAB, so you don't have to enter it yourself.

---

**Hint**

You may think some of the examples are too simple to type in yourself—that just reading the material is sufficient. However, you will remember the material better if you both read it and type it!

---

Before going any further, try Practice Exercise 1.

---

## Practice Exercise 1

Type the following expressions into MATLAB at the command prompt, and observe the results:

1. 5 + 2
2. 5 * 2
3. 5/2

4.  3 + 2 * (4 + 3)
5.  2.54 * 8/2.6
6.  6.3 − 2.1045
7.  3.6^2
8.  1 + 2^2
9.  sqrt(5)
10. cos(pi)

**Hint**

You may find it frustrating to learn that when you make a mistake, you can't just overwrite your command after you have executed it. This occurs because the command window is creating a list of all the commands you've entered. You can't "un-execute" a command, or "un-create" it. What you can do is enter the command correctly and then execute your new version. **MATLAB** offers several ways to make this easier for you. One way is to use the arrow keys, usually located on the right-hand side of your keyboard. The up arrow, ↑, allows you to move through the list of commands you have executed. Once you find the appropriate command, you can edit it and then execute your new version.

## 2 MATLAB WINDOWS

MATLAB uses several display windows. The default view, shown in Figure 1, includes on the right a large *command window* and, stacked on the left, the *current directory*, *workspace*, and *command history windows*. Notice the tabs at the top of the windows on the left; these tabs allow you to access the hidden windows. Older versions of MATLAB also included a *launch pad* window, which has been replaced by the *start* button in the lower left-hand corner. In addition, *document windows*, *graphics windows*, and *editing windows* will automatically open when needed. Each is described in the sections that follow. MATLAB also includes a built-in help function that can be accessed from the menu bar, as shown in Figure 1. To personalize your desktop, you can resize any of these windows, close the ones you aren't using with the close icon (the **x** in the upper right-hand corner of each window), or "undock" them with the undock icon, ⌐ , also located in the upper right-hand corner of each window.

### 2.1 Command Window

The command window is located in the right-hand pane of the default view of the MATLAB screen, as shown in Figure 1. The command window offers an environment similar to a scratch pad. Using it allows you to save the values you calculate, but not the *commands* used to generate those values. If you want to save the command sequence, you'll need to use the editing window to create an **M-file**. M-files are described in Section 4.2. Both approaches are valuable. Before we introduce M-files, we will concentrate on using the command window.

KEY IDEA: The command window is similar to a scratch pad

## 2.2 Command History

The *command history* window records the commands you issued in the command window. When you exit MATLAB, or when you issue the **clc** command, the command window is cleared. However, the command history window retains a list of all your commands. You may clear the command history with the edit menu. If you work on a public computer, as a security precaution, MATLAB's defaults may be set to clear the history when you exit MATLAB. If you entered the earlier sample commands, notice that they are repeated in the command history window. This window is valuable for a number of reasons, among them that it allows you to review previous MATLAB sessions and that it can be used to transfer commands to the command window. For example, first clear the contents of the command window by typing

```
clc
```

This action clears the command window but leaves the data in the command history window. You can transfer any command from the command history window to the command window by double-clicking (which also executes the command) or by clicking and dragging the line of code into the command window. Try double-clicking

```
cos(pi)
```

in the command history window. The command is copied into the command window and executed. It should return

```
ans =
        -1
```

Now click and drag

```
5^2
```

from the command history window into the command window. The command won't execute until you hit Enter, and then you'll get the result:

```
ans =
       25
```

You'll find the command history useful as you perform more and more complicated calculations in the command window.

## 2.3 Workspace Window

The *workspace window* keeps track of the *variables* you have defined as you execute commands in the command window. If you've been doing the examples, the workspace window should show just one variable, **ans**, and indicate that it has a value of 25 and is a double array:

| Name | Value | Class |
|------|-------|-------|
| ⊞ ans | 25 | double |

(Your view of the workspace window may be slightly different, depending on how your installation of MATLAB is configured.)

Set the workspace window to show more about the displayed variables by right-clicking on the bar with the column labels. (This feature is new to MATLAB 7 and won't work if you have an older version.) Check **size** and **bytes**, in addition to **name**, **value**, and **class**. Your workspace window should now display the following information, although you may need to resize the window to see all the columns:

| Name | Value | Size | Bytes | Class |
|------|-------|------|-------|-------|
| ⊞ ans | 25 | $1 \times 1$ | 8 | double |

The yellow gridlike symbol indicates that the variable **ans** is an array. The size, $1 \times 1$, tells us that it is a single value (one row by one column) and therefore a scalar. The array uses 8 bytes of memory. MATLAB was written in C, and the class designation tells us that, in the C language, **ans** is a double-precision floating-point array. For our needs, it is enough to know that the variable **ans** can store a floating-point number (a number with a decimal point). Actually, MATLAB considers every number you enter to be a floating-point number, whether you insert a decimal point or not.

KEY IDEA: The default data type is double-precision floating-point numbers stored in a matrix

In addition to information about the size of the arrays and type of data stored in them, you can also choose to display statistical information about the data. Once again right click the bar in the workspace window that displays the column headings. Notice that you can select from a number of different statistical measures, such as the max, min, and standard deviation.

You can define additional variables in the command window, and they will be listed in the workspace window. For example, typing

        A = 5

returns

        A =
            5

Notice that the variable **A** has been added to the workspace window, which lists variables in alphabetical order. Variables beginning with capital letters are listed first, followed by variables starting with lowercase letters.

| Name | Value | Size | Bytes | Class |
|------|-------|------|-------|-------|
| ⊞ A | 5 | $1 \times 1$ | 8 | double |
| ⊞ ans | 25 | $1 \times 1$ | 8 | double |

In Section 3.2 we will discuss in detail how to enter matrices into MATLAB. For now, you can enter a simple one-dimensional matrix by typing

        B = [1, 2, 3, 4]

This command returns

        B =
            1     2     3     4

The commas are optional; you'd get the same result with

        B = [ 1  2  3  4]
        B =
            1     2     3     4

Notice that the variable **B** has been added to the workspace window and that it is a 1 × 4 array:

| Name | Value | Size | Bytes | Class |
|------|-------|------|-------|-------|
| ⊞ A | 5 | 1 × 1 | 8 | double |
| ⊞ B | [1 2 3 4] | 1 × 4 | 32 | double |
| ⊞ ans | 25 | 1 × 1 | 8 | double |

You can define two-dimensional matrices in a similar fashion. Semicolons are used to separate rows. For example,

```
C = [ 1 2 3 4; 10 20 30 40; 5 10 15 20]
```

returns

```
C =
        1       2       3       4
       10      20      30      40
        5      10      15      20
```

| Name | Value | Size | Bytes | Class |
|------|-------|------|-------|-------|
| ⊞ A | 5 | 1 × 1 | 8 | double |
| ⊞ B | [1 2 3 4] | 1 × 4 | 32 | double |
| ⊞ C | <3 × 4 double> | 3 × 4 | 96 | double |
| ⊞ ans | 25 | 1 × 1 | 8 | double |

Notice that **C** appears in the workspace window as a 3 × 4 matrix. To conserve space, the values stored in the matrix are not listed.

You can recall the values for any variable by typing in the variable name. For example, entering

```
A
```

returns

```
A =
     5
```

Although the only variables we have introduced are matrices containing numbers, other types of variables are possible.

In describing the command window, we introduced the **clc** command. This command clears the command window, leaving a blank page for you to work on. However, it does not delete from memory the actual variables you have created. The **clear** command deletes all of the saved variables. The action of the **clear** command is reflected in the workspace window. Try it out by typing

```
clear
```

in the command window. The workspace window is now empty:

| Name | Value | Size | Bytes | Class |
|------|-------|------|-------|-------|

If you suppress the workspace window (closing it either from the file menu or with the close icon in the upper right-hand corner of the window), you can still find out which variables have been defined by using the **whos** command:

**whos**

If executed before we entered the **clear** command, **whos** would have returned

| Name | Size | Bytes | Class |
|------|------|-------|-------|
| A | 1x1 | 8 | double |
| B | 1x4 | 32 | double |
| C | 3x4 | 96 | double |
| ans | 1x1 | 8 | double |

## 2.4  Current Directory Window

The current directory window lists all the files in a computer folder called the current directory. When MATLAB either accesses files or saves information, it uses the current directory unless told differently. The default for the location of the current directory varies with your version of the software and the way it was installed. However, the current directory is listed at the top of the main window. The current directory can be changed by selecting another directory from the drop-down list located next to the directory listing or by browsing through your computer files. Browsing is performed with the browse button, located next to the drop-down list. (See Figure 2.)

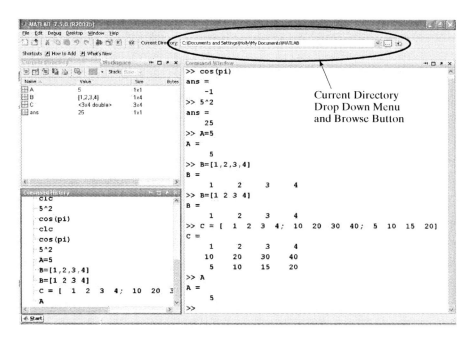

**Figure 2**
The **Current Directory Window** lists all the files in the current directory. You can change the current directory by using the drop-down menu or the browse button.

## 2.5 Document Window

Double-clicking on any variable listed in the workspace window automatically launches a document window, containing the **array editor**. Values stored in the variable are displayed in a spreadsheet format. You can change values in the array editor, or you can add new values. For example, if you haven't already entered the two-dimensional matrix C, enter the following command in the command window:

$$C = [ 1 2 3 4; 10 20 30 40; 5 10 15 20];$$

KEY IDEA: A semicolon suppresses the output from commands issued in the command window

Placing a semicolon at the end of the command suppresses the output, so that it is not repeated in the command window. However, **C** should now be listed in the workspace window. If you double-click on it, a document window will open above the command window, as shown in Figure 3. You can now add more values to the **C** matrix or change existing values.

The document window/array editor can also be used in conjunction with the workspace window to create entirely new arrays. Run your mouse slowly over the icons in the shortcut bar at the top of the workspace window. If you are patient, you should see the function of each icon appear. The new variable icon looks like a grid with a large asterisk behind it. Select the new variable icon, and a new variable called **unnamed** should appear on the variable list. You can change its name by right-clicking and selecting **rename** from the pop-up menu. To add values to this new variable, double-click on it and add your data from the array editor window. The new variable button is a new feature in MATLAB 7; if you are using an older version, you won't be able to create variables this way.

When you are finished creating new variables, close the array editor by selecting the close window icon in the upper right-hand corner of the window.

## 2.6 Graphics Window

The graphics window launches automatically when you request a graph. To demonstrate this feature, first create an array of x values:

$$x = [ 1 2 3 4 5];$$

**Figure 3**
The **Document Window** displays the **Array Editor.**

New Variable Icon

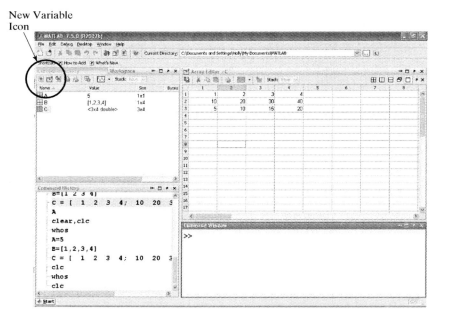

(Remember, the semicolon suppresses the output from this command; however, a new variable, x, appears in the workspace window.)

Now create a list of y values:

```
y = [10 20 30 40 50];
```

To create a graph, use the plot command:

```
plot(x,y)
```

The graphics window opens automatically. (See Figure 4.) Notice that a new window label appears on the task bar at the bottom of the windows screen. It will be titled either **<Student Version> Figure...** or simply **Figure 1**, depending on whether you are using the student or professional version, respectively, of the software. Any additional graphs you create will overwrite Figure 1, unless you specifically command MATLAB to open a new graphics window.

MATLAB makes it easy to modify graphs by adding titles, $x$ and $y$ labels, multiple lines, etc. Engineers and scientists **never** present a graph without labels!

KEY IDEA: Always add a title and axis labels to graphs

### 2.7 Edit Window

To open the edit window, choose **File** from the menu bar, then **New**, and, finally, **M-file** (**File → New → M-file**). This window allows you to type and save a series of commands without executing them. You may also open the edit window by typing **edit** at the command prompt or by selecting the New File button on the toolbar.

### 2.8 Start Button

The start button is located in the lower left-hand corner of the MATLAB window. It offers alternative access to the various MATLAB windows, as well as to the help function, Internet products, demos and MATLAB toolboxes. Toolboxes provide additional MATLAB functionality for specific content areas. The symbolic toolbox

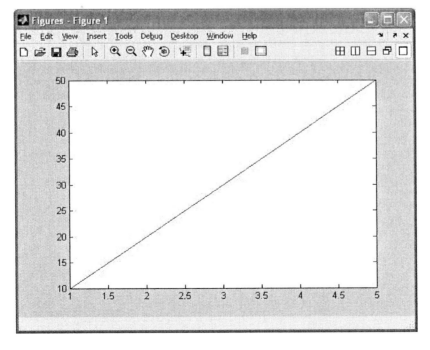

**Figure 4**
MATLAB makes it easy to create graphs.

in particular is highly useful to scientists and engineers. The start button is new to MATLAB 7 and replaces the launchpad window used in MATLAB 6.

## 3  SOLVING PROBLEMS WITH MATLAB

The command window environment is a powerful tool for solving engineering problems. To use it effectively, you'll need to understand more about how MATLAB works.

### 3.1  Using Variables

Although you can solve many problems by using MATLAB like a calculator, it is usually more convenient to give names to the values you are using. MATLAB uses the naming conventions that are common to most computer programs:

- All names must start with a letter. The names can be any length, but only the first 63 characters are used in MATLAB 7. (Use the **namelengthmax** command to confirm this.) Although MATLAB will let you create long variable names, excessive length creates a significant opportunity for error. A common guideline is to use lowercase letters and numbers in variable names and to use capital letters for the names of constants. However, if a constant is traditionally expressed as a lowercase letter, feel free to follow that convention. For example, in physics textbooks the speed of light is always lowercase $c$. Names should be short enough to remember and should be descriptive.
- The only allowable characters are letters, numbers, and the underscore. You can check to see if a variable name is allowed by using the **isvarname** command. As is standard in computer languages, the number 1 means that something is true and the number 0 means false. Hence,

```
isvarname time
ans =
      1
```

indicates that **time** is a legitimate variable name, and

```
isvarname cool-beans
ans =
      0
```

tells us that **cool-beans** is not a legitimate variable name. (Recall that the dash is not an allowed character.)
- Names are case sensitive. The variable **x** is different from the variable **X**.
- MATLAB reserves a list of keywords for use by the program, which you cannot assign as variable names. The **iskeyword** command causes MATLAB to list these reserved names:

```
iskeyword
ans =
  'break'
  'case'
  'catch'
  'classdef'
  'continue'
  'else'
  'elseif'
  'end'
```

```
'for'
'function'
'global'
'if'
'otherwise'
'parfor'
'persistent'
'return'
'switch'
'try'
'while'
```

- MATLAB allows you to reassign built-in function names as variable names. For example, you could create a new variable called **sin** with the command

```
sin = 4
```

which returns

```
sin =
     4
```

This is clearly a dangerous practice, since the **sin** (i.e., sine) function is no longer available. If you try to use the overwritten function, you'll get an error statement:

```
sin(3)
??? Index exceeds matrix dimensions.
```

You can check to see if a variable is a built-in MATLAB function by using the **which** command:

```
which sin
sin is a variable.
```

You can reset **sin** back to a function by typing

```
clear sin
```

Now when you ask

```
which sin
```

the response is

```
built-in (C:\Program
   Files\MATLAB\R2007b\toolbox\matlab\elfun\@double\sin)
% double method
```

which tells us the location of the built-in function.

## Practice Exercise 2

Which of the following names are allowed in MATLAB? Make your predictions, then test them with the **isvarname**, **iskeyword**, and **which** commands.

1. test
2. Test
3. if
4. my-book
5. my_book

6. Thisisoneverylongnamebutisitstillallowed?
7. 1stgroup
8. group_one
9. zzaAbc
10. z34wAwy?12#
11. sin
12. log

## 3.2 Matrices in MATLAB

KEY IDEA: The matrix is the primary data type in MATLAB and can hold numeric as well as other types of information

The basic data type used in MATLAB is the *matrix*. A single value, called a *scalar*, is represented as a $1 \times 1$ matrix. A list of values, arranged in either a column or a row, is a one-dimensional matrix called a *vector*. A table of values is represented as a two-dimensional matrix. Although we'll limit ourselves to scalars, vectors, and two-dimensional matrices in this chapter, MATLAB can handle higher order arrays.

VECTOR: a matrix composed of a single row or a single column

In mathematical nomenclature, matrices are represented as rows and columns inside square brackets:

$$A = [5] \quad B = [2 \quad 5] \quad C = \begin{bmatrix} 1 & 2 \\ 5 & 7 \end{bmatrix}$$

In this example, $A$ is a $1 \times 1$ matrix, $B$ is a $1 \times 2$ matrix, and $C$ is a $2 \times 2$ matrix. The advantage in using matrix representation is that whole groups of information can be represented with a single name. Most people feel more comfortable assigning a name to a single value, so we'll start by explaining how MATLAB handles scalars and then move on to more complicated matrices.

### Scalar Operations

SCALAR: a single-valued matrix

MATLAB handles arithmetic operations between two scalars much as do other computer programs and even your calculator. The syntax for addition, subtraction, multiplication, division, and exponentiation is shown in Table 1. The command

```
a = 1 + 2
```

should be read as "**a** is assigned a value of 1 plus 2," which is the addition of two scalar quantities. Arithmetic operations between two scalar variables use the same

**Table 1 Arithmetic Operations between Two Scalars (Binary Operations)**

| Operation | Algebraic Syntax | MATLAB Syntax |
|---|---|---|
| Addition | $a + b$ | **a + b** |
| Subtraction | $a - b$ | **a − b** |
| Multiplication | $a \times b$ | **a * b** |
| Division | $\dfrac{a}{b}$ or $a \div b$ | **a / b** |
| Exponentiation | $a^b$ | **a^b** |

syntax. Suppose, for example that you have defined **a** in the previous statement and that **b** has a value of 5:

```
b = 5
```

Then

```
x = a + b
```

returns the following result:

```
x =
        8
```

A single equals sign ( = ) is called an assignment operator in MATLAB. The assignment operator causes the result of your calculations to be stored in a computer memory location. In the preceding example, **x** is assigned a value of 8. If you enter the variable name

```
x
```

into MATLAB, you get the following result:

```
x =
        8
```

The assignment operator is significantly different from an equality. Consider the statement

```
x = x + 1
```

This is not a valid algebraic statement, since **x** is clearly not equal to **x + 1**. However, when interpreted as an assignment statement, it tells us to replace the current value of **x** stored in memory with a new value that is equal to the old **x** plus **1**.

Since the value stored in **x** was originally 8, the statement returns

```
x =
        9
```

KEY IDEA: The assignment operator is different from an equality

indicating that the value stored in the memory location named **x** has been changed to 9. The assignment statement is similar to the familiar process of saving a file. When you first save a word-processing document, you assign it a name. Subsequently, after you've made changes, you resave your file, but still assign it the same name. The first and second versions are not equal: You've just assigned a new version of your document to an existing memory location.

### Order of Operations

In all mathematical calculations, it is important to understand the order in which operations are performed. MATLAB follows the standard algebraic rules for the order of operation:

- First perform calculations inside parentheses, working from the innermost set to the outermost.
- Next, perform exponentiation operations.
- Then perform multiplication and division operations, working from left to right.
- Finally, perform addition and subtraction operations, working from left to right.

To better understand the importance of the order of operations, consider the calculations involved in finding the surface area of a right circular cylinder.

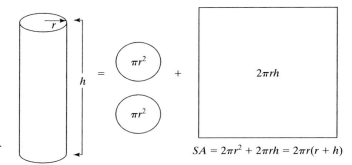

$$SA = 2\pi r^2 + 2\pi rh = 2\pi r(r + h)$$

**Figure 5**
Finding the surface area of a right circular cylinder involves addition, multiplication, and exponentiation.

The surface area is the sum of the areas of the two circular bases and the area of the curved surface between them, as shown in Figure 5. If we let the height of the cylinder be 10 cm and the radius 5 cm, the following MATLAB code can be used to find the surface area:

```
radius = 5;
height = 10;
surface_area = 2*pi*radius^2 + 2*pi*radius*height
```

The code returns

```
surface_area =
            471.2389
```

In this case, MATLAB first performs the exponentiation, raising the radius to the second power. It then works from left to right, calculating the first product and then the second product. Finally, it adds the two products together. You could instead formulate the expression as

```
surface_area = 2*pi*radius*(radius + height)
```

which also returns

```
surface_area =
            471.2389
```

In this case, MATLAB first finds the sum of the radius and height and then performs the multiplications, working from left to right. If you forgot to include the parentheses, you would have

```
surface_area = 2*pi*radius*radius + height
```

in which case the program would have first calculated the product of **2\*pi\*radius\*radius** and then added **height**—obviously resulting in the wrong answer. Note that it was necessary to include the multiplication operator before the parentheses, because MATLAB does not assume any operators and would misinterpret the expression

```
radius(radius + height)
```

as follows. The value of radius plus height is 15 (radius = 10 and height = 5), so MATLAB would have looked for the 15th value in an array called radius. This interpretation would have resulted in the following error statement.

```
??? Index exceeds matrix dimensions.
```

It is important to be extra careful in converting equations into MATLAB statements. There is no penalty for adding extra parentheses, and they often make the code easier to interpret, both for the programmer and for others who may use the code in the future.

Another way to make computer code more readable is to break long expressions into multiple statements. For example, consider the equation

$$f = \frac{\log(ax^2 + bx + c) - \sin(ax^2 + bx + c)}{4\pi x^2 + \cos(x - 2) * (ax^2 + bx + c)}$$

It would be very easy to make an error keying in this equation. To minimize the chance of that happening, break the equation into several pieces. For example, first assign values for **x**, **a**, **b**, and **c**:

```
x = 9;
a = 1;
b = 3;
c = 5;
```

Then define a polynomial and the denominator:

```
poly = a*x^2 + b*x + c;
denom = 4*pi*x^2 + cos(x - 2)*poly;
```

Combine these components into a final equation:

```
f = (log(poly) - sin(poly))/denom
```

The result is

```
f =
    0.0044
```

As mentioned, this approach minimizes your opportunity for error. Instead of keying in the polynomial three times (and risking an error each time), you need key it in only once. Your MATLAB code is more likely to be accurate, and it's easier for others to understand.

KEY IDEA: Try to minimize your opportunity for error

**Hint**

MATLAB does not read "white space," so you may add spaces to your commands without changing their meaning. A long expression is easier to read if you add a space before and after plus (+) signs and minus (−) signs, but not before and after multiplication (*) and division (/) signs.

**Practice Exercise 3**

Predict the results of the following MATLAB expressions, then check your predictions by keying the expressions into the command window:

1. 6/6 + 5
2. 2 * 6^2
3. (3 + 5) * 2
4. 3 + 5 * 2
5. 4 * 3/2 * 8
6. 3 − 2/4 + 6^2

7. $2^\wedge 3^\wedge 4$

8. $2^\wedge(3^\wedge 4)$

9. $3^\wedge 5 + 2$

10. $3^\wedge (5 + 2)$

Create and test MATLAB syntax to evaluate the following expressions, then check your answers with a handheld calculator.

11. $\dfrac{5 + 3}{9 - 1}$

12. $2^3 - \dfrac{4}{5 + 3}$

13. $\dfrac{5^{2+1}}{4 - 1}$

14. $4\dfrac{1}{2} * 5\dfrac{2}{3}$

15. $\dfrac{5 + 6 * \dfrac{7}{3} - 2^2}{\dfrac{2}{3} * \dfrac{3}{3 * 6}}$

---

### EXAMPLE 1

## Scalar Operations

Wind tunnels (see Figure 6) play an important role in our study of the behavior of high-performance aircraft. In order to interpret wind tunnel data, engineers need to understand how gases behave. The basic equation describing the properties of gases is the ideal gas law, a relationship studied in detail in freshman chemistry classes. The law states that

$$PV = nRT$$

where    $P$ = pressure in kPa,
          $V$ = volume in m³,

**Figure 6**
Wind tunnels are used to test aircraft designs. (Louis Bencze/Getty Images Inc. – Stone Allstock.)

$n$ = number of kmoles of gas in the sample,
$R$ = ideal gas constant, 8.314 kPa m$^3$/kmol K, and
$T$ = temperature, expressed in kelvins (K).

In addition, we know that the number of kmoles of gas is equal to the mass of the gas divided by the molar mass (also known as the molecular weight), or

$$n = m/\text{MW}$$

where

$m$ = mass in kg and
MW = molar mass in kg/kmol.

Different units can be used in the equations if the value of $R$ is changed accordingly.

Now suppose you know that the volume of air in the wind tunnel is 1000 m$^3$. Before the wind tunnel is turned on, the temperature of the air is 300 K, and the pressure is 100 kPa. The average molar mass (molecular weight) of air is approximately 29 kg/kmol. Find the mass of the air in the wind tunnel.

To solve this problem, use the following problem-solving methodology:

1. State the Problem
   When you solve a problem, it is a good idea to restate it in your own words: Find the mass of air in a wind tunnel.

2. Describe the Input and Output

   *Input*

   | | |
   |---|---|
   | Volume | $V$ = 1000 m$^3$ |
   | Temperature | $T$ = 300 K |
   | Pressure | $P$ = 100 kPa |
   | Molecular Weight | MW = 29 kg/kmol |
   | Gas Constant | $R$ = 8.314 kPa m$^3$/kmol K |

   *Output*

   | | |
   |---|---|
   | Mass | $m$ = ? kg |

3. Develop a Hand Example
   Working the problem by hand (or with a calculator) allows you to outline an algorithm, which you can translate to MATLAB code later. You should choose simple data that make it easy to check your work. In this problem, we know two equations relating the data:

   $PV = nRT$     ideal gas law
   $n = m/\text{MW}$     relationship between mass and moles

   Solve the ideal gas law for $n$, and plug in the given values:

$$n = PV/RT$$
$$= \frac{(100 \text{ kPa} \times 1000 \text{ m}^3)}{8.314 \text{ kPa} \dfrac{\text{m}^3}{\text{kmol K}} \times 300 \text{K}}$$
$$= 40.0930 \text{ kmol}$$

Convert moles to mass by solving the conversion equation for the mass $m$ and plugging in the values:

$$m = n \times \text{MW} = 40.0930 \text{ kmol} \times 29 \text{ kg/kmol}$$
$$m = 1162.70 \text{ kg}$$

4. Develop a MATLAB Solution
First, clear the screen and memory:

```
clear, clc
```

Now perform the following calculations in the command window:

```
P = 100
P =
          100
T = 300
T =
          300
V = 1000
V =
          1000
MW = 29
MW =
          29
R = 8.314
R =
          8.3140
n =(P*V)/(R*T)
n =
          40.0930
m = n*MW
m =
          1.1627e+003
```

There are several things you should notice about this MATLAB solution. First, because no semicolons were used to suppress the output, the values of the variables are repeated after each assignment statement. Notice also the use of parentheses in the calculation of $n$. They are necessary in the denominator, but not in the numerator. However, using parentheses in both makes the code easier to read.

5. Test the Solution
In this case, comparing the result with that obtained by hand is sufficient. More complicated problems solved in MATLAB should use a variety of input data, to confirm that your solution works in a variety of cases. The MATLAB screen used to solve this problem is shown in Figure 7.

Notice that the variables defined in the command window are listed in the workspace window. Notice also that the command history lists the commands executed in the command window. If you were to scroll up in the command history window, you would see commands from previous MATLAB sessions. All of these commands are available for you to move to the command window.

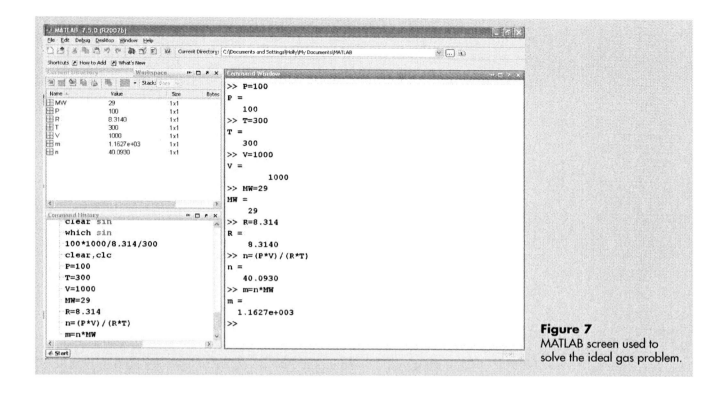

**Figure 7**
MATLAB screen used to solve the ideal gas problem.

### Array Operations

Using MATLAB as a glorified calculator is fine, but its real strength is in matrix manipulations. As described previously, the simplest way to define a matrix is to use a list of numbers, called an *explicit list*. The command

EXPLICIT LIST: a list identifying each member of a matrix

        x = [1 2 3 4]

returns the row vector

        x =
             1 2 3 4

Recall that, in defining this vector, you may list the values either with or without commas. A new row is indicated by a semicolon, so a column vector is specified as

        y = [ 1; 2; 3; 4]

and a matrix that contains both rows and columns is created with the statement

        a = [ 1 2 3 4; 2 3 4 5 ; 3 4 5 6]

and will return

        a =
             1 2 3 4
             2 3 4 5
             3 4 5 6

While a complicated matrix might have to be entered by hand, evenly spaced matrices can be entered much more readily. The command

```
b = 1:5
```

and the command

```
b = [1:5]
```

are equivalent statements. Both return a row matrix

```
b =
    1 2 3 4 5
```

(The square brackets are optional.) The default increment is 1, but if you want to use a different increment, put it between the first and final values on the right side of the command. For example,

```
c = 1:2:5
```

indicates that the increment between values will be 2 and returns

```
c =
    1    3    5
```

If you want MATLAB to calculate the spacing between elements, you may use the **linspace** command. Specify the initial value, the final value, and how many total values you want. For example,

```
d = linspace(1,10,3)
```

returns a vector with three values, evenly spaced between 1 and 10:

```
d =
    1    5.5    10
```

You can create logarithmically spaced vectors with the **logspace** command, which also requires three inputs. The first two values are powers of 10 representing the initial and final values in the array. The final value is the number of elements in the array. Thus,

```
e = logspace(1,3,3)
```

returns three values:

```
e =
    10   100   1000
```

Notice that the first element in the vector is $10^1$ and the last element in the array is $10^3$.

**Hint**

New MATLAB users often err when using the **logspace** command by entering the actual first and last values requested, insteading of the corresponding power of ten. For example,

**logspace(10,100,3)**

is interpreted by MATLAB as: Create a vector from $10^{10}$ to $10^{100}$ with three values. The result is

**ans =**
  **1.0e+100 \***
  **0.0000  0.0000  1.0000**

A common multiplier ($1 \times 10^{100}$) is specified for each result, but the first two values are so small in comparison to the third, that they are effectively 0.

**Hint**

You can include mathematical operations inside a matrix definition statement. For example, you might have **a = [ 0 : pi/10 : pi ]**.

Matrices can be used in many calculations with scalars. If **a = [ 1 2 3 ]**, we can add 5 to each value in the matrix with the syntax

    b = a + 5

which returns

    b =
        6      7      8

This approach works well for addition and subtraction; however, multiplication and division are a little different. In matrix mathematics, the multiplication operator (*) has a specific meaning. Because all MATLAB operations can involve matrices, we need a different operator to indicate element-by-element multiplication. That operator is **.\*** (called *dot multiplication or array multiplication*). For example,

    a.*b

results in element 1 of matrix **a** being multiplied by element 1 of matrix **b**,
        element 2 of matrix **a** being multiplied by element 2 of matrix **b**,
        element *n* of matrix **a** being multiplied by element *n* of matrix **b**.

For the particular case of our **a** (which is **[1 2 3]** ) and our **b** (which is **[6 7 8]**),

    a.*b

returns

    ans =
        6     14     24

(Do the math to convince yourself that these are the correct answers.)

Just using * implies a matrix multiplication, which in this case would return an error message, because **a** and **b** here do not meet the rules for multiplication in

KEY IDEA: Matrix multiplication is different from element-by-element multiplication

matrix algebra. The moral is, be careful to use the correct operator when you mean element-by-element multiplication.

The same syntax holds for element-by-element division ( ./ ) and exponentiation ( .^ ) of individual elements:

```
a./b
a.^2
```

As an exercise, predict the values resulting from the preceding two expressions, and then test your predictions by executing the commands in MATLAB.

---

### Practice Exercise 4

As you perform the following calculations, recall the difference between the * and .* operators, as well as the / and ./ and the ^ and .^ operators:

1. Define the matrix $a = [2.3 \quad 5.8 \quad 9]$ as a MATLAB variable.
2. Find the sine of **a**.
3. Add 3 to every element in **a**.
4. Define the matrix $b = [5.2 \quad 3.14 \quad 2]$ as a MATLAB variable.
5. Add together each element in matrix **a** and in matrix **b**.
6. Multiply each element in **a** by the corresponding element in **b**.
7. Square each element in matrix **a**.
8. Create a matrix named **c** of evenly spaced values from 0 to 10, with an increment of 1.
9. Create a matrix named **d** of evenly spaced values from 0 to 10, with an increment of 2.
10. Use the **linspace** function to create a matrix of six evenly spaced values from 10 to 20.
11. Use the **logspace** function to create a matrix of five logarithmically spaced values between 10 and 100.

---

KEY IDEA: The matrix capability of MATLAB makes it easy to do repetitive calculations

The matrix capability of MATLAB makes it easy to do repetitive calculations. For example, suppose you have a list of angles in degrees that you would like to convert to radians. First put the values into a matrix. For angles of 10, 15, 70, and 90, enter

```
degrees = [ 10 15 70 90];
```

To change the values to radians, you must multiply by $\pi/180$:

```
radians = degrees*pi/180
```

This command returns a matrix called **radians**, with the values in radians. (Try it!) In this case, you could use either the * or the .* operator, because the multiplication involves a single matrix (**degrees**) and two scalars (pi and 180). Thus, you could have written

```
radians = degrees.*pi/180
```

---

### Hint

The value of $\pi$ is built into MATLAB as a floating-point number called **pi**.

Because $\pi$ is an irrational number, it cannot be expressed *exactly* with a floating-point representation, so the MATLAB constant **pi** is really an approximation.

You can see this when you find **sin(pi)**. From trigonometry, the answer should be 0. However, MATLAB returns a very small number, 1.2246e–016. In most calculations, this won't make a difference in the final result.

Another useful matrix operator is transposition. The transpose operator changes rows to columns and vice versa. For example,

```
degrees'
```

returns

```
ans =
        10
        15
        70
        90
```

This makes it easy to create tables. For example, to create a table that converts degrees to radians, enter

```
table = [degrees' , radians']
```

which tells MATLAB to create a matrix named **table**, in which column 1 is degrees and column 2 is radians:

```
table =
       10.0000    0.1745
       15.0000    0.2618
       70.0000    1.2217
       90.0000    1.5708
```

If you transpose a two-dimensional matrix, all the rows become columns and all the columns become rows. For example, the command

```
table'
```

results in

```
   10.0000       15.0000       70.0000       90.0000
    0.1745        0.2618        1.2217        1.5708
```

Note that **table** is not a MATLAB command but merely a convenient variable name. We could have used any meaningful name, say, **conversions** or **degrees_to_radians.**

EXAMPLE 2

## Matrix Calculations with Scalars

Scientific data, such as data collected from wind tunnels, is usually in SI (Système International) units. However, much of the manufacturing infrastructure in the United States has been tooled in English (sometimes called American Engineering or American Standard) units. Engineers need to be fluent in both systems and should be especially careful when sharing data with other engineers. Perhaps the most notorious example of unit confusion problems is the Mars Climate Orbiter (Figure 8), which was the second flight of the Mars Surveyor Program. The spacecraft burned up in the orbit of Mars in September of 1999 because of a lookup table embedded in the craft's software. The table, probably generated from wind-tunnel testing, used pounds force (lbf) when the program expected values in newtons (N).

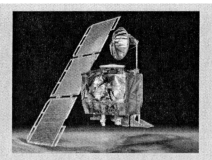

**Figure 8**
Mars Climate Orbiter.
(Courtesy of NASA/Jet
Propulsion Laboratory.)

In this example, we'll use MATLAB to create a conversion table of pounds force to newtons. The table will start at 0 and go to 1000 lbf, at 100-lbf intervals. The conversion factor is

$$1 \text{ lbf} = 4.4482216 \text{ N}$$

1. State the Problem
   Create a table converting pounds force (lbf) to newtons (N).

2. Describe the Input and Output

   ***Input***

   | | |
   |---|---|
   | The starting value in the table is | 0 lbf |
   | The final value in the table is | 1000 lbf |
   | The increment between values is | 100 lbf |
   | The conversion from lbf to N is | 1 lbf = 4.4482216 N |

   ***Output***

   Table listing pounds force (lbf) and newtons (N)

3. Develop a Hand Example
   Since we are creating a table, it makes sense to check a number of different values. Choosing numbers for which the math is easy makes the hand example simple to complete, but still valuable as a check:

   | | | |
   |---|---|---|
   | 0 | * | 4.4482216 = 0 |
   | 100 | * | 4.4482216 = 444.82216 |
   | 1000 | * | 4.4482216 = 4448.2216 |

4. Develop a MATLAB Solution

```
clear, clc
lbf = [0:100:1000];
N = lbf * 4.44822;
[lbf',N']
ans =
  1.0e+003 *
        0        0
   0.1000   0.4448
   0.2000   0.8896
   0.3000   1.3345
```

```
0.4000        1.7793
0.5000        2.2241
0.6000        2.6689
0.7000        3.1138
0.8000        3.5586
0.9000        4.0034
1.0000        4.4482
```

It is always a good idea to clear both the workspace and the command window before starting a new problem. Notice in the workspace window (Figure 9) that **lbf** and **N** are 1 × 11 matrices and that **ans** (which is where the table we created is stored) is an 11 × 2 matrix. The output from the first two commands was suppressed by adding a semicolon at the end of each line. It would be very easy to create a table with more entries by changing the increment to 10 or even to 1. Notice also that you'll need to multiply the results shown in the table by 1000 to get the correct answers. MATLAB tells you that this is necessary directly above the table, where the common scale factor is shown.

5. Test the Solution

Comparing the results of the MATLAB solution with the hand solution shows that they are the same. Once we've verified that our solution works, it's easy to use the same algorithm to create other conversion tables. For instance, modify this example to create a table that converts newtons (N) to pounds force (lbf), with an increment of 10 N, from 0 N to 1000 N.

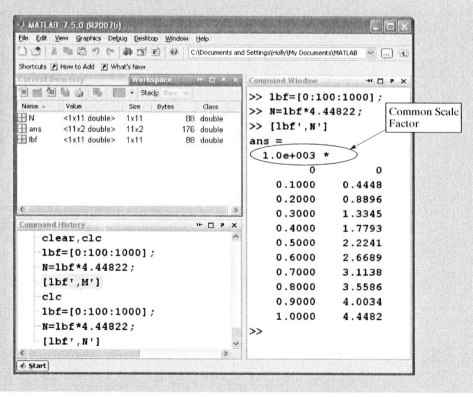

**Figure 9**
The MATLAB workspace window shows the variables as they are created.

**EXAMPLE 3**

### Calculating Drag

One performance characteristic that can be determined in a wind tunnel is drag. The friction related to drag on the Mars Climate Observer (caused by the atmosphere of Mars) resulted in the spacecraft's burning up during course corrections. Drag is extremely important in the design of terrestrial aircraft as well. (See Figure 10.)

Drag is the force generated as an object, such as an airplane, moves through a fluid. Of course, in the case of a wind tunnel, air moves past a stationary model, but the equations are the same. Drag is a complicated force that depends on many factors. One factor is skin friction, which is a function of the surface properties of the aircraft, the properties of the moving fluid (air in this case), and the flow patterns caused by the shape of the aircraft (or, in the case of the Mars Climate Observer, by the shape of the spacecraft). Drag can be calculated with the drag equation

$$\text{drag} = C_d \frac{\rho V^2 A}{2}$$

where  $C_d$ = drag coefficient, which is determined experimentally, usually in a wind tunnel,

$\rho$ = air density,
$V$ = velocity of the aircraft,
$A$ = reference area (the surface area over which the air flows).

Although the drag coefficient is not a constant, it can be taken to be constant at low speeds (less than 200 mph). Suppose the following data were measured in a wind tunnel:

| | |
|---|---|
| drag | 20,000 N |
| $\rho$ | $1 \times 10^{-6}$ kg/m$^3$ |
| $V$ | 100 mph (you'll need to convert this to meters per second) |
| $A$ | 1 m$^2$ |

Calculate the drag coefficient. Finally, use this experimentally determined drag coefficient to predict how much drag will be exerted on the aircraft at velocities from 0 mph to 200 mph.

**Figure 10**
Drag is a mechanical force generated by a solid object moving through a fluid.

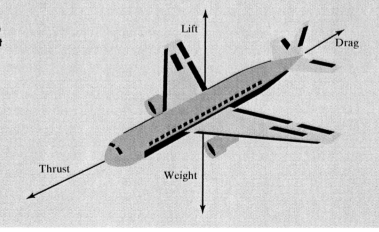

1. State the Problem

   Calculate the drag coefficient on the basis of the data collected in a wind tunnel. Use the drag coefficient to determine the drag at a variety of velocities.

2. Describe the Input and Output

   **Input**

   | | |
   |---|---|
   | Drag | 20,000 N |
   | Air density $\rho$ | $1 \times 10^{-6}$ kg/m$^3$ |
   | Velocity $V$ | 100 mph |
   | Surface area $A$ | 1 m$^2$ |

   **Output**

   Drag coefficient
   Drag at velocities from 0 to 200 mph

3. Develop a Hand Example

   First find the drag coefficient from the experimental data. Notice that the velocity is in miles/hr and must be changed to units consistent with the rest of the data (m/s). The importance of carrying units in engineering calculations cannot be overemphasized!

   $$C_d = \text{drag} \times 2/(\rho \times V^2 \times A)$$
   $$= \frac{(20{,}000 \text{ N} \times 2)}{1 \times 10^{-6} \text{ kg/m}^3 \times \left(100 \text{ miles/hr} \times 0.4470\frac{\text{m/s}}{\text{miles/hr}}\right)^2 \times 1 \text{ m}^2}$$
   $$= 2.0019 \times 10^7$$

   Since a newton is equal to a kg m/s$^2$, the drag coefficient is dimensionless. Now use the drag coefficient to find the drag at different velocities:

   $$\text{drag} = C_d \times \rho \times V^2 \times A/2$$

   Using a calculator, find the value of the drag with $V = 200$ mph:

   $$\text{drag} = \frac{2.0019 \times 10^7 \times 1 \times 10^{-6} \text{ kg/m}^3 \times \left(200 \text{ miles/hr} \times 0.4470\frac{\text{m/s}}{\text{miles/hr}}\right)^2 \times 1 \text{ m}^2}{2}$$
   $$\text{drag} = 80{,}000 \text{ N}$$

4. Develop a MATLAB Solution

   ```
   drag = 20000;                              Define the variables, and change
   density = 0.000001;                        V to SI units.
   velocity= 100*0.4470;
   area = 1;
   cd = drag*2/(density*velocity^2*area)      Calculate the coefficient of drag.
   cd =
     2.0019e+007
   velocity = 0:20:200;                       Redefine V as a matrix.
   velocity = velocity*0.4470;                Change it to SI units and
                                              calculate the drag.
   ```

```
drag = cd*density*velocity.^2*area/2;
table = [velocity', drag']
table =
  1.0e+004 *
       0           0
  0.0009      0.0800
  0.0018      0.3200
  0.0027      0.7200
  0.0036      1.2800
  0.0045      2.0000
  0.0054      2.8800
  0.0063      3.9200
  0.0072      5.1200
  0.0080      6.4800
  0.0089      8.0000
```

Notice that the equation for drag, or

```
drag = cd * density * velocity.^2 * area/2;
```

uses the **.^** operator, because we intend that each value in the matrix **velocity** be squared, not that the entire matrix **velocity** be multiplied by itself. Using

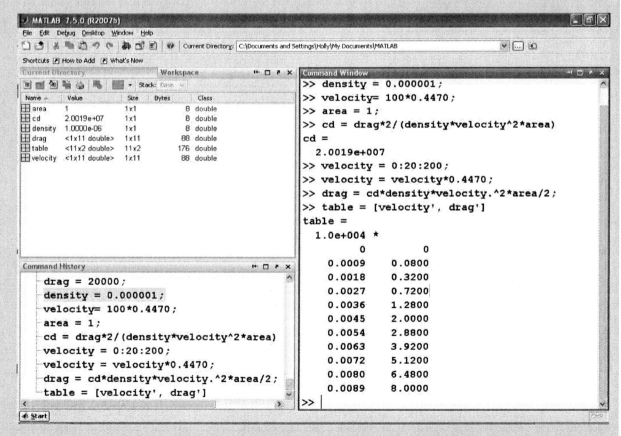

**Figure 11**
The command history window creates a record of previous commands.

just the exponentiation operator ($^\wedge$) would result in an error message. Unfortunately, it is possible to compose problems in which using the wrong operator does not give us an error message but does give us a wrong answer. This makes step 5 in our problem-solving methodology especially important.

5. Test the Solution
Comparing the hand solution with the MATLAB solution (Figure 11), we see that they give the same results. Once we have confirmed that our algorithm works with sample data, we can substitute new data and be confident that the results will be correct. Ideally, the results should also be compared with experimental data, to confirm that the equations we are using accurately model the real physical process.

## 3.3 Number Display

### Scientific Notation

Although you can enter any number in decimal notation, that isn't always the best way to represent very large or very small numbers. For example, a number that is used frequently in chemistry is Avogadro's constant, whose value, to four significant digits, is 602,200,000,000,000,000,000,000. Similarly, the diameter of an iron atom is approximately 140 picometers, which is .000000000140 meter. Scientific notation expresses a value as a number between 1 and 10, multiplied by a power of 10 (the exponent). Thus, Avogadro's number becomes $6.022 \times 10^{23}$, and the diameter of an iron atom, $1.4 \times 10^{-10}$ meter. In MATLAB, values in scientific notation are designated with an **e** between the decimal number and the exponent. (Your calculator probably uses similar notation.) For example, you might have

```
Avogadro's_constant = 6.022e23;
Iron_diameter = 140e-12; or
Iron_diameter = 1.4e-10;
```

It is important to omit blanks between the decimal number and the exponent. For instance, MATLAB will interpret

```
6.022    e23
```

as two values (6.022 and $10^{23}$).

SCIENTIFIC NOTATION: a number represented as a value between one and ten times ten to an appropriate power

---

**Hint**

Although it is a common convention to use e to identify a power of 10, students (and teachers) sometimes confuse this nomenclature with the mathematical constant $e$, which is equal to 2.7183. To raise $e$ to a power, use the **exp** function, for example **exp(3)** is equivalent to $e^3$.

---

### Display Format

A number of different display formats are available in MATLAB. No matter which display format you choose, MATLAB uses double-precision floating-point numbers in its calculations, which results in approximately 16 decimal digits of precision. Changing the display format does not change the accuracy of the results. Unlike some other computer programs, MATLAB handles both integers and decimal numbers as floating-point numbers.

KEY IDEA: MATLAB does not differentiate between integers and floating-point numbers, unless special functions are invoked

When elements of a matrix are displayed in MATLAB, integers are always printed without a decimal point. However, values with decimal fractions are printed in the default short format that shows four digits after the decimal point. Thus,

```
A = 5
```

returns

```
A =
        5
```

but

```
A = 5.1
```

KEY IDEA: No matter what display format is selected, calculations are performed using double-precision floating-point numbers

returns

```
A =
        5.1000
```

and

```
A = 51.1
```

returns

```
A =
        51.1000
```

MATLAB allows you to specify other formats that show additional digits. For example, to specify that you want values to be displayed in a decimal format with 15 digits after the decimal point, use the command

```
format long
```

which changes all subsequent displays. Thus, with **format long** specified,

```
A
```

now returns

```
A =
        51.100000000000001
```

Notice that the final digit in this case is 1, which represents a round-off error.

Two decimal digits are displayed when the format is specified as **format bank**:

```
A =
        51.10
```

The bank format displays only real numbers, so it's not appropriate when complex numbers need to be represented. Thus the command

```
A = 5+3i
```

returns the following using bank format

```
A =
        5.00
```

Using **format long** the same command returns

```
A =
        5.000000000000000 + 3.000000000000000i
```

You can return the format to four decimal digits with the command

```
format short
```

To check the results, recall the value of **A**:

```
A
```

```
A =
    5.0000 + 3.0000i
```

When numbers become too large or too small for MATLAB to display in the default format, it automatically expresses them in scientific notation. For example, if you enter Avogadro's constant into MATLAB in decimal notation as

```
a = 602000000000000000000000
```

the program returns

```
a =
    6.0200e+023
```

You can force MATLAB to display *all* numbers in scientific notation with **format short e** (with four decimal digits) or **format long e** (with 15 decimal digits). For instance,

```
format short e
x = 10.356789
```

returns

```
x =
    1.0357e+001
```

Another pair of formats that are often useful to engineers and scientists, **format short eng** and **format long eng**, are similar to scientific notation but require the power of 10 to be a multiple of three. This corresponds to common naming conventions. For example,

$$1 \text{ millimeter} = 1 \times 10^{-3} \text{ meters}$$
$$1 \text{ micrometer} = 1 \times 10^{-6} \text{ meters}$$
$$1 \text{ nanometer} = 1 \times 10^{-9} \text{ meters}$$
$$1 \text{ picometer} = 1 \times 10^{-12} \text{ meters}$$

Consider the following example. First change to engineering format and then enter a value for **y**.

```
format short eng
y = 12000
```

which gives the result

```
y =
    12.0000e+003
```

When a matrix of values is sent to the screen, and if the elements become very large or very small, a common scale factor is often applied to the entire matrix. This scale factor is printed along with the scaled values. For example, when the command window is returned to

```
format short
```

the results from Example 3 are displayed as

```
table =
1.0e+005 *
            0            0
       0.0002       0.0400
       0.0004       0.1602
       0.0006       0.3603
       0.0008       0.6406        etc...
```

Two other formats that you may occasionally find useful are **format +** and **format rat**. When a matrix is displayed in **format +**, the only characters printed are plus and minus signs. If a value is positive, a plus sign will be displayed; if a value is negative, a minus sign will be displayed. If a value is zero, nothing will be displayed. This format allows us to view a large matrix in terms of its signs:

```
format +
B = [1, -5, 0, 12; 10005, 24, -10,4]
B =
        +- +
        ++-+
```

RATIONAL NUMBER: a number that can be represented as a fraction

The **format rat** command displays numbers as rational numbers (i.e., as fractions). Thus,

```
format rat
x = 0:0.1:0.5
```

returns

```
x =
    0      1/10      1/5      3/10      2/5      1/2
```

If you're not sure which format is the best for your application, you may select **format short g** or **format long g**. This format selects the best of fixed-point or floating-point representations.

The **format** command also allows you to control how tightly information is spaced in the command window. The default (**format loose**) inserts a line feed between user-supplied expressions and the results returned by the computer. The **format compact** command removes those line feeds. The examples in this text use the compact format to save space. Table 2 shows how the value of $\pi$ is displayed in each format.

**Table 2  Numeric Display Formats**

| MATLAB Command | Display | Example |
|---|---|---|
| **format short** | 4 decimal digits | **3.1416**<br>**123.4568** |
| **format long** | 14 decimal digits | **3.14159265358979**<br>**1.234567890000000e+002** |
| **format short e** | 4 decimal digits<br>scientific notation | **3.1416e+000**<br>**1.2346e+002** |
| **format long e** | 14 decimal digits<br>scientific notation | **3.141592653589793e+000**<br>**1.234567890000000e+002** |
| **format bank** | 2 decimal digits<br>only real values are displayed | **3.14** |
| **format short eng** | 4 decimal digits<br>engineering notation | **3.1416e+000**<br>**123.4568e+000** |
| **format long eng** | 14 decimal digits<br>engineering notation | **3.141592653589793e+000**<br>**123.456789000000e+000** |
| **format +** | +, −, blank | **+** |
| **format rat** | fractional form | **355/113** |

| **format short g** | MATLAB selects the best format | **3.1416** |
| | | **123.46** |
| **format long g** | MATLAB selects the best format | **3.14159265358979** |
| | | **123.456789** |

If none of these predefined numeric display formats is right for you, you can control individual lines of output with the **fprintf** function.

## 4 SAVING YOUR WORK

Working in the command window is similar to performing calculations on your scientific calculator. When you turn off the calculator or when you exit the program, your work is gone. It *is* possible to save the *values* of the variables you defined in the command window and that are listed in the workspace window, but while doing so is useful, it is more likely that you will want to save the list of commands that generated your results. The **diary** command allows you to do just that. Also we will show you how to save and retrieve variables (the results of the assignments you made and the calculations you performed) to MAT-files or to DAT-files. Finally we'll introduce script M-files, which are created in the edit window. Script M-files allow you to save a list of commands and to execute them later. You will find script M-files especially useful for solving homework problems. When you create a program in MATLAB, it is stored in an M-file.

### 4.1 Diary

The diary function allows you to record a MATLAB session in a file, and retrieve it for later review. Both the MATLAB commands and the results are stored—including all your mistakes. To activate the diary function simply type

```
diary
```
or
```
diary on
```

at the command prompt. To end a recording session type **diary** again, or **diary off.** A file named diary should appear in the current directory. You can retrieve the file by double- clicking on the file name in the current directory window. An editor window will open with the recorded commands and results. You can also open the file in any text editor, such as Notepad. Subsequent sessions are added to the end of the file. If you prefer to store the diary session in a different file, specify the filename

```
diary <filename>     or
diary('filename')
```

In this text we'll use angle brackets ($< >$) to indicate user-defined names. Thus, to save a diary session in a file named My_diary_file type

```
diary My_diary_file     or
diary('My_diary_file')
```

### 4.2 Saving Variables

To preserve the variables you created in the **command window** (check the **workspace window** on the left-hand side of the MATLAB screen for the list of variables), you must save the contents of the **workspace window** to a file. The default format is a binary file called a MAT-file. To save the workspace (remember, this is just the variables, not the list of commands in the command window) to a file, type

```
save < file_name >
```

at the prompt. Recall that, although **save** is a MATLAB command, **file_name** is a user-defined file name. It can be any name you choose, as long as it conforms to the naming conventions for variables in MATLAB. Actually, you don't even need to supply a file name. If you don't, MATLAB names the file **matlab.mat**. You could also choose

```
File → Save Workspace As
```

from the menu bar, which will then prompt you to enter a file name for your data. To restore a workspace, type

```
load < file_name >
```

Again, **load** is a MATLAB command, but **file_name** is the user-defined file name. If you just type **load**, MATLAB will look for the default **matlab.mat** file.

The file you save will be stored in the current directory.

For example, type

```
clear, clc
```

This command will clear both the workspace and the command window. Verify that the workspace is empty by checking the workspace window or by typing

```
whos
```

Now define several variables—for example,

```
a = 5;
b = [1,2,3];
c = [ 1, 2; 3,4];
```

Check the workspace window once again, to confirm that the variables have been stored. Now, save the workspace to a file called my_example_file:

```
save my_example_file
```

Confirm that a new file has been stored in the current directory. If you prefer to save the file to another directory (for instance, onto a floppy drive), use the browse button (see Figure 2.) to navigate to the directory of your choice. Remember that in a public computer lab the current directory is probably purged after each user logs off the system.

Now, clear the workspace and command window by typing

```
clear, clc
```

The workspace window should be empty. You can recover the missing variables and their values by loading the file (my_example_file.mat) back into the workspace:

```
load my_example_file
```

The file you want to load must be in the current directory, or MATLAB won't be able to find it. In the command window, type

```
a
```

which returns

```
a =
     5
```

Similarly,

```
b
```

returns

        **b =**
            **1   2   3**

and typing

        **c**

returns

        **c =**
            **1   2**
            **3   4**

MATLAB can also store individual matrices or lists of matrices into the current directory with the command

        **save <file_name> <variable_list>**

where **file_name** is the user-defined file name designating the location in memory at which you wish to store the information, and **variable_list** is the list of variables to be stored in the file. For example,

        **save my_new_file a b**

would save just the variables **a** and **b** into **my_new_file.mat**.

If your saved data will be used by a program other than MATLAB (such as C or C++), the .mat format is not appropriate, because .mat files are unique to MAT-LAB. The ASCII format is standard between computer platforms and is more appropriate if you need to share files. MATLAB allows you to save files as ASCII files by modifying the save command to

        **save <file_name> <variable_list> -ascii**

The command **-ascii** tells MATLAB to store the data in a standard eight-digit text format. ASCII files should be saved into a .dat file or .txt file instead of a .mat file; be sure to add .the extension to your file name:

        **save my_new_file.dat a b -ascii**

If you don't add .dat, MATLAB will default to .mat.

If more precision is needed, the data can be stored in a 16-digit text format:

        **save file_name variable_list -ascii -double**

You can retrieve the data from the current directory with the load command:

        **load <file_name>**

For example, to create the matrix **z** and save it to the file **data_2.dat** in eight-digit text format, use the following commands:

        **z = [5 3 5; 6 2 3];**
        **save data_2.dat z -ascii**

Together, these commands cause each row of the matrix **z** to be written to a separate line in the data file. You can view the data_2.dat file by double-clicking the file name in the current directory window. (See Figure 12.) Perhaps the easiest way to retrieve data from an ASCII .dat file is to enter the **load** command followed by the file name. This causes the information to be read into a matrix with the same name as the data file. However, it is also quite easy to use MATLAB's interactive Import Wizard to load the data. When you double-click a data file name in the current directory to view the contents of the file, the Import Wizard will automatically launch. Just follow the directions to load the data into the workspace, with the same name as the data file. You can use this same technique to import data from other

ASCII: binary data storage format

KEY IDEA: When you save the workspace, you save only the variables and their values; you do not save the commands you've executed

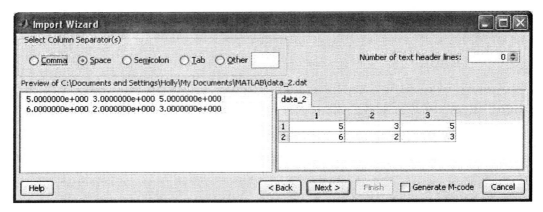

**Figure 12**
Double-clicking the file name in the command directory launches the Import Wizard.

programs, including Excel spreadsheets, or you can select **File → Import Data...** from the menu bar.

### 4.3  Script M-Files

Using the command window for calculations is an easy and powerful tool. However, once you close the MATLAB program, all of our calculations are gone. Fortunately, MATLAB contains a powerful programming language. As a programmer, you can create and save code in files called M-files. These files can be reused anytime you wish to repeat your calculations. An M-file is an ASCII text file similar to a C or FORTRAN source-code file. It can be created and edited with the MATLAB M-file editor/debugger (the edit window discussed in Section 2.7), or you can use another text editor of your choice. To open the editing window, select

```
File → New → M-file
```

from the MATLAB menu bar. The MATLAB edit window is shown in Figure 13. Many programmers prefer to dock the editing window onto the MATLAB desktop, using the docking arrow in the upper right-hand corner of the window. This allows you to see both the contents of the M-file and the results displayed when the

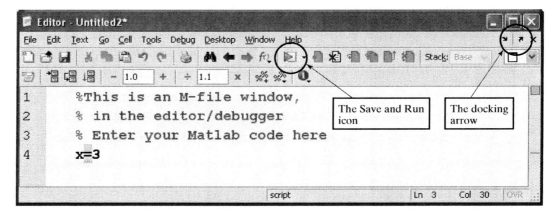

**Figure 13**
The MATLAB edit window, also called the editor/debugger.

program is executed. The results from an M-file program are displayed in the command window.

If you choose a different text editor, make sure that the files you save are ASCII files. Notepad is an example of a text editor that defaults to an ASCII file structure. Other word processors, such as WordPerfect or Word, will require you to specify the ASCII structure when you save the file. These programs default to proprietary file structures that are not ASCII compliant and may yield some unexpected results if you try to use code written in them without specifying that the files be saved in ASCII format.

When you save an M-file, it is stored in the current directory. You'll need to name your file with a valid MATLAB variable name—that is, a name starting with a letter and containing only letters, numbers, and the underscore (_). Spaces are not allowed. (See Section 3.1.)

There are two types of M-files, called scripts and functions. A script M-file is simply a list of MATLAB statements that are saved in a file with a .m file extension. The script can use any variables that have been defined in the workspace, and any variables created in the script are added to the workspace when the script finishes. You can execute a script created in the MATLAB edit window by selecting the Save and Run icon from the menu bar, as shown in Figure 13. (The Save and Run icon changed appearance with MATLAB 7.5. Previous versions of the program used an icon similar to an exclamation point.) You can also execute a script by typing a file name or by using the run command from the command window as shown in Table 3.

You can find out what M-files and MAT files are in the current directory by typing

    what

into the command window. You can also browse through the current directory by looking in the current directory window.

Using script M-files allows you to work on a project and to save the list of commands for future use. Because you will be using these files in the future, it is a good idea to sprinkle them liberally with comments. The comment operator in MATLAB is the percentage sign, as in

    % This is a comment

MATLAB will not execute any code on a commented line.

You can also add comments after a command, but on the same line:

    a = 5        %The variable a is defined as 5

MATLAB code that could be entered into an M-file and used to solve Example 3 is as follows:

    clear, clc
    % A Script M-file to find Drag
    % First define the variables

**M-FILE**: a list of MATLAB commands stored in a separate file

**KEY IDEA**: The two types of M-files are scripts and functions

### Table 3  Approaches to Executing a Script M-File from the Command Window

| MATLAB Command | Comments |
| --- | --- |
| myscript | Type the file name. The .m file extension is assumed. |
| run myscript | Use the run command with the file name. |
| run('myscript') | Use the functional form of the run command. |

```
drag = 20000;              %Define drag in Newtons
density= 0.000001;         %Define air density in kg/m^3
velocity = 100*0.4470;     %Define velocity in m/s
area = 1;                  %Define area in m^2
% Calculate coefficient of drag
cd = drag *2/(density*velocity^2*area)
% Find the drag for a variety of velocities
velocity = 0:20:200;          %Redefine velocity
velocity = velocity*.4470  %Change velocity to m/s
drag = cd*density*velocity.^2*area/2;    %Calculate drag
table = [velocity',drag']  %Create a table of results
```

This code can be run either from the M-file or from the command window. The results will appear in the command window in either case, and the variables will be stored in the workspace. The advantage of an M-file is that you can save your program to run again later.

---

**Hint**

You can execute a portion of an M-file by highlighting a section and then right-clicking and selecting **Evaluate Section**. You can also comment or "uncomment" whole sections of code from this menu; doing so is useful when you are creating programs while you are still debugging your work.

---

The final example in this chapter uses a script M-file to find the velocity and acceleration that a spacecraft might reach in leaving the solar system.

**EXAMPLE 4**

### Creating an M-File to Calculate the Acceleration of a Spacecraft

In the absence of drag, the propulsion power requirements for a spacecraft are determined fairly simply. Recall from basic physical science that

$$F = ma$$

In other words, force ($F$) is equal to mass ($m$) times acceleration ($a$). Work ($W$) is force times distance ($d$), and since power ($P$) is work per unit time, power becomes force times velocity ($v$):

$$W = Fd$$
$$P = \frac{W}{t} = F \times \frac{d}{t} = F \times v = m \times a \times v$$

This means that the power requirements for the spacecraft depend on its mass, how fast it's going, and how quickly it needs to speed up or slow down. If no power is applied, the spacecraft just keeps traveling at its current velocity. As long as we don't want to do anything quickly, course corrections can be made with very little power. Of course, most of the power requirements for spacecraft are not related to navigation. Power is required for communication, for housekeeping, and for science experiments and observations.

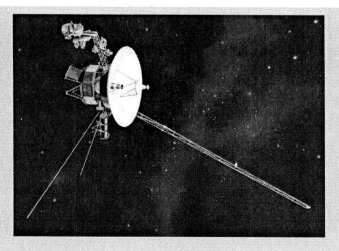

**Figure 14**
The *Voyager 1* and *Voyager 2* spacecraft were launched in 1977 and have since left the solar system. (Courtesy of NASA/Jet Propulsion Laboratory.)

The *Voyager 1* and *2* spacecraft explored the outer solar system during the last quarter of the 20th century. (See Figure 14.) *Voyager 1* encountered both Jupiter and Saturn; *Voyager 2* not only encountered Jupiter and Saturn but continued on to Uranus and Neptune. The *Voyager* program was enormously successful, and the *Voyager* spacecraft continue to gather information as they leave the solar system. The power generators (low-level nuclear reactors) on each spacecraft are expected to function until at least 2020. The power source is a sample of plutonium-238, which, as it decays, generates heat that is used to produce electricity. At the launch of each spacecraft, its generator produced about 470 watts of power. Because the plutonium is decaying, the power production had decreased to about 335 watts in 1997, almost 20 years after launch. This power is used to operate the science package, but if it were diverted to propulsion, how much acceleration would it produce in the spacecraft? *Voyager 1* is currently traveling at a velocity of 3.50 AU/year (an AU is an astronomical unit), and *Voyager 2* is traveling at 3.15 AU/year. Each spacecraft weighs 721.9 kg.

1. State the Problem
   Find the acceleration that is possible with the power output from the spacecraft power generators.

2. Describe the Input and Output

   ***Input***

   Mass = 721.9 kg
   Power = 335 watts = 335 J/s
   Velocity = 3.50 AU/year (*Voyager* 1)
   Velocity = 3.15 AU/year (*Voyager* 2)

   ***Output***

   Acceleration of each spacecraft, in m/sec/sec

3. Develop a Hand Example
   We know that

   $$P = m \times a \times v$$

   which can be rearranged to give

   $$a = P/(m \times v)$$

The hardest part of this calculation will be keeping the units straight. First let's change the velocity to m/s. For *Voyager 1*,

$$v = 3.50 \frac{AU}{year} \times \frac{150 \times 10^9 \, m}{AU} \times \frac{year}{365 \, days} \times \frac{day}{24 \, hours} \times \frac{hour}{3600 \, s} = 16{,}650 \frac{m}{s}$$

Then we calculate the acceleration:

$$a = \frac{335 \frac{J}{s} \times 1 \frac{kg \times m^2}{s^2 \, J}}{721.9 \, kg \times 16{,}650 \frac{m}{s}} = 2.7 \times 10^{-5} \frac{m}{s^2}$$

4. Develop a MATLAB Solution

```
clear, clc
%Example 4
%Find the possible acceleration of the Voyager 1
%and Voyager 2 Spacecraft using the on board power
%generator
format short
mass=721.9;          %mass in kg
power=335;           % power in watts
velocity=[3.5 3.15];          % velocity in AU/year
%Change the velocity to m/sec
velocity=velocity*150e9/365/24/3600
%Calculate the acceleration
acceleration=power./(mass.*velocity)
```

The results are printed in the command window, as shown in Figure 15.

**Figure 15**
The results of an M-file execution print into the command window. The variables created are reflected in the workspace and the M-file is listed in the current directory window. The commands issued in the M-file are not mirrored in the command history.

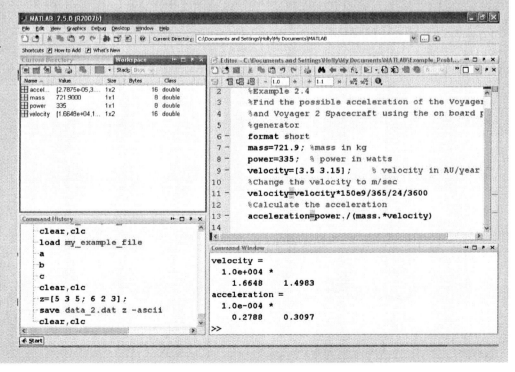

5. Test the Solution

Compare the MATLAB results with the hand example results. Notice that the velocity and acceleration calculated from the hand example and the MATLAB solution for *Voyager 1* match. The acceleration seems quite small, but applied over periods of weeks or months such an acceleration can achieve significant velocity changes. For example, a constant acceleration of $2.8 \times 10^{-5}$ m/s$^2$ results in a velocity change of about 72 m/sec over the space of a month:

$$2.8 \times 10^{-5} \text{ m/s}^2 \times 3600 \text{ s/hour}$$
$$\times 24 \text{ hour/day} \times 30 \text{ days/month} = 72.3 \text{ m/s}$$

Now that you have a MATLAB program that works, you can use it as the starting point for other, more complicated calculations.

---

**SUMMARY**

In this chapter, we introduced the basic MATLAB structure. The MATLAB environment includes multiple windows, four of which are open in the default view:

- Command window
- Command history window
- Workspace window
- Current directory window

In addition, the

- Document window
- Graphics window
- Edit window

open as needed during a MATLAB session.

Variables defined in MATLAB follow common computer naming conventions:

- Names must start with a letter.
- Letters, numbers, and the underscore are the only characters allowed.
- Names are case sensitive.
- Names may be any length, although only the first 63 characters are used by MATLAB.
- Some keywords are reserved by MATLAB and cannot be used as variable names.
- MATLAB allows the user to reassign function names as variable names, although doing so is not good practice.

The basic computational unit in MATLAB is the matrix. Matrices may be

- Scalars ($1 \times 1$ matrix)
- Vectors ($1 \times n$ or $n \times 1$ matrix, either a row or a column)
- Two-dimensional arrays ($m \times n$ or $n \times m$)
- Multidimensional arrays

Matrices often store numeric information, although they can store other kinds of information as well. Data can be entered into a matrix manually or can be retrieved from stored data files. When entered manually, a matrix is enclosed in square brackets, elements in a row are separated by either commas or spaces, and a new row is indicated by a semicolon:

```
a = [1 2 3 4; 5 6 7 8]
```

Evenly spaced matrices can be generated with the colon operator. Thus, the command

```
b = 0:2:10
```

creates a matrix starting at 0, ending at 10, and with an increment of 2. The **linspace** and **logspace** functions can be used to generate a matrix of specified length from given starting and ending values, spaced either linearly or logarithmically. The **help** function or the MATLAB Help menu can be used to determine the appropriate syntax for these and other functions.

MATLAB follows the standard algebraic order of operations. The operators supported by MATLAB are listed in the "MATLAB Summary" section of this chapter.

MATLAB supports both standard (decimal) and scientific notation. It also supports a number of different display options, described in the "MATLAB Summary" section. No matter how values are displayed, they are stored as double-precision floating-point numbers.

Collections of MATLAB commands can be saved in script M-files. MATLAB variables can be saved or imported from either .MAT or .DAT files. The .MAT format is proprietary to MATLAB and is used because it stores data more efficiently than other file formats. The .DAT format employs the standard ASCII format and is used when data created in MATLAB will be shared with other programs.

**MATLAB SUMMARY**    The following MATLAB summary lists all the special characters, commands, and functions that were defined in this chapter:

| Special Characters | |
| --- | --- |
| [ ] | forms matrices |
| ( ) | used in statements to group operations |
| | used with a matrix name to identify specific elements |
| , | separates subscripts or matrix elements |
| ; | separates rows in a matrix definition |
| | suppresses output when used in commands |
| : | used to generate matrices |
| | indicates all rows or all columns |
| = | assignment operator assigns a value to a memory location; |
| | not the same as an equality |
| % | indicates a comment in an M-file |
| + | scalar and array addition |
| - | scalar and array subtraction |
| * | scalar multiplication and multiplication in matrix algebra |
| .* | array multiplication (dot multiply or dot star) |
| / | scalar division and division in matrix algebra |
| ./ | array division (dot divide or dot slash) |
| ^ | scalar exponentiation and matrix exponentiation in matrix algebra |
| .^ | array exponentiation (dot power or dot caret) |

## Commands and Functions

| | |
|---|---|
| **ans** | default variable name for results of MATLAB calculations |
| **ascii** | indicates that data should be saved in standard ASCII format |
| **clc** | clears command window |
| **clear** | clears workspace |
| **diary** | creates a copy of all the commands issued in the workspace window, and most of the results |
| **exit** | terminates MATLAB |
| **format +** | sets format to plus and minus signs only |
| **format compact** | sets format to compact form |
| **format long** | sets format to 14 decimal places |
| **format long e** | sets format to scientific notation with 14 decimal places |
| **format long eng** | sets format to engineering notation with 14 decimal places |
| **format long g** | allows MATLAB to select the best format (either fixed point or floating point), using 14 decimal digits |
| **format loose** | sets format to the default, noncompact form |
| **format short** | sets format to the default, 4 decimal places |
| **format short e** | sets format to scientific notation with 4 decimal places |
| **format short eng** | sets format to engineering notation with 4 decimal places |
| **format short g** | allows MATLAB to select the best format (either fixed point or floating point), using 4 decimal digits |
| **format rat** | sets format to rational (fractional) display |
| **help** | invokes help utility |
| **linspace** | linearly spaced vector function |
| **load** | loads matrices from a file |
| **logspace** | logarithmically spaced vector function |
| **pi** | numeric approximation of the value of $\pi$ |
| **quit** | terminates MATLAB |
| **save** | saves variables in a file |
| **who** | lists variables in memory |
| **whos** | lists variables and their sizes |

**KEY TERMS**

arguments
array
array editor
ASCII
assignment
command history
command window
current directory

document window
edit window
function
graphics window
M-file
matrix
operator
prompt

scalar
scientific notation
script
start button
transpose
vector
workspace

## PROBLEMS

You can either solve these problems in the command window, using Matlab as an electronic calculator, or you can create an M-file of the solutions. If you are solving these problems as a homework assignment, you will probably want to use an M-file, so that you can turn in your solutions.

### Getting Started

**1**   Predict the outcome of the following MATLAB calculations:

$1 + 3/4$

$5 * 6 * 4/2$

$5/2 * 6 * 4$

$5^2 * 3$

$5^ (2 * 3)$

$1 + 3 + 5/5 + 3 + 1$

$(1 + 3 + 5)(5 + 3 + 1)$

Check your results by entering the calculations into the command window.

### Using Variables

**2**   Identify which name in each of the following pairs is a legitimate MATLAB variable name:

| | |
|---|---|
| fred | fred! |
| book_1 | book-1 |
| 2ndplace | Second_Place |
| #1 | No_1 |
| vel_5 | vel.5 |
| tan | while |

Test your answers by using **isvarname**—for example,

```
isvarname fred
```

Remember, **isvarname** returns a 1 if the name is valid and a 0 if it is not. Although it is possible to reassign a function name as a variable name, doing so is not a good idea. Use **which** to check whether the preceding names are function names—for example,

```
which sin
```

In what case would MATLAB tell you that **sin** is a variable name, not a function name?

### Scalar Operations and Order of Operations

**3**   Create MATLAB code to perform the following calculations:

$5^2$

$\dfrac{5 + 3}{5 \cdot 6}$

$\sqrt{4 + 6^3}$    (*Hint*: A square root is the same thing as a $^1\!/_2$ power.)

$9\dfrac{6}{12} + 7 \cdot 5^{3+2}$

$1 + 5 \cdot 3/6^2 + 2^{2-4} \cdot 1/5.5$

Check your code by entering it into MATLAB and performing the calculations on your scientific calculator.

**Figure P4(a)**

4  **(a)** The area of a circle is $\pi r^2$. Define $r$ as 5, then find the area of a circle, using MATLAB.
   **(b)** The surface area of a sphere is $4\pi r^2$. Find the surface area of a sphere with a radius of 10 ft.
   **(c)** The volume of a sphere is $^4\!/_3\pi r^3$. Find the volume of a sphere with a radius of 2 ft.

5  **(a)** The area of a square is the edge length squared. ($A = $ edge$^2$.) Define the edge length as 5, then find the area of a square, using MATLAB.
   **(b)** The surface area of a cube is 6 times the edge length squared. (SA $= 6 \times$ edge$^2$.) Find the surface area of a cube with edge length 10.
   **(c)** The volume of a cube is the edge length cubed. (V $=$ edge$^3$.) Find the volume of a cube with edge length 12.

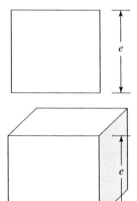

**Figure P5(a-c)**

6  Consider the barbell shown in Figure P6.
   **(a)** Find the volume of the figure, if the radius of each sphere is 10 cm, the length of the bar connecting them is 15 cm, and the diameter of the bar is 1 cm.
   **(b)** Find the surface area of the figure.

**Figure P6**
The geometry of a barbell can be modeled as two spheres and a cylindrical rod.

7  The ideal gas law was introduced in Example 1. It describes the relationship between pressure ($P$), temperature ($T$), volume ($V$) and the number of moles of gas ($n$).

$$PV = nRT$$

The additional symbol, $R$, represents the ideal-gas constant. The ideal-gas law is a good approximation of the behavior of gases when the pressure is low and the temperature is high. (What constitutes low pressure and high temperature varies with different gases.) In 1873, Johannes Diderik van der Waals (Figure P7) proposed a modified version of the ideal gas law that

**Figure P7**
Johannes Diderik van der Waals

better models the behavior of real gases over a wider range of temperature and pressure.

$$\left(P + \frac{n^2 a}{V^2}\right)(V - nb) = nRT$$

In this equation the additional variables $a$ and $b$ represent values characteristic of individual gases.

Use both the ideal gas law and Van der Waals' equation to calculate the temperature of water vapor (steam), given the following data.

| | |
|---|---|
| pressure, $P$ | 220 bar |
| moles, $n$ | 2 mol |
| volume, V | 1 L |
| $a$ | 5.536 $L^2 bar/mol^2$    * |
| $b$ | 0.03049 L/mol    * |
| ideal gas constant, $R$ | .08314472 L bar /K mol |

*Source: Weast,. R. C. (Ed.), *Handbook of Chemistry and Physics (53rd Edn.)*, Cleveland:Chemical Rubber Co., 1972.

### Array Operations

**Figure P8(a)**

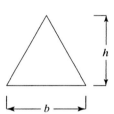

**Figure P8(b)**

8   (a)  The volume of a cylinder is $\pi r^2 h$. Define $r$ as 3 and $h$ as the matrix

    h = [1, 5, 12]

Find the volume of the cylinders. (See Figure P8a.)

   (b)  The area of a triangle is $\frac{1}{2}$ the length of the base of the triangle, times the height of the triangle. Define the base as the matrix

    b = [ 2, 4, 6]

and the height $h$ as 12, and find the area of the triangles. (See Figure P8b.)

   (c)  The volume of any right prism is the area of the base of the prism, times the vertical dimension of the prism. The base of the prism can be any shape—for example, a circle, a rectangle or a triangle.

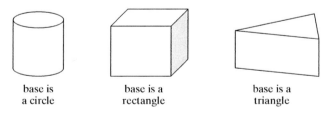

base is          base is a          base is a
a circle         rectangle          triangle

**Figure P8(c)**

Find the volume of the prisms created from the triangles of part (b). Assume that the vertical dimension of these prisms is 6. (See Figure P8c.)

9   Burning one gallon of gasoline in your car produces 19.4 pounds of $CO_2$. Calculate the amount of $CO_2$ emitted during a year for the following vehicles, assuming they all travel 12,000 miles per year. The reported fuel-efficiency numbers were extracted from the manufacturers' websites based on the EPA 2008 criteria; they are an average of the city and highway estimates.

| 2008 | Smart Car Fortwo | 37 mpg |
|------|------------------|--------|
| 2008 | Civic Coupe | 29 mpg |
| 2008 | Civic Hybrid | 43 mpg |
| 2008 | Chevrolet Cobalt | 30 mpg |
| 2008 | Toyota Prius (Hybrid) | 46 mpg |
| 2008 | Toyota Yaris | 32 mpg |

**10**  **(a)** Create an evenly spaced vector of values from 1 to 20 in increments of 1.

**(b)** Create a vector of values from zero to $2\pi$ in increments of $\pi/10$.

**(c)** Create a vector containing 15 values, evenly spaced between 4 and 20. (*Hint*: Use the **linspace** command. If you can't remember the syntax, type **help linspace**.)

**(d)** Create a vector containing 10 values, spaced logarithmically between 10 and 1000. (*Hint*: Use the **logspace** command.)

**11**  **(a)** Create a table of conversions from feet to meters. Start the feet column at 0, increment it by 1, and end it at 10 feet. (Look up the conversion factor in a textbook or online.)

**(b)** Create a table of conversions from radians to degrees. Start the radians column at 0 and increment by $0.1\pi$ radian, up to $\pi$ radians. (Look up the conversion factor in a textbook or online.)

**(c)** Create a table of conversions from mi/h to ft/s. Start the mi/h column at 0 and end it at 100 mi/h. Print 15 values in your table. (Look up the conversion factor in a textbook or online.)

**(d)** The acidity of solutions is generally measured in terms of $pH$. The $pH$ of a solution is defined as $-\log_{10}$ of the concentration of hydronium ions. Create a table of conversions from concentration of hydronium ion to $pH$, spaced logarithmically from .001 to .1 mol/liter with 10 values. Assuming that you have named the concentration of hydronium ions **H_conc**, the syntax for calculating the logarithm of the concentration is

```
log10(H_conc)
```

**12**  The general equation for the distance that a freely falling body has traveled (neglecting air friction) is

$$d = \frac{1}{2}gt^2$$

Assume that $g = 9.8$ m/s$^2$. Generate a table of time versus distance traveled for values of time from 0 to 100 seconds. Choose a suitable increment for your time vector. (*Hint*: Be careful to use the correct operators; $t^2$ is an array operation!)

**13**  Newton's law of universal gravitation tells us that the force exerted by one particle on another is

$$F = G\frac{m_1 m_2}{r^2}$$

where the universal gravitational constant $G$ is found experimentally to be

$$G = 6.673 \times 10^{-11} \text{ N m}^2/\text{kg}^2$$

The mass of each particle is $m_1$ and $m_2$, respectively, and $r$ is the distance between the two particles. Use Newton's law of universal gravitation to find the force exerted by the earth on the moon, assuming that the mass of the earth is approximately $6 \times 10^{24}$ kg,

the mass of the moon is approximately $7.4 \times 10^{22}$ kg, and

the earth and the moon are an average of $3.9 \times 10^8$ m apart.

**14** We know that the earth and the moon are not always the same distance apart. Find the force the moon exerts on the earth for 10 distances between $3.8 \times 10^8$ m and $4.0 \times 10^8$ m.

**15** Recall from problem 7 that the ideal gas law is:

$$PV = nRT$$

and that the Van der Waals modification of the ideal gas law is

$$\left( P + \frac{n^2a}{V^2} \right)(V - nb) = nRT$$

Using the data from Problem 7, find the value of temperature ($T$), for

**(a)** 10 values of pressure from 0 bar to 400 bar for volume of 1 L

**(b)** 10 values of volume from 0.1 L to 10 L for a pressure of 220 bar

## Number Display

**16** Create a matrix **a** equal to $[-1/3, 0, 1/3, 2/3]$, and use each of the built-in format options to display the results:

> **format short (which is the default)**
> **format long**
> **format bank**
> **format short e**
> **format long e**
> **format short eng**
> **format long eng**
> **format short g**
> **format long g**
> **format +**
> **format rat**

## Saving Your Work in Files

**17** • Create a matrix called D_to_R composed of two columns, one representing degrees and the other representing the corresponding value in radians. Any value set will do for this exercise.
  • Save the matrix to a file called degrees.dat.
  • Once the file is saved, clear your workspace and then load the data from the file back into MATLAB.

**18** Create a script M-file and use it to do the homework problems you've been assigned from this chapter. Your file should include appropriate comments to identify each problem and to describe your calculation process. Don't forget to include your name, the date, and any other information your instructor requests.

## SOLUTIONS TO PRACTICE EXERCISES

### Practice Exercises 1

1. 7
2. 10
3. 2.5000
4. 17
5. 7.8154
6. 4.1955
7. 12.9600
8. 5
9. 2.2361
10. −1

### Practice Exercises 2

1. **test** is a valid name.
2. **Test** is a valid name, but is a different variable from **test**.
3. **if** is not allowed. It is a reserved keyword.
4. **my-book** is not allowed because it contains a hyphen.
5. **my_book** is a valid name
6. **Thisisoneverylongnamebutisitstillallowed?** is not allowed because it includes a question mark. Even without the question mark, it is not a good idea.
7. **1stgroup** is not allowed because it starts with a number.
8. **group_one** is a valid name.
9. **zzaAbc** is a valid name, although it's not a very good one because it combines uppercase and lowercase letters and is not meaningful.
10. **z34wAwy%12#** is not valid because it includes the percent and pound signs.
11. **sin** is a valid name, but a poor choice since it is also a function name.
12. **log** is a valid name, but a poor choice since it is also a function name.

### Practice Exercises 3

1. 6
2. 72
3. 16
4. 13
5. 48
6. 38.5
7. 4096
8. $2.4179e + 024$
9. 245
10. 2187
11. $(5 + 3)/(9 - 1) = 1$

12. $2^3 - 4/(5 + 3) = 7.5$
13. $5^(2 + 1)/(4 - 1) = 41.6667$
14. $(4 + 1/2) * (5 + 2/3) = 25.5$
15. $(5 + 6 * 7/3 - 2^2)/(2/3 * 3/(3 * 6)) = 135$

## Practice Exercises 4

1. `a = [2.3 5.8 9]`
2. `sin(a)`
   ```
   ans =
       0.7457 -0.4646 0.4121
   ```
3. `a + 3`
   ```
   ans =
       5.3000 8.8000 12.0000
   ```
4. `b = [5.2 3.14 2]`
5. `a + b`
   ```
   ans =
       7.5000 8.9400 11.0000
   ```
6. `a .* b`
   ```
   ans =
       11.9600 18.2120 18.0000
   ```
7. `a.^2`
   ```
   ans =
       5.2900 33.6400 81.0000
   ```
8. `c = 0:10 or`
   `c = [0:10]`
9. `d = 0:2:10 or`
   `d = [0:2:10]`
10. `linspace(10,20, 6)`
    ```
    ans =
        10 12 14 16 18 20
    ```
11. `logspace(1, 2, 5)`
    ```
    ans =
        10.0000 17.7828 31.6228 56.2341 100.0000
    ```

# 3

# Built-In MATLAB Functions

## INTRODUCTION

The vast majority of engineering computations require quite complicated mathematical functions, including logarithms, trigonometric functions, and statistical analysis functions. MATLAB has an extensive library of built-in functions to allow you to perform these calculations.

## 1 USING BUILT-IN FUNCTIONS

Many of the names for MATLAB's built-in functions are the same as those defined not only in the C programming language, but in Fortran and Java as well. For example, to take the square root of the variable **x**, we type

```
b = sqrt(x)
```

A big advantage of MATLAB is that function arguments can generally be either scalars or matrices. In our example, if **x** is a scalar, a scalar result is returned. Thus, the statement

```
x = 9;
b = sqrt(x)
```

returns a scalar:

```
b =
    3
```

However, the square-root function, **sqrt**, can also accept matrices as input. In this case, the square root of each element is calculated, so

```
x = [4, 9, 16];
b = sqrt(x)
```

returns

```
b =
    2    3    4
```

KEY IDEA: Most of the MATLAB function names are the same as those used in other computer programs

ARGUMENT: input to a function

All functions can be thought of as having three components: a name, input, and output. In the preceding example, the name of the function is **sqrt**, the required input (also called the *argument*) goes inside the parentheses and can be a scalar or a matrix, and the output is a calculated value or values. In this example, the output was assigned the variable name **b**.

Some functions require multiple inputs. For example, the remainder function, **rem**, requires two inputs: a dividend and a divisor. We represent this as **rem(x,y)**, so

```
rem(10,3)
```

calculates the remainder of 10 divided by 3:

```
ans =
     1
```

The **size** function is an example of a function that returns two outputs, which are stored in a single array. It determines the number of rows and columns in a matrix. Thus,

```
d = [1,  2,  3;  4,  5,  6];
f = size(d)
```

returns the $1 \times 2$ result matrix

```
f =
    2    3
```

You can also assign variable names to each of the answers by representing the left-hand side of the assignment statement as a matrix. For example,

```
[rows,cols] = size(d)
```

gives

```
rows =
        2
cols =
        3
```

NESTING: using one function as the input to another

You can create more complicated expressions by nesting functions. For instance,

```
g = sqrt(sin(x))
```

finds the square root of the sine of whatever values are stored in the matrix named **x**. If **x** is assigned a value of 2,

```
x = 2;
```

the result is

```
g =
      0.9536
```

Nesting functions can result in some complicated MATLAB code. Be sure to include the arguments for each function inside their own set of parentheses. Often, your code will be easier to read if you break nested expressions into two separate statements. Thus,

```
a = sin(x);
g = sqrt(a)
```

gives the same result as **g = sqrt(sin(x))** and is easier to follow.

---

**Hint**

You can probably *guess* the name and syntax for many MATLAB functions. However, check to make sure that the function of interest is working the way you assume it is, before you do any important calculations.

---

## 2  USING THE HELP FEATURE

MATLAB includes extensive help tools, which are especially useful in understanding how to use functions. There are two ways to get help from within MATLAB: a command-line help function (**help**) and an HTML-based set of documentation available by selecting **Help** from the menu bar or by using the *F1* function key, usually located at the top of your keyboard (or found by typing **helpwin** in the command window). There is also an online help set of documentation, available through the Start button or the Help icon on the menu bar. However, the online help usually just reflects the HTML-based documentation. You should use both help options, since they provide different information and insights into how to use a specific function.

To use the command-line help function, type **help** in the command window:

```
help
```

A list of help topics will appear:

```
HELP topics:

MATLAB\general     — General-purpose commands
MATLAB\ops         — Operators and special characters
MATLAB\lang        — Programming language constructs
MATLAB\elmat       — Elementary matrices and matrix
                     manipulation
MATLAB\elfun       — Elementary math functions
MATLAB\specfun     — Specialized math functions

and so on
```

KEY IDEA: Use the help function to help you use MATLAB's built-in functions

To get help on a particular topic, type **help <topic>**. (Recall that the angle brackets ,< and >, identify where you should type your input; they are not included in your actual MATLAB statement.)

For example, to get help on the **tangent** function, type

```
help tan
```

The following should be displayed:

```
TAN        Tangent of argument in radians.
  TAN(X)   is the tangent of the elements of X.
See also atan, tand, atan2.
```

To use the windowed help screen, select **Help** → **MATLAB Help** from the menu bar. A windowed version of the help list will appear. (See Figure 1.) You can then navigate to the appropriate topic. To access this version of the help utility directly from the command window, type **doc <topic>.** Thus, to access the windowed help for tangent, type

```
doc tan
```

The contents of the two methods for getting help on a function are different. If your question isn't immediately answered by whichever method you try first, it's often

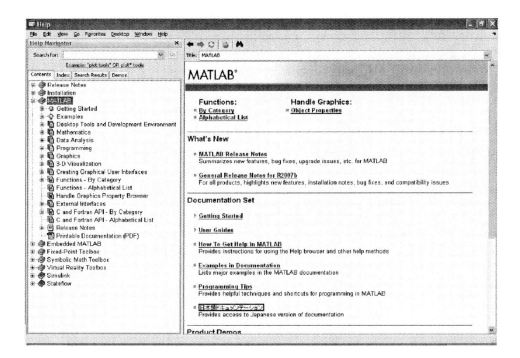

**Figure 1**
The MATLAB help
environment.

useful to try the other technique. The windowed help utility includes a MATLAB tutorial that you will find extremely useful. The list in the left-hand window is a table of contents. Notice that it includes a link to a list of functions, organized both by category and alphabetically by name. You can use this link to find out what MATLAB functions are available to solve many problems. For example, you might want to round a number you've calculated. Use the MATLAB help window to determine whether an appropriate MATLAB function is available.

Select the **MATLAB Functions-By Category** link (see Figure 1) and then the **Mathematics** link (see Figure 2).

Near the middle of the page is the category Elementary Math, (Figure 3) which lists rounding as a topic. Follow the links and you will find a whole category devoted to rounding functions. For example, **round** rounds to the nearest integer.

You could have also found the syntax for the round function by selecting **Functions—Alphabetical List.**

---

### Practice Exercises 1

1. Use the help command in the command window to find the appropriate syntax for the following functions:

   **a.** cos

   **b.** sqrt

   **c.** exp

2. Use the windowed help function from the menu bar to learn about the functions in Exercise 1.

3. Go to the online help function at www.mathworks.com to learn about the functions in Exercise 1.

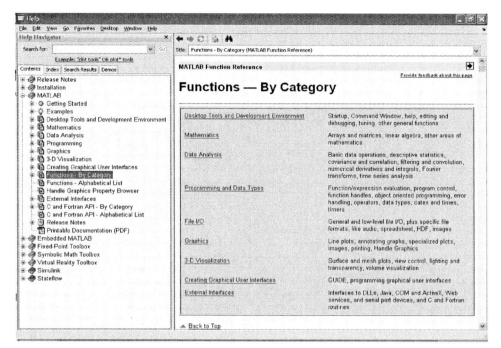

**Figure 2**
Functions-By Category help window. Notice the link to Mathematics functions in the righthand pane.

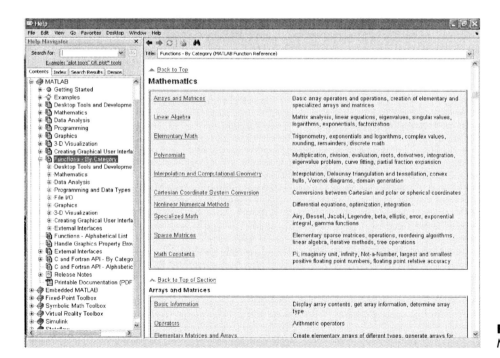

**Figure 3**
Mathematics Help Window

## 3 ELEMENTARY MATH FUNCTIONS

Elementary math functions include logarithms, exponentials, absolute value, rounding functions, and functions used in discrete mathematics.

### 3.1 Common Computations

KEY IDEA: Most functions accept either scalars, vectors or matrices as input

The functions listed in Table 1 accept either a scalar or a matrix of **x** values.

---

**Hint**

As a rule, the function **log** in all computer languages means the **natural logarithm**. Although not the standard in mathematics textbooks, it *is* the standard in computer programming. Not knowing this distinction is a common source of errors, especially for new users. If you want logarithms to the base 10, you'll need to use the **log10** function. A **log2** function is also included in MATLAB, but logarithms to any other base will need to be computed; there is no general logarithm function that allows the user to input the base.

---

### Practice Exercises 2

1. Create a vector **x** from −2 to +2 with an increment of 1. Your vector should be

$$\mathbf{x} = \begin{bmatrix} -2, & -1, & 0, & 1, & 2 \end{bmatrix}$$

   **a.** Find the absolute value of each member of the vector.
   **b.** Find the square root of each member of the vector.

2. Find the square root of both −3 and +3.
   **a.** Use the **sqrt** function.
   **b.** Use the **nthroot** function. (You should get an error statement for −3.)
   **c.** Raise −3 and +3 to the ½ power.

   How do the results vary?

3. Create a vector **x** from −9 to 12 with an increment of 3.
   **a.** Find the result of **x** divided by 2.
   **b.** Find the remainder of **x** divided by 2.

4. Using the vector from Exercise 3, find $\mathbf{e^x}$.

5. Using the vector from Exercise 3,
   **a.** find ln(**x**) (the natural logarithm of **x**).
   **b.** find $\log_{10}(\mathbf{x})$ (the common logarithm of **x**).

   Explain your results.

6. Use the **sign** function to determine which of the elements in vector **x** are positive.

7. Change the **format** to **rat**, and display the value of the **x** vector divided by 2.
   (Don't forget to change the format back to **format short** when you are done with this exercise set.)

**Table 1  Common Math Functions**

| | | |
|---|---|---|
| **abs(x)** | Finds the absolute value of **x**. | **abs(-3)** <br> **ans = 3** |
| **sqrt(x)** | Finds the square root of **x**. | **sqrt(85)** <br> **ans = 9.2195** |
| **nthroot(x,n)** | Finds the real *n*th root of **x**. This function will not return complex results. Thus, <br> **(-2)^(1/3)** <br> does not return the same result, yet both answers are legitimate third roots of $-2$. | **nthroot(-2,3)** <br> **ans =** <br> **-1.2599** <br><br> **(-2)^(1/3)** <br><br> **ans =** <br> **0.6300 + 1.0911i** |
| **sign(x)** | Returns a value of $-1$ if **x** is less than zero, a value of 0 if **x** equals zero, and a value of $+1$ if **x** is greater than zero. | **sign(-8)** <br> **ans = -1** |
| **rem(x,y)** | Computes the remainder of **x/y**. | **rem(25,4)** <br> **ans = 1** |
| **exp(x)** | Computes the value of $e^x$, where $e$ is the base for natural logarithms, or approximately 2.7183. | **exp(10)** <br> **ans = 2.2026e+004** |
| **log(x)** | Computes ln(**x**), the natural logarithm of **x** (to the base $e$). | **log(10)** <br> **ans = 2.3026** |
| **log10(x)** | Computes $\log_{10}(\mathbf{x})$, the common logarithm of **x** (to the base 10). | **log10(10)** <br> **ans = 1** |

**Hint**

The mathematical notation and MATLAB syntax for raising $e$ to a power are not the same. To raise $e$ to the third power, the mathematical notation would be $e^3$. However, the MATLAB syntax is **exp(3)**. Students also sometimes confuse the syntax for scientific notation with exponentials. The number **5e3** should be interpreted as $5 \times 10^3$.

**EXAMPLE 1**

## Using the Clausius–Clapeyron Equation

Meteorologists study the atmosphere in an attempt to understand and ultimately predict the weather. (See Figure 4.) Weather prediction is a complicated process, even with the best data. Meteorologists study chemistry, physics, thermodynamics, and geography, in addition to specialized courses about the atmosphere.

One equation used by meteorologists is the Clausius–Clapeyron equation, which is usually introduced in chemistry classes and examined in more detail in advanced thermodynamics classes. Rudolf Clausius and Emile Clapeyron were physicists responsible for the early development of thermodynamic principles during the mid-1800s. (See Figures 5a and Figure 5b.)

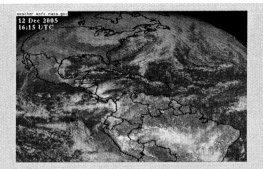

**Figure 4**
View of the earth's weather from space. (Courtesy of NASA/Jet Propulsion Laboratory.)

In meteorology, the Clausius–Clapeyron equation is employed to determine the relationship between saturation water-vapor pressure and the atmospheric temperature. The saturation water-vapor pressure can be used to calculate relative humidity, an important component of weather prediction, when the actual partial pressure of water in the air is known.

The Clausius–Clapeyron equation is

$$\ln\left(\frac{P^0}{6.11}\right) = \left(\frac{\Delta H_v}{R_{air}}\right) * \left(\frac{1}{273} - \frac{1}{T}\right)$$

where

$P^0$     =   saturation vapor pressure for water, in mbar, at temperature $T$,
$\Delta H_v$   =   latent heat of vaporization for water, $2.453 \times 10^6$ J/kg,
$R_{air}$   =   gas constant for moist air, 461 J/kg, and
$T$       =   temperature in kelvins (K).

It is rare that temperatures on the surface of the earth are lower than $-60°$F or higher than $120°$F. Use the Clausius–Clapeyron equation to find the saturation vapor pressure for temperatures in this range. Present your results as a table of Fahrenheit temperatures and saturation vapor pressures.

1. State the Problem
   Find the saturation vapor pressure at temperatures from $-60°$F to $120°$F, using the Clausius–Clapeyron equation.

2. Describe the Input and Output

**Figure 5a**
Rudolf Clausius.

**Figure 5b**
Emile Clapeyron.

*Input*

$$\Delta H_v = 2.453 \times 10^6 \text{ J/kg}$$
$$R_{air} = 461 \text{ J/kg}$$
$$T = -60°\text{F to } 120°\text{F}$$

Since the number of temperature values was not specified, we'll choose to recalculate every 10°F.

*Output*

Saturation vapor pressures

3. Develop a Hand Example

The Clausius–Clapeyron equation requires that all the variables have consistent units. This means that temperature ($T$) needs to be in kelvins. To change Fahrenheit degrees to kelvins, we use the conversion equation

$$T_k = \frac{(T_f + 459.6)}{1.8}$$

(There are lots of places to find units conversions. The Internet is one source, as are science and engineering textbooks.)

Now we need to solve the Clausius–Clapeyron equation for the saturation vapor pressure $P^0$. We have

$$\ln\left(\frac{P^0}{6.11}\right) = \left(\frac{\Delta H_v}{R_{air}}\right) \times \left(\frac{1}{273} - \frac{1}{T}\right)$$

$$P^0 = 6.11 \times e\left(\left(\frac{\Delta H_v}{R_{air}}\right) \times \left(\frac{1}{273} - \frac{1}{T}\right)\right)$$

Next, we solve for one temperature—for example, $T = 0°\text{F}$. Since the equation requires temperature in kelvins we must perform the unit conversion to obtain

$$T = \frac{(0 + 459.6)}{1.8} = 255.3333 \text{ K}$$

Finally, we substitute values to get

$$P^0 = 6.11 \times e\left(\left(\frac{2.453 \times 10^6}{461}\right) \times \left(\frac{1}{273} - \frac{1}{255.3333}\right)\right) = 1.5836 \text{ mbar}$$

4. Develop a MATLAB Solution

Create the MATLAB solution in an M-file, and then run it in the command environment:

```
%Example 1
%Using the Clausius-Clapeyron Equation, find the
%saturation vapor pressure for water at different
temperatures

TempF=[-60:10:120];          %Define temp matrix in F
TempK=(TempF + 459.6)/1.8;   %Convert temp to K
Delta_H=2.45e6;              %Define latent heat of
                             %vaporization
```

```
R_air = 461;                    %Define ideal gas constant for air
%
%Calculate the vapor pressures
Vapor_Pressure=6.11*exp((Delta_H/R_air)*(1/273 - 1./TempK));
%Display the results in a table
my_results = [TempF',Vapor_Pressure']
```

When you create a MATLAB program, it is a good idea to comment liberally (lines beginning with %). This makes your program easier for others to understand and may make it easier for you to "debug." Notice that most of the lines of code end with a semicolon, which suppresses the output. Therefore, the only information that displays in the command window is the table **my_results**:

```
my_results =
   -60.0000      0.0698
   -50.0000      0.1252
   -40.0000      0.2184
   ...
   120.0000    118.1931
```

5. Test the Solution
   Compare the MATLAB solution when $T = 0°F$ with the hand solution:

   Hand solution:      $P^0 = 1.5888$ mbar
   MATLAB solution:    $P^0 = 1.5888$ mbar

   The Clausius–Clapeyron equation can be used for more than just humidity problems. By changing the values of $\Delta H$ and $R$, you could generalize the program to deal with any condensing vapor.

### 3.2 Rounding Functions

MATLAB contains functions for a number of different rounding techniques (Table 2). You are probably most familiar with rounding to the closest integer; however, you may want to round either up or down, depending on the situation. For example, suppose you want to buy apples at the grocery store. The apples cost $0.52 apiece. You have $5.00. How many apples can you buy? Mathematically,

$$\frac{\$5.00}{\$0.52/\text{apple}} = 9.6154 \text{ apples}$$

But clearly, you can't buy part of an apple, and the grocery store won't let you round to the nearest number of apples. Instead, you need to round down. The MATLAB function to accomplish this is **fix.** Thus,

```
fix(5/0.52)
```

returns the maximum number of apples you can buy:

```
ans =
     9
```

**Table 2  Rounding Functions**

| | | |
|---|---|---|
| **round(x)** | Rounds **x** to the nearest integer. | **round(8.6)** <br> **ans = 9** |
| **fix(x)** | Rounds (or truncates) **x** to the nearest integer toward zero. Notice that 8.6 truncates to 8, not 9, with this function. | **fix(8.6)** <br> **ans = 8** <br> **fix(-8.6)** <br> **ans = -8** |
| **floor(x)** | Rounds **x** to the nearest integer toward negative infinity. | **floor(-8.6)** <br> **ans = -9** |
| **ceil(x)** | Rounds **x** to the nearest integer toward positive infinity. | **ceil(-8.6)** <br> **ans = -8** |

## 3.3  Discrete Mathematics

MATLAB includes functions to factor numbers, find common denominators and multiples, calculate factorials, and explore prime numbers (Table 3). All of these functions require integer scalars as input. In addition, MATLAB includes the **rats** function, which expresses a floating-point number as a rational number—i.e., a fraction. Discrete mathematics is the mathematics of whole numbers. Factoring, calculating common denominators, and finding least common multiples are functions usually covered in intermediate algebra courses. Factorials are usually covered in statistics or probability courses.

A factorial is the product of all the positive integers from 1 to a given value. Thus 3 factorial (indicated as 3!) is $3 \times 2 \times 1 = 6$. Many problems involving probability can be solved with factorials. For example, the number of ways that five cards can be arranged is $5 \times 4 \times 3 \times 2 \times 1 = 5! = 120$. When you select the first card, you have five choices; when you select the second card, you have only four choices remaining, then three, two, and one. This approach is called combinatorial mathematics, or combinatorics. To calculate a factorial in MATLAB use the factorial function. Thus

```
        factorial(5)
ans =
        120
```

gives the same result as

```
5*4*3*2*1
ans =
        120
```

The value of a factorial quickly becomes very large. Ten factorial is 3,628,800. MATLAB can handle up to 170!—anything larger gives **Inf** for an answer, because the maximum value for a real number is exceeded.

```
factorial(170)
        ans =
        7.2574e+306
factorial(171)
        ans =
              Inf
```

**Table 3  Functions Used in Discrete Mathematics**

| | | |
|---|---|---|
| **factor(x)** | Finds the prime factors of **x**. | **factor(12)**<br>**ans =**<br>    **2   2   3** |
| **gcd(x,y)** | Finds the greatest common denominator of **x** and **y**. | **gcd(10,15)**<br>**ans =**<br>    **5** |
| **lcm(x,y)** | Finds the least common multiple of **x** and **y**. | **lcm(2,5)**<br>**ans =**<br>    **10**<br>**lcm(2,10)**<br>**ans =**<br>    **10** |
| **rats(x)** | Represents **x** as a fraction. | **rats(1.5)**<br>**ans =**<br>    **3/2** |
| **factorial(x)** | Finds the value of **x** factorial (**x!**). A factorial is the product of all the integers less than **x**. For example, $6! = 6 \times 5 \times 4 \times 3 \times 2 \times 1 = 720$ | **factorial(6)**<br>**ans =**<br>    **720** |
| **nchoosek(n,k)** | Finds the number of possible combinations of $k$ items from a group of $n$ items. For example, use this function to determine the number of possible subgroups of 3 chosen from a group of 10. | **nchoosek(10,3)**<br>**ans =**<br>    **120** |
| **primes(x)** | Finds all the prime numbers less than **x**. | **primes(10)**<br>**ans =**<br>    **2   3   5   7** |
| **isprime(x)** | Checks to see if **x** is a prime number. If it is, the function returns 1; if not, it returns 0. | **isprime(7)**<br>**ans =**<br>    **1**<br>**isprime(10)**<br>**ans =**<br>    **0** |

Factorials are used to calculate the number of permutations and combinations of possible outcomes. A permutation is the number of subgroups that can be formed when sampling from a larger group, *when the order matters*. Consider the following problem. How many different teams of two people can you form from a group of four? Assume that the order matters, since for this problem the first person chosen is the group leader. If we represent each person as a letter, the possibilities are:

    AB   BA   CA   DA
    AC   BC   CB   DB
    AD   BD   CD   DC

For the first member of the team there are four choices, and for the second there are three choices, so the number of possible teams is $4 \times 3 = 12$. We could also express this as 4!/2!. More generally, if you have a large group to choose from, call the group size $n$, and the size of the subgroup (team) $m$. Then the possible number of permutations is

$$\frac{n!}{(n-m)!}$$

If there are 100 people to choose from, the number of teams of two (where order matters) is

$$\frac{100!}{(100 - 2)!} = 9900$$

But what if the order doesn't matter? In this case team AB is the same as team BA, and we refer to all the possibilities as combinations instead of permutations. The possible number of combinations is

$$\frac{n!}{(n - m)! \times m!}$$

Although you could use MATLAB's factorial function to calculate the number of combinations, the **nchoosek** function will do it for you, and it offers some advantages when using larger numbers. If we want to know the number of possible teams of 2, chosen from a pool of 100 (100 choose 2),

```
nchoosek(100,2)
ans =
    4950
```

The **nchoosek** function allows us to calculate the number of combinations even if the pool size is greater than 170, which would not be possible using the factorial approach.

```
nchoosek(200,2)
ans =
    19900
        factorial(200)/(factorial(198)*factorial(2))
        ans =
            NaN
```

---

### Practice Exercises 3

1. Factor the number 322.
2. Find the greatest common denominator of 322 and 6.
3. Is 322 a prime number?
4. How many primes occur between 0 and 322?
5. Approximate $\pi$ as a rational number.
6. Find 10! (10 factorial).
7. Find the number of possible of groups containing 3 people from a group of 20, when order does not matter. (20 choose 3)

---

## 4 TRIGONOMETRIC FUNCTIONS

MATLAB includes a complete set of the standard trigonometric functions and the hyperbolic trigonometric functions. Most of these functions assume that angles are expressed in radians. To convert radians to degrees or degrees to radians, we need to take advantage of the fact that $\pi$ radians equals 180 degrees:

$$\text{degrees} = \text{radians}\left(\frac{180}{\pi}\right) \quad \text{and} \quad \text{radians} = \text{degrees}\left(\frac{\pi}{180}\right)$$

**Table 4  Trigonometric Functions**

| | | |
|---|---|---|
| **sin(x)** | Finds the sine of **x** when **x** is expressed in radians. | **sin(0)**<br>**ans = 0** |
| **cos(x)** | Finds the cosine of **x** when **x** is expressed in radians. | **cos(pi)**<br>**ans = -1** |
| **tan(x)** | Finds the tangent of **x** when **x** is expressed in radians. | **tan(pi)**<br>**ans =**<br>**-1.2246**<br>**e-016** |
| **asin(x)** | Finds the arcsine, or inverse sine, of **x**, where **x** must be between $-1$ and 1. The function returns an angle in radians between $\pi/2$ and $-\pi/2$. | **asin(-1)**<br>**ans =**<br>**-1.5708** |
| **sinh(x)** | Finds the hyperbolic sine of **x** when **x** is expressed in radians. | **sinh(pi)**<br>**ans =**<br>**11.5487** |
| **asinh(x)** | Finds the inverse hyperbolic sin of **x**. | **asinh(1)**<br>**ans =**<br>**0.8814** |
| **sind(x)** | Finds the sin of **x** when **x** is expressed in degrees. | **sind(90)**<br>**ans =**<br>**1** |
| **asind(x)** | Finds the inverse sin of **x** and reports the result in degrees. | **asind(90)**<br>**ans =**<br>**1** |

KEY IDEA: Most trig functions require input in radians

The MATLAB code to perform these conversions is

```
degrees = radians * 180/pi;
radians = degrees * pi/180;
```

To carry out these calculations, we need the value of $\pi$, so a constant, **pi**, is built into MATLAB. However, since $\pi$ cannot be expressed as a floating-point number, the constant **pi** in MATLAB is only an approximation of the mathematical quantity $\pi$. Usually this is not important; however, you may notice some surprising results. For example, for

```
sin(pi)
ans =
      1.2246e-016
```

when you expect an answer of zero.

You may access the help function from the menu bar for a complete list of trigonometric functions available in MATLAB. Table 4 shows some of the more common ones.

---

**Hint**

Math texts often use the notation $\sin^{-1}(x)$ to indicate an inverse sine function, also called an arcsine. Students are often confused by this notation and try to create parallel MATLAB code. Note, however, that

$$\mathbf{a = sin^\wedge -1(x)}$$

is *not* a valid MATLAB statement, but instead should be

    a = asin(x)

---

### Practice Exercises 4

Calculate the following (remember that mathematical notation is not necessarily the same as MATLAB notation):

1. $\sin(2\theta)$ for $\theta = 3\pi$.
2. $\cos(\theta)$ for $0 \le \theta \le 2\pi$; let $\theta$ change in steps of $0.2\pi$.
3. $\sin^{-1}(1)$.
4. $\cos^{-1}(x)$ for $-1 \le x \le 1$; let $x$ change in steps of $0.2$.
5. Find the cosine of $45°$.
    a. Convert the angle from degrees to radians, and then use the **cos** function.
    b. Use the **cosd** function.
6. Find the angle whose sine is 0.5. Is your answer in degrees or radians?
7. Find the cosecant of 60 degrees. You may have to use the help function to find the appropriate syntax.

---

**EXAMPLE 2**

## Using Trigonometric Functions

A basic calculation in engineering is finding the resulting force on an object that is being pushed or pulled in multiple directions. Adding up forces is the primary calculation performed in both statics and dynamics classes. Consider a balloon that is acted upon by the forces shown in Figure 6.

To find the net force acting on the balloon, we need to add up the force due to gravity, the force due to buoyancy, and the force due to the wind. One approach is to find the force in the $x$ direction and the force in the $y$ direction for each individual force and then to recombine them into a final result.

The forces in the $x$ and $y$ directions can be found by trigonometry:

$F$ = total force
$F_x$ = force in the $x$ direction
$F_y$ = force in the $y$ direction

We know from trigonometry that the sine is the opposite side over the hypotenuse, so

$$\sin(\theta) = F_y/F$$

and therefore,

$$F_y = F \sin(\theta)$$

Similarly, since the cosine is the adjacent side over the hypotenuse,

$$F_x = F \cos(\theta)$$

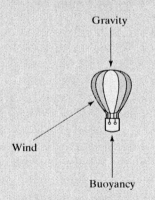

Gravity

Wind

Buoyancy

**Figure 6**
Force balance on a balloon.

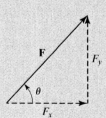

We can add up all the forces in the $x$ direction and all the forces in the $y$ direction and use these totals to find the resulting force:

$$F_{x\,\text{total}} = \Sigma F_{xi} \qquad F_{y\,\text{total}} = \Sigma F_{yi}$$

To find the magnitude and angle for $F_{\text{total}}$, we use trigonometry again. The tangent is the opposite side over the adjacent side. Therefore,

$$\tan(\theta) = \frac{F_{y\,\text{total}}}{F_{x\,\text{total}}}$$

We use an inverse tangent to write

$$\theta = \tan^{-1}\left(\frac{F_{y\,\text{total}}}{F_{X\,\text{total}}}\right)$$

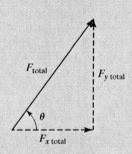

(The inverse tangent is also called the *arctangent*; you'll see it on your scientific calculator as atan.)

Once we know $\theta$, we can find $F_{\text{total}}$, using either the sine or the cosine. We have

$$F_{x\,\text{total}} = F_{\text{total}} \cos(\theta)$$

and rearranging terms gives

$$F_{\text{total}} = \frac{F_{x\,\text{total}}}{\cos(\theta)}$$

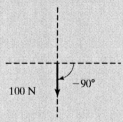

100 N    $-90°$

Gravitational Force

Now consider again the balloon shown in Figure 5. Assume that the force due to gravity on this particular balloon is 100 N, pointed downward. Assume further that the buoyant force is 200 N, pointed upward. Finally, assume that the wind is pushing on the balloon with a force of 50 N, at an angle of 30 degrees from horizontal. Find the resulting force on the balloon.

1. State the Problem
   Find the resulting force on a balloon. Consider the forces due to gravity, buoyancy, and the wind.

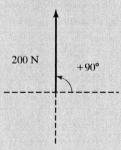

200 N    $+90°$

Buoyant Force

2. Describe the Input and Output

   *Input*

| Force | Magnitude | Direction |
|-------|-----------|-----------|
| Gravity | 100 N | −90 degrees |
| Buoyancy | 200 N | +90 degrees |
| Wind | 50 N | +30 degrees |

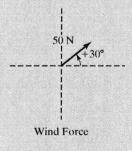

50 N    $+30°$

Wind Force

   *Output*

We'll need to find both the magnitude and the direction of the resulting force.

3. Develop a Hand Example
   First find the $x$ and $y$ components of each force and sum the components:

| Force | Horizontal Component | Vertical Component |
|---|---|---|
| Gravity | $F_x = F\cos(\theta)$ | $F_y = F\sin(\theta)$ |
|  | $F_x = 100\cos(-90°) = 0\,N$ | $F_y = 100\sin(-90°) = -100\,N$ |
| Buoyancy | $F_x = F\cos(\theta)$ | $F_y = F\sin(\theta)$ |
|  | $F_x = 200\cos(+90°) = 0\,N$ | $F_y = 200\sin(+90°) = +200\,N$ |
| Wind | $F_x = F\cos(\theta)$ | $F_y = F\sin(\theta)$ |
|  | $F_x = 50\cos(+30°) = 43.301\,N$ | $F_y = 50\sin(+30°) = +25\,N$ |
| Sum | $F_{x\,total} = 0 + 0 + 43.301$ | $F_{y\,total} = -100 + 200 + 25$ |
|  | $= 43.301\,N$ | $= 125\,N$ |

Find the resulting angle:

$$\theta = \tan^{-1}\left(\frac{F_{y\,total}}{F_{x\,total}}\right)$$

$$\theta = \tan^{-1}\frac{125}{43.301} = 70.89°$$

Find the magnitude of the total force:

$$F_{total} = \frac{F_{x\,total}}{\cos(\theta)}$$

$$F_{total} = \frac{43.301}{\cos(70.89°)} = 132.29\,N$$

4. Develop a MATLAB Solution
   One solution is

```
%Example 2
clear, clc
%Define the input
Force =[100, 200, 50];
theta = [-90, +90, +30];
%convert angles to radians
theta = theta*pi/180;
%Find the x components
ForceX = Force.*cos(theta);
%Sum the x components
ForceX_total = sum(ForceX);
%Find and sum the y components in the same step
ForceY_total = sum(Force.*sin(theta));
%Find the resulting angle in radians
result_angle = atan(ForceY_total/ForceX_total);
%Find the resulting angle in degrees
result_degrees = result_angle*180/pi
%Find the magnitude of the resulting force
Force_total = ForceX_total/cos(result_angle)
```

which returns

```
result_degrees =
      70.8934

Force_total =
     132.2876
```

Notice that the values for the force and the angle were entered into an array. This makes the solution more general. Notice also that the angles were converted to radians. In the program listing, the output from all but the final calculations was suppressed. However, while developing the program, we left off the semicolons so that we could observe the intermediate results.

5. Test the Solution

Compare the MATLAB solution with the hand solution. Now that you know it works, you can use the program to find the resultant of multiple forces. Just add the additional information to the definitions of the force vector **Force** and the angle vector **theta**. Note that we assumed a two-dimensional world in this example, but it would be easy to extend our solution to forces in all three dimensions.

## 5  DATA ANALYSIS FUNCTIONS

Analyzing data statistically in MATLAB is particularly easy, partly because whole data sets can be represented by a single matrix and partly because of the large number of built-in data analysis functions.

### 5.1  Maximum and Minimum

Table 5 lists functions that find the minimum and maximum in a data set and the element at which those values occur.

**Table 5  Maxima and Minima**

| | | |
|---|---|---|
| **max(x)** | Finds the largest value in a **vector x**. For example, if $x = [1\quad 5\quad 3]$, the maximum value is 5. | x=[1, 5, 3];<br>max(x)<br>ans =<br>  5 |
| | Creates a row vector containing the maximum element from each column of a **matrix x**. For example, if $x = \begin{bmatrix} 1 & 5 & 3 \\ 2 & 4 & 6 \end{bmatrix}$, then the maximum value in column 1 is 2, the maximum value in column 2 is 5, and the maximum value in column 3 is 6. | x=[1, 5, 3; 2, 4, 6];<br>max(x)<br><br>ans =<br>  2  5  6 |
| **[a,b]=max(x)** | Finds both the largest value in a **vector x** and its location in vector **x**. For $x = [1\quad 5\quad 3]$ the maximum value is named **a** and is found to be 5. The location of the maximum value is element 2 and is named **b**. | x=[1, 5, 3];<br>[a,b]=max(x)<br>a =<br>  5<br>b =<br>  2 |

|  |  |  |
|---|---|---|
|  | Creates a row vector containing the maximum element from each column of a matrix **x** and returns a row vector with the location of the maximum in each column of matrix **x**. For example, if $x = \begin{bmatrix} 1 & 5 & 3 \\ 2 & 4 & 6 \end{bmatrix}$, then the maximum value in column 1 is 2, the maximum value in column 2 is 5, and the maximum value in column 3 is 6. These maxima occur in row 2, row 1, and row 2, respectively. | x=[1, 5, 3; 2, 4, 6];<br>[a,b]=max(x)<br>a =<br>  2  5  6<br>b =<br>  2  1  2 |
| **max(x,y)** | Creates a matrix the same size as **x** and **y**. (Both **x** and **y** must have the same number of rows and columns.) Each element in the resulting matrix contains the maximum value from the corresponding positions in **x** and **y**. For example, if $x = \begin{bmatrix} 1 & 5 & 5 \\ 2 & 4 & 6 \end{bmatrix}$ and $y = \begin{bmatrix} 10 & 2 & 4 \\ 1 & 8 & 7 \end{bmatrix}$ then the resulting matrix will be $x = \begin{bmatrix} 10 & 5 & 4 \\ 2 & 8 & 7 \end{bmatrix}$ | x=[1, 5, 3; 2, 4, 6];<br>y=[10,2,4; 1, 8, 7];<br>max(x,y)<br>ans =<br>  10  5  4<br>  2  8  7 |
| **min(x)** | Finds the smallest value in a **vector x**. For example, if $x = \begin{bmatrix} 1 & 5 & 3 \end{bmatrix}$ the minimum value is 1. | x=[1, 5, 3];<br>min(x)<br>ans =<br>  1 |
|  | Creates a row vector containing the minimum element from each column of a **matrix x**. For example, if $x = \begin{bmatrix} 1 & 5 & 3 \\ 2 & 4 & 6 \end{bmatrix}$, then the minimum value in column 1 is 1, the minimum value in column 2 is 4, and the minimum value in column 3 is 3. | x=[1, 5, 3; 2, 4, 6];<br>min(x)<br>ans =<br>  1  4  3 |
| **[a,b]=min(x)** | Finds both the smallest value in a **vector x** and its location in vector **x**. For $x = \begin{bmatrix} 1 & 5 & 3 \end{bmatrix}$, the minimum value is named **a** and is found to be 1. The location of the minimum value is element 1 and is named **b**. | x=[1, 5, 3];<br>[a,b]=min(x)<br>a =<br>  1<br>b =<br>  1 |
|  | Creates a row vector containing the minimum element from each column of a matrix **x** and returns a row vector with the location of the minimum in each column of matrix **x**. For example, if $x = \begin{bmatrix} 1 & 5 & 3 \\ 2 & 4 & 6 \end{bmatrix}$, then the minimum value in column 1 is 1, the minimum value in column 2 is 4, and the minimum value in column 3 is 3. These minima occur in row 1, row 2, and row 1, respectively. | x=[1, 5, 3; 2, 4, 6];<br>[a,b]=min(x)<br>a =<br>  1  4  3<br>b =<br>  1  2  1 |
| **min(x,y)** | Creates a matrix the same size as **x** and **y**. (Both **x** and **y** must have the same number of rows and columns.) Each element in the resulting matrix contains the minimum value from the corresponding positions in **x** and **y**. For example, if $x = \begin{bmatrix} 1 & 5 & 3 \\ 2 & 4 & 6 \end{bmatrix}$ and $y = \begin{bmatrix} 10 & 2 & 4 \\ 1 & 8 & 7 \end{bmatrix}$, then the resulting matrix will be $= \begin{bmatrix} 1 & 2 & 3 \\ 1 & 4 & 6 \end{bmatrix}$ | x=[1, 5, 3; 2, 4, 6];<br>y=[10,2,4; 1, 8, 7];<br>min(x,y)<br>ans =<br>  1  2  3<br>  1  4  6 |

**Hint**

All of the functions in this section work on the *columns* in two-dimensional matrices. If your data analysis requires you to evaluate data in rows, the data must be transposed. (In other words, the rows must become columns and the columns must become rows.) The transpose operator is a single quote ( ' ). For example, if you want to find the maximum value in each *row* of the matrix

$$x = \begin{bmatrix} 1 & 5 & 3 \\ 2 & 4 & 6 \end{bmatrix}$$

use the command

```
max(x')
```

which returns

```
ans=
    5    6
```

---

**Practice Exercises 5**

Consider the following matrix:

$$x = \begin{bmatrix} 4 & 90 & 85 & 75 \\ 2 & 55 & 65 & 75 \\ 3 & 78 & 82 & 79 \\ 1 & 84 & 92 & 93 \end{bmatrix}$$

1. What is the maximum value in each column?
2. In which row does that maximum occur?
3. What is the maximum value in each row? (You'll have to transpose the matrix to answer this question.)
4. In which column does the maximum occur?
5. What is the maximum value in the entire table?

---

### 5.2 Mean and Median

MEAN: the average of all the values in the data set

MEDIAN: the middle value in a data set

There are several ways to find the "average" value in a data set. In statistics, the **mean** of a group of values is probably what most of us would call the average. The mean is the sum of all the values, divided by the total number of values. Another kind of average is the **median**, or the middle value. There are an equal number of values both larger and smaller than the median. The **mode** is the value that appears most often in a data set. MATLAB provides functions for finding the mean, median and the mode, as shown in Table 6.

### 5.3 Sums and Products

Often it is useful to add up (sum) all of the elements in a matrix or to multiply all of the elements together. MATLAB provides a number of functions to calculate both sums and products, as shown in Table 7.

## Table 6  Averages

| | | |
|---|---|---|
| **mean(x)** | Computes the mean value (or average value) of a **vector x**. For example if $x = \begin{bmatrix} 1 & 5 & 3 \end{bmatrix}$, the mean value is 3. | **x=[1, 5, 3];**<br>**mean(x)**<br>**ans =**<br>  **3.0000** |
| | Returns a row vector containing the mean value from each column of a **matrix x**.<br><br>For example, if $x = \begin{bmatrix} 1 & 5 & 3 \\ 2 & 4 & 6 \end{bmatrix}$<br><br>then the mean value of column 1 is 1.5, the mean value of column 2 is 4.5, and the mean value of column 3 is 4.5. | **x=[1, 5, 3; 2, 4, 6];**<br>**mean(x)**<br>**ans =**<br>  **1.5  4.5  4.5** |
| **median(x)** | Finds the median of the elements of a **vector x**. For example, if $x = \begin{bmatrix} 1 & 5 & 3 \end{bmatrix}$, the median value is 3. | **x=[1, 5, 3];**<br>**median(x)**<br>**ans =**<br>  **3** |
| | Returns a row vector containing the median value from each column of a **matrix x**.<br><br>For example, if $x = \begin{bmatrix} 1 & 5 & 3 \\ 2 & 4 & 6 \\ 3 & 8 & 4 \end{bmatrix}$,<br><br>then the median value from column 1 is 2, the median value from column 2 is 5, and the median value from column 3 is 4. | **x=[1, 5, 3;**<br>**2, 4, 6;**<br>**3, 8, 4];**<br>**median(x)**<br>**ans =**<br>  **2  5  4** |
| **mode(x)** | Finds the value that occurs most often in an array. Thus, for the array<br>$x = \begin{bmatrix} 1, & 2, & 3, & 3 \end{bmatrix}$<br>the mode is 3. | **x=[1,2,3,3]**<br>**mode(x)**<br>**ans =**<br>  **3** |

## Practice Exercises 6

Consider the following matrix:

$$x = \begin{bmatrix} 4 & 90 & 85 & 75 \\ 2 & 55 & 65 & 75 \\ 3 & 78 & 82 & 79 \\ 1 & 84 & 92 & 93 \end{bmatrix}$$

1. What is the mean value in each column?
2. What is the median for each column?
3. What is the mean value in each row?
4. What is the median for each row?
5. What is returned when you request the mode?
6. What is the mean for the entire matrix?

**Table 7   Sums and Products**

| | | |
|---|---|---|
| **sum(x)** | Sums the elements in **vector x**. For example, if $x = \begin{bmatrix} 1 & 5 & 3 \end{bmatrix}$, the sum is 9. | x=[1, 5, 3];<br>sum(x)<br>ans =<br>    9 |
| | Computes a row vector containing the sum of the elements in each column of a **matrix x**. For example, if $x = \begin{bmatrix} 1 & 5 & 3 \\ 2 & 4 & 6 \end{bmatrix}$ then the sum of column 1 is 3, the sum of column 2 is 9, and the sum of column 3 is 9. | x=[1, 5, 3; 2, 4, 6];<br>sum(x)<br>ans =<br>    3  9  9 |
| **prod(x)** | Computes the product of the elements of a **vector x**. For example, if $x = \begin{bmatrix} 1 & 5 & 3 \end{bmatrix}$, the product is 15. | x=[1, 5, 3];<br>prod(x)<br>ans =<br>    15 |
| | Computes a row vector containing the product of the elements in each column of a **matrix x**. For example, if $x = \begin{bmatrix} 1 & 5 & 3 \\ 2 & 4 & 6 \end{bmatrix}$, then the product of column 1 is 2, the product of column 2 is 20, and the product of column 3 is 18. | x=[1, 5, 3; 2, 4, 6];<br>prod(x)<br>ans =<br>    2  20  18 |
| **cumsum(x)** | Computes a vector of the same size as, and containing cumulative sums of the elements of, a **vector x**. For example, if $x = \begin{bmatrix} 1 & 5 & 3 \end{bmatrix}$, the resulting vector is $x = \begin{bmatrix} 1 & 6 & 9 \end{bmatrix}$. | x=[1, 5, 3];<br>cumsum(x)<br>ans =<br>    1  6  9 |
| | Computes a matrix containing the cumulative sum of the elements in each column of a **matrix x**. For example, if $x = \begin{bmatrix} 1 & 5 & 3 \\ 2 & 4 & 6 \end{bmatrix}$, the resulting matrix is $x = \begin{bmatrix} 1 & 5 & 3 \\ 3 & 9 & 9 \end{bmatrix}$. | x=[1, 5, 3; 2, 4, 6];<br>cumsum(x)<br>ans =<br>    1  5  3<br>    3  9  9 |
| **cumprod(x)** | Computes a vector of the same size as, and containing cumulative products of the elements of, a **vector x**. For example, if $x = \begin{bmatrix} 1 & 5 & 3 \end{bmatrix}$, the resulting vector is $x = \begin{bmatrix} 1 & 5 & 15 \end{bmatrix}$. | x=[1, 5, 3];<br>cumprod(x)<br>ans =<br>    1  5  15 |
| | Computes a matrix containing the cumulative product of the elements in each column of a **matrix x.** For example, if $x = \begin{bmatrix} 1 & 5 & 3 \\ 2 & 4 & 6 \end{bmatrix}$, the resulting matrix is $x = \begin{bmatrix} 1 & 5 & 3 \\ 2 & 20 & 18 \end{bmatrix}$. | x=[1, 5, 3; 2, 4, 6];<br>cumprod(x)<br>ans =<br>    1  5  3<br>    2  20  18 |

In addition to simply adding up all the elements, which returns a single value for each column in the array, the **cumsum** function (cumulative sum) adds all of the previous elements in an array and creates a new array of these intermediate totals. This is useful when dealing with the sequences of numbers in a series. Consider the harmonic series

$$\sum_{k=1}^{n} \frac{1}{k}$$

which is equivalent to

$$\frac{1}{1} + \frac{1}{2} + \frac{1}{3} + \frac{1}{4} + \ldots + \frac{1}{n}$$

We could use MATLAB to create a sequence representing the first five values in the sequence as follows

```
k = 1:5;
sequence = 1./5
```

which gives us

```
sequence =
   1.0000    0.5000    0.3333    0.2500    0.2000
```

We could view the series as a sequence of fractions by changing the format to rational with the following code

```
format rat
sequence =
      1       1/2      1/3      1/4      1/5
```

Now we could use the **cumsum** function to find the value of the entire series for values of $n$ from 1 to 5

```
format short
series = cumsum(sequence)
series =
   1.0000   1.5000   1.8333   2.0833   2.2833
```

Similarly the **cumprod** function finds the cumulative product of a sequence of numbers stored in an array.

## 5.4 Sorting Values

Table 8 lists several commands to sort data in a matrix into ascending or descending order. For example, if we define an array **x**

```
x = [ 1 6 3 9 4]
```

we can use the **sort** function to rearrange the values.

```
sort(x)
ans =
    1    3    4    6    9
```

The default is ascending order, but adding the string 'descend' to the second field will force the function to list the values in descending order.

```
sort(x, 'descend')
ans =
    9    6    4    3    1
```

You can also use the sort command to rearrange entire matrices. This function is consistent with other MATLAB functions, and sorts based on columns. Each column will be sorted independently. Thus

```
x = [ 1 3; 10 2; 3 1; 82 4; 5 5]
```

**Table 8 Sorting Functions**

| | | |
|---|---|---|
| **sort(x)** | Sorts the elements of a vector **x** into ascending order. For example, if $x = \begin{bmatrix} 1 & 5 & 3 \end{bmatrix}$, the resulting vector is $x = \begin{bmatrix} 1 & 3 & 5 \end{bmatrix}$. | **x=[1, 5, 3];** **sort(x)** **ans =**   1 3 5 |
| | Sorts the elements in each column of a matrix **x** into ascending order. For example, if $x = \begin{bmatrix} 1 & 5 & 3 \\ 2 & 4 & 6 \end{bmatrix}$, the resulting matrix is $x = \begin{bmatrix} 1 & 4 & 3 \\ 2 & 5 & 6 \end{bmatrix}$. | **x=[1, 5, 3; 2, 4, 6];** **sort(x)** **ans =**   1 4 3   2 5 6 |
| **sort(x,'descend')** | Sorts the elements in each column in descending order. | **x=[1, 5, 3; 2, 4, 6];** **sort(x,'descend')** **ans =**   2 5 6   1 4 3 |
| **sortrows(x)** | Sorts the rows in a matrix in ascending order on the basis of the values in the first column, and keeps each row intact. For example, if $x = \begin{bmatrix} 3 & 1 & 2 \\ 1 & 9 & 3 \\ 4 & 3 & 6 \end{bmatrix}$, then using the **sortrows** command will move the middle row into the top position. The first column defaults to the basis for sorting. | **x=[3, 1, 3; 1, 9, 3; 4, 3, 6]** **sortrows(x)** **ans =**   1 9 3   3 1 2   4 3 6 |
| **sortrows(x,n)** | Sorts the rows in a matrix on the basis of the values in column n. If n is negative, the values are sorted in descending order. If n is not specified, the default column used as the basis for sorting is column 1. | **sortrows(x,2)** **ans =**   3 1 2   4 3 6   1 9 3 |

gives

```
        x =
               1     3
              10     2
               3     1
              82     4
               5     5
```

When we sort the array

```
        sort(x)
```

each column is sorted in ascending order.

```
        ans =
               1     1
               3     2
               5     3
              10     4
              82     5
```

The **sortrows** allows you to sort entire rows, based on the value in a specified column. Thus

```
sortrows(x,1)
```

sorts based on the first column, but maintains the relationship between values in columns one and two.

```
ans =
      1   3
      3   1
      5   5
     10   2
     82   4
```

Similarly you can sort based on values in the second column.

```
sortrows(x,2)
ans =
      3   1
     10   2
      1   3
      2   4
      5   5
```

These functions are particularly useful in analyzing data. Consider the results of the Men's 2006 Olympic 500-meter speed skating event shown in Table 9.

The skaters were given a random number for this illustration, but once the race is over we'd like to sort the table in ascending order, based on the times in the second column.

```
skating_results =   [1.0000   42.0930
                     2.0000   42.0890
                     3.0000   41.9350
                     4.0000   42.4970
                     5.0000   42.0020]

sortrows(skating_results,2)

ans =
      3.0000   41.9350
      5.0000   42.0020
      2.0000   42.0890
      1.0000   42.0930
      4.0000   42.4970
```

As you may remember, the winning time was posted by Apolo Anton Ohno, who in our example, is skater number 3.

Table 9  2006 Olympic Speed Skating Times

| Skater Number | Time (min) |
| --- | --- |
| 1 | 42.093 |
| 2 | 42.089 |
| 3 | 41.935 |
| 4 | 42.497 |
| 5 | 42.002 |

The **sortrows** function can also sort in descending order but uses a different syntax from the **sort** function. To sort in descending order, place a minus sign in front of the column number used for sorting. Thus

```
sortrows(skating_results, -2)
```

sorts the array in descending order, based on the second column. The result of this command is

```
ans =
      4.0000   42.4970
      1.0000   42.0930
      2.0000   42.0890
      5.0000   42.0020
      3.0000   41.9350
```

### 5.5  Determining Matrix Size

MATLAB offers two functions (Table 10) that allow us to determine how big a matrix is: **size** and **length**. The **size** function returns the number of rows and columns in a matrix. The **length** function returns the larger of the matrix dimensions. For example, if

```
x = [1 2 3; 4 5 6];

size(x);
```

MATLAB returns the following result

```
ans =
     2     3
```

This tells us that the **x** array has two rows and three columns. However, if we use the **length** function

```
length(x)
```

the result is

```
ans =
     3
```

**Table 10  Size Functions**

| | | |
|---|---|---|
| **size(x)** | Determines the number of rows and columns in matrix **x**. (If **x** is a multidimensional array, **size** determines how many dimensions exist and how big they are.) | x=[1, 5, 3; 2, 4, 6];<br>size(x)<br>ans =<br>  2  3 |
| **[a,b] = size(x)** | Determines the number of rows and columns in matrix **x** and assigns the number of rows to **a** and the number of columns to **b**. | [a,b]=size(x)<br>a =<br>  2<br>b =<br>  3 |
| **length(x)** | Determines the largest dimension of a matrix **x**. | x=[1, 5, 3; 2, 4, 6];<br>length(x)<br>ans =<br>  3 |

because the largest of the array dimensions is 3. The **length** function is particularly useful when used with a loop structure, since it can easily determine how many times to execute the loop—based on the dimensions of an array.

**EXAMPLE 3**

### Weather Data

The National Weather Service collects massive amounts of weather data every day (Figure 7). Those data are available to all of us on the agency's online service at http://cdo.ncdc.noaa.gov/CDO/cdo. Analyzing large amounts of data can be confusing, so it's a good idea to start with a small data set, develop an approach that works, and then apply it to the larger data set that we are interested in.

We have extracted precipitation information from the National Weather Service for one location for all of 1999 and stored it in a file called Weather_Data.xls. (The .xls indicates that the data are in an Excel spreadsheet.) Each row represents a month, so there are 12 rows, and each column represents the day of the month (1 to 31), so there are 31 rows. Since not every month has the same number of days, data are missing for some locations in the last several columns. We place the number −99999 in those locations. The precipitation information is presented in hundredths of an inch. For example, on February 1 there was 0.61 inch of precipitation, and on April 1, 2.60 inches. A sample of the data is displayed in Table 11, with labels added for clarity; however, **the data in the file contain only numbers**.

Use the data in the file to find the following:

**a.** the total precipitation in each month.
**b.** the total precipitation for the year.
**c.** the month and day on which the maximum precipitation during the year was recorded.

**Figure 7**
Satellite photo of a hurricane. (Courtesy of NASA/Jet Propulsion Laboratory.)

**Table 11  Precipitation Data from Asheville, North Carolina**

| 1999 | Day1 | Day2 | Day3 | Day4 | | Day28 | Day29 | Day30 | Day31 |
|------|------|------|------|------|------|------|------|------|------|
| January | 0 | 0 | 272 | 0 | etc.... | 0 | 0 | 33 | 33 |
| February | 61 | 103 | 0 | 2 | | 62 | −99999 | −99999 | −99999 |
| March | 2 | 0 | 17 | 27 | | 0 | 5 | 8 | 0 |
| April | 260 | 1 | 0 | 0 | | 13 | 86 | 0 | −99999 |
| May | 47 | 0 | 0 | 0 | | 0 | 0 | 0 | 0 |
| June | 0 | 0 | 30 | 42 | | 14 | 14 | 8 | −99999 |
| July | 0 | 0 | 0 | 0 | | 5 | 0 | 0 | 0 |
| August | 0 | 45 | 0 | 0 | | 0 | 0 | 0 | 0 |
| September | 0 | 0 | 0 | 0 | | 138 | 58 | 10 | −99999 |
| October | 0 | 0 | 0 | 14 | | 0 | 0 | 0 | 1 |
| November | 1 | 163 | 5 | 0 | | 0 | 0 | 0 | −99999 |
| December | 0 | 0 | 0 | 0 | | 0 | 0 | 0 | 0 |

1. State the Problem

    Using the data in the file Weather_Data.xls, find the total monthly precipitation, the total precipitation for the year, and the day on which it rained the most.

2. Describe the Input and Output

    ***Input*** The input for this example is included in a data file called Weather_Data. xls and consists of a two-dimensional matrix. Each row represents a month, and each column represents a day.

    ***Output*** The output should be the total precipitation for each month, the total precipitation for the year, and the day on which the precipitation was a maximum. We have decided to present precipitation in inches, since no other units were specified in the statement of the problem.

3. Develop a Hand Example

    For the hand example, deal only with a small subset of the data. The information included in Table 11 is enough. The total for January, days 1 to 4, is

    $$total\_1 = (0 + 0 + 272 + 0)/100 = 2.72 \text{ inches}$$

    The total for February, days 1 to 4, is

    $$total\_2 = (61 + 103 + 0 + 2)/100 = 1.66 \text{ inches}$$

    Now add the months together to get the combined total. If our sample "year" is just January and February, then

    $$total = total\_1 + total\_2 = 2.72 + 1.66 = 4.38 \text{ inches}$$

    To find the day on which the maximum precipitation occurred, first find the maximum in the table, and then determine which row and which column it is in.

    Working through a hand example allows you to formulate the steps required to solve the problem in MATLAB.

4. Develop a MATLAB Solution

    First we'll need to save the data file into MATLAB as a matrix. Because the file is an Excel spreadsheet, the easiest approach is to use the Import Wizard. Double-click on the file in the current directory window to launch the Import Wizard.

    Once the Import Wizard has completed execution, the variable name **Sheet1** will appear in the workspace window. (See Figure 8; your version may name the variable **Weather_data**.)

    Because not every month has 31 days, there are a number of entries for nonexistent days. The value $-99999$ was inserted into those fields. You can double-click the variable name, **Sheet1**, in the workspace window, to edit this matrix and change the "phantom" values to 0. (See Figure 9.)

    Now write the script M-file to solve the problem:

```
clc
%Example 3 - Weather Data
%In this example we will find the total precipitation
%for each month, and for the entire year, using a data file
%We will also find the month and day on which the
%precipitation was the maximum
```

```
weather_data=Sheet1;
%Use the transpose operator to change rows to columns
weather_data = weather_data';
%Find the sum of each column, which is the sum for each
%month
monthly_total=sum(weather_data)/100
%Find the annual total
yearly_total = sum(monthly_total)
%Find the annual maximum and the day on which it occurs
[maximum_precip,month]=max(max(weather_data))
%Find the annual maximum and the month in which it occurs
[maximum_precip,day]=max(max(weather_data'))
```

Notice that the code did not start with our usual **clear, clc** commands, because that would clear the workspace, effectively deleting the **Sheet1** variable. Next we rename **Sheet1** to **weather_data**.

Next, the matrix **weather_data** is transposed, so that the data for each month are in a column instead of a row. That allows us to use the **sum** command to add up all the precipitation values for the month.

Now we can add up all the monthly totals to get the total for the year. An alternative syntax is

```
yearly_total = sum(sum(weather_data))
```

Finding the maximum daily precipitation is easy; what makes this example hard is determining the day and month on which the maximum occurred. The command

```
[maximum_precip,month] = max(max(weather_data))
```

is easier to understand if we break it up into two commands. First,

```
[a,b] = max(weather_data)
```

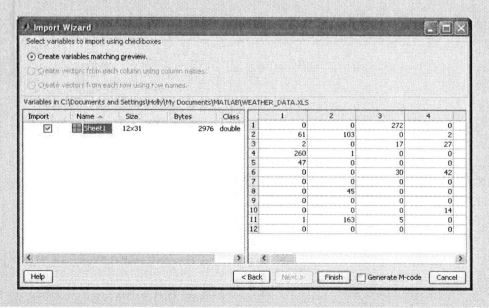

**Figure 8**
MATLAB Import Wizard.

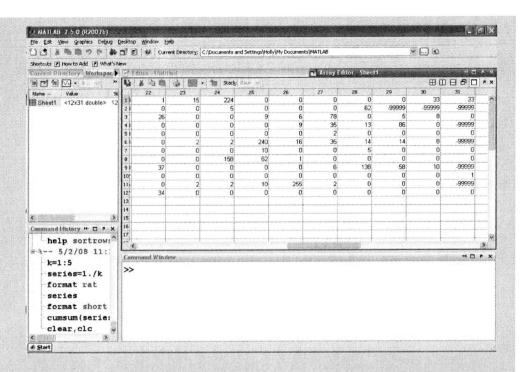

**Figure 9**
MATLAB array editor. You can edit the array in this window and change all of the "phantom values" from −99999 to 0.

returns a matrix of maxima for each column, which in this case is the maximum for each month. This value is assigned to the variable name **a**. The variable **b** becomes a matrix of index numbers that represent the row in each column at which the maximum occurred. The result, then, is

```
a =
      Columns 1 through 9
        272    135     78    260    115    240    157    158    138
      Columns 10 through 12
        156    255     97
b =
      Columns 1 through 9
          3     18     27      1      6     25     12     24     28
      Columns 10 through 12
          5     26     14
```

Now when we execute the **max** command the second time, we determine the maximum precipitation for the entire data set, which is the maximum value in matrix **a**. Also, from matrix **a**, we find the index number for that maximum:

```
[c,d]=max(a)
c =
        272
d =
          1
```

These results tell us that the maximum precipitation occurred in column 1 of the **a** matrix, which means that it occurred in the first month.

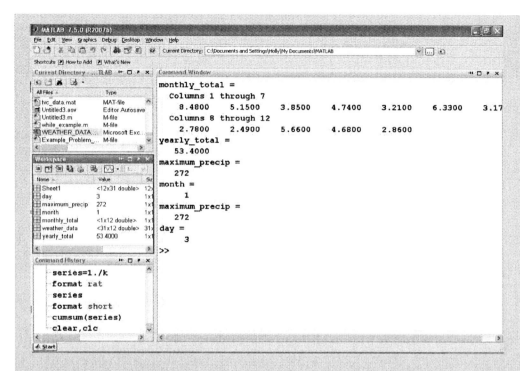

**Figure 10**
Results from the precipitation calculations.

Similarly, transposing the **weather_data** matrix (i.e., obtaining **weather_data'**) and finding the maximum twice allows us to find the day of the month on which the maximum occurred.

There are several things you should notice about the MATLAB screen shown in Figure 10. In the **workspace window**, both **Sheet1** and **weather_data** are listed. **Sheet1** is a 12 × 31 matrix, whereas **weather_data** is a 31 × 12 matrix. All of the variables created when the M-file was executed are now available to the command window. This makes it easy to perform additional calculations in the command window after the M-file has completed running. For example, notice that we forgot to change the **maximum_precip** value to inches from hundredths of an inch. Adding the command

```
maximum_precip = maximum_precip/100
```

would correct that oversight. Notice also that the Weather_Data.xls file is still in the current directory. Finally, notice that the **command history window** reflects only commands issued from the **command window**; it does not show commands executed from an M-file.

5. Test the Solution

Open the Weather_Data.xls file, and confirm that the maximum precipitation occurred on January 3. Once you've confirmed that your M-file program works, you can use it to analyze other data. The National Weather Service maintains similar records for all of its recording stations.

### 5.6 Variance and Standard Deviation

STANDARD DEVIATION: a measure of the spread of values in a data set

The standard deviation and variance are measures of how much elements in a data set vary with respect to each other. Every student knows that the average score on a test is important, but you also need to know the high and low scores to get an idea of how well you did. Test scores, like many kinds of data that are important in engineering, are often distributed in a "bell"-shaped curve. In a normal (Gaussian) distribution of a large amount of data, approximately 68% of the data falls within one standard deviation (sigma) of the mean (± one sigma). If you extend the range to a two-sigma variation (± two sigma), approximately 95% of the data should fall inside these bounds, and if you go out to three sigma, over 99% of the data should fall in this range (Figure 11). Usually, measures such as the standard deviation and variance are meaningful only with large data sets.

---

## Practice Exercises 7

Consider the following matrix:

$$x = \begin{bmatrix} 4 & 90 & 85 & 75 \\ 2 & 55 & 65 & 75 \\ 3 & 78 & 82 & 79 \\ 1 & 84 & 92 & 93 \end{bmatrix}$$

1. Use the **size** function to determine the number of rows and columns in this matrix.
2. Use the **sort** function to sort each column in ascending order.
3. Use the **sort** function to sort each column in descending order.
4. Use the **sortrows** function to sort the matrix so that the first column is in ascending order, but each row still retains its original data. Your matrix should look like this:

$$x = \begin{bmatrix} 1 & 84 & 92 & 93 \\ 2 & 55 & 65 & 75 \\ 3 & 78 & 82 & 79 \\ 4 & 90 & 85 & 75 \end{bmatrix}$$

5. Use the **sortrows** function to sort the matrix from Exercise 4 in descending order, based on the third column.

---

**Figure 11**
Normal distribution.

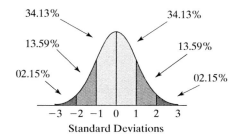

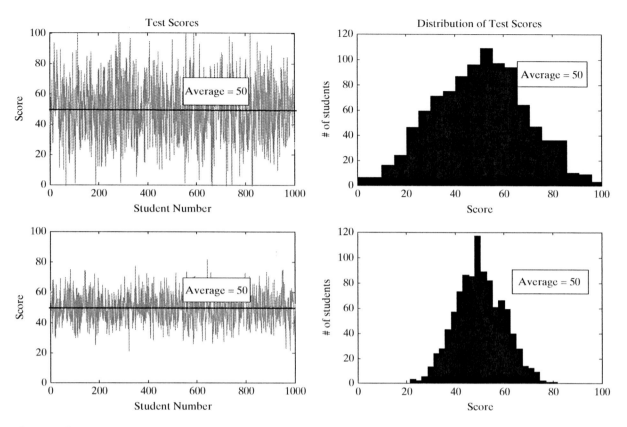

**Figure 12**
Test scores from two different tests.

Consider the data graphed in Figure 12. Both sets of data have the same average (mean) value of 50. However, it is easy to see that the first data set has more variation than the second.

The mathematical definition of variance is

VARIANCE: the standard deviation squared

$$\text{variance} = \sigma^2 = \frac{\sum\limits_{k=1}^{N}(x_k - \mu)^2}{N - 1}$$

In this equation, the symbol $\mu$ represents the mean of the values $x_k$ in the data set. Thus, the term $x_k - \mu$ is simply the difference between the actual value and the average value. The terms are squared and added together:

$$\sum_{k=1}^{N}(x_k - \mu)^2$$

Finally, we divide the summation term by the number of values in the data set ($N$), minus 1.

The standard deviation ($\sigma$), which is used more often than the variance, is the square root of the variance.

**Table 12  Statistical Functions**

| | | |
|---|---|---|
| **std(x)** | Computes the standard deviation of the values in a vector **x**. For example, if $x = \begin{bmatrix} 1 & 5 & 3 \end{bmatrix}$, the standard deviation is 2. However, standard deviations are not usually calculated for small samples of data. | **x=[1, 5, 3];**<br>**std(x)**<br>**ans =**<br>**2** |
| | Returns a row vector containing the standard deviation calculated for each column of a matrix **x**. For example, if $x = \begin{bmatrix} 1 & 5 & 3 \\ 2 & 4 & 6 \end{bmatrix}$ the standard deviation in column 1 is 0.7071, the standard deviation in column 2 is 0.7071, and standard deviation in column 3 is 2.1213.<br>Again, standard deviations are not usually calculated for small samples of data. | **x=[1, 5, 3; 2, 4, 6];**<br>**std(x)**<br>**ans =**<br>**0.7071   0.7071**<br>**2.1213** |
| **var(x)** | Calculates the variance of the data in **x**. For example, if $x = \begin{bmatrix} 1 & 5 & 3 \end{bmatrix}$, the variance is 4. However, variance is not usually calculated for small samples of data. Notice that the standard deviation in this example is the square root of the variance. | **var(x)**<br>**ans =**<br>**4** |

The MATLAB function used to find the standard deviation is **std**. When we applied this function on the large data set shown in Figure 12, we obtained the following output:

```
std(scores1)

ans =
      20.3653
std(scores2)

ans =
      9.8753
```

In other words, approximately 68% of the data in the first data set fall between the average, 50, and ±20.3653. Similarly 68% of the data in the second data set fall between the same average, 50, and ±9.8753.

The variance is found in a similar manner with the **var** function:

```
var(scores1)

ans =
    414.7454
var(scores2)

ans =
    97.5209
```

The syntax for calculating both standard deviation and variance is shown in Table 12.

### Practice Exercises 8

Consider the following matrix:

$$x = \begin{bmatrix} 4 & 90 & 85 & 75 \\ 2 & 55 & 65 & 75 \\ 3 & 78 & 82 & 79 \\ 1 & 84 & 92 & 93 \end{bmatrix}$$

1. Find the standard deviation for each column.
2. Find the variance for each column.
3. Calculate the square root of the variance you found for each column.
4. How do the results from Exercise 3 compare against the standard deviation you found in Exercise 1?

EXAMPLE 4

## Climatologic Data

Climatologists examine weather data over long periods of time, trying to find a pattern. Weather data have been kept reliably in the United States since the 1850s; however, most reporting stations have been in place only since the 1930s and 1940s (Figure 13). Climatologists perform statistical calculations on the data they collect. Although the data in Weather_Data.xls represent just one location for one year, we can use them to practice statistical calculations. Find the mean daily precipitation for each month and the mean daily precipitation for the year, and then find the standard deviation for each month and for the year.

1. State the Problem
   Find the mean daily precipitation for each month and for the year, on the basis of the data in Weather_Data.xls. Also, find the standard deviation of the data during each month and during the entire year.

2. Describe the Input and Output

   ***Input*** Use the Weather_Data.xls file as input to the problem.

   ***Output*** Find

   The mean daily precipitation for each month.
   The mean daily precipitation for the year.
   The standard deviation of the daily precipitation data for each month.
   The standard deviation of the daily precipitation data for the year.

3. Develop a Hand Example
   Use just the data for the first four days of the month:
        January average $= (0 + 0 + 272 + 0)/4 = 68$ hundredths of an inch of precipitation, or 0.68 inch.

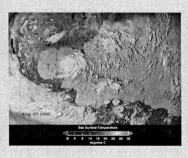

**Figure 13**
A hurricane over Florida.
(Courtesy of NASA/Jet Propulsion Laboratory.)

The standard deviation is found from the following equation:

$$\sigma = \sqrt{\frac{\sum_{k=1}^{N}(x_k - \mu)^2}{N - 1}}$$

Using just the first four days of January, first calculate the sum of the squares of the difference between the mean and the actual value:

$$(0 - 68)^2 + (0 - 68)^2 + (272 - 68)^2 + (0 - 68)^2 = 55{,}488$$

Divide by the number of data points minus 1:

$$55{,}488/(4 - 1) = 18{,}496$$

Finally, take the square root, to give 136 hundredths of an inch of precipitation, or 1.36 inches.

4. Develop a MATLAB Solution

First we need to load the Weather_Data.xls file and edit out the −99999 entries. Although we could do that as described in Example 3, there is an easier way: The data from Example 3 could be saved to a file, so that they are available to use later. If we want to save the entire workspace, just type

```
save <filename>
```

where **filename** is a user-defined file name. If you just want to save one variable, type

```
save <filename>   <variable_name>
```

which saves a single variable or a list of variables to a file. All we need to save is the variable **weather_data**, so the following command is sufficient:

```
save weather_data weather_data
```

This command saves the matrix **weather_data** into the **weather_data.mat** file. Check the current directory window to make sure that **weather_data.mat** has been stored (Figure 14).

Now the M-file we create to solve this example can load the data automatically:

```
clear, clc
%  Example 4 Climatological Data
%  In this example, we find the mean daily
%  precipitation for each month
%  and the mean daily precipitation for the year
%  We also find the standard deviation of the data
%
%  Changing the format to bank often makes the output
%  easier to read
format bank
%  By saving the variable weather_data from the last exam-
ple, it is
```

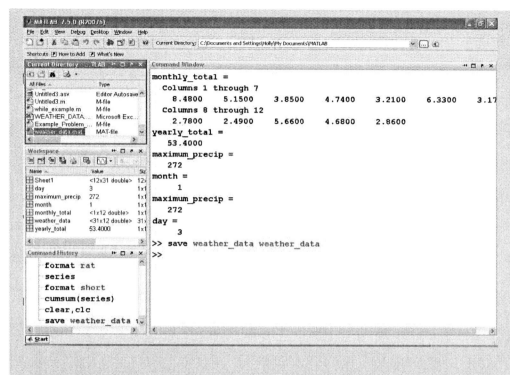

**Figure 14**
The current directory records the name of the saved file.

```
% available to use in this problem
load weather_data
Average_daily_precip_monthly = mean(weather_data)
Average_daily_precip_yearly = mean(weather_data(:))
% Another way to find the average yearly precipitation
Average_daily_precip_yearly = mean(mean(weather_data))
% Now calculate the standard deviation
Monthly_Stdeviation = std(weather_data)
Yearly_Stdeviation = std(weather_data(:))
```

The results, shown in the command window, are

```
Average_daily_precip_monthly =
  Columns 1 through 3
    27.35  16.61  12.42
  Columns 4 through 6
    15.29  10.35  20.42
  Columns 7 through 9
    10.23   8.97   8.03
  Columns 10 through 12
    18.26  15.10   9.23
Average_daily_precip_yearly =
    14.35
Average_daily_precip_yearly =
    14.35
Monthly_Stdeviation =
  Columns 1 through 3
    63.78      35.06      20.40
```

```
Columns 4 through 6
    48.98      26.65        50.46
Columns 7 through 9
    30.63      30.77        27.03
Columns 10 through 12
    42.08      53.34        21.01
Yearly_Stdeviation =
    39.62
```

The mean daily precipitation for the year was calculated in two equivalent ways. The mean of each month was found, and then the mean (average) of the monthly values was found. This works out to be the same as taking the mean of all the data at once. Some new syntax was introduced in this example. The command

```
weather_data(:)
```

converts the two-dimensional matrix **weather_data** into a one-dimensional matrix, thus making it possible to find the mean in one step.

The situation is different for the standard deviation of daily precipitation for the year. Here, we need to perform just one calculation:

```
std(weather_data(:))
```

Otherwise you would find the standard deviation of the standard deviation—not what you want at all.

5. Test the Solution

First, check the results to make sure they make sense. For example, the first time we executed the M-file, the **weather_data** matrix still contained −99999 values. That resulted in mean values less than 1. Since it isn't possible to have negative rainfall, checking the data for reasonability alerted us to the problem. Finally, although calculating the mean daily rainfall for one month by hand would serve as an excellent check, it would be tedious. You can use MATLAB to help you by calculating the mean without using a predefined function. The command window is a convenient place to perform these calculations:

```
load weather_data
sum(weather_data(:,1))      %Find the sum of all the rows in
                            %column one of matrix weather_data
ans =
   848.00
ans/31
ans =
    27.35
```

Compare these results with those for January (month 1).

---

**Hint**

Use the colon operator to change a two-dimensional matrix into a single column:

$$A = X(:)$$

# 6 RANDOM NUMBERS

Random numbers are often used in engineering calculations to simulate measured data. Measured data rarely behave exactly as predicted by mathematical models, so we can add small values of random numbers to our predictions to make a model behave more like a real system. Random numbers are also used to model games of chance. Two different types of random numbers can be generated in MATLAB: uniform random numbers and Gaussian random numbers (often called a normal distribution).

## 6.1 Uniform Random Numbers

Uniform random numbers are generated with the **rand** function. These numbers are evenly distributed between 0 and 1. (Consult the help function for more details.) Table 13 lists several MATLAB commands for generating random numbers.

We can create a set of random numbers over other ranges by modifying the numbers created by the **rand** function. For example, to create a set of 100 evenly distributed numbers between 0 and 5, first create a set over the default range with the command

```
r = rand(100,1);
```

This results in a $100 \times 1$ matrix of values. Now we just to multiply by 5 to expand the range to 0 to 5:

```
r = r * 5;
```

If we want to change the range to 5 to 10, we can add 5 to every value in the array:

```
r = r + 5;
```

The result will be random numbers varying from 5 to 10. We can generalize these results with the equation

$$x = (\text{max} - \text{min}) \cdot \text{random\_number\_set} + \text{mean}$$

## Table 13 Random-Number Generators

| | | |
|---|---|---|
| **rand(n)** | Returns an $n \times n$ matrix. Each value in the matrix is a random number between 0 and 1. | **rand(2)**<br>**ans =**<br>　0.9501　0.6068<br>　0.2311　0.4860 |
| **rand(m,n)** | Returns an $m \times n$ matrix. Each value in the matrix is a random number between 0 and 1. | **rand(3,2)**<br>**ans =**<br>　0.8913　0.0185<br>　0.7621　0.8214<br>　0.4565　0.4447 |
| **randn(n)** | Returns an $n \times n$ matrix. Each value in the matrix is a Gaussian (or normal) random number with a mean of 0 and a variance of 1. | **randn(2)**<br>**ans =**<br>　−0.4326　0.1253<br>　−1.6656　0.2877 |
| **randn(m,n)** | Returns an $m \times n$ matrix. Each value in the matrix is a Gaussian (or normal) random number with a mean of 0 and a variance of 1. | **randn(3,2)**<br>**ans =**<br>　−1.1465　−0.0376<br>　1.1909　0.3273<br>　1.1892　0.1746 |

## 6.2 Gaussian Random Numbers

Gaussian random numbers have the normal distribution shown in Figure 11. There is no absolute upper or lower bound to a data set of this type; we are just less and less likely to find data, the farther away from the mean we get. Gaussian random-number sets are described by specifying their average and the standard deviation of the data set.

MATLAB generates Gaussian values with a mean of 0 and a variance of 1.0, using the **randn** function. For example,

```
randn(3)
```

returns a 3 × 3 matrix

```
ans =
 -0.4326    0.2877    1.1892
 -1.6656   -1.1465   -0.0376
  0.1253    1.1909    0.3273
```

If we need a data set with a different average or a different standard deviation, we start with the default set of random numbers and then modify it. Since the default standard deviation is 1, we must *multiply* by the required standard deviation for the new data set. Since the default mean is 0, we'll need to *add* the new mean:

$$x = \text{standard\_deviation} \cdot \text{random\_data\_set} + \text{mean}$$

For example, to create a sequence of 500 Gaussian random variables with a standard deviation of 2.5 and a mean of 3, type

```
x = randn(1,500)*2.5 + 3;
```

Notice that both **rand** and **randn** can accept either one or two input values. If only one is specified the result is a square matrix. If two values are specified they represent the number of rows and the number of columns in the resulting matrix.

---

### Practice Exercises 9

1. Create a 3 × 3 matrix of evenly distributed random numbers.
2. Create a 3 × 3 matrix of normally distributed random numbers.
3. Create a 100 × 5 matrix of evenly distributed random numbers. Be sure to suppress the output.
4. Find the maximum, the standard deviation, the variance, and the mean for each column in the matrix that you created in Exercise 3.
5. Create a 100 × 5 matrix of normally distributed random numbers. Be sure to suppress the output.
6. Find the maximum, the standard deviation, the variance, and the mean for each column in the matrix you created in Exercise 5.
7. Explain why your results for Exercises 4 and 6 are different.

**EXAMPLE 5**

## Noise

Random numbers can be used to simulate the noise we hear as static on the radio. By adding this noise to data files that store music, we can study the effect of static on recordings.

MATLAB has the ability to play music files by means of the **sound** function. To demonstrate this function, it also has a built-in music file with a short segment of Handel's *Messiah*. In this example, we will use the **randn** function to create noise, and then we'll add the noise to the music clip.

Music is stored in MATLAB as an array with values from −1 to 1. To convert this array into music, the **sound** function requires a sample frequency. The **handel.mat** file contains both an array representing the music and the value of the sample frequency. To hear the *Messiah*, you must first load the file, using the command

```
load handel
```

Notice that two new variables—**y** and **Fs**—were added to the workspace window when the **handel** file was loaded. To play the clip, type

```
sound(y, Fs)
```

Experiment with different values of **Fs** to hear the effect of different sample frequencies on the music. (Clearly, the sound must be engaged on your computer, or you won't be able to hear the playback.)

1. State the Problem
   Add a noise component to the recording of Handel's *Messiah* included with MATLAB.

2. Describe the Input and Output

   *Input*  MATLAB data file of Handel's *Messiah*, stored as the built-in file **handel**

   *Output*  An array representing the *Messiah*, with static added
   A graph of the first 200 elements of the data file

3. Develop a Hand Example
   Since the data in the music file vary between −1 and +1, we should add noise values of a smaller order of magnitude. First we'll try values centered on 0 and with a standard deviation of 0.1.

**Figure 15**
Utah Symphony Orchestra.

4. Develop a MATLAB Solution

```
%Example 5
%Noise
load handel      %Load the music data file
sound(y,Fs)      %Play the music data file
pause            %Pause to listen to the music
% Be sure to hit enter to continue after playing the music
% Add random noise
noise=randn(length(y),1)*0.10;
sound(y+noise,Fs)
```

This program allows you to play the recording of the *Messiah*, both with and without the added noise. You can adjust the multiplier on the noise line to observe the effect of changing the magnitude of the added static. For example:

```
noise=randn(length(y),1)*0.20
```

5. Test the Solution

In addition to playing back the music both with and without the added noise, we could plot the results. Because the file is quite large (73,113 elements), we'll just plot the first 200 points:

```
%   Plot the first 200 data points in each file
t=1:length(y);
noisy = y + noise;
plot(t(1,1:200),y(1:200,1),t(1,1:200),noisy(1:200,1),':')
title('Handel"s Messiah')
xlabel('Element Number in Music Array')
ylabel('Frequency')
```

**Figure 16**
Handel's *Messiah*. The solid line represents the original data, and the dotted line is the data to which we've added noise

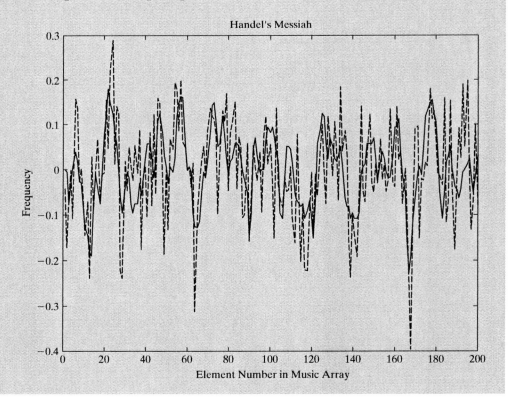

These commands tell MATLAB to plot the index number of the data on the *x*-axis and the value stored in the music arrays on the *y*-axis.

In Figure 16, the solid line represents the original data and the dotted line the data to which we've added noise. As expected, the noisy data has a bigger range and doesn't always follow the same pattern as the original.

## 7 COMPLEX NUMBERS

MATLAB includes several functions used primarily with complex numbers. Complex numbers consist of two parts: a real and an imaginary component. For example,

$$5 + 3i$$

is a complex number. The real component is 5, and the imaginary component is 3. Complex numbers can be entered into MATLAB in two ways: as an addition problem, such as

**COMPLEX NUMBER:** a number with both real and imaginary components

```
A = 5 + 3i          or          A = 5+3*i
```

or with the **complex** function, as in

```
A = complex(5,3)
```

which returns

```
A =
   5.0000 + 3.0000i
```

As is standard in MATLAB, the input to the **complex** function can be either two scalars or two arrays of values. Thus, if **x** and **y** are defined as

```
x = 1:3;
y = [-1,5,12];
```

then the **complex** function can be used to define an array of complex numbers as follows:

```
complex(x,y)
ans =
   1.0000 - 1.0000i   2.0000 + 5.0000i   3.0000 +12.0000i
```

The **real** and **imag** functions can be used to separate the real and imaginary components of complex numbers. For example, for **A = 5 + 3*i**, we have

```
real(A)
ans =
   5
imag(A)
ans =
   3
```

The **isreal** function can be used to determine whether a variable is storing a complex number. It returns a 1 if the variable is real and a 0 if it is complex. Since **A** is a complex number, we get

```
isreal(A)
ans =
   0
```

Thus, the **isreal** function is false and returns a value of 0.

The complex conjugate of a complex number consists of the same real component, but an imaginary component of the opposite sign. The **conj** function returns the complex conjugate:

```
conj(A)
ans =
   5.0000 - 3.0000i
```

The transpose operator also returns the complex conjugate of an array, in addition to converting rows to columns and columns to rows. Thus, we have

```
A'
ans =
   5.0000 - 3.0000i
```

Of course, in this example **A** is a scalar. We can create a complex array **B** by using **A** and performing both addition and multiplication operations:

```
B = [A, A+1, A*3]
B =
   5.0000 + 3.0000i   6.0000 + 3.0000i   15.0000 + 9.0000i
```

The transpose of **B** is

```
B'
ans =
    5.0000 - 3.0000i
    6.0000 - 3.0000i
   15.0000 - 9.0000i
```

Complex numbers are often thought of as describing a position on an *x–y* plane. The real part of the number corresponds to the *x*-value, and the imaginary component corresponds to the *y*-value, as shown in Figure 17a. Another way to think about this point is to describe it with polar coordinates—that is, with a radius and an angle (Figure 17b).

MATLAB includes functions to convert complex numbers from Cartesian to polar form.

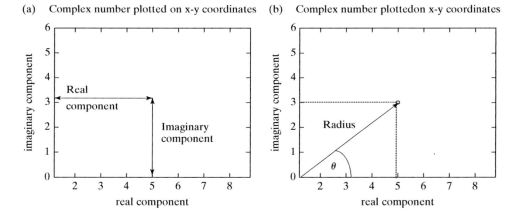

**Figure 17**
(a) Complex number represented in a Cartesian coordinate system. (b) A complex number can also be described with polar coordinates.

When the absolute-value function is used with a complex number, it calculates the radius, using the Pythagorean theorem:

```
abs(A)
ans =
    5.8310
```

POLAR COORDINATES: a technique for describing a location using an angle and a distance

$$\text{radius} = \sqrt{(\text{real component})^2 + (\text{imaginary component})^2}$$

Since, in this example, the real component is 5 and the imaginary component is 3,

$$\text{radius} = \sqrt{5^2 + 3^2} = 5.8310$$

We could also calculate the radius in MATLAB, using the **real** and **imag** functions described earlier:

```
sqrt(real(A).^2 + imag(A).^2)
ans =
    5.8310
```

### Table 14  Functions Used with Complex Numbers

| | | |
|---|---|---|
| **abs(x)** | Computes the absolute value of a complex number, using the Pythagorean theorem. This is equivalent to the radius if the complex number is represented in polar coordinates.<br><br>For example, if $x = 3 + 4i$, the absolute value is $\sqrt{3^2 + 4^2} = 5$. | x=3+4i;<br>**abs(x)**<br>ans =<br>    5 |
| **angle(x)** | Computes the angle from the horizontal in radians when a complex number is represented in polar coordinates. | x=3+4i;<br>**angle(x)**<br>ans =<br>    0.9273 |
| **complex(x,y)** | Generates a complex number with a real component $x$ and an imaginary component $y$. | x=3;<br>y=4;<br>**complex(x,y)**<br>ans =<br>    3.0000 +<br>    4.0000i |
| **real(x)** | Extracts the real component from a complex number. | x=3+4i;<br>**real(x)**<br>ans =<br>    3 |
| **imag(x)** | Extracts the imaginary component from a complex number. | x=3+4i;<br>**imag(x)**<br>ans =<br>    4 |
| **isreal(x)** | Determines whether the values in an array are real. If they are real, the function returns a 1; if they are complex, it returns a 0. | x=3+4i;<br>**isreal(x)**<br>ans =<br>    0 |
| **conj(x)** | Generates the complex conjugate of a complex number. | x=3+4i;<br>**conj(x)**<br>ans =<br>    3.0000 - 4.0000i |

Similarly, the angle is found with the angle function:

```
angle(A)
ans =
      0.5404
```

The result is expressed in radians. Both functions, **abs** and **angle**, will accept scalars or arrays as input. Recall that B is a 1 × 3 array of complex numbers:

```
B =
   5.0000 + 3.0000i   6.0000 + 3.0000i   15.0000 + 9.0000i
```

The **abs** function returns the radius if the number is represented in polar coordinates:

```
abs(B)
ans =
      5.8310    6.7082    17.4929
```

The angle from the horizontal can be found with the **angle** function:

```
angle(B)
ans =
      0.5404    0.4636    0.5404
```

The MATLAB functions commonly used with complex numbers are summarized in Table 14.

---

### Practice Exercises 10

1. Create the following complex numbers:
   **a.** $A = 1 + i$
   **b.** $B = 2 - 3i$
   **c.** $C = 8 + 2i$
2. Create a vector **D** of complex numbers whose real components are 2, 4, and 6 and whose imaginary components are −3, 8, and −16.
3. Find the magnitude (absolute value) of each of the vectors you created in Exercises 1 and 2.
4. Find the angle from the horizontal of each of the complex numbers you created in Exercises 1 and 2.
5. Find the complex conjugate of vector **D**.
6. Use the transpose operator to find the complex conjugate of vector **D**.
7. Multiply **A** by its complex conjugate, and then take the square root of your answer. How does this value compare against the magnitude (absolute value) of **A**?

---

## 8  COMPUTATIONAL LIMITATIONS

KEY IDEA: There is a limit to how small or how large a number can be handled by computer programs

The variables stored in a computer can assume a wide range of values. On the majority of computers, the range extends from about $10^{-308}$ to $10^{308}$, which should be enough to accommodate most computations. MATLAB includes functions to identify the largest real numbers and the largest integers the program can process (Table 15).

**Table 15  Computational Limits**

| | | |
|---|---|---|
| **realmax** | Returns the largest possible floating-point number used in MATLAB. | **realmax** <br> **ans =** <br>    **1.7977e+308** |
| **realmin** | Returns the smallest possible floating-point number used in MATLAB. | **realmin** <br> **ans =** <br>    **2.2251e-308** |
| **intmax** | Returns the largest possible integer number used in MATLAB. | **intmax** <br> **ans =** <br>    **2147483647** |
| **intmin** | Returns the smallest possible integer number used in MATLAB. | **intmin** <br> **ans =** <br>    **–2147483648** |

The value of **realmax** corresponds roughly to $2^{1024}$, since computers actually perform their calculations in binary (base-2) arithmetic. Of course, it is possible to formulate a problem in which the result of an expression is larger or smaller than the permitted maximum. For example, suppose that we execute the following commands:

```
x = 2.5e200;
y = 1.0e200;
z = x*y
```

MATLAB responds with

```
z =
    Inf
```

because the answer (2.5e400) is outside the allowable range. This error is called *exponent overflow*, because the exponent of the result of an arithmetic operation is too large to store in the computer's memory.

Exponent underflow is a similar error, caused by the exponent of the result of an arithmetic operation being too *small* to store in the computer's memory. Using the same allowable range, we obtain an exponent underflow with the following commands:

```
x = 2.5e-200;
y = 1.0e200
z = x/y
```

Together, these commands return

```
z = 0
```

The result of an exponent underflow is zero.

We also know that division by zero is an invalid operation. If an expression results in a division by zero, the result of the division is infinity:

```
z = y/0
z =
    Inf
```

MATLAB may print a warning telling you that division by zero is not possible.

OVERFLOW: a calculational result that is too large for the computer program to handle

UNDERFLOW: a calculational result that is too small for the computer program to distinguish from zero

KEY IDEA: Careful planning can help you avoid calculational overflow or underflow

In performing calculations with very large or very small numbers, it may be possible to reorder the calculations to avoid an underflow or an overflow. Suppose, for example, that you would like to perform the following string of multiplications:

$$(2.5 \times 10^{200}) \times (2 \times 10^{200}) \times (1 \times 10^{-100})$$

The answer is $5 \times 10^{300}$, within the bounds allowed by MATLAB. However, consider what happens when we enter the problem into MATLAB:

```
2.5e200*2e200*1e-100
ans =
        Inf
```

Because MATLAB executes the problem from left to right, the first multiplication yields a value outside the allowable range ($5 \times 10^{400}$), resulting in an answer of infinity. However, by rearranging the problem to

```
2.5e200*1e-100*2e200
ans =
5.0000e+300
```

we avoid the overflow and find the correct answer.

## 9   SPECIAL VALUES AND MISCELLANEOUS FUNCTIONS

Most, but not all, functions require an input argument. Although used as if they were scalar constants, the functions listed in Table 16 do *not* require any input.

MATLAB allows you to redefine these special values as variable names; however, doing so can have unexpected consequences. For example, the following MATLAB code is allowed, even though it is not wise:

```
pi = 12.8;
```

From this point on, whenever the variable **pi** is called, the new value will be used. Similarly, you can redefine **any** function as a variable name, such as

```
sin = 10;
```

To restore **sin** to its job as a trigonometric function (or to restore the default value of **pi**), you must clear the workspace with

```
clear
```

Now check to see the result by issuing the command for $\pi$.

```
pi
```

This command returns

```
pi =
        3.1416
```

---

### Hint

The function $i$ is the most common of these functions to be unintentionally renamed by MATLAB users.

**Practice Exercises 11**

1. Use the **clock** function to add the time and date to your work sheet.
2. Use the **date** function to add the date to your work sheet.
3. Convert the following calculations to MATLAB code and explain your results:
   **a.** 322! (Remember that, to a mathematician, the symbol ! means factorial.)
   **b.** $5 \times 10^{500}$
   **c.** $1/5 \times 10^{500}$
   **d.** 0/0

## Table 16  Special Functions

| | | |
|---|---|---|
| **pi** | Mathematical constant $\pi$. | **pi**<br>**ans =**<br>  **3.1416** |
| **i** | Imaginary number. | **i**<br>**ans =**<br>  **0 + 1.0000i** |
| **j** | Imaginary number. | **j**<br>**ans =**<br>  **0 + 1.0000i** |
| **Inf** | Infinity, which often occurs during a calculational overflow or when a number is divided by zero. | **5/0**<br>**Warning: Divide by zero.**<br>**ans =**<br>  **Inf** |
| **NaN** | Not a number.<br>Occurs when a calculation is undefined. | **0/0**<br>**Warning: Divide by zero.**<br>**ans =**<br>  **NaN**<br>**inf/inf**<br>**ans =**<br>  **NaN** |
| **clock** | Current time.<br>Returns a six-member array [year month day hour minute second]. When the **clock** function was called on July 19, 2008, at 5:19 P.M. and 30.0 seconds, MATLAB returned the output shown at the right. | **clock**<br>**ans =**<br>  **1.0e+003 ***<br>**2.0080  0.0070  0.0190**<br>**0.0170  0.0190  0.0300** |
| | The **fix** and **clock** functions together result in a format that is easier to read.<br>The **fix** function rounds toward zero. A similar result could be obtained by setting **format bank**. | **fix(clock)**<br>**ans =**<br>  **2008    7    19**<br>  **17    19    30** |
| **date** | Current date.<br>Similar to the **clock** function. However, it returns the date in a "string format." | **date**<br>**ans =**<br>  **19-Jul-2008** |
| **eps** | The distance between 1 and the next-larger double-precision floating-point number. | **eps**<br>**ans =**<br>  **2.2204e-016** |

## SUMMARY

In this chapter, we explored a number of predefined MATLAB functions, including the following:

- general mathematical functions, such as
  - exponential functions
  - logarithmic functions
  - roots
- rounding functions
- functions used in discrete mathematics, such as
  - factoring functions
  - prime-number functions
- trigonometric functions, including
  - standard trigonometric functions
  - inverse trigonometric functions
  - hyperbolic trigonometric functions
  - trigonometric functions that use degrees instead of radians
- data analysis functions, such as
  - maxima and minima
  - averages (mean and median)
  - sums and products
  - sorting
  - standard deviation and variance
- random-number generation for both
  - uniform distributions
  - Gaussian (normal) distributions
- functions used with complex numbers

We explored the computational limits inherent in MATLAB and introduced special values, such as **pi**, that are built into the program.

**MATLAB SUMMARY**

The following MATLAB summary lists and briefly describes all of the special characters, commands, and functions that were defined in this chapter:

| Special Characters and Functions | |
| --- | --- |
| **eps** | smallest difference recognized |
| **i** | imaginary number |
| **clock** | returns the time |
| **date** | returns the date |
| **Inf** | infinity |
| **intmax** | returns the largest possible integer number used in MATLAB |
| **intmin** | returns the smallest possible integer number used in MATLAB |
| **j** | imaginary number |
| **NaN** | not a number |
| **pi** | mathematical constant $\pi$ |
| **realmax** | returns the largest possible floating-point number used in MATLAB |
| **realmin** | returns the smallest possible floating-point number used in MATLAB |

## Commands and Functions

| | |
|---|---|
| **abs** | computes the absolute value of a real number or the magnitude of a complex number |
| **angle** | computes the angle when complex numbers are represented in polar coordinates |
| **asin** | computes the inverse sine (arcsine) |
| **asind** | computes the inverse sine and reports the result in degrees |
| **ceil** | rounds to the nearest integer toward positive infinity |
| **complex** | creates a complex number |
| **conj** | creates the complex conjugate of a complex number |
| **cos** | computes the cosine |
| **cumprod** | computes a cumulative product of the values in an array |
| **cumsum** | computes a cumulative sum of the values in an array |
| **erf** | calculates the error function |
| **exp** | computes the value of $e^x$ |
| **factor** | finds the prime factors |
| **factorial** | calculates the factorial |
| **fix** | rounds to the nearest integer toward zero |
| **floor** | rounds to the nearest integer toward minus infinity |
| **gcd** | finds the greatest common denominator |
| **help** | opens the help function |
| **helpwin** | opens the windowed help function |
| **imag** | extracts the imaginary component of a complex number |
| **isprime** | determines whether a value is prime |
| **isreal** | determines whether a value is real or complex |
| **lcn** | finds the least common denominator |
| **length** | determines the largest dimension of an array |
| **log** | computes the natural logarithm, or the logarithm to the base $e$ ($\log_e$) |
| **log10** | computes the common logarithm, or the logarithm to the base 10 ($\log_{10}$) |
| **log2** | computes the logarithm to the base 2 ($\log_2$) |
| **max** | finds the maximum value in an array and determines which element stores the maximum value |
| **mean** | computes the average of the elements in an array |
| **median** | finds the median of the elements in an arry |
| **min** | finds the minimum value in an array and determines which element stores the minimum value |
| **mode** | finds the most common number in an array |
| **nchoosek** | finds the number of possible combinations when a subgroup of $k$ values is chosen from a group of $n$ values. |
| **nthroot** | find the real $n$th root of the input matrix |
| **primes** | finds the prime numbers less than the input value — |
| **prod** | multiplies the values in an array |
| **rand** | calculates evenly distributed random numbers |

*(Continued)*

| Commands and Functions (Continued) | |
|---|---|
| **randn** | calculates normally distributed (Gaussian) random numbers |
| **rats** | converts the input to a rational representation (i.e., a fraction) |
| **real** | extracts the real component of a complex number |
| **rem** | calculates the remainder in a division problem |
| **round** | rounds to the nearest integer |
| **sign** | determines the sign (positive or negative) |
| **sin** | computes the sine, using radians as input |
| **sind** | computes the sine, using angles in degrees as input |
| **sinh** | computes the hyperbolic sine |
| **size** | determines the number of rows and columns in an array |
| **sort** | sorts the elements of a vector |
| **sortrows** | sorts the rows of a vector on the basis of the values in the first column |
| **sound** | plays back music files |
| **sqrt** | calculates the square root of a number |
| **std** | determines the standard deviation |
| **sum** | sums the values in an array |
| **tan** | computes the tangent, using radians as input |
| **var** | computes the variance |

**KEY TERMS**

argument
average
complex numbers
discrete mathematics
function
function input
Gaussian random variation

mean
median
nesting
normal random variation
overflow
rational numbers
real numbers

seed
standard deviation
underflow
uniform random number
variance

**PROBLEMS**

## Elementary Math Functions

1  Find the cube root of $-5$, both by using the **nthroot** function and by raising $-5$ to the 1/3 power. Explain the difference in your answers. Prove that both results are indeed correct answers by cubing them and showing that they equal $-5$.

2  MATLAB contains functions to calculate the natural logarithm (**log**), the logarithm to the base 10 (**log10**), and the logarithm to the base 2 (**log2**). However, if you want to find a logarithm to another base—for example, base $b$—you'll have to do the math yourself with the formula

$$\log_b(x) = \frac{\log_e(x)}{\log_e(b)}$$

What is the $\log_b$ of 10 when $b$ is defined from 1 to 10 in increments of 1?

3  Populations tend to expand exponentially. That is,

$$P = P_0 e^{rt}$$

where

$P$ = current population,

$P_0$ = original population,

$r$ = continuous growth rate, expressed as a fraction, and

$t$ = time.

If you originally have 100 rabbits that breed at a continuous growth rate of 90% ($r = 0.9$) per year, find how many rabbits you will have at the end of 10 years.

4   Chemical reaction rates are proportional to a rate constant $k$ that changes with temperature according to the Arrhenius equation

$$k = k_0 e^{-Q/RT}$$

For a certain reaction,

$Q = 8000$ cal/mol

$R = 1.987$ cal/mol K

$k_0 = 1200$ min$^{-1}$

Find the values of $k$ for temperatures from 100 K to 500 K, in 50-degree increments. Create a table of your results.

5   Consider the air-conditioning requirements of the large home shown in Figure P5. The interior of the house is warmed by waste heat from lighting and electrical appliances, by heat leaking in from the outdoors, and by heat generated by the people in the home. An air conditioner must be able to remove all this thermal energy in order to keep the inside temperature from rising. Suppose there are 20 light bulbs emitting 100 J/s of energy each and four appliances emitting 500 J/s each. Suppose also that heat leaks in from the outside at a rate of 3000 J/s.

   **(a)** How much heat must the air conditioner be able to remove from the home per second?

   **(b)** One particular air-conditioning unit can handle 2000 J/s. How many of these units are needed to keep the home at a constant temperature?

6   **(a)** If you have four people, how many different ways can you arrange them in a line?

   **(b)** If you have 10 different tiles, how many different ways can you arrange them?

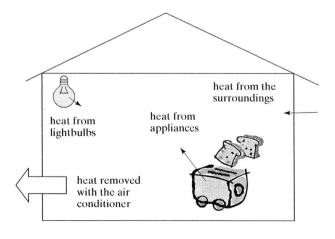

**Figure P5**
Air conditioning must remove heat from a number of sources.

**7** **(a)** If you have 12 people, how many different committees of two people each can you create? Remember that a committee of Bob and Alice is the same as a committee of Alice and Bob.
**(b)** How many different soccer teams of 11 players can you form from a class of 30 students? (Combinations—order does not matter)
**(c)** Since each player on a soccer team is assigned a particular role, order *does* matter. Recalculate the possible number of different soccer teams that can be formed when order is taken into account.

**8** There are 52 *different* cards in a deck. How many different hands of 5 cards each are possible? Remember, every hand can be arranged 120 (5!) different ways.

**9** Very large prime numbers are used in cryptography. How many prime numbers are there between 10,000 and 20,000? (These aren't big enough primes to be useful in ciphers.) (*Hint*: Use the **primes** function and the **length** command.)

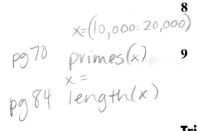

$$x = (10,000 : 20,000)$$

pg 70  primes(x)

pg 84  $x =$ length(x)

### Trigonometric Functions

**10** Sometimes it is convenient to have a table of sine, cosine, and tangent values instead of using a calculator. Create a table of all three of these trigonometric functions for angles from 0 to $2\pi$, with a spacing of 0.1 radian. Your table should contain a column for the angle and then for the sine, cosine, and tangent.

**11** The displacement of the oscillating spring shown in Figure P11 can be described by

$$x = A \cos(\omega t)$$

where

$x =$ displacement at time $t$,
$A =$ maximum displacement,
$\omega =$ angular frequency, which depends on the spring constant and the mass attached to the spring, and
$t =$ time.

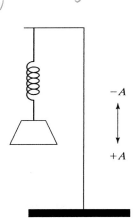

**Figure P11**
An oscillating spring.

Find the displacement $x$ for times from 0 to 10 seconds when the maximum displacement $A$ is 4 cm and the angular frequency is 0.6 radian/sec. Present your results in a table of displacement and time values.

**12** The acceleration of the spring described in the preceding exercise is

$$a = -A\omega^2 \cos(\omega t)$$

Find the acceleration for times from 0 to 10 seconds, using the constant values from the preceding problem. Create a table that includes the time, the displacement from corresponding values in the previous exercise, and the acceleration.

**13** You can use trigonometry to find the height of a building as shown in Figure P13. Suppose you measure the angle between the line of sight and the horizontal line connecting the measuring point and the building. You can calculate the height of the building with the following formulas:

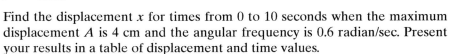

$$\tan(\theta) = h/d$$
$$h = d \tan(\theta)$$

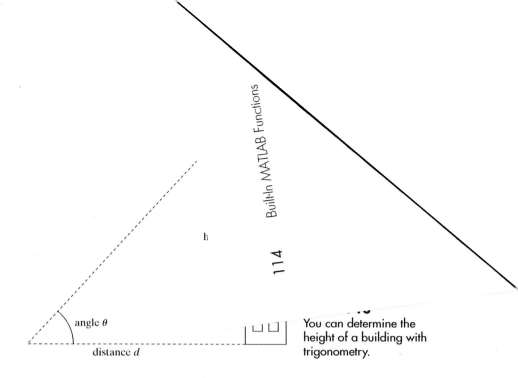

You can determine the height of a building with trigonometry.

Assume that the distance to the building along the ground is 120 meters and the angle measured along the line of sight is $30° \pm 3°$. Find the maximum and minimum heights the building can be.

14 Consider the building from the previous exercise.

(a) If it is 200 feet tall and you are 20 feet away, at what angle from the ground will you have to tilt your head to see the top of the building? (Assume that your head is even with the ground.)

(b) How far is it from your head to the top of the building?

## Data Analysis Functions

15 Consider the following table of data representing temperature readings in a reactor:

| Thermocouple 1 | Thermocouple 2 | Thermocouple 3 |
|:---:|:---:|:---:|
| 84.3 | 90.0 | 86.7 |
| 86.4 | 89.5 | 87.6 |
| 85.2 | 88.6 | 88.3 |
| 87.1 | 88.9 | 85.3 |
| 83.5 | 88.9 | 80.3 |
| 84.8 | 90.4 | 82.4 |
| 85.0 | 89.3 | 83.4 |
| 85.3 | 89.5 | 85.4 |
| 85.3 | 88.9 | 86.3 |
| 85.2 | 89.1 | 85.3 |
| 82.3 | 89.5 | 89.0 |
| 84.7 | 89.4 | 87.3 |
| 83.6 | 89.8 | 87.2 |

Your instructor may provide you with a file named **thermocouple.dat**, or you may need to enter the data yourself.

Use MATLAB to find

**(a)** the maximum temperature measured by each thermocouple.

**(b)** the minimum temperature measured by each thermocouple.

**16** The range of an object shot at an angle $\theta$ with respect to the x-axis and an initial velocity $v_0$ (Figure P16) is given by

$$\text{Range} = \frac{v_0^2}{g} \sin(2\theta)$$

for $0 \le \theta \le \pi/2$ and neglecting air resistance. Use $g = 9.81$ m/s$^2$ and an initial velocity $v_0$ of 100 m/s. Show that the maximum range is obtained at approximately $\theta = \pi/4$ by computing the range in increments of $\pi/100$ between $0 \le \theta \le \pi/2$. You won't be able to find the exact angle that results in the maximum range, because your calculations are at evenly spaced angles of $\pi/100$ radian.

**17** The vector

$$G = [68, 83, 61, 70, 75, 82, 57, 5, 76, 85, 62, 71, 96, 78, 76, 68, 72, 75, 83, 93]$$

represents the distribution of final grades in a dynamics course. Compute the mean, median, mode, and standard deviation of **G**. Which better represents the "most typical grade," the mean, median or mode? Why? Use MATLAB to determine the number of grades in the array (don't just count them) and to sort them into ascending order.

**18** Generate 10,000 Gaussian random numbers with a mean of 80 and standard deviation of 23.5. (You'll want to suppress the output so that you don't overwhelm the command window with data.) Use the **mean** function to confirm that your array actually has a mean of 80. Use the **std** function to confirm that your standard deviation is actually 23.5.

**19** Use the **date** function to add the current date to your homework.

## Random Numbers

**20** Many games require the player to roll two dice. The number on each die can vary from 1 to 6.

pg 97

**(a)** Use the **rand** function in combination with a rounding function to create a simulation of one roll of one die.

**(b)** Use your results from part (a) to create a simulation of the value rolled with a second die.

**(c)** Add your two results to create a value representing the total rolled during each turn.

**(d)** Use your program to determine the values rolled in a favorite board game, or use the game shown in Figure P20.

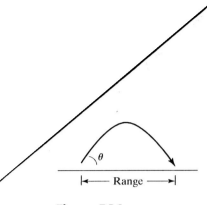

**Figure P16**
The range depends on the launch angle and the launch velocity.

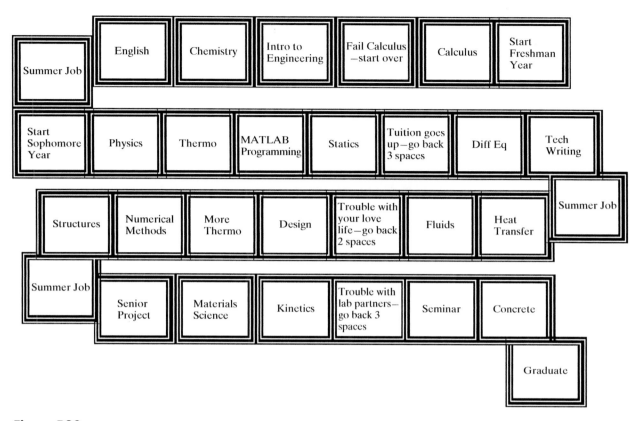

**Figure P20**
The college game.

21  Suppose you are designing a container to ship sensitive medical materials
    between hospitals. The container needs to keep the contents within a speci-
    fied temperature range. You have created a model predicting how the con-
    tainer responds to the exterior temperature, and you now need to run a
    simulation.

    **(a)** Create a normal distribution (Gaussian distribution) of temperatures
    with a mean of 70°F and a standard deviation of 2°, corresponding to two
    hours' duration. You'll need a temperature for each time value from 0 to
    120 minutes. (That's 121 values.)

    **(b)** Plot the data on an x–y plot. Don't worry about labels. Recall that the
    MATLAB function for plotting is **plot(x,y)**.

    **(c)** Find the maximum temperature, the minimum temperature, and the
    times at which they occur.

## SOLUTIONS TO PRACTICE EXERCISES

### Practice Exercises 1

1. In the command window, type

   ```
   help cos
   help sqrt
   help exp
   ```

2. Select **Help → MATLAB Help** from the menu bar.

   Use the left-hand pane to navigate to either **Functions - Categorical List** or **Functions - Alphabetical List**

3. Select **Help → Web Resources → The Mathworks Web Site**

### Practice Exercises 2

1. ```
   x = -2:1:2
   x =
    -2 -1 0 1 2
   abs(x)
   ans =
    2  1 0 1 2
   sqrt(x)
   ans =
      0 + 1.4142i 0 + 1.0000i 0 1.0000 1.4142
   ```

2. **a.** ```
   sqrt(-3)
   ans =
      0 + 1.7321i
   sqrt(3)
   ans =
      1.7321
   ```

   **b.** ```
   nthroot(-3,2)
   ??? Error using ==> nthroot at 33
   If X is negative, N must be an odd integer.
   nthroot(3,2)
   ans =
      1.7321
   ```

   **c.** ```
   -3^(1/2)
   ans =
     -1.7321
   3^(1/2)
   ans =
      1.7321
   ```

3. ```
   x = -9:3:12
   x =
    -9 -6 -3 0 3 6 9 12
   rem(x,2)
   ans =
    -1 0 -1 0 1 0 1 0
   ```

4. ```
   exp(x)
   ans =
    1.0e+005 *
   0.0000 0.0000 0.0000 0.0000 0.0002 0.0040 0.0810 1.6275
   ```

5. ```
   log(x)
   ans =
    Columns 1 through 4
    2.1972 + 3.1416i 1.7918 + 3.1416i 1.0986 + 3.1416i -Inf
    Columns 5 through 8
   ```
   ```

```
   1.0986 1.7918 2.1972 2.4849
log10(x)
ans =
  Columns 1 through 4
  0.9542 + 1.3644i 0.7782 + 1.3644i 0.4771 + 1.3644i -Inf
  Columns 5 through 8
  0.4771 0.7782 0.9542 1.0792
```

6. `sign(x)`
```
ans =
 -1 -1 -1 0 1 1 1 1
```

7. `format rat`
`x/2`
```
ans =
    -9/2 -3 -3/2 0 3/2 3 9/2 6
```

## Practice Exercises 3

1. `factor(322)`
```
ans =
 2 7 23
```

2. `gcd(322,6)`
```
ans =
 2
```

3. `isprime(322)`
```
ans =
 0
```
   Because the result of **isprime** is the number 0, 322 is not a prime number.

4. `length(primes(322))`
```
ans =
 66
```

5. `rats(pi)`
```
ans =
 355/113
```

6. `factorial(10)`
```
ans =
 3628800
```

7. `nchoosek(20,3)`
```
ans =
 1140
```

## Practice Exercises 4

1. `theta = 3*pi;`
`sin(2*theta)`
```
ans =
-7.3479e-016
```

2. `theta = 0:0.2*pi:2*pi;`
`cos(theta)`
```
ans =
 Columns 1 through 7
  1.0000 0.8090 0.3090 -0.3090 -0.8090 -1.0000 -0.8090
 Columns 8 through 11
  -0.3090 0.3090 0.8090 1.0000
```

3. `asin(1)`
```
ans =
 1.5708
```
   This answer is in radians.

4. `x = -1:0.2:1;`
`acos(x)`

```
ans =
Columns 1 through 7
  3.1416 2.4981 2.2143 1.9823 1.7722 1.5708 1.3694
Columns 8 through 11
  1.1593 0.9273 0.6435 0
```

5. `cos(45*pi/180)`
```
ans =
  0.7071
```
   `cosd(45)`
```
ans =
  0.7071
```

6. `asin(0.5)`
```
ans =
  0.5236  This answer is in radians. You could also find the result in degrees.
asind(0.5)
ans =
  30.0000
```

7. `csc(60*pi/180)`
```
ans =
  1.1547
```
   or...
   `cscd(60)`
```
ans =
  1.1547
```

## Practice Exercises 5

`x = [4 90 85 75; 2 55 65 75; 3 78 82 79;1 84 92 93];`

1. `max(x)`
```
ans =
  4 90 92 93
```
2. `[maximum, row]=max(x)`
```
maximum =
  4 90 92 93
row =
  1 1 4 4
```
3. `max(x')`
```
ans =
  90 75 82 93
```
4. `[maximum, column]=max(x')`
```
maximum =
  90 75 82 93
column =
  2 4 3 4
```
5. `max(max(x))`
```
ans =
  93
```

## Practice Exercises 6

`x = [4 90 85 75; 2 55 65 75; 3 78 82 79;1 84 92 93];`

1. `mean(x)`
```
ans =
  2.5000 76.7500 81.0000 80.5000
```
2. `median(x)`
```
ans =
  2.5000 81.0000 83.5000 77.0000
```

3. `mean(x')`
   ```
   ans =
      63.5000 49.2500 60.5000 67.5000
   ```
4. `median(x')`
   ```
   ans =
   80.0000 60.0000 78.5000 88.0000
   ```
5. `mode(x)`
   ```
   ans =
      1 55 65 75
   ```
6. `mean(mean(x))`
   ```
   ans =
      60.1875
   ```
   or . . .
   `mean(x(:))`
   ```
   ans =
           60.1875
   ```

## Practice Exercises 7

`x = [4 90 85 75; 2 55 65 75; 3 78 82 79;1 84 92 93];`

1. `size(x)`
   ```
   ans =
      4 4
   ```
2. `sort(x)`
   ```
   ans =
      1 55 65 75
      2 78 82 75
      3 84 85 79
      4 90 92 93
   ```
3. `sort(x,'descend')`
   ```
   ans =
      4 90 92 93
      3 84 85 79
      2 78 82 75
      1 55 65 75
   ```
4. `sortrows(x)`
   ```
   ans =
      1 84 92 93
      2 55 65 75
      3 78 82 79
      4 90 85 75
   ```
5. `sortrows(x,-3)`
   ```
   ans =
      1 84 92 93
      4 90 85 75
      3 78 82 79
      2 55 65 75
   ```

## Practice Exercises 8

`x = [4 90 85 75; 2 55 65 75; 3 78 82 79;1 84 92 93];`

1. `std(x)`
   ```
   ans =
      1.2910 15.3052 11.4601 8.5440
   ```
2. `var(x)`
   ```
   ans =
      1.6667 234.2500 131.3333 73.0000
   ```

3. `sqrt(var(x))`
   ```
   ans =
      1.2910 15.3052 11.4601 8.5440
   ```
4. The square root of the variance is equal to the standard deviation.

## Practice Exercises 9

1. `rand(3)`
   ```
   ans =
      0.9501 0.4860 0.4565
      0.2311 0.8913 0.0185
      0.6068 0.7621 0.8214
   ```
2. `randn(3)`
   ```
   ans =
      -0.4326 0.2877 1.1892
      -1.6656 -1.1465 -0.0376
       0.1253 1.1909 0.3273
   ```
3. `x = rand(100,5);`
4. `max(x)`
   ```
   ans =
      0.9811 0.9785 0.9981 0.9948 0.9962
   ```
   `std(x)`
   ```
   ans =
      0.2821 0.2796 0.3018 0.2997 0.2942
   ```
   `var(x)`
   ```
   ans =
      0.0796 0.0782 0.0911 0.0898 0.0865
   ```
   `mean(x)`
   ```
   ans =
      0.4823 0.5026 0.5401 0.4948 0.5111
   ```
5. `x = randn(100,5);`
6. `max(x)`
   ```
   ans =
      2.6903 2.6289 2.7316 2.4953 1.7621
   ```
   `std(x)`
   ```
   ans =
      0.9725 0.9201 0.9603 0.9367 0.9130
   ```
   `var(x)`
   ```
   ans =
      0.9458 0.8465 0.9221 0.8774 0.8335
   ```
   `mean(x)`
   ```
   ans =
      -0.0277 0.0117 -0.0822 0.0974 -0.1337
   ```

## Practice Exercises 10

1. `A = 1+i`
   ```
   A =
      1.0000 + 1.0000i
   ```
   `B = 2-3i`
   ```
   B =
      2.0000 - 3.0000i
   ```
   `C = 8+2i`
   ```
   C =
       8.0000 + 2.0000i
   ```
2. `imagD = [-3,8,-16];`
   `realD = [2,4,6];`
   `D = complex(realD,imagD)`

```
ans =
  2.0000 - 3.0000i 4.0000 + 8.0000i 6.0000 -16.0000i
```
3. `abs(A)`
```
ans =
  1.4142
```
`abs(B)`
```
ans =
  3.6056
```
`abs(C)`
```
ans =
  8.2462
```
`abs(D)`
```
ans =
  3.6056 8.9443 17.0880
```
4. `angle(A)`
```
ans =
  0.7854
```
`angle(B)`
```
ans =
  -0.9828
```
`angle(C)`
```
ans =
  0.2450
```
`angle(D)`
```
ans =
  -0.9828 1.1071 -1.2120
```
5. `conj(D)`
```
ans =
  2.0000 + 3.0000i 4.0000 - 8.0000i 6.0000 +16.0000i
```
6. `D'`
```
ans =
  2.0000 + 3.0000i
  4.0000 - 8.0000i
  6.0000 +16.0000i
```
7. `sqrt(A.*A')`
```
ans =
  1.4142
```

## Practice Exercises 11

1. `clock`
```
ans =
  1.0e+003 *
  2.0080 0.0050 0.0270 0.0160 0.0010 0.0220
```
2. `date`
```
ans =
27-May-2008
```
3. **a.** `factorial(322)`
```
   ans =
    Inf
```
   **b.** `5*10^500`
```
   ans =
     Inf
```
   **c.** `1/5*10^500`
```
   ans =
    Inf
```
   **d.** `0/0`
```
   Warning: Divide by zero.
   ans =
    NaN
```

# 4

# Manipulating MATLAB Matrices

## Objectives

After reading this chapter, you should be able to

- manipulate matrices
- extract data from matrices
- solve problems with two matrix variables of different size
- create and use special matrices

## 1 MANIPULATING MATRICES

As you solve more and more complicated problems with MATLAB, you'll find that you will need to combine small matrices into larger matrices, extract information from large matrices, create very large matrices, and use matrices with special properties.

### 1.1 Defining Matrices

In MATLAB, you can define a matrix by typing in a list of numbers enclosed in square brackets. You can separate the numbers by spaces or by commas, at your discretion. (You can even combine the two techniques in the same matrix definition.) To indicate a new row, you can use a semicolon. For example,

```
A = [3.5];
B = [1.5, 3.1]; or B = [1.5    3.1];
C = [-1, 0, 0; 1, 1, 0; 0, 0, 2];
```

You can also define a matrix by listing each row on a separate line, as in the following set of MATLAB commands:

```
C =      [-1,   0,  0;
           1,   1,  0;
           1,  -1,  0;
           0,   0,  2]
```

You don't even need to enter the semicolon to indicate a new row. MATLAB interprets

```
C =      [-1,   0,  0
           1,   1,  0
           1,  -1,  0
           0,   0,  2]
```

as a 4 $\times$ 3 matrix. You could also enter a column matrix in this manner:

```
A =
    1
    2
    3
```

If there are too many numbers in a row to fit on one line, you can continue the statement on the next line, but a comma and an ellipsis ( ... ) are required at the end of the line, indicating that the row is to be continued. You can also use the ellipsis to continue other long assignment statements in MATLAB.

ELLIPSIS: a set of three periods used to indicate that a row is continued on the next line

If we want to define **F** with 10 values, we can use either of the following statements:

```
F = [1, 52, 64, 197, 42, -42, 55, 82, 22, 109];    or

F = [1, 52, 64, 197, 42, -42, ...
        55, 82, 22, 109];
```

MATLAB also allows you to define a matrix in terms of another matrix that has already been defined. For example, the statements

```
B = [1.5, 3.1];
S = [3.0, B]
```

return

```
S =
    3.0    1.5    3.1
```

Similarly,

```
T = [ 1, 2, 3; S]
```

returns

```
T =
    1      2      3
    3      1.5    3.1
```

We can change values in a matrix, or include additional values, by using an index number to specify a particular element. This process is called *indexing into an array*. Thus, the command

INDEX: a number used to identify elements in an array

```
S(2) = -1.0;
```

changes the second value in the matrix **S** from 1.5 to $-1$. If we type the matrix name

```
S
```

into the command window, then MATLAB returns

```
S =
    3.0    -1.0    3.1
```

We can also extend a matrix by defining new elements. If we execute the command

```
S(4) = 5.5;
```

we extend the matrix **S** to four elements instead of three. If we define element

```
S(8) = 9.5;
```

matrix **S** will have eight values, and the values of **S(5)**, **S(6)**, and **S(7)** will be set to 0. Thus,

```
S
```

returns

```
S =
        3.0    -1.0    3.1    5.5    0    0    0    9.5
```

### 1.2 Using the Colon Operator

The colon operator is very powerful for defining new matrices and modifying existing ones. First, we can use it to define an evenly spaced matrix. For example,

```
H = 1:8
```

returns

```
H =
        1    2    3    4    5    6    7    8
```

The default spacing is 1. However, when colons are used to separate three numbers, the middle value becomes the spacing. Thus,

```
time = 0.0 : 0.5 : 2.0
```

returns

```
time =
        0    0.5000    1.0000    1.5000    2.0000
```

The colon operator can also be used to extract data from matrices, a feature that is very useful in data analysis. When a colon is used in a matrix reference in place of a specific index number, the colon represents the entire row or column.

Suppose we define **M** as

```
M =    [1 2 3 4 5;
        2 3 4 5 6;
        3 4 5 6 7];
```

We can extract column 1 from matrix **M** with the command

```
x = M(:, 1)
```

which returns

```
x =
        1
        2
        3
```

We read this syntax as "all the rows in column 1." We can extract any of the columns in a similar manner. For instance,

```
y = M(:, 4)
```

returns

```
y =
        4
        5
        6
```

and can be interpreted as "all the rows in column 4." Similarly, to extract a row,

```
z = M(1,:)
```

returns

```
z =
        1    2    3    4    5
```

and is read as "row 1, all the columns."

We don't have to extract an entire row or an entire column. The colon operator can also be used to mean "from row _ to row _" or "from column _ to column _." To extract the two bottom rows of the matrix **M**, type

```
w = M(2:3,:)
```

which returns

```
w =
        2    3    4    5    6
        3    4    5    6    7
```

and reads "rows 2 to 3, all the columns." Similarly, to extract just the four numbers in the lower right-hand corner of matrix **M**,

```
w = M(2:3, 4:5)
```

returns

```
w =
        5    6
        6    7
```

and reads "rows 2 to 3 in columns 4 to 5."

In MATLAB, it is valid to have a matrix that is empty. For example, each of the following statements will generate an empty matrix:

```
a = [ ];
b = 4:-1:5;
```

Finally, using the matrix name with a single colon, such as

```
M(:)
```

transforms the matrix into one long column.

```
M =
  1
  2
  3
  2
  3
  4
  3
  4
  5
  4
  5
  6
  5
  6
  7
```

The matrix was formed by first listing column 1, then adding column 2 onto the end, tacking on column 3, and so on. Actually, the computer does not store two-dimensional arrays in a two-dimensional pattern. Rather, it "thinks" of a matrix as one long list, just like the matrix **M** at the left. There are two ways you can extract a single value from an array: by using a single index number or by using the row, column notation. To find the value in row 2, column 3, use the following commands:

```
M
M =
        1    2    3    4    5
        2    3    4    5    6
        3    4    5    6    7
M(2, 3)
ans =
             4
```

KEY IDEA: You can identify an element using either a single number, or indices representing the row and column

Alternatively, you can use a single index number. The value in row 2, column 3 of matrix **M** is element number 8. (Count down column 1, then down column 2, and finally down column 3 to the correct element.) The associated MATLAB command is

```
M(8)
ans = 4
```

**Hint**

You can use the word "end" to identify the final row or column in a matrix, even if you don't know how big it is. For example,

```
M(1,end)
```
returns
```
M(1,end)
ans =
      5
```
and
```
M(end, end)
```
returns
```
ans =
      7
```
as does
```
M(end)
ans =
      7
```

**Practice Exercises 1**

Create MATLAB variables to represent the following matrices, and use them in the exercises that follow:

$$a = \begin{bmatrix} 12 & 17 & 3 & 6 \end{bmatrix} \quad b = \begin{bmatrix} 5 & 8 & 3 \\ 1 & 2 & 3 \\ 2 & 4 & 6 \end{bmatrix} \quad c = \begin{bmatrix} 22 \\ 17 \\ 4 \end{bmatrix}$$

1. Assign to the variable **x1** the value in the second column of matrix $a$. This is sometimes represented in mathematics textbooks as element $a_{1,2}$ and could be expressed as $x1 = a_{1,2}$.
2. Assign to the variable **x2** the third column of matrix $b$.
3. Assign to the variable **x3** the third row of matrix $b$.
4. Assign to the variable **x4** the values in matrix $b$ along the diagonal (i.e., elements $b_{1,1}$, $b_{2,2}$, and $b_{3,3}$).
5. Assign to the variable **x5** the first three values in matrix $a$ as the first row and all the values in matrix $b$ as the second through the fourth row.

6. Assign to the variable **x6** the values in matrix *c* as the first column, the values in matrix *b* as columns 2, 3, and 4, and the values in matrix *a* as the last row.

7. Assign to the variable **x7** the value of element 8 in matrix *b*, using the single-index-number identification scheme.

8. Convert matrix *b* to a column vector named **x8**.

---

**EXAMPLE 1**

## Using Temperature Data

The data collected by the National Weather Service are extensive but are not always organized in exactly the way we would like (Figure 1). Take, for example, the summary of the 1999 Asheville, North Carolina, Climatological Data. We'll use these data to practice manipulating matrices—both extracting elements and recombining elements to form new matrices.

The numeric information has been extracted from the table and is in an Excel file called **Asheville_1999.xls** (Table B.1, located at the end of this selection). Use MATLAB to confirm that the reported values on the annual row are correct for the mean maximum temperature and the mean minimum temperature, as well as for the annual high temperature and the annual low temperature. Combine these four columns of data into a new matrix called **temp_data**.

1. State the Problem
   Calculate the annual mean maximum temperature, the annual mean minimum temperature, the highest temperature reached during the year, and the lowest temperature reached during the year for 1999 in Asheville, North Carolina.

2. Describe the Input and Output

   ***Input*** Import a matrix from the Excel file **Asheville_1999.xls**.

   ***Output*** Find the following four values:   annual mean maximum temperature
   annual mean minimum temperature
   highest temperature
   lowest temperature

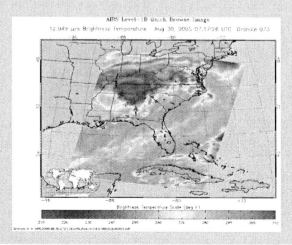

**Figure 1**
Temperature data collected from a weather satellite were used to create this composite false-color image. (Courtesy of NASA/Jet Propulsion Laboratory.)

Create a matrix composed of the mean maximum temperature values, the mean minimum temperature values, the highest monthly temperatures, and the lowest monthly temperatures. Do not include the annual data.

3. Develop a Hand Example

Using a calculator, add the values in column 2 of the table and divide by 12.

4. Develop a MATLAB Solution

First import the data from Excel, then save them in the current directory as **Asheville_1999**. Save the variable **Asheville_1999** as the file **Asheville_1999.mat**. This makes it available to be loaded into the workspace from our M-file program:

```
%  Example 1
%  In this example, we extract data from a large matrix and
%  use the data analysis functions to find the mean high
%  and mean low temperatures for the year and to find the
%  high temperature and the low temperature for the year
%
clear, clc
%  load the data matrix from a file
load asheville_1999
%  extract the mean high temperatures from the large matrix
mean_max = asheville_1999(1:12,2);
%  extract the mean low temperatures from the large matrix
mean_min = asheville_1999(1:12,3);
%  Calculate the annual means
annual_mean_max = mean(mean_max)
annual_mean_min = mean(mean_min)
%  extract the high and low temperatures from the large
%  matrix
high_temp = asheville_1999(1:12,8);
low_temp = asheville_1999(1:12,10);
%  Find the max and min temperature for the year
max_high = max(high_temp)
min_low = min(low_temp)
%  Create a new matrix with just the temperature
%  information
new_table =[mean_max, mean_min, high_temp, low_temp]
```

The results are displayed in the command window:

```
annual_mean_max =
   68.0500
annual_mean_min =
   46.3250
max_high =
   96
min_low =
   9
new_table =
   51.4000    31.5000    78.0000     9.0000
   52.6000    32.1000    66.0000    16.0000
   52.7000    32.5000    76.0000    22.0000
   70.1000    48.2000    83.0000    34.0000
   75.0000    51.5000    83.0000    40.0000
   80.2000    60.9000    90.0000    50.0000
   85.7000    64.9000    96.0000    56.0000
```

| | | | |
|---|---|---|---|
| 86.4000 | 63.0000 | 94.0000 | 54.0000 |
| 79.1000 | 54.6000 | 91.0000 | 39.0000 |
| 67.6000 | 45.5000 | 78.0000 | 28.0000 |
| 62.2000 | 40.7000 | 76.0000 | 26.0000 |
| 53.6000 | 30.5000 | 69.0000 | 15.0000 |

5. Test the Solution

Compare the results against the bottom line of the table from the Asheville, North Carolina, Climatological Survey. It is important to confirm that the results are accurate before you start to use any computer program to process data.

## 2 PROBLEMS WITH TWO VARIABLES

All of the calculations we have done thus far have used only one variable. Of course, most physical phenomena can vary with many different factors. In this section, we consider how to perform the same calculations when the variables are represented by vectors.

Consider the following MATLAB statements:

```
x = 3;
y = 5;
A = x * y
```

Since **x** and **y** are scalars, it's an easy calculation: $x \cdot y = 15$, or

```
A =
        15
```

Now let's see what happens if **x** is a matrix and **y** is still a scalar:

```
x = 1:5;
```

returns five values of **x**. Because **y** is still a scalar with only one value (5),

```
A = x * y
```

returns

```
A =
        5      10      15      20      25
```

This is still all review. But what happens if **y** is now a vector? Then

```
y = 1:3;
A = x * y
```

returns an error statement:

```
??? Error using ==> *
Inner matrix dimensions must agree.
```

This error statement reminds us that the asterisk is the operator for matrix multiplication—which is not what we want. We want the dot-asterisk operator (.*), which will perform an element-by-element multiplication. However, the two vectors, **x** and **y**, will need to be the same length for this to work. Thus,

```
y = linspace(1,3,5)
```

**KEY IDEA:** When formulating problems with two variables, the matrix dimensions must agree

creates a new vector **y** with five evenly spaced elements:

```
y =
       1.0000     1.5000     2.0000     2.5000     3.0000
A = x .* y
A =
       1      3      6     10     15
```

However, although this solution works, the result is probably not what you really want. You can think of the results as the diagonal on a matrix (Table 1).

What if we want to know the result for element 3 of vector **x** and element 5 of vector **y**? This approach obviously doesn't give us all the possible answers. We want a two-dimensional matrix of answers that corresponds to all the combinations of **x** and **y**. In order for the answer, **A**, to be a two-dimensional matrix, the input vectors must be two-dimensional matrices. MATLAB has a built-in function called **meshgrid** that will help us accomplish this—and **x** and **y** don't even have to be the same size.

First let's change **y** back to a three-element vector:

```
y = 1:3;
```

Then we'll use **meshgrid** to create a new two-dimensional version of both **x** and **y** that we'll call **new_x** and **new_y**:

```
[new_x, new_y]=meshgrid(x,y)
```

KEY IDEA: Use the meshgrid function to map two one-dimensional variables into two-dimensional variables of equal size

The **meshgrid** command takes the two input vectors and creates two two-dimensional matrices. Each of the resulting matrices has the same number of rows and columns. The number of columns is determined by the number of elements in the **x** vector, and the number of rows is determined by the number of elements in the **y** vector. This operation is called *mapping the vectors into a two-dimensional array*:

```
new_x =
       1      2      3      4      5
       1      2      3      4      5
       1      2      3      4      5
new_y =
       1      1      1      1      1
       2      2      2      2      2
       3      3      3      3      3
```

**Table 1  Results of an Element-by-Element Calculation**

| | | x | | | | |
|---|---|---|---|---|---|---|
| | | **1** | **2** | **3** | **4** | **5** |
| | **1.0** | 1 | | | | |
| | **1.5** | | 3 | | | |
| **y** | **2.0** | | | 6 | | |
| | **2.5** | | | | 10 | |
| | **3.0** | | | ? | | 15 |

Notice that all the rows in **new_x** are the same and all the columns in **new_y** are the same. Now it's possible to multiply **new_x** by **new_y** and get the two-dimensional grid of results we really want:

```
A = new_x.*new_y
A =
        1     2     3     4     5
        2     4     6     8    10
        3     6     9    12    15
```

---

**Practice Exercises 2**
**Using Meshgrid**

1. The area of a rectangle (Figure 2) is length times width (area = length × width). Find the areas of rectangles with lengths of 1, 3, and 5 cm and with widths of 2, 4, 6, and 8 cm. (You should have 12 answers.)

2. The volume of a circular cylinder is volume = $\pi r^2 h$. Find the volume of cylindrical containers with radii from 0 to 12 meters and heights from 10 to 20 meters. Increment the radius dimension by 3 meters and the height by 2 meters as you span the two ranges.

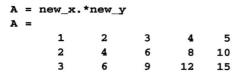

**Figure 2**
Dimensions of a rectangle and a circular cylinder.

width $w$

length $l$

radius $r$

height $h$

---

**EXAMPLE 2**

**Distance to the Horizon**

You've probably experienced standing on the top of a hill or a mountain and feeling like you can see forever. How far can you really see? It depends on the height of the mountain and the radius of the earth, as shown in Figure 3. The distance to

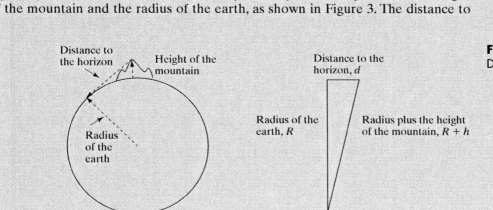

**Figure 3**
Distance to the horizon.

Distance to the horizon

Height of the mountain

Radius of the earth

Distance to the horizon, $d$

Radius of the earth, $R$

Radius plus the height of the mountain, $R + h$

the horizon is quite different on the moon than on the earth, because the radius is different for each.

Using the Pythagorean theorem, we see that

$$R^2 + d^2 = (R + h)^2$$

and solving for $d$ yields $d = \sqrt{h^2 + 2Rh}$.

From this last expression, find the distance to the horizon on the earth and on the moon, for mountains from 0 to 8000 meters. (Mount Everest is 8850 meters tall.) The radius of the earth is 6378 km and the radius of the moon is 1737 km.

1. State the Problem

   Find the distance to the horizon from the top of a mountain on the moon and on the earth.

2. Describe the Input and Output

   *Input*

   | | |
   |---|---|
   | Radius of the moon | 1737 km |
   | Radius of the earth | 6378 km |
   | Height of the mountains | 0 to 8000 meters |

   *Output*

   Distance to the horizon, in kilometers

3. Develop a Hand Example

   $$d = \sqrt{h^2 + 2Rh}$$

   Using the radius of the earth and an 8000-meter mountain yields

   $$d = \sqrt{(8\,\text{km})^2 + 2 \times 6378\,\text{km} \times 8\,\text{km}} = 319\,\text{km}$$

4. Develop a MATLAB Solution

   ```
   %Example 2
   %Find the distance to the horizon
   %Define the height of the mountains
   % in meters
   clear, clc
   format bank
   %Define the height vector
   height=0:1000:8000;
   %Convert meters to km
   height=height/1000;
   %Define the radii of the moon and earth
   radius = [1737     6378];
   %Map the radii and heights onto a 2D grid
   [Radius,Height]=meshgrid(radius,height);
   %Calculate the distance to the horizon
   distance=sqrt(Height.^2 + 2*Height.*Radius)
   ```

Executing the preceding M-file returns a table of the distances to the horizon on both the moon and the earth:

```
distance =
           0           0
       58.95      112.95
```

| 83.38 | 159.74 |
|---|---|
| 102.13 | 195.65 |
| 117.95 | 225.92 |
| 131.89 | 252.60 |
| 144.50 | 276.72 |
| 156.10 | 298.90 |
| 166.90 | 319.55 |

5. Test the Solution

Compare the MATLAB solution with the hand solution. The distance to the horizon from near the top of Mount Everest (8000 m) is over 300 km and matches the value calculated in MATLAB.

**EXAMPLE 3**

## Free Fall

The general equation for the distance that a freely falling body has traveled (neglecting air friction) is

$$d = \frac{1}{2}gt^2$$

where

$d$  = distance,
$g$  = acceleration due to gravity, and
$t$  = time.

When a satellite orbits a planet, it is in free fall. Many people believe that when the space shuttle enters orbit, it leaves gravity behind. Gravity, though, is what keeps the shuttle in orbit. The shuttle (or any satellite) is actually falling toward the earth (Figure 4). If it is going fast enough horizontally, it stays in orbit; if it's going too slowly, it hits the ground.

The value of the constant $g$, the acceleration due to gravity, depends on the mass of the planet. On different planets, $g$ has different values (Table 2).

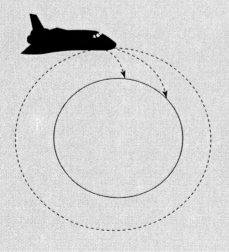

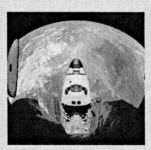

**Figure 4**
The space shuttle is constantly falling toward the earth. (Courtesy of NASA/Jet Propulsion Laboratory.)

| Table 2 Acceleration Due to Gravity in Our Solar System | |
|---|---|
| Mercury | $g = 3.7$ m/s$^2$ |
| Venus | $g = 8.87$ m/s$^2$ |
| Earth | $g = 9.8$ m/s$^2$ |
| Moon | $g = 1.6$ m/s$^2$ |
| Mars | $g = 3.7$ m/s$^2$ |
| Jupiter | $g = 23.12$ m/s$^2$ |
| Saturn | $g = 8.96$ m/s$^2$ |
| Uranus | $g = 8.69$ m/s$^2$ |
| Neptune | $g = 11.0$ m/s$^2$ |
| Pluto | $g = .58$ m/s$^2$ |

Find how far an object would fall at times from 0 to 100 seconds on each planet in our solar system and on our moon.

1. State the Problem
   Find the distance traveled by a freely falling object on planets with different gravities.
2. Describe the Input and Output
   **Input**  Value of $g$, the acceleration due to gravity, on each of the planets and the moon

$$\text{Time} = 0 \text{ to } 100 \text{ s}$$

   **Output**  Distances calculated for each planet and the moon
3. Develop a Hand Example

   $d = \frac{1}{2} gt^2$, so on Mercury at 100 seconds:

   $d = \frac{1}{2} \times 3.7$ m/s$^2 \times 100^2$ s$^2$

   $d = 18,500$ m

4. Develop a MATLAB Solution

```
%Example 3
%Free fall
clear, clc
%Try the problem first with only two planets, and a coarse
%  grid
format bank
%Define constants for acceleration due to gravity on
%Mercury and Venus
acceleration_due_to_gravity = [3.7, 8.87];
time=0:10:100;     %Define time vector
%Map acceleration_due_to_gravity and time into 2D matrices
[g,t]=meshgrid(acceleration_due_to_gravity, time);
%Calculate the distances
distance=1/2*g.*t.^2
```

Executing the preceding M-file returns the following values of distance traveled on Mercury and on Venus.

```
distance =
                  0                0
             185.00           443.50
             740.00          1774.00
            1665.00          3991.50
            2960.00          7096.00
            4625.00         11087.50
            6660.00         15966.00
            9065.00         21731.50
           11840.00         28384.00
           14985.00         35923.50
           18500.00         44350.00
```

5. Test the Solution

Compare the MATLAB solution with the hand solution. We can see that the distance traveled on Mercury at 100 seconds is 18,500 m, which corresponds to the hand calculation.

The M-file included the calculations for just the first two planets and was performed first to work out any programming difficulties. Once we've confirmed that the program works, it is easy to redo with the data for all the planets:

```
%Redo the problem with all the data
clear, clc
format bank
%Define constants
acceleration_due_to_gravity  = [3.7, 8.87, 9.8, 1.6, 3.7,
23.12 8.96, 8.69, 11.0, 0.58];
time=0:10:100;
%Map acceleration_due_to_gravity and time into 2D matrices
[g,t]=meshgrid(acceleration_due_to_gravity,time);
%Calculate the distances
d=1/2*g.*t.^2
```

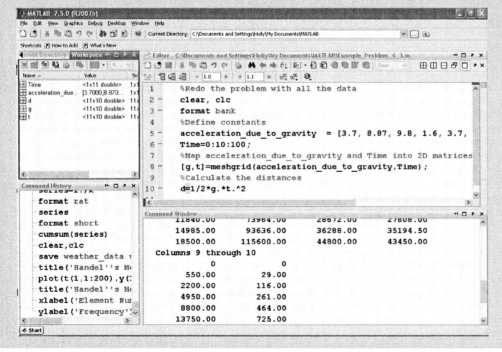

**Figure 5**
Results of the distance calculations for an object falling on each of the planets.

There are several important things to notice about the results shown in Figure 5. First, look at the workspace window **acceleration_due_to_gravity** is a $1 \times 10$ matrix (one value for each of the planets and the moon), and **time** is a $1 \times 11$ matrix (11 values of time). However, both **g** and **t** are $11 \times 10$ matrices—the result of the **meshgrid** operation. The results shown in the command window were formatted with the **format bank** command to make the output easier to read; otherwise there would have been a common scale factor.

### Hint

As you create a MATLAB program in the editing window, you may want to comment out those parts of the code which you know work and then uncomment them later. Although you can do this by adding one % at a time to each line, it's easier to select **text** from the menu bar. Just highlight the part of the code you want to comment out, and then choose **comment** from the **text** drop-down menu. To delete the comments, highlight and select **uncomment** from the **text** drop-down menu (text → uncomment). You can also access this menu by right-clicking in the edit window.

## 3 SPECIAL MATRICES

MATLAB contains a group of functions that generate special matrices; we present some of these functions in Table 3.

**Table 3  Functions to Create and Manipulate Matrices**

| **zeros(m)** | Creates an $m \times m$ matrix of zeros. | **zeros(3)**<br>**ans =**<br>   0  0  0<br>   0  0  0<br>   0  0  0 |
| --- | --- | --- |
| **zeros(m,n)** | Creates an $m \times n$ matrix of zeros. | **zeros(2,3)**<br>**ans =**<br>   0  0  0<br>   0  0  0 |
| **ones(m)** | Creates an $m \times m$ matrix of ones. | **ones(3)**<br>**ans =**<br>   1  1  1<br>   1  1  1<br>   1  1  1 |
| **ones(m,n)** | Creates an $m \times n$ matrix of ones. | **ones(2,3)**<br>**ans =**<br>   1  1  1<br>   1  1  1 |

*(Continued)*

**Table 3    (Continued)**

| | | |
|---|---|---|
| **diag(A)** | Extracts the diagonal of a two-dimensional matrix **A**. | **A=[1 2 3; 3 4 5; 1 2 3];**<br>**diag(A)**<br>**ans =**<br>  **1**<br>  **4**<br>  **3** |
| | For any vector **A,** creates a square matrix with **A** as the diagonal. Check the **help** function for other ways the **diag** function can be used. | **A=[1 2 3];**<br>**diag(A)**<br>**ans =**<br>  **1  0  0**<br>  **0  2  0**<br>  **0  0  3** |
| **fliplr** | Flips a matrix into its mirror image, from right to left. | **A=[1 0 0; 0 2 0; 0 0 3];**<br>**fliplr(A)**<br>**ans =**<br>  **0  0  1**<br>  **0  2  0**<br>  **3  0  0** |
| **flipud** | Flips a matrix vertically. | **flipud(A)**<br>**ans =**<br>  **0  0  3**<br>  **0  2  0**<br>  **1  0  0** |
| **magic(m)** | Creates an $m \times m$ "magic" matrix. | **magic(3)**<br>**ans =**<br>  **8  1  6**<br>  **3  5  7**<br>  **4  9  2** |

### 3.1 Matrix of Zeros

It is sometimes useful to create a matrix of all zeros. When the **zeros** function is used with a single scalar input argument, a square matrix is generated:

```
A = zeros(3)
A =
      0      0      0
      0      0      0
      0      0      0
```

If we use two scalar arguments, the first value specifies the number of rows and the second the number of columns:

```
B = zeros(3,2)
B =
      0      0
      0      0
      0      0
```

### 3.2 Matrix of Ones

The **ones** function is similar to the **zeros** function but creates a matrix of ones:

```
A = ones(3)
A =
     1     1     1
     1     1     1
     1     1     1
```

As with the **zeros** function, if we use two inputs, we can control the number of rows and columns:

```
B = ones(3,2)
B =
     1     1
     1     1
     1     1
```

The **zeros** and **ones** functions are useful for creating matrices with "placeholder" values that will be filled in later. For example, if you wanted a vector of five numbers, all of which were equal to $\pi$, you might first create a vector of ones:

```
a = ones(1,5)
```

This gives

```
a =
     1     1     1     1     1
```

Then multiply by $\pi$:

```
b = a*pi
```

The result is

```
b =
     3.1416     3.1416     3.1416     3.1416     3.1416
```

The same result could be obtained by adding $\pi$ to a matrix of zeros. For example,

```
a = zeros(1,5);
b = a+pi
```

gives

```
b =
     3.1416     3.1416     3.1416     3.1416     3.1416
```

A placeholder matrix is especially useful in MATLAB programs with a loop structure, because it can reduce the time required to execute the loop.

### 3.3 Diagonal Matrices

We can use the **diag** function to extract the diagonal from a matrix. For example, if we define a square matrix

```
A = [1 2 3; 3 4 5; 1 2 3];
```

then using the function

```
diag(A)
```

extracts the main diagonal and gives the following results:

```
ans =
    1.00
    4.00
    3.00
```

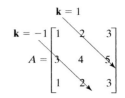

**Figure 6**
Each diagonal in a matrix can be described by means of the parameter **k**.

Other diagonals can be extracted by defining a second input, **k**, to **diag**. Positive values of **k** specify diagonals in the upper right-hand corner of the matrix, and negative values specify diagonals in the lower left-hand corner. (See Figure 6.)
    Thus, the command

```
diag(A,1)
```

returns

```
ans =
    2
    5
```

If, instead of using a two-dimensional matrix as input to the **diag** function, we use a vector such as

```
B = [1 2 3];
```

then MATLAB uses the vector for the values along the diagonal of a new matrix and fills in the remaining elements with zeros:

```
diag(B)
ans =
    1    0    0
    0    2    0
    0    0    3
```

By specifying a second parameter, we can move the diagonal to any place in the matrix:

```
diag(B,1)
ans =
    0    1    0    0
    0    0    2    0
    0    0    0    3
    0    0    0    0
```

## 3.4 Magic Matrices

MATLAB includes a matrix function called **magic** that generates a matrix with unusual properties. There does not seem to be any practical use for magic matrices—except that they are fun. In a magic matrix, the sums of the columns are the same, as are the sums of the rows. An example is

```
A = magic(4)
A =
    16     2     3    13
     5    11    10     8
     9     7     6    12
     4    14    15     1
```

```
sum(A)
ans =
      34        34        34        34
```

To find the sums of the rows, we need to transpose the matrix:

```
sum(A')
ans =
      34        34        34        34
```

Not only are the sums of all the columns and rows the same, but the sums of the diagonals are the same. The diagonal from left to right is

```
diag(A)
ans =
   16
   11
    6
    1
```

The sum of the diagonal is the same number as the sums of the rows and columns:

```
sum(diag(A))
ans =
   34
```

Finally, to find the diagonal from lower left to upper right, we first have to "flip" the matrix and then find the sum of the diagonal:

```
fliplr(A)
ans =
      13         3         2        16
       8        10        11         5
      12         6         7         9
       1        15        14         4
diag(ans)
ans =
   13
   10
    7
    4
sum(ans)
ans =
   34
```

Figure 7 shows one of the earliest documented examples of a magic square—Albrecht Dürer's woodcut "Melancholia," created in 1514. Scholars believe the square was a reference to alchemical concepts popular at the time. The date 1514 is included in the two middle squares of the bottom row. (See Figure 8.)

Magic squares have fascinated both professional and amateur mathematicians for centuries. For example, Benjamin Franklin experimented with magic squares. You can create magic squares of any size greater than 2 × 2 in MATLAB. MATLAB's solution is not the only one; other magic squares are possible;

**Figure 7**
"Melancholia" by Albrecht
Dürer, 1514. (Courtesy of
the Library of Congress.)

**Figure 8**
Albrecht Dürer included the
date of the woodcut (1514)
in the magic square. (Courtesy of the Library of Congress.)

**Practice Exercises 3**

1. Create a 3 × 3 matrix of zeros.
2. Create a 3 × 4 matrix of zeros.
3. Create a 3 × 3 matrix of ones.
4. Create a 5 × 3 matrix of ones.
5. Create a 4 × 6 matrix in which all the elements have a value of pi.

6. Use the **diag** function to create a matrix whose diagonal has values of 1, 2, 3.
7. Create a 10 × 10 magic matrix.
   **a.** Extract the diagonal from this matrix.
   **b.** Extract the diagonal that runs from lower left to upper right from this matrix.
   **c.** Confirm that the sums of the rows, columns, and diagonals are all the same.

## SUMMARY

This chapter concentrated on manipulating matrices, a capability that allows the user to create complicated matrices by combining smaller ones. It also lets you extract portions of an existing matrix. The colon operator is especially useful for these operations. The colon operator should be interpreted as "all of the rows" or "all of the columns" when used in place of a row or column designation. It should be interpreted as "from _ to _" when it is used between row or column numbers. For example,

```
A(:,2:3)
```

should be interpreted as "all the rows in matrix **A**, and all the columns from 2 to 3." When used alone as the sole index, as in **A(:)**, it creates a matrix that is a single column from a two-dimensional representation. The computer actually stores all array information as a list, making both single-index notation and row–column notation useful alternatives for specifying the location of a value in a matrix.

The **meshgrid** function is extremely useful, since it can be used to map vectors into two-dimensional matrices, making it possible to perform array calculations with vectors of unequal size.

MATLAB contains a number of functions that make it easy to create special matrices:

- **zeros**, which is used to create a matrix composed entirely of zeros
- **ones**, which is used to create a matrix composed entirely of ones
- **diag**, which can be used to extract the diagonal from a matrix or, if the input is a vector, to create a square matrix
- **magic**, which can be used to create a matrix with the unusual property that all the rows and columns add up to the same value, as do the diagonals.

In addition, a number of functions were included that allow the user to "flip" the matrix either from left to right or from top to bottom.

**MATLAB SUMMARY**    The following MATLAB summary lists and briefly describes all of the special characters, commands, and functions that were defined in this chapter:

| Special Characters | |
| --- | --- |
| : | colon operator |
| ... | ellipsis, indicating continuation on the next line |
| [] | empty matrix |

| Commands and Functions | |
| --- | --- |
| meshgrid | maps vectors into a two-dimensional array |
| zeros | creates a matrix of zeros |
| ones | creates a matrix of ones |
| diag | extracts the diagonal from a matrix |
| fliplr | flips a matrix into its mirror image, from left to right |
| flipud | flips a matrix vertically |
| magic | creates a "magic" matrix |

**KEY TERMS**

subscripts

magic matrices
mapping

elements
index numbers

**PROBLEMS**

## Manipulating Matrices

**1** Create the following matrices, and use them in the exercises that follow:

$$a = \begin{bmatrix} 15 & 3 & 22 \\ 3 & 8 & 5 \\ 14 & 3 & 82 \end{bmatrix} \qquad b = \begin{bmatrix} 1 \\ 5 \\ 6 \end{bmatrix} \qquad c = \begin{bmatrix} 12 & 18 & 5 & 2 \end{bmatrix}$$

**(a)** Create a matrix called **d** from the third column of matrix **a**.

**(b)** Combine matrix **b** and matrix **d** to create matrix **e**, a two-dimensional matrix with three rows and two columns.

**(c)** Combine matrix **b** and matrix **d** to create matrix **f**, a one-dimensional matrix with six rows and one column.

**(d)** Create a matrix **g** from matrix **a** and the first three elements of matrix **c**, with four rows and three columns.

**(e)** Create a matrix **h** with the first element equal to $a_{1,3}$, the second element equal to $c_{1,2}$, and the third element equal to $b_{2,1}$.

**2** Load the file **thermo_scores.dat** provided by your instructor, or enter the matrix found in the table after part e of this problem and name it **thermo_scores**. (Enter only the numbers.)

**(a)** Extract the scores and student number for student 5 into a row vector named **student_5**.

**(b)** Extract the scores for Test 1 into a column vector named **test_1**.

**(c)** Find the standard deviation and variance for each test.

(d) Assuming that each test was worth 100 points, find each student's final total score and final percentage. (Be careful not to add in the student number.)

(e) Create a table that includes the final percentages and the scores from the original table.

| Student No. | Test 1 | Test 2 | Test 3 |
|---|---|---|---|
| 1 | 68 | 45 | 92 |
| 2 | 83 | 54 | 93 |
| 3 | 61 | 67 | 91 |
| 4 | 70 | 66 | 92 |
| 5 | 75 | 68 | 96 |
| 6 | 82 | 67 | 90 |
| 7 | 57 | 65 | 89 |
| 8 | 5 | 69 | 89 |
| 9 | 76 | 62 | 97 |
| 10 | 85 | 52 | 94 |
| 11 | 62 | 34 | 87 |
| 12 | 71 | 45 | 85 |
| 13 | 96 | 56 | 45 |
| 14 | 78 | 65 | 87 |
| 15 | 76 | 43 | 97 |
| 16 | 68 | 76 | 95 |
| 17 | 72 | 65 | 89 |
| 18 | 75 | 67 | 88 |
| 19 | 83 | 68 | 91 |
| 20 | 93 | 90 | 92 |

(f) Sort the matrix on the basis of the final percentage, from high to low (in descending order), keeping the data in each row together. (You may need to consult the **help** function to determine the proper syntax.)

3    Consider the following table:

| Time (hr) | Thermocouple 1 °F | Thermocouple 2 °F | Thermocouple 3 °F |
|---|---|---|---|
| 0 | 84.3 | 90.0 | 86.7 |
| 2 | 86.4 | 89.5 | 87.6 |
| 4 | 85.2 | 88.6 | 88.3 |
| 6 | 87.1 | 88.9 | 85.3 |
| 8 | 83.5 | 88.9 | 80.3 |
| 10 | 84.8 | 90.4 | 82.4 |
| 12 | 85.0 | 89.3 | 83.4 |

| 14 | 85.3 | 89.5 | 85.4 |
| 16 | 85.3 | 88.9 | 86.3 |
| 18 | 85.2 | 89.1 | 85.3 |
| 20 | 82.3 | 89.5 | 89.0 |
| 22 | 84.7 | 89.4 | 87.3 |
| 24 | 83.6 | 89.8 | 87.2 |

**(a)** Create a column vector named **times** going from 0 to 24 in 2-hour increments.

**(b)** Your instructor may provide you with the thermocouple temperatures in a file called **thermocouple.dat**, or you may need to create a matrix named **thermocouple** yourself by typing in the data.

**(c)** Combine the **times** vector you created in part (a) with the data from **thermocouple** to create a matrix corresponding to the table in this problem.

**(d)** Recall that both the **max** and **min** functions can return not only the maximum values in a column, but also the element number where those values occur. Use this capability to determine the values of **times** at which the maxima and minima occur in each column.

**4** Suppose that a file named **sensor.dat** contains information collected from a set of sensors. Your instructor may provide you with this file, or you may need to enter it by hand from the following data:

| Time (s) | Sensor 1 | Sensor 2 | Sensor 3 | Sensor 4 | Sensor 5 |
|---|---|---|---|---|---|
| 0.0000 | 70.6432 | 68.3470 | 72.3469 | 67.6751 | 73.1764 |
| 1.0000 | 73.2823 | 65.7819 | 65.4822 | 71.8548 | 66.9929 |
| 2.0000 | 64.1609 | 72.4888 | 70.1794 | 73.6414 | 72.7559 |
| 3.0000 | 67.6970 | 77.4425 | 66.8623 | 80.5608 | 64.5008 |
| 4.0000 | 68.6878 | 67.2676 | 72.6770 | 63.2135 | 70.4300 |
| 5.0000 | 63.9342 | 65.7662 | 2.7644 | 64.8869 | 59.9772 |
| 6.0000 | 63.4028 | 68.7683 | 68.9815 | 75.1892 | 67.5346 |
| 7.0000 | 74.6561 | 73.3151 | 59.7284 | 68.0510 | 72.3102 |
| 8.0000 | 70.0562 | 65.7290 | 70.6628 | 63.0937 | 68.3950 |
| 9.0000 | 66.7743 | 63.9934 | 77.9647 | 71.5777 | 76.1828 |
| 10.0000 | 74.0286 | 69.4007 | 75.0921 | 77.7662 | 66.8436 |
| 11.0000 | 71.1581 | 69.6735 | 62.0980 | 73.5395 | 58.3739 |
| 12.0000 | 65.0512 | 72.4265 | 69.6067 | 79.7869 | 63.8418 |
| 13.0000 | 76.6979 | 67.0225 | 66.5917 | 72.5227 | 75.2782 |
| 14.0000 | 71.4475 | 69.2517 | 64.8772 | 79.3226 | 69.4339 |
| 15.0000 | 77.3946 | 67.8262 | 63.8282 | 68.3009 | 71.8961 |
| 16.0000 | 75.6901 | 69.6033 | 71.4440 | 64.3011 | 74.7210 |
| 17.0000 | 66.5793 | 77.6758 | 67.8535 | 68.9444 | 59.3979 |
| 18.0000 | 63.5403 | 66.9676 | 70.2790 | 75.9512 | 66.7766 |
| 19.0000 | 69.6354 | 63.2632 | 68.1606 | 64.4190 | 66.4785 |

Each row contains a set of sensor readings, with the first row containing values collected at 0 seconds, the second row containing values collected at 1.0 seconds, and so on.

**(a)** Read the data file and print the number of sensors and the number of seconds of data contained in the file. (*Hint*: Use the **size** function—don't just count the two numbers.)

**(b)** Find both the maximum value and the minimum value recorded on each sensor. Use MATLAB to determine at what times they occurred.

**(c)** Find the mean and standard deviation for each sensor and for all the data values collected. Remember, column 1 does not contain sensor data; it contains time data.

### Problems with Two Variables

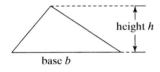

**5** The area of a triangle is area $= \frac{1}{2}$base $\times$ height. (See Figure P5.) Find the area of a group of triangles whose base varies from 0 to 10 meters and whose height varies from 2 to 6 meters. Choose an appropriate spacing for your calculational variables. Your answer should be a two-dimensional matrix.

**Figure P5**
The area of a triangle.

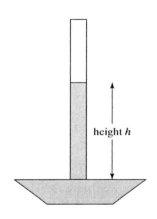

**6** A barometer (see Figure P6) is used to measure atmospheric pressure and is filled with a high-density fluid. In the past, mercury was used, but because of its toxic properties it has been replaced with a variety of other fluids. The pressure $P$ measured by a barometer is the height of the fluid column, $h$, times the density of the liquid, $\rho$, times the acceleration due to gravity, $g$, or

$$P = h\rho g$$

This equation could be solved for the height:

$$h = \frac{P}{\rho g}$$

Find the height to which the liquid column will rise for pressures from 0 to 100 kPa for two different barometers. Assume that the first uses mercury, with a density of 13.56 g/cm$^3$ (13,560 kg/m$^3$), and the second uses water, with a density of 1.0 g/cm$^3$ (1000 kg/m$^3$). The acceleration due to gravity is 9.81 m/s$^2$. Before you start calculating, be sure to check the units in this calculation. The metric measurement of pressure is a pascal (Pa), equal to 1 kg/m s$^2$ A kPa is 1000 times as big as a Pa. Your answer should be a two-dimensional matrix.

**Figure P6**
Barometer.

**7** The ideal gas law, $Pv = RT$, describes the behavior of many gases. When solved for $v$ (the specific volume, m$^3$/kg), the equation can be written

$$v = \frac{RT}{P}$$

Find the specific volume for air, for temperatures from 100 to 1000 K and for pressures from 100 kPa to 1000 kPa. The value of $R$ for air is 0.2870 kJ/(kg K). In this formulation of the ideal gas law, $R$ is different for every gas. There are other formulations in which $R$ is a constant, and the molecular weight of the gas must be included in the calculation. You'll learn more about this equation in chemistry classes and thermodynamics classes. Your answer should be a two-dimensional matrix.

### Special Matrices

**8** Create a matrix of zeros the same size as each of the matrices **a, b,** and **c** from Problem 1. (Use the **size** function to help you accomplish this task.)

**9**   Create a 6 × 6 magic matrix.

    **(a)** What is the sum of each of the rows?
    **(b)** What is the sum of each of the columns?
    **(c)** What is the sum of each of the diagonals?

**10**   Extract a 3 × 3 matrix from the upper left-hand corner of the magic matrix you created in Problem 9. Is this also a magic matrix?

**11**   Create a 5 × 5 magic matrix named **a**.

    **(a)** Is **a** times a constant such as 2 also a magic matrix?
    **(b)** If you square each element of **a**, is the new matrix a magic matrix?
    **(c)** If you add a constant to each element, is the new matrix a magic matrix?
    **(d)** Create a 10 × 10 matrix out of the following components (see Figure P11):
        • the matrix **a**
        • 2 times the matrix **a**
        • a matrix formed by squaring each element of a
        • 2 plus the matrix **a**

Is your result a magic matrix? Does the order in which you arrange the components affect your answer?

| a | 2*a |
|---|-----|
| a^2 | a+2 |

**Figure P11**
Create a matrix out of other matrices.

## SOLUTIONS TO PRACTICE EXERCISES

### Practice Exercises 1

```
    a = [12 17 3 6]
    a =
       12 17 3 6
    b = [5 8 3; 1 2 3; 2 4 6]
    b =
       5 8 3
       1 2 3
       2 4 6
    c = [22;17;4]
    c =
       22
       17
       4
```

1. ```
   x1 = a(1,2)
   x1 =
   17
   ```
2. ```
   x2 = b(:,3)
   x2 =
      3
      3
      6
   ```
3. ```
   x3 = b(3,:)
   x3 =
      2 4 6
   ```
4. ```
   x4 = [b(1,1), b(2,2), b(3,3)]
   x4 =
      5 2 6
   ```
5. ```
   x5 = [a(1:3);b]
   x5 =
      12 17 3
       5  8 3
       1  2 3
       2  4 6
   ```
   ```

6. ```
   x6 = [c,b;a]
   x6 =
       22 5 8 3
       17 1 2 3
       4 2 4 6
       12 17 3 6
   ```
7. ```
   x7 = b(8)
   x7 =
       3
   ```
8. ```
   x8 = b(:)
   x8 =
       5
       1
       2
       8
       2
       4
       3
       3
       6
   ```

## Practice Exercises 2

1. ```
   length = [1, 3, 5];
   width = [2,4,6,8];
   [L,W] = meshgrid(length,width);
   area = L.*W
   area =
       2  6 10
       4 12 20
       6 18 30
       8 24 40
   ```
2. ```
   radius = 0:3:12;
   height = 10:2:20;
   [R,H] = meshgrid(radius,height);
   volume = pi*R.^2.*H
   volume =
     1.0e+003 *
           0   0.2827   1.1310   2.5447   4.5239
           0   0.3393   1.3572   3.0536   5.4287
           0   0.3958   1.5834   3.5626   6.3335
           0   0.4524   1.8096   4.0715   7.2382
           0   0.5089   2.0358   4.5804   8.1430
           0   0.5655   2.2619   5.0894   9.0478
   ```

## Practice Exercises 3

1. ```
   zeros(3)
   ans =
       0  0  0
       0  0  0
       0  0  0
   ```
2. ```
   zeros(3,4)
   ans =
       0  0  0  0
       0  0  0  0
       0  0  0  0
   ```
   ```

3. `ones(3)`
```
ans =
   1  1  1
   1  1  1
   1  1  1
```
4. `ones(5,3)`
```
ans =
   1  1  1
   1  1  1
   1  1  1
   1  1  1
   1  1  1
```
5. `ones(4,6)*pi`
```
ans =
   3.1416   3.1416   3.1416   3.1416   3.1416   3.1416
   3.1416   3.1416   3.1416   3.1416   3.1416   3.1416
   3.1416   3.1416   3.1416   3.1416   3.1416   3.1416
   3.1416   3.1416   3.1416   3.1416   3.1416   3.1416
```
6. `x = [1,2,3];`
   `diag(x)`
```
ans =
   1  0  0
   0  2  0
   0  0  3
```
7. `x = magic(10)`
```
x =
   92   99    1    8   15   67   74   51   58   40
   98   80    7   14   16   73   55   57   64   41
    4   81   88   20   22   54   56   63   70   47
   85   87   19   21    3   60   62   69   71   28
   86   93   25    2    9   61   68   75   52   34
   17   24   76   83   90   42   49   26   33   65
   23    5   82   89   91   48   30   32   39   66
   79    6   13   95   97   29   31   38   45   72
   10   12   94   96   78   35   37   44   46   53
   11   18  100   77   84   36   43   50   27   59
```
   a. `diag(x)`
```
   ans =
   92   80   88   21    9   42   30   38   46   59
```
   b. `diag(fliplr(x))`
```
   ans =
   40   64   63   62   61   90   89   13   12   11
```
   c. `sum(x)`
```
   ans =
    505 505 505 505 505 505 505 505 505 505
   sum(x')
   ans =
    505 505 505 505 505 505 505 505 505 505
   sum(diag(x))
   ans =
    505
   sum(diag(fliplr(x)))
   ans =
    505
```

**Table B.1 Annual Climatological Summary, Station: 310301/13872, Asheville, North Carolina, 1999 (Elev. 2240 ft. above sea level; Lat. 35°36'N, Lon. 82°32'W)**

| Date | Temperature (°F) | | | | | | | | | | | | | | Precipitation (inches) | | | | | | | | | |
|---|---|---|---|---|---|---|---|---|---|---|---|---|---|---|---|---|---|---|---|---|---|---|---|---|
| Elem-> | MMXT | MMNT | MNTM | DPNT | HTDD | CLDD | EMXT | | EMNP | | DT90 | DX32 | DT32 | DT00 | TPCP | DPNP | EMXP | | TSNW | MXSD | | DP01 | DP05 | DP10 |
| | Mean Max. | Mean Min. | Mean | Depart. from Normal | Heating Degree Days | Cooling Degree Days | Highest | High Date | Lowest | Low Date | Max >=90° | Max <=32° | Min <=32° | Min <=0° | Total | Depart. from Normal | Greatest Day | Observed Date | Total Fall | Max Depth | Max Date | >=.10 | >=.50 | >=1.0 |
| 1999 Month | | | | | | | | | | | Number of Days | | | | | | | | Snow, Sleet | | | Number of Days | | |
| 1 | 51.4 | 31.5 | 41.5 | 5.8 | 725 | 0 | 78 | 27 | 9 | 5 | 0 | 2 | 16 | 0 | 4.56 | 2.09 | 1.61 | 2 | 2.7 | 1 | 31 | 9 | 2 | 2 |
| 2 | 52.6 | 32.1 | 42.4 | 3.5 | 628 | 0 | 66 | 8 | 16 | 14 | 0 | 2 | 16 | 0 | 3.07 | -0.18 | 0.79 | 17 | 1.2 | 0T | 1 | 6 | 3 | 0 |
| 3 | 52.7 | 32.5 | 42.6 | -4.8 | 687 | 0 | 76 | 17 | 22 | 8 | 0 | 0 | 19 | 0 | 2.47 | -1.41 | 0.62 | 3 | 5.3 | 1 | 26 | 8 | 1 | 0 |
| 4 | 70.1 | 48.2 | 59.2 | 3.6 | 197 | 30 | 83 | 10 | 34 | 19 | 0 | 0 | 0 | 0 | 2.10 | -1.02 | 0.48 | 27 | 0.0T | 0T | 2 | 6 | 0 | 0 |
| 5 | 75.0 | 51.5 | 63.3 | -0.1 | 69 | 25 | 83 | 29 | 40 | 2 | 0 | 0 | 0 | 0 | 2.49 | -1.12 | 0.93 | 7 | 0.0 | 0 | | 5 | 2 | 0 |
| 6 | 80.2 | 60.9 | 70.6 | 0.3 | 4 | 181 | 90 | 8 | 50 | 18 | 1 | 0 | 0 | 0 | 2.59 | -0.68 | 0.69 | 29 | 0.0 | 0 | | 6 | 2 | 0 |
| 7 | 85.7 | 64.9 | 75.3 | 1.6 | 7 | 336 | 96 | 31 | 56 | 13 | 8 | 0 | 0 | 0 | 3.87 | 0.94 | 0.80 | 11 | 0.0 | 0 | | 10 | 4 | 0 |
| 8 | 86.4 | 63.0 | 74.7 | 1.9 | 0 | 311 | 94 | 13 | 54 | 31 | 7 | 0 | 0 | 0 | 0.90 | -2.86 | 0.29 | 8 | 0.0 | 0 | | 4 | 0 | 0 |
| 9 | 79.1 | 54.6 | 66.9 | 0.2 | 43 | 106 | 91 | 2 | 39 | 23 | 3 | 0 | 0 | 0 | 1.72 | -1.48 | 0.75 | 28 | 0.0 | 0 | | 4 | 1 | 0 |
| 10 | 67.6 | 45.5 | 56.6 | 0.4 | 255 | 1 | 78 | 15 | 28 | 25 | 0 | 0 | 2 | 0 | 1.53 | -1.24 | 0.59 | 4 | 0.0 | 0 | | 3 | 2 | 0 |
| 11 | 62.2 | 40.7 | 51.5 | 4.0 | 397 | 0 | 76 | 9 | 26 | 30 | 0 | 0 | 8 | 0 | 3.48 | 0.56 | 1.71 | 25 | 0.3 | 0 | | 5 | 3 | 1 |
| 12 | 53.6 | 30.5 | 42.1 | 2.7 | 706 | 0 | 69 | 4 | 15 | 25 | 0 | 0 | 20 | 0 | 1.07 | -1.72 | 0.65 | 13 | 0.0T | 0T | | 3 | 1 | 0 |
| Annual | 68.0 | 46.3 | 57.2 | 1.6 | 3718 | 990 | 96 | Jul | 9 | Jan | 19 | 4 | 81 | 0 | 29.85 | -8.12 | 1.71 | Nov | 9.5 | 1 | Mar | 69 | 21 | 3 |

## Notes

(blank) Not reported.

+  Occurred on one or more previous dates during the month. The date in the Date field is the last day of occurrence. Used through December 1983 only.

A  Accumulated amount. This value is a total that may include data from a previous month or months or year (for annual value).

B  Adjusted Total. Monthly value totals based on proportional available data across the entire month.

E  An estimated monthly or annual total.

X  Monthly means or totals based on incomplete time series. 1 to 9 days are missing. Annual means or totals include one or more months which had 1 to 9 days that were missing.

M  Used to indicate data element missing.

T  Trace of precipitation, snowfall, or snowdepth. The precipitation data value will = zero.

S  Precipitation amount is continuing to be accumulated. Total will be included in a subsequent monthly or yearly value. Example: Days 1–20 had 1.35 inches of precipitation, then a period of accumulation began. The element TPCP would then be 00135S and the total accumulated amount value appears in a subsequent monthly value. If TPCP = "M", there was no precipitation measured during the month. Flag is set to "S" and the total accumulated amount appears in a subsequent monthly value.

U.S. Department of Commerce National Oceanic & Atmospheric Administration

# 5

# Plotting

## Objectives

After reading this chapter, you should be able to

- create and label two-dimensional plots
- adjust the appearance of your plots
- divide the plotting window into subplots
- create three-dimensional plots
- use the interactive MATLAB plotting tools

## INTRODUCTION

Large tables of data are difficult to interpret. Engineers use graphing techniques to make the information easier to understand. With a graph, it is easy to identify trends, pick out highs and lows, and isolate data points that may be measurement or calculation errors. Graphs can also be used as a quick check to determine whether a computer solution is yielding expected results.

## 1 TWO-DIMENSIONAL PLOTS

The most useful plot for engineers is the $x$–$y$ plot. A set of ordered pairs is used to identify points on a two-dimensional graph; the points are then connected by straight lines. The values of $x$ and $y$ may be measured or calculated. Generally, the independent variable is given the name $x$ and is plotted on the $x$-axis, and the dependent variable is given the name $y$ and is plotted on the $y$-axis.

### 1.1 Basic Plotting

#### Simple x–y Plots

Once vectors of $x$-values and $y$-values have been defined, MATLAB makes it easy to create plots. Suppose a set of time-versus-distance data were obtained through measurement.

We can store the time values in a vector called **x** (the user can define any convenient name) and the distance values in a vector called **y**:

```
x = [0:2:18];
y = [0, 0.33, 4.13, 6.29, 6.85, 11.19, 13.19, 13.96,
    16.33, 18.17];
```

To plot these points, use the **plot** command, with **x** and **y** as arguments:

```
plot(x,y)
```

| Time, sec | Distance, ft |
|-----------|--------------|
| 0 | 0 |
| 2 | 0.33 |
| 4 | 4.13 |
| 6 | 6.29 |
| 8 | 6.85 |
| 10 | 11.19 |
| 12 | 13.19 |
| 14 | 13.96 |
| 16 | 16.33 |
| 18 | 18.17 |

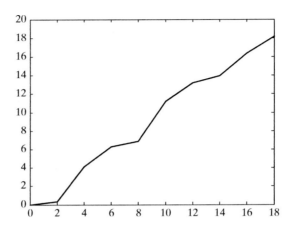

**Figure 1**
Simple plot of time versus distance created in MATLAB.

A graphics window automatically opens, which MATLAB calls Figure 1. The resulting plot is shown in Figure 1. (Slight variations in scaling of the plot may occur, depending on the size of the graphics window.)

### Titles, Labels, and Grids

Good engineering practice requires that we include units and a title in our plot. The following commands add a title, $x$- and $y$-axis labels, and a background grid:

KEY IDEA: Always include units on axis labels

```
plot(x,y)
xlabel('Time, sec' )
ylabel('Distance, ft')
grid on
```

These commands generate the plot in Figure 2. They could also be combined onto one or two lines, separated by commas:

```
plot(x,y) , title('Laboratory Experiment 1')
xlabel('Time, sec' ), ylabel('Distance, ft'), grid
```

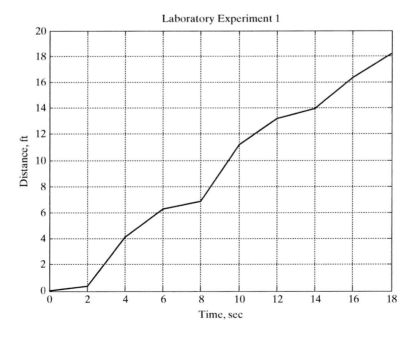

**Figure 2**
Adding a grid, a title, and labels makes a plot easier to interpret.

STRING: a list of characters enclosed by single quotes

As you type the preceding commands into MATLAB, notice that the text color changes to red when you enter a single quote ('). This alerts you that you are starting a string. The color changes to purple when you type the final single quote ('), indicating that you have completed the string. Paying attention to these visual aids will help you avoid coding mistakes. MATLAB 6 used different color cues, but the idea is the same.

If you are working in the command window, the graphics window will open on top of the other windows. (See Figure 3.) To continue working, either click in the command window or minimize the graphics window. You can also resize the graphics window to whatever size is convenient for you or add it to the MATLAB desktop by selecting the docking arrow underneath the exit icon in the upper right-hand corner of the figure window.

---

**Hint**

Once you click in the command window, the figure window is hidden behind the current window. To see the changes to your figure, you will need to select the figure from the Windows task bar at the bottom of the screen.

---

**Hint**

You must create a graph *before* you add the title and labels. If you specify the title and labels first, they are erased when the plot command executes.

---

**Figure 3**
The graphics window opens on top of the command window. You can resize it to a convenient shape, or dock it with the MATLAB desktop.

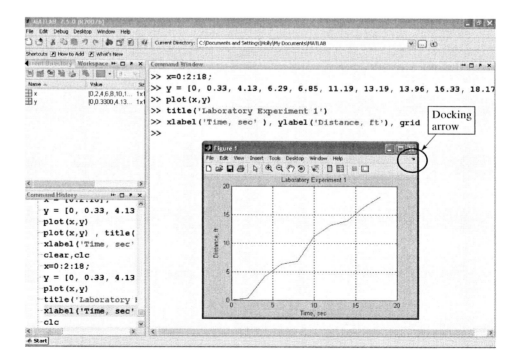

---

**Hint**

Because a single quote is used to end the string used in **xlabel**, **ylabel**, and **title** commands, MATLAB interprets an apostrophe (as in the word *it's*) as the end of the string. Entering the single quote twice, as in **xlabel('Holly"s Data')**, will allow you to use apostrophes in your text. (Don't use a double quote, which is a different character)

---

### Creating Multiple Plots

If you are working in an M-file when you request a plot, and then you continue with more computations, MATLAB will generate and display the graphics window and then return immediately to execute the rest of the commands in the program. If you request a second plot, the graph you created will be overwritten. There are two possible solutions to this problem: Use the **pause** command to temporarily halt the execution of your M-file program, or create a second figure, using the **figure** function.

The **pause** command stops the program execution until any key is pressed. If you want to pause for a specified number of seconds, use the **pause(n)** command, which will cause execution to pause for **n** seconds before continuing.

The **figure** command allows you to open a new figure window. The next time you request a plot, it will be displayed in this new window. For example,

```
figure(2)
```

opens a window named Figure 2, which then becomes the window used for subsequent plotting. Executing **figure** without an input parameter causes a new window to open, numbered consecutively one up from the current window. For example, if the current figure window is named "Figure 2", executing **figure** will cause "Figure 3" to open. The commands used to create a simple plot are summarized in Table 1.

### Plots with More than One Line

A plot with more than one line can be created in several ways. By default, the execution of a second **plot** statement will erase the first plot. However, you can layer plots on top of one another by using the **hold on** command. Execute the following

### Table 1 Basic Plotting Functions

| | | |
|---|---|---|
| **plot** | Creates an x–y plot | **plot(x,y)** |
| **title** | Adds a title to a plot | **title('My Graph')** |
| **xlabel** | Adds a label to the x-axis | **xlabel('Independent Variable')** |
| **ylabel** | Adds a label to the y-axis | **ylabel('Dependent Variable')** |
| **grid** | Adds a grid to the graph | **grid**<br>**grid on**<br>**grid off** |
| **pause** | Pauses the execution of the program, allowing the user to view the graph | **pause** |
| **figure** | Determines which figure will be used for the current plot | **figure**<br>**figure(2)** |
| **hold** | Freezes the current plot, so that an additional plot can be overlaid | **hold on**<br>**hold off** |

statements to create a plot with both functions plotted on the same graph, as shown in Figure 4:

```
x = 0:pi/100:2*pi;
y1 = cos(x*4);
plot(x,y1)
y2 = sin(x);
hold on;
plot(x, y2)
```

Semicolons are optional on both the **plot** statement and the **hold on** statement. MATLAB will continue to layer the plots until the **hold off** command is executed:

```
hold off
```

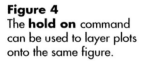

KEY IDEA: The most common plot used in engineering is the *x–y* scatter plot

Another way to create a graph with multiple lines is to request both lines in a single **plot** command. MATLAB interprets the input to **plot** as alternating *x* and *y* vectors, as in

```
plot(X1, Y1, X2,Y2)
```

where the variables **X1, Y1** form an ordered set of values to be plotted and **X2, Y2** form a second ordered set of values. Using the data from the previous example,

```
plot(x,y1, x, y2)
```

produces the same graph as Figure 4, with one exception: The two lines are different colors. MATLAB uses a default plotting color (blue) for the first line drawn in a **plot** command. In the **hold on** approach, each line is drawn in a separate plot command and thus is the same color. By requesting two lines in a single command, such as **plot(x,y1, x, y2),** the second line defaults to green, allowing the user to distinguish between the two plots.

If the **plot** function is called with a single matrix argument, MATLAB draws a separate line for each column of the matrix. The *x*-axis is labeled with the row index vector, 1:*k*, where *k* is the number of rows in the matrix. This produces an evenly spaced plot, sometimes called a line plot. If **plot** is called with two arguments, one a vector and the other a matrix, MATLAB successively plots a line for each row in the matrix. For example, we can combine **y1** and **y2** into a single matrix and plot against **x**:

```
Y = [y1; y2];
plot(x,Y)
```

This creates the same plot as Figure 4, with each line a different color.

**Figure 4**
The **hold on** command can be used to layer plots onto the same figure.

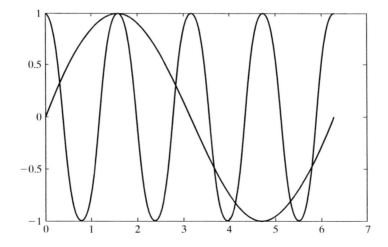

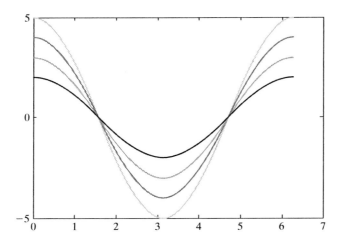

**Figure 5**
Multiple plots on the same graph.

Here's another more complicated example:

```
X = 0:pi/100:2*pi;
Y1 = cos(X)*2;
Y2 = cos(X)*3;
Y3 = cos(X)*4;
Y4 = cos(X)*5;
Z = [Y1; Y2; Y3; Y4];
plot(X, Y1, X, Y2, X, Y3, X, Y4)
```

This code produces the same result (Figure 5) as

```
plot(X, Z)
```

A function of two variables, the **peaks** function produces sample data that are useful for demonstrating certain graphing functions. (The data are created by scaling and translating Gaussian distributions.) Calling **peaks** with a single argument **n** will create an $n \times n$ matrix. We can use **peaks** to demonstrate the power of using a matrix argument in the **plot** function. The command

```
plot(peaks(100))
```

results in the impressive graph in Figure 6. The input to the plot function created by peaks is a $100 \times 100$ matrix. Notice that the *x*-axis goes from 1 to 100, the index

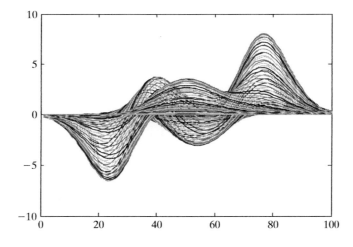

**Figure 6**
The **peaks** function, plotted with a single argument in the **plot** command.

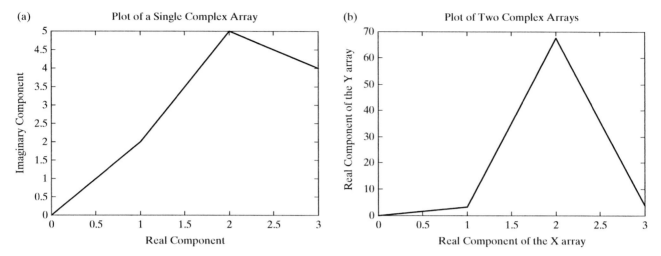

**Figure 7**
(a) Complex numbers are plotted with the real component on the *x*-axis and the imaginary component on the *y*-axis when a single array is used as input. (b) When two complex arrays are used in the **plot** function, the imaginary components are ignored.

numbers of the data. You undoubtedly can't tell, but there are 100 lines drawn to create this graph—one for each column.

### Plots of Complex Arrays

If the input to the **plot** command is a single array of complex numbers, MATLAB plots the real component on the *x*-axis and the imaginary component on the *y*-axis. For example, if

```
A = [0+0i,1+2i, 2+5i, 3+4i]
```

then

```
plot(A)
title('Plot of a Single Complex Array')
xlabel('Real Component')
ylabel('Imaginary Component')
```

returns the graph shown in Figure 7a.

If we attempt to use two arrays of complex numbers in the **plot** function, the imaginary components are ignored. The real portion of the first array is used for the *x*-values, and the real portion of the second array is used for the *y*-values. To illustrate, first create another array called **B** by taking the sine of the complex array **A**:

```
B = sin(A)
```

returns

```
B =
    0   3.1658 + 1.9596i   67.4789 -30.8794i   3.8537 -27.0168i
```

and

```
plot(A,B)
title('Plot of Two Complex Arrays')
xlabel('Real Component of the X array')
ylabel('Real Component of the Y array')
```

gives us an error statement.

```
Warning: Imaginary parts of complex X and/or Y arguments
ignored.
```

The data are still plotted, as shown in Figure 7b.

### 1.2 Line, Color, and Mark Style

You can change the appearance of your plots by selecting user-defined line styles and line colors and by choosing to show the data points on the graph with user-specified mark styles. The command

```
help plot
```

returns a list of the available options. You can select solid (the default), dashed, dotted, and dash-dot line styles, and you can choose to show the points. The choices among marks include plus signs, stars, circles, and x-marks, among others. There are seven different color choices. (See Table 2 for a complete list.)

The following commands illustrate the use of line, color, and mark styles:

```
x = [1:10];
y = [ 58.5, 63.8, 64.2, 67.3, 71.5, 88.3, 90.1, 90.6,
    89.5,90.4];
plot(x,y,':ok')
```

The resulting plot (Figure 8a) consists of a dashed line, together with data points marked with circles. The line, the points, and the circles are drawn in black. The indicators were listed inside a string, denoted with single quotes. The order in which they are entered is arbitrary and does not affect the output.

To specify line, mark, and color styles for multiple lines, add a string containing the choices after each pair of data points. If the string is not included, the defaults are used. For example,

```
plot(x,y,':ok',x,y*2,'--xr',x,y/2,'-b')
```

results in the graph shown in Figure 8b.

### Table 2  Line, Mark, and Color Options

| Line Type | Indicator | Point Type | Indicator | Color | Indicator |
|---|---|---|---|---|---|
| solid | - | point | . | blue | b |
| dotted | : | circle | o | green | g |
| dash-dot | -. | x-mark | x | red | r |
| dashed | -- | plus | + | cyan | c |
| | | star | * | magenta | m |
| | | square | s | yellow | y |
| | | diamond | d | black | k |
| | | triangle down | v | white | w |
| | | triangle up | ^ | | |
| | | triangle left | < | | |
| | | triangle right | > | | |
| | | pentagram | p | | |
| | | hexagram | h | | |

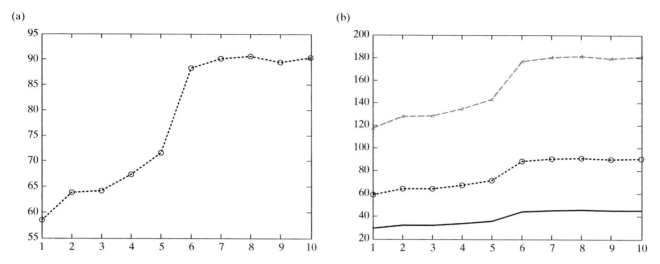

**Figure 8**
(a) Adjusting the line, mark, and color style. (b) Multiple plots with varying line styles, colors, and point styles.

The **plot** command offers additional options to control the way the plot appears. For example, the line width can be controlled. Plots intended for overhead presentations may look better with thicker lines. Use the **help** function to learn more about controlling the appearance of the plot, or use the interactive controls described in Section 5.

### 1.3 Axis Scaling and Annotating Plots

MATLAB automatically selects appropriate *x*-axis and *y*-axis scaling. Sometimes it is useful for the user to be able to control the scaling. Control is accomplished with the **axis** function, shown in Table 3. Executing the **axis** function without any input

```
axis
```

freezes the scaling of the plot. If you use the **hold on** command to add a second line to your graph, the scaling cannot change. To return control of the scaling to MATLAB, simply re-execute the **axis** function.

The **axis** function also accepts input defining the *x*-axis and *y*-axis scaling. The argument is a single matrix, with four values representing

- the minimum *x* value shown on the *x*-axis
- the maximum *x* value shown on the *x*-axis
- the minimum *y* value shown on the *y*-axis
- the maximum *y* value shown on the *y*-axis

Thus the command

```
axis([-2, 3, 0, 10])
```

fixes the plot axes to *x* from −2 to +3 and *y* from 0 to 10.

MATLAB offers several additional functions, also listed in Table 3, that allow you to annotate your plots. The **legend** function requires the user to specify a legend in the form of a string for each line plotted, and displays it in the upper right-hand corner of the plot. The **text** function allows you to add a text box to your plot, which is useful for describing features on the graph. It requires the user to specify the location of the lower left-hand corner of the box in the plot window as the first two input fields, with a string specifying the contents of the text box in the third

**Table 3  Axis Scaling and Annotating Plots**

| | |
|---|---|
| **axis** | When the **axis** function is used without inputs, it freezes the axis at the current configuration. Executing the function a second time returns axis control to MATLAB. |
| **axis(v)** | The input to the **axis** command must be a four-element vector that specifies the minimum and maximum values for both the *x*- and *y*-axes—for example, **[xmin, xmax,ymin,ymax]** |
| **legend('string1', 'string 2', etc)** | Allows you to add a legend to your graph. The legend shows a sample of the line and lists the string you have specified. |
| **text(x_coordinate,y_coordinate, 'string')** | Allows you to add a text box to the graph. The box is placed at the specified *x*- and *y*-coordinates and contains the string value specified. |
| **gtext('string')** | Similar to text. The box is placed at a location determined interactively by the user by clicking in the figure window. |

input field. The use of both **legend** and **text** is demonstrated in the following code, which modifies the graph from Figure 8b.

```
legend('line 1', 'line 2', 'line3')
text(1,100,'Label plots with the text command')
```

We added a title, *x* and *y* labels, and adjusted the axis with the following commands:

```
xlabel('My x label'), ylabel('My y label')
title('Example graph for Plotting Chapter')
axis([0,11,0,200])
```

The results are shown in Figure 9.

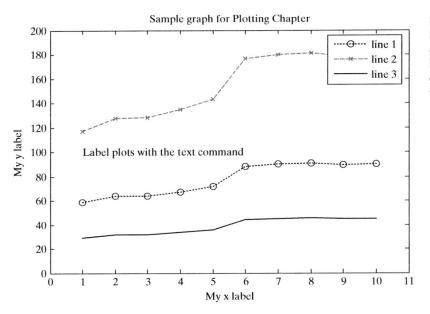

**Figure 9**
Final version of the sample graph, annotated with a legend, a text box, a title, *x* and *y* labels, and a modified axis.

**Hint**

You can use Greek letters in your titles and labels by putting a backslash (\) before the name of the letter. For example,

        `title('\alpha \beta \gamma')`

creates the plot title

$$\alpha\beta\gamma$$

To create a superscript, use a caret. Thus,

        `title('x^2')`

gives

$$x^2$$

To create a subscript, use an underscore.

        `title('x_5')`

gives

$$x_5$$

If your expression requires a group of characters as either a subscript or superscript, enclose them in curly braces. For example,

        `title('k^{-1}')`

which returns

$$k^{-1}$$

MATLAB has the ability to create more complicated mathematical expressions for use as titles, axis labels, and other text strings, using the TEX markup language. To learn more, consult the **help** feature. (Search on "text properties".)

---

### Practice Exercises 1

1. Plot $x$ versus $y$ for $y = \sin(x)$. Let $x$ vary from 0 to $2\pi$ in increments of $0.1\pi$.
2. Add a title and labels to your plot.
3. Plot $x$ versus $y_1$ and $y_2$ for $y_1 = \sin(x)$ and $y_2 = \cos(x)$. Let $x$ vary from 0 to $2\pi$ in increments of $0.1\pi$. Add a title and labels to your plot.
4. Re-create the plot from Exercise 3, but make the $\sin(x)$ line dashed and red. Make the $\cos(x)$ line green and dotted.
5. Add a legend to the graph in Exercise 4.
6. Adjust the axes so that the $x$-axis goes from $-1$ to $2\pi + 1$ and the $y$-axis from $-1.5$ to $+1.5$.
7. Create a new vector, **a** = cos(**x**). Let **x** vary from 0 to $2\pi$ in increments of $0.1\pi$. Plot just **a** (**plot(a)**) and observe the result. Compare this result with the graph produced by plotting **x** versus **a** (**plot(x,a)**).

EXAMPLE 1

## Using the Clausius–Clapeyron Equation

The Clausius–Clapeyron equation can be used to find the saturation vapor pressure of water in the atmosphere, for different temperatures. The saturation water vapor pressure is useful to meteorologists because it can be used to calculate relative humidity, an important component of weather prediction, when the actual partial pressure of water in the air is known.

The following table presents the results of calculating the saturation vapor pressure of water in the atmosphere for various air temperatures with the use of the Clausius–Clapeyron equation:

| Air Temperature, °F | Saturation Vapor Pressure, mbar |
|---|---|
| −60.0000 | 0.0698 |
| −50.0000 | 0.1252 |
| −40.0000 | 0.2184 |
| −30.0000 | 0.3714 |
| −20.0000 | 0.6163 |
| −10.0000 | 1.0000 |
| 0 | 1.5888 |
| 10.0000 | 2.4749 |
| 20.0000 | 3.7847 |
| 30.0000 | 5.6880 |
| 40.0000 | 8.4102 |
| 50.0000 | 12.2458 |
| 60.0000 | 17.5747 |
| 70.0000 | 24.8807 |
| 80.0000 | 34.7729 |
| 90.0000 | 48.0098 |
| 100.0000 | 65.5257 |
| 110.0000 | 88.4608 |
| 120.0000 | 118.1931 |

Let us present these results graphically as well.

The Clausius–Clapeyron equation is

$$\ln\left(P^{0}/6.11\right) = \left(\frac{\Delta H_{v}}{R_{\text{air}}}\right) * \left(\frac{1}{273} - \frac{1}{T}\right)$$

where

$P^{0}$  = saturation vapor pressure for water, in mbar, at temperature $T$,
$\Delta H_{v}$ = latent heat of vaporization for water, $2.453 \times 10^{6}$ J/kg,
$R_{v}$  = gas constant for moist air, 461 J/kg, and
$T$  = temperature in kelvins

1. State the Problem

Find the saturation vapor pressure at temperatures from $-60°F$ to $120°F$, using the Clausius–Clapeyron equation.

2. Describe the Input and Output

*Input*

$$\Delta H_v = 2.453 \times 10^6 \text{ J/kg}$$
$$R_{air} = 461 \text{ J/kg}$$
$$T = -60°F \text{ to } 120°F$$

Since the number of temperature values was not specified, we'll choose to recalculate every $10°F$.

*Output*

Table of temperature versus saturation vapor pressures
Graph of temperature versus saturation vapor pressures

3. Develop a Hand Example

Change the temperatures from Fahrenheit to Kelvin:

$$T_k = \frac{(T_f + 459.6)}{1.8}$$

Solve the Clausius–Clapeyron equation for the saturation vapor pressure ($P^0$):

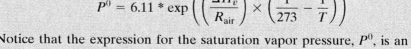

$$\ln\left(\frac{P^0}{6.11}\right) = \left(\frac{\Delta H_v}{R_{air}}\right) \times \left(\frac{1}{273} - \frac{1}{T}\right)$$
$$P^0 = 6.11 * \exp\left(\left(\frac{\Delta H_v}{R_{air}}\right) \times \left(\frac{1}{273} - \frac{1}{T}\right)\right)$$

Notice that the expression for the saturation vapor pressure, $P^0$, is an exponential equation. We would thus expect the graph to have the following shape:

4. Develop a MATLAB Solution

```
%Example 1
%Using the Clausius-Clapeyron equation, find the
%saturation vapor pressure for water at different
%temperatures
%
  TF=[-60:10:120];          %Define temp matrix in F
  TK=(TF + 459.6)/1.8;      %Convert temp to K
  Delta_H=2.45e6;           %Define latent heat of
                            %vaporization
  R_air = 461;              %Define ideal gas constant
                            %for air
%
%Calculate the vapor pressures
  Vapor_Pressure=6.11*exp((Delta_H/R_air)*(1/273 - 1./TK));
  %Display the results in a table
    my_results = [TF',Vapor_Pressure']
%
```

The figure to the left shows axes labeled Pressure (vertical) and Temperature (horizontal) with an exponential curve.

```
%Create an x-y plot
   plot(TF,Vapor_Pressure)
   title('Clausius-Clapeyron Behavior')
   xlabel('Temperature, F')
   ylabel('Saturation Vapor Pressure, mbar')
```

The resulting table is

```
my_results =
        -60.0000     0.0698
        -50.0000     0.1252
        -40.0000     0.2184
        -30.0000     0.3714
        -20.0000     0.6163
        -10.0000     1.0000
               0     1.5888
         10.0000     2.4749
         20.0000     3.7847
         30.0000     5.6880
         40.0000     8.4102
         50.0000    12.2458
         60.0000    17.5747
         70.0000    24.8807
         80.0000    34.7729
         90.0000    48.0098
        100.0000    65.5257
        110.0000    88.4608
        120.0000   118.1931
```

A figure window opens to display the graphical results, shown in Figure 10.

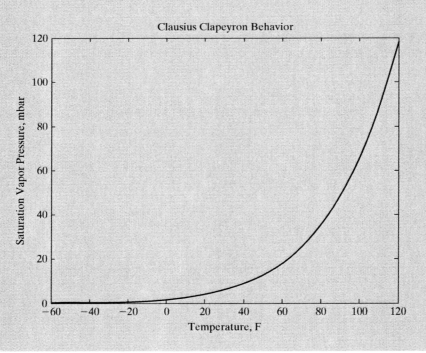

**Figure 10**
A plot of the
Clausius–Clapeyron
equation.

5. Test the Solution

The plot follows the expected trend. It is almost always easier to determine whether computational results make sense if a graph is produced. Tabular data are extremely difficult to interpret.

**EXAMPLE 2**

### Ballistics

The range of an object (see Figure 11) shot at an angle $\theta$ with respect to the $x$-axis and an initial velocity $v_0$ is given by

$$R(\theta) = \frac{v^2}{g}\sin(2\theta) \quad \text{for } 0 \le \theta \le \frac{\pi}{2} \text{ (neglecting air resistance)}$$

Use $g = 9.9 \text{ m/s}^2$ and an initial velocity of 100 m/s. Show that the maximum range is obtained at $\theta = \pi/4$ by computing and plotting the range for values of theta from

$$0 \le \theta \le \frac{\pi}{2}$$

in increments of 0.05.

Repeat your calculations with an initial velocity of 50 m/s, and plot both sets of results on a single graph.

1. State the Problem

Calculate the range as a function of the launch angle.

2. Describe the Input and Output

**Input**

$g$  = 9.9 m/s$^2$
$\theta$  = 0 to $\pi/2$, incremented by 0.05
$v_0$ = 50 m/s and 100 m/s

**Output**

Range $R$
Present the results as a plot.

3. Develop a Hand Example

If the cannon is pointed straight up, we know that the range is zero, and if the cannon is horizontal, the range is also zero. (See Figure 12.)

**Figure 11**
Ballistic motion.

**Figure 12**
The range is zero if the cannon is perfectly vertical, or perfectly horizontal.

This means that the range must increase with the cannon angle up to some maximum and then decrease. A sample calculation at 45 degrees ($\pi/4$ radians) shows that

$$R(\theta) = \frac{v^2}{g}\sin(2\theta)$$

$$R\left(\frac{\pi}{4}\right) = \frac{100^2}{9.9}\sin\left(\frac{2\cdot\pi}{4}\right) = 1010 \text{ meters when the initial velocity is 100 m/s}$$

4. Develop a MATLAB Solution

```
%Example 2
%The program calculates the range of a ballistic projectile
%
% Define the constants
  g = 9.9;
  v1 = 50;
  v2 = 100;
% Define the angle vector
  angle = 0:0.05:pi/2;
% Calculate the range
  R1 = v1^2/g*sin(2*angle);
  R2 = v2^2/g*sin(2*angle);
%Plot the results
  plot(angle,R1,angle,R2,':')
  title('Cannon Range')
  xlabel('Cannon Angle')
  ylabel('Range, meters')
  legend('Initial Velocity=50 m/s', 'Initial Velocity=100 m/s')
```

Notice that in the **plot** command we requested MATLAB to print the second set of data as a dashed line. A title, labels, and a legend were also added. The results are plotted in Figure 13.

5. Test the Solution
Compare the MATLAB results with those from the hand example. Both graphs start and end at zero. The maximum range for an initial velocity of 100 m/s is approximately 1000 m, which corresponds well to the calculated

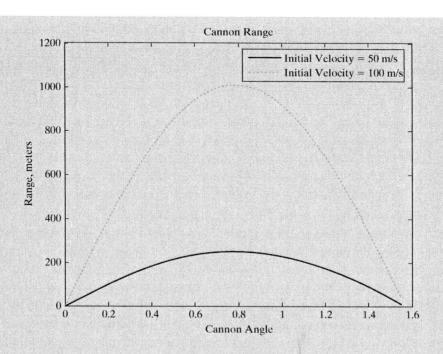

**Figure 13**
The predicted range of a projectile.

value of 1010 m. Notice that both solutions peak at the same angle, approximately 0.8 radian. The numerical value for $\pi/4$ is 0.785 radian, confirming the hypothesis presented in the problem statement that the maximum range is achieved by pointing the cannon at an angle of $\pi/4$ radians (45 degrees).

**Hint**

To clear a figure, use the **clf** command. To close a figure window, use the **close** command.

A function similar to **text** is **gtext**, which allows the user to interactively place a text box in an existing plot. The **gtext** function requires a single input, the string to be displayed.

```
gtext('This string will display on the graph')
```

Once executed, a crosshair appears on the graph. The user positions the crosshair to the appropriate position. The text is added to the graph when any key on the keyboard is depressed, or a mouse button is selected.

## 2 SUBPLOTS

The **subplot** command allows you to subdivide the graphing window into a grid of *m* rows and *n* columns. The function

```
subplot(m,n,p)
```

splits the figure into an $m \times n$ matrix. The variable **p** identifies the portion of the window where the next plot will be drawn. For example, if the command

```
subplot(2,2,1)
```

is used, the window is divided into two rows and two columns, and the plot is drawn in the upper left-hand window (Figure 14).

The windows are numbered from left to right, top to bottom. Similarly, the following commands split the graph window into a top plot and a bottom plot:

```
x = 0:pi/20:2*pi;
subplot(2,1,1)
plot(x,sin(x))
subplot(2,1,2)
plot(x,sin(2*x))
```

| $p = 1$ | $p = 2$ |
| --- | --- |
| $p = 3$ | $p = 4$ |

**Figure 14**
Subplots are used to subdivide the figure window into an $m \times n$ matrix.

The first graph is drawn in the top window, since **p** = 1. Then the **subplot** command is used again to draw the next graph in the bottom window. Figure 15 shows both graphs.

Titles are added above each subwindow as the graphs are drawn, as are *x*- and *y*-axis labels and any annotation desired. The use of the **subplot** command is illustrated in several of the sections that follow.

**Practice Exercises 2**

1. Subdivide a figure window into two rows and one column.
2. In the top window, plot $y = \tan(x)$ for $-1.5 \le x \le 1.5$. Use an increment of 0.1.
3. Add a title and axis labels to your graph.
4. In the bottom window, plot $y = \sinh(x)$ for the same range.
5. Add a title and labels to your graph.
6. Try the preceding exercises again, but divide the figure window vertically instead of horizontally.

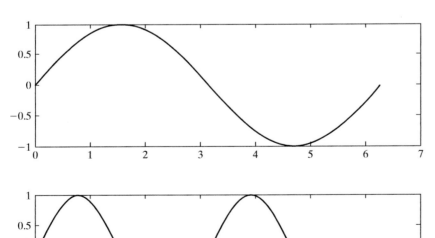

**Figure 15**
The **subplot** command allows the user to create multiple graphs in the same figure window.

## 3 OTHER TYPES OF TWO-DIMENSIONAL PLOTS

Although simple *x–y* plots are the most common type of engineering plot, there are many other ways to represent data. Depending on the situation, these techniques may be more appropriate than an *x–y* plot.

### 3.1 Polar Plots

MATLAB provides plotting capability with polar coordinates:

```
polar(theta, r)
```

generates a polar plot of angle theta (in radians) and radial distance *r*.

For example, the code

```
x = 0:pi/100:pi;
y = sin(x);
polar(x,y)
```

generates the plot in Figure 16. A title was added in the usual way:

```
title('The sine function plotted in polar coordinates is a
circle.')
```

---

**Practice Exercises 3**

1. Define an array called **theta**, from 0 to $2\pi$, in steps of $0.01\pi$.

   Define an array of distances **r = 5*cos(4*theta)**.

   Make a polar plot of **theta** versus **r**.

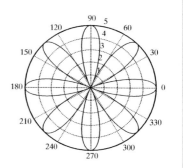

2. Use the **hold on** command to freeze the graph.

   Assign **r = 4*cos(6*theta)** and plot.

   Add a title.

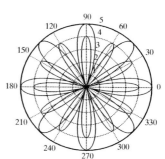

3. Create a new figure.

   Use the **theta** array from the preceding exercises.

   Assign **r = 5 − 5*sin(theta)** and create a new polar plot.

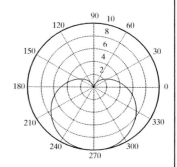

4. Create a new figure.
   Use the **theta** array from the preceding exercises.
   Assign
   **r = sqrt(5^2*cos(2*theta))**
   and create a new polar plot.

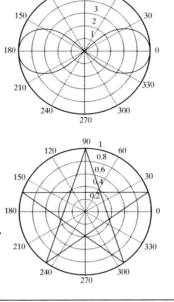

5. Create a new figure.
   Define a theta array such that
   **theta = pi/2:4/5*pi:4.8*pi;**
   Create a six-member array of ones called **r**.
   Create a new polar plot of **theta** versus **r**.

## 3.2 Logarithmic Plots

For most plots that we generate, the *x*- and *y*-axes are divided into equally spaced intervals; these plots are called *linear* or *rectangular* plots. Occasionally, however, we may want to use a logarithmic scale on one or both of the axes. A logarithmic scale (to the base 10) is convenient when a variable ranges over many orders of magnitude, because the wide range of values can be graphed without compressing the smaller values. Logarithmic plots are also useful for representing data that vary exponentially.

KEY IDEA: Logarithmic plots are especially useful if the data vary exponentially

The sine function plotted in polar coordinates is a circle.

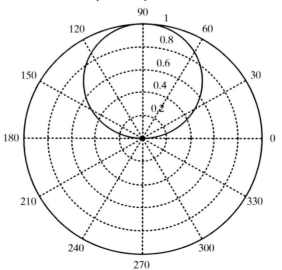

**Figure 16**
A polar plot of the sine function.

## Table 4  Rectangular and Logarithmic Plots

| | |
|---|---|
| **plot(x,y)** | Generates a linear plot of the vectors **x** and **y** |
| **semilogx(x,y)** | Generates a plot of the values of **x** and **y**, using a logarithmic scale for **x** and a linear scale for **y** |
| **semilogy(x,y)** | Generates a plot of the values of **x** and **y**, using a linear scale for **x** and a logarithmic scale for **y** |
| **loglog(x,y)** | Generates a plot of the vectors **x** and **y**, using a logarithmic scale for both **x** and **y** |

The MATLAB commands for generating linear and logarithmic plots of the vectors **x** and **y** are listed in Table 4.

Remember that the logarithm of a negative number or of zero does not exist. If your data include these values, MATLAB will issue a warning message and will not plot the points in question. However, it will generate a plot based on the remaining points.

Each command for logarithmic plotting can be executed with one argument, as we saw in **plot(y)** for a linear plot. In these cases, the plots are generated with the values of the indices of the vector **y** used as **x** values.

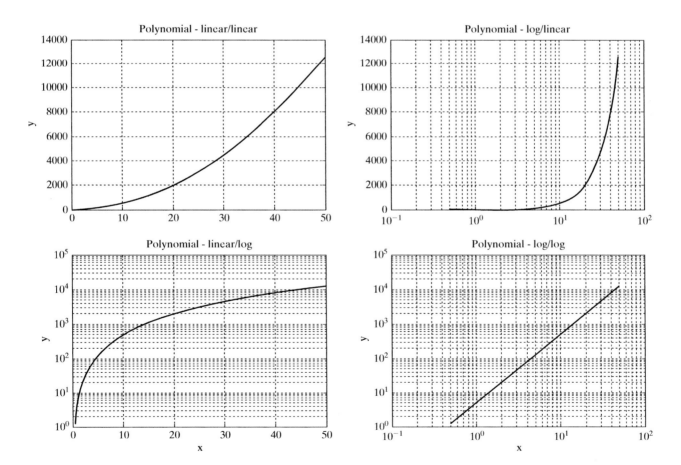

**Figure 17**
Linear and logarithmic plots, displayed using the subplot function.

As an example, plots of $y = 5x^2$ were created using all four scaling approaches, as shown in Figure 17. The linear (rectangular) plot, semilog plot along the *x*-axis, semilog plot along the *y*-axis, and log–log plot are all shown on one figure, plotted with the **subplot** function in the following code:

```
x = 0:0.5:50;
y = 5*x.^2;
subplot(2,2,1)
plot(x,y)
    title('Polynomial - linear/linear')
    ylabel('y'), grid
subplot(2,2,2)
semilogx(x,y)
    title('Polynomial - log/linear')
    ylabel('y'), grid
subplot(2,2,3)
semilogy(x,y)
    title('Polynomial - linear/log')
    xlabel('x'), ylabel('y'), grid
subplot(2,2,4)
loglog(x,y)
    title('Polynomial - log/log')
    xlabel('x'), ylabel('y'), grid
```

The indenting is intended to make the code easier to read—MATLAB ignores white space. As a matter of style, notice that only the bottom two subplots have *x*-axis labels.

KEY IDEA: Since MATLAB ignores white space, use it to make your code more readable

### EXAMPLE 3

## Rates of Diffusion

Metals are often treated to make them stronger and therefore wear longer. One problem with making a strong piece of metal is that it becomes difficult to form it into a desired shape. A strategy that gets around this problem is to form a soft metal into the shape you desire and then harden the surface. This makes the metal wear well without making it brittle.

A common hardening process is called *carburizing*. The metal part is exposed to carbon, which diffuses into the part, making it harder. This is a very slow process if performed at low temperatures, but it can be accelerated by heating the part. The diffusivity is a measure of how fast diffusion occurs and can be modeled as

$$D = D_0 \exp\left(\frac{-Q}{RT}\right)$$

where

$D$ = diffusivity, cm$^2$/s,
$D_0$ = diffusion coefficient, cm$^2$/s,
$Q$ = activation energy, J/mol, 8.314 J/mol K,
$R$ = ideal gas constant, J/mol K, and
$T$ = temperature, K.

As iron is heated, it changes structure and its diffusion characteristics change. The values of $D_0$ and $Q$ are shown in the following table for carbon diffusing through each of iron's structures:

| Type of Metal | $D_0$ (cm$^2$/s) | $Q$ (J/mol K) |
|---|---|---|
| alpha Fe (BCC) | .0062 | 80,000 |
| gamma Fe (FCC) | 0.23 | 148,000 |

Create a plot of diffusivity versus inverse temperature ($1/T$), using the data provided. Try the rectangular, semilog and log–log plots to see which you think might represent the results best. Let the temperature vary from room temperature (25°C) to 1200°C.

1. State the Problem
   Calculate the diffusivity of carbon in iron.
2. Describe the Input and Output

   **Input**

   For C in alpha iron, $D_0 = 0.0062$ cm$^2$/s and $Q = 80,000$ J/mol K
   For C in gamma iron, $D_0 = 0.23$ cm$^2$/s and $Q = 148,000$ J/mol K
   $R = 8.314$ J/mol K
   $T$ varies from 25°C to 1200°C

   **Output**

   Calculate the diffusivity and plot it.
3. Develop a Hand Example
   The diffusivity is given by

   $$D = D_0 \exp\left(\frac{-Q}{RT}\right)$$

   At room temperature, the diffusivity for carbon in alpha iron is

   $$D = .0062 \exp\left(\frac{-80,000}{8.314 \cdot (25 + 273)}\right)$$
   $$D = 5.9 \times 10^{-17}$$

   (Notice that the temperature had to be changed from Celsius to Kelvin.)
4. Develop a MATLAB Solution

```
% Example 3
% Calculate the diffusivity of carbon in iron
   clear, clc
% Define the constants
   D0alpha = .0062;
   D0gamma = 0.23;
   Qalpha = 80000;
   Qgamma = 148000;
   R = 8.314;
   T = 25:5:1200;
```

```
% Change T from C to K
  T = T+273;
% Calculate the diffusivity
  Dalpha = D0alpha*exp(-Qalpha./(R*T));
  Dgamma = D0gamma*exp(-Qgamma./(R*T));
% Plot the results
  subplot(2,2,1)
  plot(1./T,Dalpha, 1./T,Dgamma)
  title('Diffusivity of C in Fe')
  xlabel('Inverse Temperature, K^{-1}'),
  ylabel('Diffusivity, cm^2/s')
  grid on

  subplot(2,2,2)
  semilogx(1./T,Dalpha, 1./T,Dgamma)
  title('Diffusivity of C in Fe')
  xlabel('Inverse Temperature, K^{-1}'),
  ylabel('Diffusivity, cm^2/s')
  grid on

  subplot(2,2,3)
  semilogy(1./T,Dalpha, 1./T,Dgamma)
  title('Diffusivity of C in Fe')
  xlabel('Inverse Temperature, K^{-1}'),
  ylabel('Diffusivity, cm^2/s')
  grid on

  subplot(2,2,4)
  loglog(1./T,Dalpha, 1./T,Dgamma)
  title('Diffusivity of C in Fe')
  xlabel('Inverse Temperature, K^{-1}'),
  ylabel('Diffusivity, cm^2/s')
  grid on
```

Subplots were used in Figure 18, so that all four variations of the plot are in the same figure. Notice that $x$-labels were added only to the bottom two graphs, to reduce clutter, and that a legend was added only to the first plot. The **semilogy** plot resulted in straight lines and allows a user to read values off the graph easily over a wide range of both temperatures and diffusivities. This is the plotting scheme usually used in textbooks and handbooks to present diffusivity values.

5. Test the Solution

Compare the MATLAB results with those from the hand example.

We calculated the diffusivity to be

$$5.9 \times 10^{-17} \text{ cm}^2/\text{s at } 25°\text{C}$$

for carbon in alpha iron. To check our answer, we'll need to change 25°C to kelvins and take the inverse:

$$\frac{1}{(25 + 273)} = 3.36 \times 10^{-3}$$

**From the semilogy** graph (lower left-hand corner), we can see that the diffusivity for alpha iron is approximately $10^{-17}$.

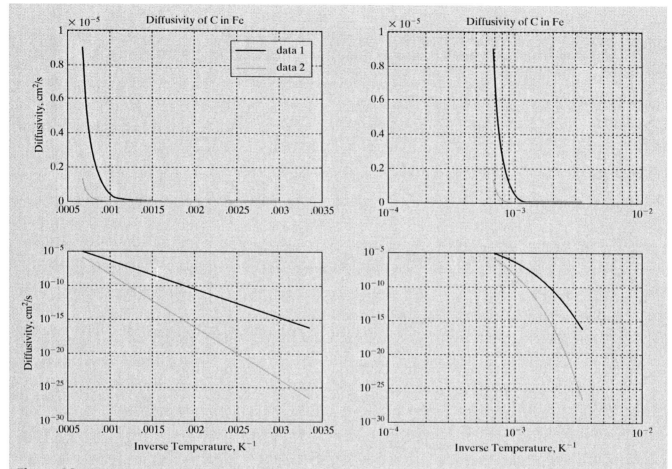

**Figure 18**
Diffusivity data plotted on different scales. The data follows a straight line when the $\log_{10}$ of the diffusivity is plotted on the y-axis vs. the inverse temperature on the x-axis.

### Practice Exercises 4

Create appropriate **x** and **y** arrays to use in plotting each of the expressions that follow. Use the **subplot** command to divide your figures into four sections, and create each of these four graphs for each expression:

- rectangular
- semilogx
- semilogy
- loglog

1. $y = 5x + 3$
2. $y = 3x^2$
3. $y = 12e^{(x+2)}$
4. $y = 1/x$

Physical data usually are plotted so that they fall on a straight line. Which of the preceding types of plot results in a straight line for each problem?

**Table 5  Bar Graphs and Pie Charts**

| | |
|---|---|
| **bar(x)** | When **x** is a vector, **bar** generates a vertical bar graph. When **x** is a two-dimensional matrix, **bar** groups the data by row. |
| **barh(x)** | When **x** is a vector, **barh** generates a horizontal bar graph. When **x** is a two-dimensional matrix, **barh** groups the data by row. |
| **bar3(x)** | Generates a three-dimensional bar chart |
| **bar3h(x)** | Generates a three-dimensional horizontal bar chart |
| **pie(x)** | Generates a pie chart. Each element in the matrix is represented as a slice of the pie. |
| **pie3(x)** | Generates a three-dimensional pie chart. Each element in the matrix is represented as a slice of the pie. |
| **hist(x)** | Generates a histogram |

### 3.3  Bar Graphs and Pie Charts

Bar graphs, histograms, and pie charts are popular forms for reporting data. Some of the commonly used MATLAB functions for creating bar graphs and pie charts are listed in Table 5.

Examples of some of these graphs are shown in Figure 19. The graphs make use of the **subplot** function to allow four plots in the same figure window:

```
clear, clc
x = [1,2,5,4,8];
y = [x;1:5];
subplot(2,2,1)
  bar(x),title('A bar graph of vector x')
subplot(2,2,2)
  bar(y),title('A bar graph of matrix y')
subplot(2,2,3)
  bar3(y),title('A three-dimensional bar graph')
subplot(2,2,4)
  pie(x),title('A pie chart of x')
```

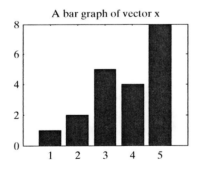

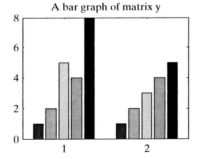

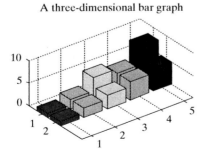

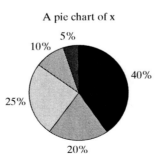

**Figure 19**
Sample bar graphs and pie charts. The **subplot** function was used to divide the window into quadrants.

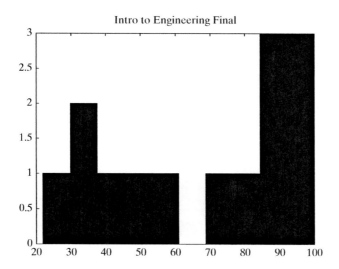

**Figure 20**
A histogram of grade data.

### 3.4 Histograms

KEY IDEA: Histograms are useful in statistical analysis

A histogram is a special type of graph that is particularly useful for the statistical analysis of data. It is a plot showing the distribution of a set of values. In MATLAB, the histogram computes the number of values falling into 10 bins (categories) that are equally spaced between the minimum and maximum values. For example, if we define a matrix **x** as the set of grades from the Introduction to Engineering final, the scores could be represented in a histogram, shown in Figure 20 and generated with the following code:

```
x = [100,95,74,87,22,78,34,35,93,88,86,42,55,48];
hist(x)
```

The default number of bins is 10, but if we have a large data set, we may want to divide the data up into more bins. For example, to create a histogram with 25 bins, the command would be

```
hist(x, 25)
```

If you set the **hist** function equal to a variable, as in

```
A = hist(x)
```

the data used in the plot are stored in **A**:

```
A =
    1   2   1   1   1   0   1   1   3   3
```

---

**EXAMPLE 4**

## Weight Distributions

The average 18-year-old American male weighs 152 pounds. A group of 100 young men were weighed and the data stored in a file called **weight.dat**. Create a graph to represent the data.

1. State the Problem
   Use the data file to create a line graph and a histogram. Which is a better representation of the data?

2. Describe the Input and Output

   ***Input***    **weight.dat**, an ASCII data file that contains weight data

   ***Output***  A line plot of the data
              A histogram of the data

3. Develop a Hand Example

   Since this is a sample of actual weights, we would expect the data to approximate a normal random distribution (a Gaussian distribution). The histogram should be bell shaped.

4. Develop a MATLAB Solution

   The following code generates the plots shown in Figure 21:

```
% Example 4
% Using Weight Data
%
load weight.dat
% Create the line plot of weight data
subplot(1,2,1)
plot(weight)
title('Weight of Freshman Class Men')
xlabel('Student Number')
ylabel('Weight, lb')
grid on
% Create the histogram of the data
subplot(1,2,2)
hist(weight)
xlabel('Weight, lb')
ylabel('Number of students')
title('Weight of Freshman Class Men')
```

5. Test the Solution

   The graphs match our expectations. The weight appears to average about 150 lb and varies in what looks like a normal distribution. We can use MATLAB to

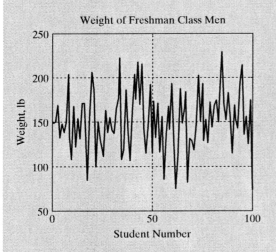
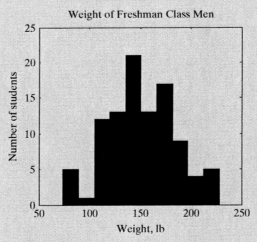

**Figure 21**
Histograms and line plots are two different ways to visualize numeric information.

find the average and the standard deviation of the data, as well as the maximum and minimum weights in the data set. The MATLAB code

```
average_weight    = mean(weight)
standard_deviation = std(weight)
maximum_weight    = max(weight)
minimum_weight    = min(weight)
```

returns

```
average_weight =
   151.1500
standard_deviation =
   32.9411
maximum_weight =
   228
minimum_weight =
   74
```

### 3.5  *X–Y* Graphs with Two *Y*-Axes

Sometimes it is useful to overlay two x–y plots onto the same figure. However, if the orders of magnitude of the y-values are quite different, it may be difficult to see how the data behave. Consider, for example, a graph of sin(x) and $e^x$ drawn on the same figure. The results, obtained with the following code, are shown in Figure 22:

```
x = 0:pi/20:2*pi;
y1 = sin(x);
y2 = exp(x);
subplot(2,1,1)
plot(x,y1,x,y2)
```

**Figure 22**
MATLAB allows the *y*-axis to be scaled differently on the left-hand and right-hand sides of the figure. In the top graph both lines were drawn using the same scaling. In the bottom graph the sine curve was drawn using the scaling on the left axis, while the exponential curve was drawn using the scaling on the right axis.

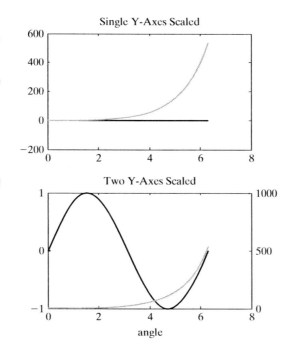

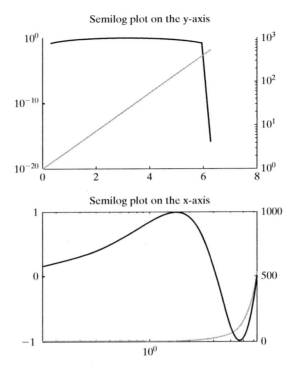

**Figure 23**
The **plotyy** function can generate several types of graphs, including semilogx, semilogy, and loglog.

The plot of sin(x) looks like it runs straight along the line x = 0, because of the scale. The **plotyy** function allows us to create a graph with two y-axes, the one on the left for the first set of ordered pairs and the one on the right for the second set of ordered pairs:

```
subplot(2,1,2)
plotyy(x,y1,x,y2)
```

Titles and labels were added in the usual way. The y-axis was not labeled, because the results are dimensionless.

The **plotyy** function can create a number of different types of plots by adding a string with the name of the plot type after the second set of ordered pairs. In Figure 23, the plots were created with the following code and have a logarithmically scaled axis:

```
subplot(2,1,1)
plotyy(x,y1,x,y2, 'semilogy')
subplot(2,1,2)
plotyy(x,y1,x,y2,'semilogx')
```

**EXAMPLE 5**

## Periodic Properties of the Elements

The properties of elements in the same row or column in the periodic table usually display a recognizable trend as we move across a row or down a column. For example, the melting point usually goes down as we move down a column, because the atoms are farther apart and the bonds between the atoms are therefore weaker. Similarly, the radius of the atoms goes up as we move down a column, because there are more electrons in each atom and correspondingly

**Table 6  Group I Elements and Selected Physical Properties**

| Element | Atomic Number | Melting Point, °C | Atomic Radius, pm |
|---------|---------------|-------------------|-------------------|
| Lithium | 3 | 181 | 0.1520 |
| Sodium | 11 | 98 | 0.1860 |
| Potassium | 19 | 63 | 0.2270 |
| Rubidium | 37 | 34 | 0.2480 |
| Cesium | 55 | 28.4 | 0.2650 |

bigger orbitals. It is instructive to plot these trends against atomic weight on the same graph.

1. State the Problem

    Plot the melting point and the atomic radius of the Group I elements against the atomic weight, and comment on the trends you observe.

2. Describe the Input and Output

    ***Input***    The atomic weights, melting points, and atomic radii of the Group I elements are listed in Table 6.

    ***Output***  Plot with both melting point and atomic radius on the same graph

3. Develop a Hand Example

    We would expect the graph to look something like the sketch shown in Figure 24.

4. Develop a MATLAB Solution

    The following code produces the plot shown in Figure 25:

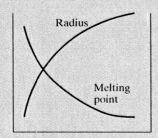

**Figure 24**
Sketch of the predicted data behavior.

```
% Example 5
clear, clc
% Define the variables
atomic_number = [ 3, 11, 19, 37, 55];
melting_point = [181, 98, 63, 34, 28.4];
atomic_radius = [0.152, 0.186, 0.227, 0.2480, 0.2650];
% Create the plot with two lines on the same scale
subplot(1,2,1)
plot(atomic_number,melting_point,atomic_number,atomic_radius)
title('Periodic Properties')
xlabel('Atomic Number')
ylabel('Properties')
% Create the second plot with two different y scales
subplot(1,2,2)
plotyy(atomic_number,melting_point,atomic_number,atomic_radius)
title('Periodic Properties')
xlabel('Atomic Number')
ylabel('Melting Point, C')
```

On the second graph, which has two different *y* scales, we used the **plotyy** function instead of the **plot** function. This forced the addition of a second scale, on the right-hand side of the plot. We needed it because atomic radius and melting point have different units and the values for each have different magnitudes. Notice that in the first plot it is almost impossible to see the atomic-radius line; it

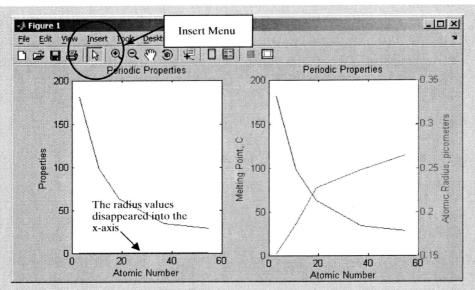

**Figure 25**
In the left-hand figure the two sets of values were plotted using the same scale. Using two y-axes allows us to plot data with different units on the same graph, as shown in the right-hand figure.

is on top of the *x*-axis because the numbers are so small. It's possible, but difficult, to add the right-hand *y*-axis label from the command line. Instead, we used the **Insert** option from the menu bar. Just remember, if you rerun your program, you'll lose the right-hand label.

5. Test the Solution
   Compare the MATLAB results with those from the hand example. The trend matches our prediction. Clearly, the graph with two *y*-axes is the superior representation, because we can see the property trends.

## 3.6 Function Plots

The **fplot** function allows you to plot a function without defining arrays of corresponding *x*- and *y*-values. For example,

```
fplot('sin(x)',[-2*pi,2*pi])
```

creates a plot (Figure 26) of *x* versus sin(*x*) for *x*-values from $-2\pi$ to $2\pi$. MATLAB automatically calculates the spacing of *x*-values to create a smooth curve. Notice that the first argument in the **fplot** function is a string containing the function and the second argument is an array. For more complicated functions that may be inconvenient to enter as a string, you may define an anonymous function and enter the function handle.

---

### Practice Exercises 5

Create a plot of the functions that follow, using **fplot**. You'll need to select an appropriate range for each plot. Don't forget to title and label your graphs.

1. $f(t) = 5t^2$
2. $f(t) = 5\sin^2(t) + t\cos^2(t)$
3. $f(t) = te^t$
4. $f(t) = \ln(t) + \sin(t)$

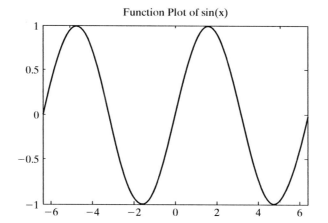

Function Plot of sin(x)

**Figure 26**
Function plots do not require the user to define arrays of ordered pairs.

**Hint**

The correct MATLAB syntax for the mathematical expression $\sin^2(t)$ is **sin(t).^2.**

## 4 THREE-DIMENSIONAL PLOTTING

MATLAB offers a variety of three-dimensional plotting commands, several of which are listed in Table 7.

### 4.1 Three-Dimensional Line Plot

The **plot3** function is similar to the **plot** function, except that it accepts data in three dimensions. Instead of just providing **x** and **y** vectors, the user must also provide a **z** vector. These ordered triples are then plotted in three-space and connected with straight lines. For example

```
clear, clc
x = linspace(0,10*pi,1000);
y = cos(x);
```

### Table 7 Three-Dimensional Plots

| | |
|---|---|
| **plot3(x,y,z)** | Creates a three-dimensional line plot |
| **comet3(x,y,z)** | Generates an animated version of **plot3** |
| **mesh(z) or mesh(x,y,z)** | Creates a meshed surface plot |
| **surf(z) or surf(x,y,z)** | Creates a surface plot; similar to the mesh function |
| **shading interp** | Interpolates between the colors used to illustrate surface plots |
| **shading flat** | Colors each grid section with a solid color |
| **colormap(map_name)** | Allows the user to select the color pattern used on surface plots |
| **contour(z) or contour(x,y,z)** | Generates a contour plot |
| **surfc(z) or surfc(x,y,z)** | Creates a combined surface plot and contour plot |
| **pcolor(z) or pcolor(x,y,z)** | Creates a pseudo color plot |

```
z = sin(x);
plot3(x,y,z)
grid
xlabel('angle'), ylabel('cos(x)') zlabel('sin(x)') title('A Spring')
```

The title, labels, and grid are added to the graph in Figure 27 in the usual way, with the addition of **zlabel** for the $z$-axis.

The coordinate system used with **plot3** is oriented using the right-handed coordinate system familiar to engineers.

**KEY IDEA:** The axes used for three-dimensional plotting correspond to the right-hand rule

---

**Hint**

Just for fun, re-create the plot shown in Figure 27, but this time with the **comet3** function:

```
comet3(x,y,z)
```

This plotting function "draws" the graph in an animation sequence. If your animation runs too quickly, add more data points. For two-dimensional line graphs, use the **comet** function.

---

## 4.2 Surface Plots

Surface plots allow us to represent data as a surface. We will be experimenting with two types of surface plots: **mesh** plots and **surf** plots.

### Mesh Plots

There are several ways to use **mesh** plots. They can be used to good effect with a single two-dimensional $m \times n$ matrix. In this application, the value in the matrix represents the **z**-value in the plot. The **x-** and **y**-values are based on the matrix dimensions. Take, for example, the following very simple matrix:

```
z = [1,  2,  3,  4,  5,  6,  7,  8,  9,  10;
     2,  4,  6,  8, 10, 12, 14, 16, 18,  20;
     3,  4,  5,  6,  7,  8,  9, 10, 11,  12];
```

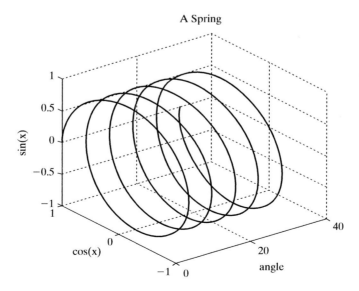

**Figure 27**
A three-dimensional plot of a spring. MATLAB uses a coordinate system consistent with the right-hand rule.

The code

```
mesh(z)
xlabel('x-axis')
ylabel('y-axis')
zlabel('z-axis')
```

generates the graph in Figure 28.

The graph is a "mesh" created by connecting the points defined in **z** into a rectilinear grid. Notice that the x-axis goes from 0 to 10 and y goes from 0 to 3. The matrix index numbers were used for the axis values. For example, note that $z_{1,5}$—the value of z in row 1, column 5—is equal to 5. This element is circled in Figure 28.

The **mesh** function can also be used with three arguments: **mesh(x,y,z)**. In this case, **x** is a list of x-coordinates, **y** is a list of y-coordinates, and **z** is a list of z-coordinates.

```
x = linspace(1,50,10)
y = linspace(500,1000,3)
z = [1,  2,  3,  4,  5,  6,  7,  8,  9, 10;
     2,  4,  6,  8, 10, 12, 14, 16, 18, 20;
     3,  4,  5,  6,  7,  8,  9, 10, 11, 12]
```

The **x** vector must have the same number of elements as the number of columns in the **z** vector; the **y** vector must have the same number of elements as the number of rows in the **z** vector. The command

```
mesh(x,y,z)
```

creates the plot in Figure 29a. Notice that the x-axis varies from 0 to 60, with data plotted from 1 to 50. Compare this scaling with that in Figure 28, which used the **z** matrix index numbers for the x- and y-axes.

### Surf Plots

Surf plots are similar to **mesh** plots, but **surf** creates a three-dimensional colored surface instead of a mesh. The colors vary with the value of **z**.

The **surf** command takes the same input as **mesh**: either a single input—for example, **surf(z)**, in which case it uses the row and column indices as x- and y-coordinates—or three matrices. Figure 29b was generated with the same commands as those used to generate Figure 29a, except that **surf** replaced **mesh**.

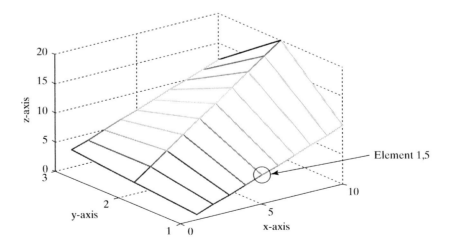

**Figure 28**
Simple mesh created with a single two-dimensional matrix.

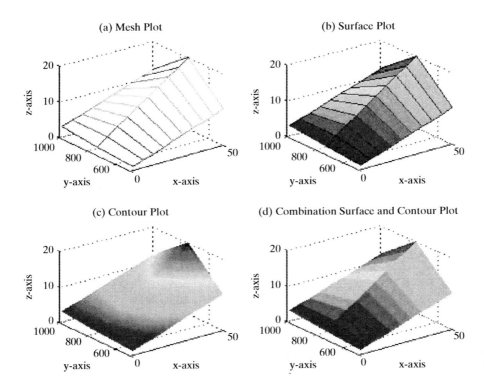

**Figure 29**
Mesh and surf plots created with three input arguments.

The shading scheme for surface plots is controlled with the shading command. The default, shown in Figure 29b, is "faceted flat." Interpolated shading can create interesting effects. The plot shown in Figure 29c was created by adding

    **shading interp**

to the previous list of commands. Flat shading without the grid is generated when

    **shading flat**

is used, as shown in Figure 29d.

The color scheme used in surface plots can be controlled with the **colormap** function. For example,

    **colormap(gray)**

forces a grayscale representation for surface plots. This may be appropriate if you'll be making black-and-white copies of your plots. Other available **colormaps** are

KEY IDEA: The colormap function controls the colors used on surface plots

| | | |
|---|---|---|
| **autumn** | **bone** | **hot** |
| **spring** | **colorcube** | **hsv** |
| **summer** | **cool** | **pink** |
| **winter** | **copper** | **prism** |
| **jet (default)** | **flag** | **white** |

Use the **help** command to see a description of the various options:

    **help colormap**

### Another Example

A more complicated surface can be created by calculating the values of **Z**:

```
x= [-2:0.2:2];
y= [-2:0.2:2];
[X,Y] = meshgrid(x,y);
Z = X.*exp(-X.^2 - Y.^2);
```

In the preceding code, the **meshgrid** function is used to create the two-dimensional matrices **X** and **Y** from the one-dimensional vectors **x** and **y**. The values in **Z** are then calculated. The following code plots the calculated values:

```
subplot(2,2,1)
mesh(X,Y,Z)
title('Mesh Plot'), xlabel('x-axis'), ylabel('y-axis'),
zlabel('z-axis')

subplot(2,2,2)
surf(X,Y,Z)
title('Surface Plot'), xlabel('x-axis'), ylabel('y-axis'),
zlabel('z-axis')
```

Either the **x**, **y** vectors or the **X**, **Y** matrices can be used to define the *x*- and *y*-axes. Figure 30a is a **mesh** plot of the given function, and Figure 30b is a **surf** plot of the same function.

---

**Hint**

If a single vector is used in the **meshgrid** function, the program interprets it as

```
[X,Y] = meshgrid(x,x)
```

You could also use the vector definition as input to **meshgrid**:

```
[X,Y] = meshgrid(-2:0.2:2)
```

Both of these lines of code would produce the same result as the commands listed in the example.

---

### Contour Plots

Contour plots are two-dimensional representations of three-dimensional surfaces. The **contour** command was used to create Figure 30c, and the **surfc** command was used to create Figure 30d:

```
subplot(2,2,3)
contour(X,Y,Z)

xlabel('x-axis'), ylabel('y-axis'), title('Contour Plot')
subplot(2,2,4)
surfc(X,Y,Z)
xlabel('x-axis'), ylabel('y-axis')
title('Combination Surface and Contour Plot')
```

### Pseudo Color Plots

Pseudo color plots are similar to contour plots, except that instead of lines outlining a specific contour, a two-dimensional shaded map is generated over a grid. MATLAB

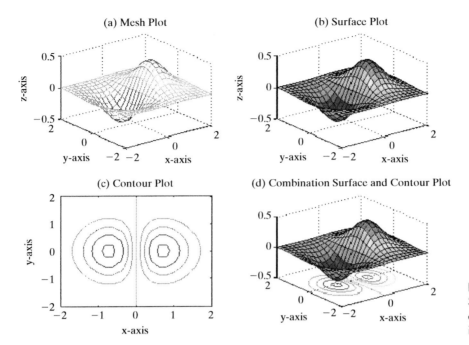

**Figure 30**
Surface and contour plots are different ways of visualizing the same data.

includes a sample function called **peaks** that generates the **x**, **y**, and **z** matrices of an interesting surface that looks like a mountain range:

```
[x,y,z] = peaks;
```

With the following code, we can use this surface to demonstrate the use of pseudo color plots, shown in Figure 31:

```
subplot(2,2,1)
pcolor(x,y,z)
```

The grid is deleted when interpolated shading is used:

```
subplot(2,2,2)
pcolor(x,y,z)
shading interp
```

You can add contours to the image by overlaying a contour plot:

```
subplot(2,2,3)
pcolor(x,y,z)
shading interp
hold on
contour(x,y,z,20,'k')
```

The number **20** specifies that 20 contour lines are drawn, and the **'k'** indicates that the lines should be black. If we hadn't specified black lines, they would have been the same color as the pseudo color plot and would have disappeared into the image. Finally, a simple contour plot was added to the figure for comparison:

```
subplot(2,2,4)
contour(x,y,z)
```

Additional options for using all the three-dimensional plotting functions are included in the help window.

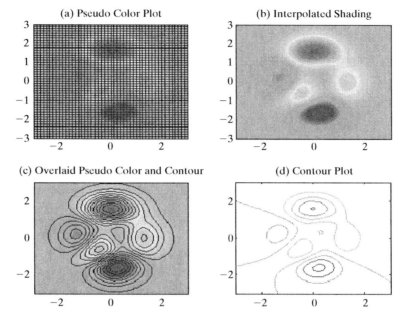

**Figure 31**
A variety of contour plots is available in MATLAB.

## 5  EDITING PLOTS FROM THE MENU BAR

KEY IDEA: When you interactively edit a plot, your changes will be lost if you rerun the program

In addition to controlling the way your plots look by using MATLAB commands, you can edit a plot once you've created it. The plot in Figure 32 was created with the **sphere** command, which is one of several sample functions, like **peaks**, used to demonstrate plotting.

```
sphere
```

In the figure, the **Insert menu** has been selected. Notice that you can insert labels, titles, legends, text boxes, and so on, all by using this menu. The **Tools menu** allows you to change the way the plot looks, by zooming in or out, changing the aspect ratio, etc. The figure toolbar, underneath the menu toolbar, offers icons that allow you to do the same thing.

The plot in Figure 32 doesn't really look like a sphere; it's also missing labels and a title, and the meaning of the colors may not be clear. We edited this plot by first adjusting the shape:

- Select **Edit** ➡ **Axis Properties** from the menu toolbar.
- From the **Property Editor – Axis window**, select More Properties ➡ **Data Aspect Ratio Mode**.
- Set the mode to manual. (See Figure 33).

Similarly, labels, a title, and a color bar were added (Figure 34) using the Property Editor. They could also have been added by using **the Insert menu** option on the menu bar. Editing your plot in this manner is more interactive and allows you to fine-tune the plot's appearance. The only problem with editing a figure interactively is that if you run your MATLAB program again, you will lose all of your improvements.

---

### Hint

You can force a plot to space the data equally on all the axes by using the **axis equal** command. This approach has the advantage that you can program **axis equal** into an M-file and retain your improvements.

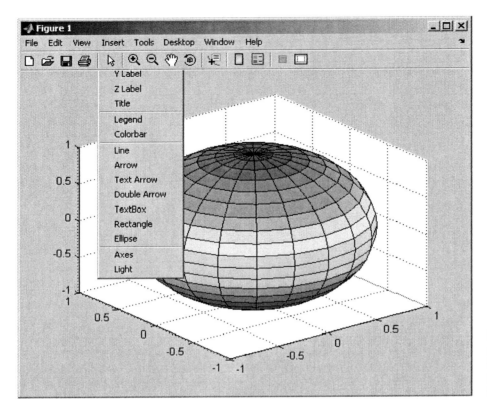

**Figure 32**
MATLAB offers interactive tools, such as the insert tool, that allow the user to adjust the appearance of graphs.

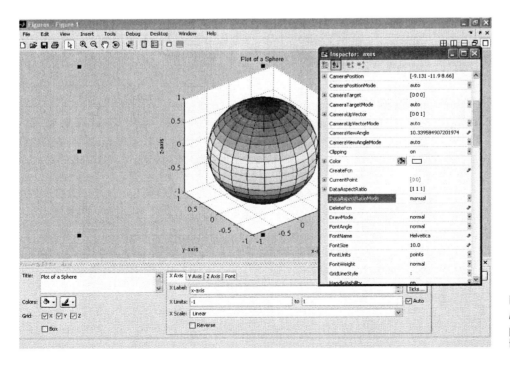

**Figure 33**
MATLAB allows you to edit plots by using commands from the toolbar.

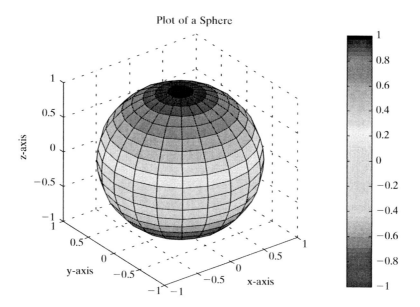

**Figure 34**
Edited plot of a sphere.

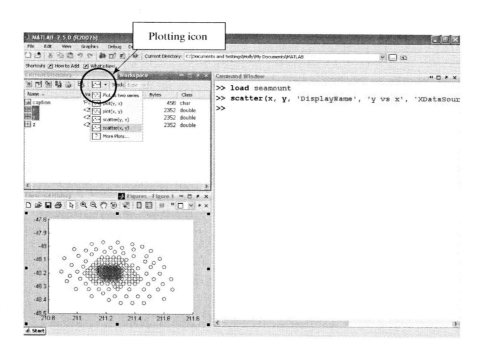

**Figure 35**
Plotting from the workspace window, using the interactive plotting feature.

## 6  CREATING PLOTS FROM THE WORKSPACE WINDOW

A great feature of MATLAB 7 is its ability to create plots interactively from the workspace window. In this window, select a variable, then select the drop-down menu on the **plotting icon** (shown in Figure 35). MATLAB will list the plotting options it "thinks" are reasonable for the data stored in your variable. Simply select the appropriate option, and your plot is created in the current **figure window**. If you don't like any of the suggested types of plot, choose **More plots...** from the drop-down menu, and a new window will open with the complete list of available plotting options for you to choose from. This is especially useful, because it may suggest options that had not occurred to you. For example, Figure 35 shows a scatter plot of the **x and y** matrices highlighted in the figure. The matrices were created by loading the seamount data set, which is built into MATLAB.

If you want to plot more than one variable, highlight the first, then hold down the *Ctrl* key and select the additional variables. To annotate your plots, use the interactive editing process described in Section 5. The interactive environment is a rich resource. You'll get the most out of it by exploring and experimenting.

## 7 SAVING YOUR PLOTS

There are several ways to save plots created in MATLAB:

- If you created the plot with programming code stored in an M-file, simply rerunning the code will re-create the figure.
- You can also save the figure from the file menu, using the **Save As...** option. You'll be presented with several choices:

  1. You may save the figure as a **.fig** file, which is a MATLAB-specific file format. To retrieve the figure, just double-click on the file name in the current directory.
  2. You may save the figure in a number of different standard graphics formats, such as jpeg (**.jpg**) and enhanced metafile (**.emf**). These versions of the figure can be inserted into other documents, such as a Word document.
  3. You can select Edit from the menu bar, then select **copy figure**, and paste the figure into another document.
  4. You can use the file menu to create an M-file that will re-create the figure.

---

**Practice Exercises 6**

Create a plot of $y = \cos(x)$. Practice saving the file and inserting it into a Word document.

---

**SUMMARY**

The most commonly used graph in engineering is the $x$–$y$ plot. This two-dimensional plot can be used to graph data or to visualize mathematical functions. No matter what a graph represents, it should always include a title and $x$- and $y$-axis labels. Axis labels should be descriptive and should include units, such as ft/s or kJ/kg.

MATLAB includes extensive options for controlling the appearance of your plots. The user can specify the color, line style, and marker style for each line on a graph. A grid can be added to the graph, and the axis range can be adjusted. Text boxes and a legend can be employed to describe the graph. The subplot function is used to divide the plot window into an $m \times n$ grid. Inside each of these subwindows, any of the MATLAB plots can be created and modified.

In addition to $x$–$y$ plots, MATLAB offers a variety of plotting options, including polar plots, pie charts, bar graphs, histograms, and $x$–$y$ graphs with two $y$-axes. The scaling on $x$–$y$ plots can be modified to produce logarithmic plots on either or both $x$- and $y$-axes. Engineers often use logarithmic scaling to represent data as a straight line.

The function **fplot** allows the user to plot a function without defining a vector of $x$- and $y$-values. MATLAB automatically chooses the appropriate number of points and spacing to produce a smooth graph. Additional function-plotting capability is available in the symbolic toolbox.

The three-dimensional plotting options in MATLAB include a line plot, a number of surface plots, and contour plots. Most of the options available in two-dimensional plotting also apply to these three-dimensional plots. The **meshgrid** function is especially useful in creating three-dimensional surface plots.

Interactive tools allow the user to modify existing plots. These tools are available from the figure menu bar. Plots can also be created with the interactive plotting option from the workspace window. The interactive environment is a rich resource. You'll get the most out of it by exploring and experimenting.

Figures created in MATLAB can be saved in a variety of ways, either to be edited later or to be inserted into other documents. MATLAB offers both proprietary file formats that minimize the storage space required to store figures and standard file formats suitable to import into other applications.

**MATLAB SUMMARY**   The following MATLAB summary lists all the special characters, commands, and functions that were defined in this chapter:

**Special Characters**

| Line Type | Indicator | Point Type | Indicator | Color | Indicator |
|-----------|-----------|------------|-----------|-------|-----------|
| solid | - | point | . | blue | **b** |
| dotted | : | circle | **o** | green | **g** |
| dash-dot | -. | x-mark | **x** | red | **r** |
| dashed | -- | plus | + | cyan | **c** |
| | | star | * | magenta | **m** |
| | | square | **s** | yellow | **y** |
| | | diamond | **d** | black | **k** |
| | | triangle down | **v** | white | **w** |
| | | triangle up | ∧ | | |
| | | triangle left | < | | |
| | | triangle right | > | | |
| | | pentagram | **p** | | |
| | | hexagram | **h** | | |

**Commands and Functions**

| | |
|---|---|
| **autumn** | optional colormap used in surface plots |
| **axis** | freezes the current axis scaling for subsequent plots or specifies the axis dimensions |
| **axis equal** | forces the same scale spacing for each axis |
| **bar** | generates a bar graph |
| **bar3** | generates a three-dimensional bar graph |
| **barh** | generates a horizontal bar graph |
| **bar3h** | generates a horizontal three-dimensional bar graph |
| **bone** | optional colormap used in surface plots |
| **colorcube** | optional colormap used in surface plots |

## Commands and Functions (Continued)

| | |
|---|---|
| **colormap** | color scheme used in surface plots |
| **comet** | draws an *x–y* plot in a pseudo animation sequence |
| **comet3** | draws a three-dimensional line plot in a pseudo animation sequence |
| **contour** | generates a contour map of a three-dimensional surface |
| **cool** | optional colormap used in surface plots |
| **copper** | optional colormap used in surface plots |
| **figure** | opens a new figure window |
| **flag** | optional colormap used in surface plots |
| **fplot** | creates an *x–y* plot based on a function |
| **gtext** | similar to text; the box is placed at a location determined interactively by the user by clicking in the figure window |
| **grid** | adds a grid to the current plot only |
| **grid off** | turns the grid off |
| **grid on** | adds a grid to the current and all subsequent graphs in the current figure |
| **hist** | generates a histogram |
| **hold off** | instructs MATLAB **to** erase figure contents before adding new information |
| **hold on** | instructs MATLAB **not to** erase figure contents before adding new information |
| **hot** | optional colormap used in surface plots |
| **hsv** | optional colormap used in surface plots |
| **jet** | default colormap used in surface plots |
| **legend** | adds a legend to a graph |
| **linspace** | creates a linearly spaced vector |
| **loglog** | generates an *x–y* plot with both axes scaled logarithmically |
| **mesh** | generates a mesh plot of a surface |
| **meshgrid** | places each of two vectors into separate two-dimensional matrices, the size of which is determined by the source vectors |
| **pause** | pauses the execution of a program until any key is hit |
| **pcolor** | creates a pseudo color plot similar to a contour map |
| **peaks** | creates a sample matrix used to demonstrate graphing functions |
| **pie** | generates a pie chart |
| **pie3** | generates a three-dimensional pie chart |
| **pink** | optional colormap used in surface plots |
| **plot** | creates an *x–y* plot |
| **plot3** | generates a three-dimensional line plot |
| **plotyy** | creates a plot with two *y*-axes |
| **polar** | creates a polar plot |
| **prism** | optional colormap used in surface plots |
| **semilogx** | generates an *x–y* plot with the *x*-axis scaled logarithmically |
| **semilogy** | generates an *x–y* plot with the *y*-axis scaled logarithmically |
| **shading flat** | shades a surface plot with one color per grid section |
| **shading interp** | shades a surface plot by interpolation |
| **sphere** | sample function used to demonstrate graphing |

*(Continued)*

| Commands and Functions (Continued) | |
| --- | --- |
| spring | optional colormap used in surface plots |
| subplot | divides the graphics window into sections available for plotting |
| summer | optional colormap used in surface plots |
| surf | generates a surface plot |
| surfc | generates a combination surface and contour plot |
| text | adds a text box to a graph |
| title | adds a title to a plot |
| white | optional colormap used in surface plots |
| winter | optional colormap used in surface plots |
| xlabel | adds a label to the $x$-axis |
| ylabel | adds a label to the $y$-axis |
| zlabel | adds a label to the $z$-axis |

## PROBLEMS

### Two-Dimensional (x–y) Plots

**1** Create plots of the following functions from $x = 0$ to 10.

(a) $y = e^x$
(b) $y = \sin(x)$
(c) $y = ax^2 + bx + c$, where $a = 5$, $b = 2$, and $c = 4$
(d) $y = \sqrt{x}$

Each of your plots should include a title, an $x$-axis label, a $y$-axis label, and a grid.

**2** Plot the following set of data:

$$y = [12, 14, 12, 22, 8, 9]$$

Allow MATLAB to use the matrix index number as the parameter for the $x$-axis.

**3** Plot the following functions on the same graph for $x$ values from $-\pi$ to $\pi$, selecting spacing to create a smooth plot:

$$y_1 = \sin(x)$$
$$y_2 = \sin(2x)$$
$$y_3 = \sin(3x)$$

(*Hint*: Recall that the appropriate MATLAB syntax for $2x$ is **2 * x**.)

**4** Adjust the plot created in Problem 3 so that

- line 1 is red and dashed.
- line 2 is blue and solid.
- line 3 is green and dotted.

Do not include markers on any of the graphs. In general, markers are included only on plots of measured data, not for calculated values.

**5** Adjust the plot created in Problem 4 so that the $x$-axis goes from $-6$ to $+6$.

- Add a legend.
- Add a text box describing the plots.

### *x–y* Plotting with Projectiles

Use the following information in Problems 6 through 10:

The distance a projectile travels when fired at an angle $\theta$ is a function of time and can be divided into horizontal and vertical distances according to the formulas

$$\text{horizontal}(t) = tV_0 \cos(\theta)$$

and

$$\text{vertical}(t) = tV_0 \sin(\theta) - \tfrac{1}{2}gt^2$$

where

| | |
|---|---|
| horizontal | = distance traveled in the $x$ direction, |
| vertical | = distance traveled in the $y$ direction, |
| $V_0$ | = initial velocity, |
| $g$ | = acceleration due to gravity, 9.8 m/s$^2$, |
| $t$ | = time, s. |

**6** Suppose the projectile just described is fired at an initial velocity of 100 m/s and a launch angle of $\pi/4$ (45°). Find the distance traveled both horizontally and vertically (in the $x$ and $y$ directions) for times from 0 to 20 s with a spacing of .01 seconds.

   **(a)** Graph horizontal distance versus time.

   **(b)** In a new figure window, plot vertical distance versus time (with time on the $x$-axis).

   Don't forget a title and labels.

**7** In a new figure window, plot horizontal distance on the $x$-axis and vertical distance on the $y$-axis.

**8** Replot horizontal distance on the $x$-axis and vertical distance on the $y$-axis using the comet function. If the plot draws too quickly or too slowly on your computer, adjust the number of time values used in your calculations.

**9** Calculate three new vectors for each of the vertical ($v_1$, $v_2$, $v_3$) and horizontal ($h_1$, $h_2$, $h_3$) distances traveled, assuming launch angles of $\pi/2$, $\pi/4$, and $\pi/6$.

   • In a new figure window, graph horizontal distance on the $x$-axis and vertical distance on the $y$-axis, for all three cases. (You'll have three lines.)
   • Make one line solid, one dashed, and one dotted. Add a legend to identify which line is which.

**10** Re-create the plot from Problem 9. This time, create a matrix **theta** of the three angles, $\pi/2$, $\pi/4$, and $\pi/6$. Use the **meshgrid** function to create a mesh of **theta** and the time vector (**t**). Then use the two new meshed variables you create to recalculate vertical distance (**v**) and horizontal distance (**h**) traveled. Each of your results should be a 2001 × 3 matrix. Use the **plot** command to plot **h** on the $x$-axis and **v** on the $y$-axis.

**11** A tensile testing machine such as the one shown in Figures P11a and P11b is used to determine the behavior of materials as they are deformed. In the typical test a specimen is stretched at a steady rate. The force (load) required to deform the material is measured, as is the resulting deformation.

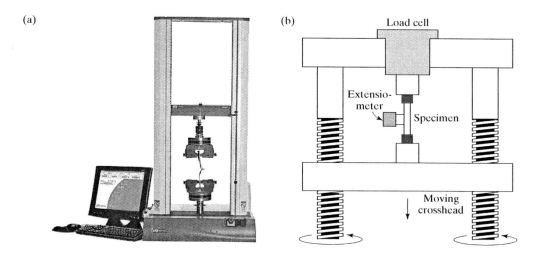

**Figure P11a**   A tensile testing machine is used to measure stress and strain and to characterize the behavior of materials as they are deformed. (Photo courtesy of Instron®.)

**Table P11  Tensile Testing Data**
(From William Callister, *Materials Science and Engineering, An Introduction,* 5th ed., p. 149.)

| load, lbf | length, inches |
|---|---|
| 0 | 2 |
| 1650 | 2.002 |
| 3400 | 2.004 |
| 5200 | 2.006 |
| 6850 | 2.008 |
| 7750 | 2.010 |
| 8650 | 2.020 |
| 9300 | 2.040 |
| 10100 | 2.080 |
| 10400 | 2.120 |

An example set of data measured in one such test is shown in Table P11. These data can be used to calculate the applied stress and the resulting strain with the following equations.

$$\sigma = \frac{F}{A} \quad \text{and} \quad \varepsilon = \frac{l - l_0}{l_0}$$

where

$\sigma$ is the stress in $lb_f/in.^2$   (psi)

$F$ is the applied force in $lb_f$

$A$ is the sample cross sectional area in in.$^2$

$\varepsilon$ is the strain in in./in.

$l$ is the sample length

$l_0$ is the original sample length

(a) Use the provided data to calculate the stress and the corresponding strain for each data pair. The tested sample was a rod of diameter 0.505 in., so you'll need to find the cross sectional area to use in your calculations.

(b) Create an $x$–$y$ plot with strain on the $x$-axis and stress on the $y$-axis. Connect the data points with a solid black line, and use circles to mark each data point.

(c) Add a title and appropriate axis labels.

(d) The point where the graph changes from a straight line with a steep slope to a flattened curve is called the yield stress or yield point. This corresponds to a significant change in the material behavior. Before the yield point the material is elastic, returning to its original shape if the load is removed—much like a rubber band. Once the material has been deformed past the yield point, the change in shape becomes permanent and is called plastic deformation. Use a text box to mark the yield point on your graph.

## Using Subplots

12    In Problem 1, you created four plots. Combine these into one figure with four subwindows, using the **subplot** function of MATLAB.

13    In Problems 6, 7 and 9, you created a total of four plots. Combine these into one figure with four subwindows, using the **subplot** function of MATLAB.

## Polar Plots

14    Create a vector of angles from 0 to $2\pi$. Use the **polar** plotting function to create graphs of the functions that follow. Remember, polar plots expect the angle and the radius as the two inputs to the **polar** function. Use the **subplot** function to put all four of your graphs in the same figure.

(a) $r = \sin^2(\theta) + \cos^2(\theta)$

(b) $r = \sin(\theta)$

(c) $r = e^{\theta/5}$

(d) $r = \sinh(\theta)$

15    In Practice Exercises 3, you created a number of interesting shapes in polar coordinates. Use those exercises as a help in creating the following figures:

(a) Create a "flower" with three petals.

(b) Overlay your figure with eight additional petals half the size of the three original ones.

(c) Create a heart shape.

(d) Create a six-pointed star.

(e) Create a hexagon.

### Logarithmic Plots

**16** When interest is compounded continuously, the following equation represents the growth of your savings:

$$P = P_0 e^{rt}$$

In this equation,

$P$ = current balance,

$P_0$ = initial balance,

$r$ = growth constant, expressed as a decimal fraction, and

$t$ = time invested.

Determine the amount in your account at the end of each year if you invest $1000 at 8% (0.08) for 30 years. (Make a table.)

Create a figure with four subplots. Plot time on the $x$-axis and current balance $P$ on the $y$-axis.

**(a)** In the first quadrant, plot $t$ versus $P$ in a rectangular coordinate system.
**(b)** In the second quadrant, plot $t$ versus $P$, scaling the $x$-axis logarithmically.
**(c)** In the third quadrant, plot $t$ versus $P$, scaling the $y$-axis logarithmically.
**(d)** In the fourth quadrant, plot $t$ versus $P$, scaling both axes logarithmically.

Which of the four plotting techniques do you think displays the data best?

**Figure P17**
Gordon Moore, a pioneer of the semiconductor industry. (Copyright © 2005 Intel Corporation.)

**17** According to Moore's law (an observation made in 1965 by Gordon Moore, a cofounder of Intel Corporation; see Figure P17), the number of transistors that would fit per square inch on a semiconductor integrated circuit doubles approximately every two years. Although Moore's law is often reported as predicting doubling every 18 months, this is incorrect. A colleague of Moore's took into account the fact that transistor performance is also improving, and when combined with the increased number of transistors results in doubling of *performance* every 18 months. The year 2005 was the fortieth anniversary of the law. Over the last 40 years, Moore's projection has been consistently met. In 1965, the then state-of-the-art technology allowed for 30 transistors per square inch. Moore's law says that transistor density can be predicted by $d(t) = 30\,(2^{t/2})$, where $t$ is measured in years.

**(a)** Letting $t = 0$ represent the year 1965 and $t = 45$ represent 2010, use this model to calculate the predicted number of transistors per square inch for the 45 years from 1965 to 2010. Let $t$ increase in increments of two years. Display the results in a table with two columns—one for the year and one for the number of transistors.
**(b)** Using the **subplot** feature, plot the data in a linear $x$–$y$ plot, a semilog $x$ plot, a semilog $y$ plot and a log–log plot. Be sure to title the plots and label the axes.

**18** The total number of transistor count on integrated circuits produced over the last 35 years is shown in Table P18. Create a semilog plot (with the $y$-axis scaled logarithmically) of the actual data, using circles only to indicate the data points (no lines). Include a second line representing the predicted values using Moore's law, based on the 1971 count as the starting point. Add a legend to your plot.

**19** Many physical phenomena can be described by the Arrhenius equation. For example, reaction-rate constants for chemical reactions are modeled as

$$k = k_0 e^{(-Q/RT)}$$

**Table P18 Exponential Increase in Transistor Count on Integrated Circuits***

| Processor | Transistor Count | Date of Introduction | Manufacturer |
|---|---|---|---|
| Intel 4004 | 2300 | 1971 | Intel |
| Intel 8008 | 2500 | 1972 | Intel |
| Intel 8080 | 4500 | 1974 | Intel |
| Intel 8088 | 29000 | 1979 | Intel |
| Intel 80286 | 134000 | 1982 | Intel |
| Intel 80386 | 275000 | 1985 | Intel |
| Intel 80486 | 1200000 | 1989 | Intel |
| Pentium | 3100000 | 1993 | Intel |
| AMD K5 | 4300000 | 1996 | AMD |
| Pentium II | 7500000 | 1997 | Intel |
| AMD K6 | 8800000 | 1997 | AMD |
| Pentium III | 9500000 | 1999 | Intel |
| AMD K6-III | 21300000 | 1999 | AMD |
| AMD K7 | 22000000 | 1999 | AMD |
| Pentium 4 | 42000000 | 2000 | Intel |
| Barton | 54300000 | 2003 | AMD |
| AMD K8 | 105900000 | 2003 | AMD |
| Itanium 2 | 220000000 | 2003 | Intel |
| Itanium 2 with 9MB cache | 592000000 | 2004 | Intel |
| Cell | 241000000 | 2006 | Sony/IBM/Toshiba |
| Core 2 Duo | 291000000 | 2006 | Intel |
| Core 2 Quad | 582000000 | 2006 | Intel |
| G80 | 681000000 | 2006 | NVIDIA |
| POWER6 | 789000000 | 2007 | IBM |
| Dual-Core Itanium 2 | 1700000000 | 2006 | Intel |
| Quad-Core Itanium Tukwila (processor)[1] | 2000000000 | 2008 | Intel |

*Data from *Wikipedia*, http://en.wikipedia.org/wiki/Transistor_count.

where

$k_0$ = constant with units that depend upon the reaction,

$Q$ = activation energy, kJ/kmol,

$R$ = ideal gas constant, kJ/kmol K, and

$T$ = temperature in K.

For a certain chemical reaction, the values of the constants are

$$Q = 1000 \text{ J/mol},$$

$$k_0 = 10 \text{ sec}^{-1}, \text{ and}$$

$$R = 8.314 \text{ J/mol K},$$

for $T$ from 300 K to 1000 K. Find the values of $k$. Create the following two graphs of your data in a single figure window:

**(a)** Plot $T$ on the $x$-axis and $k$ on the $y$-axis.

**(b)** Plot your results as the $\log_{10}$ of $k$ on the $y$-axis and $1/T$ on the $x$-axis.

## Bar Graphs, Pie Charts, and Histograms

**20** Let the vector

$$G = [68, 83, 61, 70, 75, 82, 57, 5, 76, 85, 62, 71, 96, 78, 76, 68, 72, 75, 83, 93]$$

represent the distribution of final grades in an engineering course.

**(a)** Use MATLAB to sort the data and create a bar graph of the scores.

**(b)** Create a histogram of the scores.

**21** In the engineering class mentioned in Problem 20, there are

2 A's

4 B's

8 C's

4 D's

2 E's

**(a)** Create a vector of the grade distribution

$$\text{grades} = [2, 4, 8, 4, 2]$$

Create a pie chart of the grades vector. Add a legend listing the grade names (A, B, C, etc.)

**(b)** Use the **menu** text option instead of a legend to add a text box to each slice of pie, and save your modified graph as a **.fig** file.

**(c)** Create a three-dimensional pie chart of the same data. MATLAB has trouble with legends for many three-dimensional figures, so don't be surprised if your legend doesn't match the pie chart.

**22** The inventory of a certain type of screw in a warehouse at the end of each month is listed in the following table:

|            | 2004 | 2005 |
|------------|------|------|
| **January**   | 2345 | 2343 |
| **February**  | 4363 | 5766 |
| **March**     | 3212 | 4534 |
| **April**     | 4565 | 4719 |
| **May**       | 8776 | 3422 |
| **June**      | 7679 | 2200 |
| **July**      | 6532 | 3454 |
| **August**    | 2376 | 7865 |
| **September** | 2238 | 6543 |
| **October**   | 4509 | 4508 |
| **November**  | 5643 | 2312 |
| **December**  | 1137 | 4566 |

Plot the data in a bar graph.

**23** Use the **randn** function to create 1000 values in a normal (Gaussian) distribution of numbers with a mean of 70 and a standard deviation of 3.5. Create a histogram of the data set you calculated.

## Graphs with Two y-Axes

**24** In the introduction to Problems 6 through 9, we learned that the equations for the distance traveled by a projectile as a function of time are

$$\text{Horizontal}(t) = tV_0 \cos(\theta)$$

$$\text{Vertical}(t) = tV_0 \sin(\theta) - \tfrac{1}{2} g t^2$$

For time from 0 to 20 s, plot both the horizontal distance versus time and the vertical distance versus time on the same graph, using separate y-axes for each line. Assume a launch angle of 45 degrees ($\pi/4$ radians) and an initial velocity of 100 m/s. Assume also that the acceleration due to gravity, $g$, is 9.8 m/s.

**25** If the equation modeling the vertical distance traveled by a projectile as a function of time is

$$\text{Vertical}(t) = tV_0 \sin(\theta) - 1/2 \, g t^2$$

then, from calculus, the velocity in the vertical direction is

$$\text{Velocity}(t) = V_0 \sin(\theta) - gt$$

Create a vector $t$ from 0 to 20 s, and calculate both the vertical position and the velocity in the vertical direction, assuming a launch angle $\theta$ of $\pi/4$ radians and an initial velocity of 100 m/s. Plot both quantities on the same graph with separate y-axes.

The velocity should be zero at the point where the projectile is the highest in the vertical direction. Does your graph support this prediction?

**26** For many metals, deformation changes their physical properties. In a process called *cold work*, metal is intentionally deformed to make it stronger. The following data tabulate both the strength and ductility of a metal that has been cold worked to different degrees:

| Percent Cold Work | Yield Strength, MPa | Ductility, % |
|---|---|---|
| 10 | 275 | 43 |
| 15 | 310 | 30 |
| 20 | 340 | 23 |
| 25 | 360 | 17 |
| 30 | 375 | 12 |
| 40 | 390 | 7 |
| 50 | 400 | 4 |
| 60 | 407 | 3 |
| 68 | 410 | 2 |

Plot these data on a single x–y plot with two y-axes.

## Three-Dimensional Line Plots

**27** Create a vector **x** of values from 0 to 20 $\pi$, with a spacing of $\pi/100$. Define vectors **y** and **z** as

$$y = x \sin(x)$$

and
$$z = x \cos(x)$$

**(a)** Create an $x$–$y$ plot of **x** and **y**.
**(b)** Create a polar plot of **x** and **y**.
**(c)** Create a three-dimensional line plot of **x**, **y**, and **z**. Don't forget a title and labels.

28    Figure out how to adjust your input to **plot3** in Problem 27 so as to create a graph that looks like a tornado. (See Figure P28.)  Use **comet3** instead of **plot3** to create the graph.

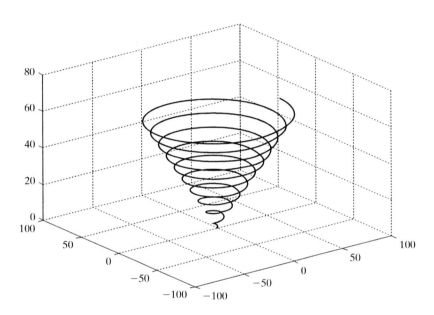

**Figure P28**
Tornado plot.

**Three-Dimensional Surface and Contour Plots**

29    Create **x** and **y** vectors from $-5$ to $+5$ with a spacing of 0.5. Use the **meshgrid** function to map **x** and **y** onto two new two-dimensional matrices called **X** and **Y**. Use your new matrices to calculate vector **Z**, with magnitude
$$Z = \sin\left(\sqrt{X^2 + Y^2}\right)$$

**(a)** Use the **mesh** plotting function to create a three-dimensional plot of **Z**.
**(b)** Use the **surf** plotting function to create a three-dimensional plot of **Z**. Compare the results you obtain with a single input (**Z**) with those obtained with inputs for all three dimensions (**X**, **Y**, **Z**).
**(c)** Modify your surface plot with interpolated shading. Try using different **colormaps**.
**(d)** Generate a contour plot of **Z**.
**(e)** Generate a combination surface and contour plot of **Z**.

## SOLUTIONS TO PRACTICE EXERCISES

### Practice Exercises 1

1. ```
clear,clc
x = 0:0.1*pi:2*pi;
y = sin(x);
plot(x,y)
```

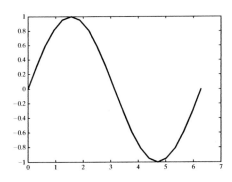

2. ```
title('Sinusoidal Curve')
xlabel('x values')
ylabel('sin(x)')
```

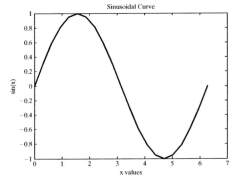

3. ```
figure(2)
y1 = sin(x);
y2 = cos(x);
plot(x,y1,x,y2)
title('Sine and
 Cosine Plots')
xlabel('x values')
ylabel('y values')
```

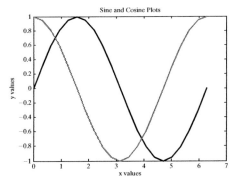

4. ```
figure(3)
plot(x,y1,'-- r',
 x,y2,': g')
title('Sine and Cosine
 Plots')
xlabel('x values')
ylabel('y values')
```

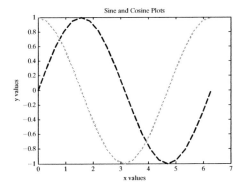

5. `legend('sin(x)','cos(x)')`

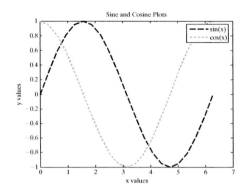

6. `axis([-1,2*pi+1,`
   `    -1.5,1.5])`

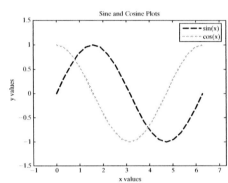

7. `figure(4)`
   `a = cos(x);`
   `plot(a)`

   A line graph is created,
   with **a** plotted against the
   vector index number.

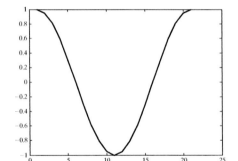

## Practice Exercises 2

1. `subplot(2,1,1)`

2. `x = -1.5:0.1:1.5;`
   `y = tan(x);`
   `plot(x,y)`

3. `title('Tangent(x)')`
   `xlabel('x value')`
   `ylabel('y value')`

4. `subplot(2,1,2)`
   `y = sinh(x);`
   `plot(x,y)`

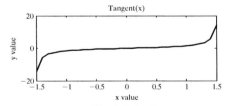

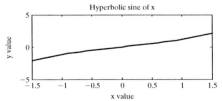

5. ```
title('Hyperbolic
       sine of x')
xlabel('x value')
ylabel('y value')
```

6. ```
figure(2)
subplot(1,2,1)
plot(x,y)
title('Tangent(x)')
xlabel('x value')
ylabel('y value')
subplot(1,2,2)
y = sinh(x);
plot(x,y)
title('Hyperbolic
   sine of x')
xlabel('x value')
ylabel('y value')
```

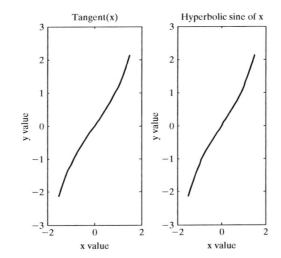

## Practice Exercises 3

1. ```
theta = 0:0.01*pi:2*pi;
r = 5*cos(4*theta);
polar(theta,r)
```

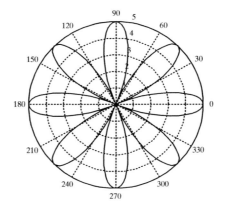

2. ```
hold on
r = 4*cos(6*theta);
polar(theta,r)
title('Flower Power')
```

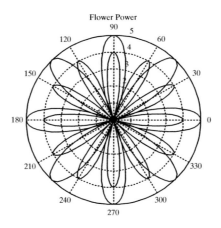

3. ```
figure(2)
r = 5-5*sin(theta);
polar(theta,r)
```

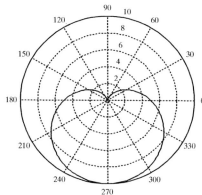

4. ```
figure(3)
r = sqrt(5^2*cos(2*theta));
polar(theta3,r)
```

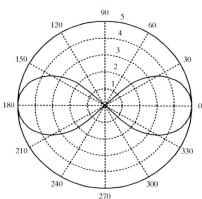

5. ```
figure(4)
theta = pi/2:4/5*pi:4.8*pi;
r = ones(1,6);
polar(theta,r)
```

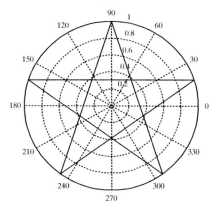

## Practice Exercises 4

1. ```
figure(1)
x = -1:0.1:1;
y = 5*x+3;
subplot(2,2,1)
plot(x,y)
title('Rectangular Coordinates')
ylabel('y-axis')
grid on
```

```
subplot(2,2,2)
semilogx(x,y)
title('Semilog x Coordinate System')
grid on
subplot(2,2,3)
semilogy(x,y)
title('Semilog y Coordinate System')
ylabel('y-axis')
xlabel('x-axis')
grid on
subplot(2,2,4)
loglog(x,y)
title('Log Plot')
xlabel('x-axis')
grid on
```

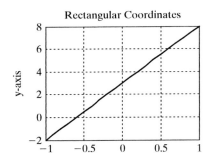

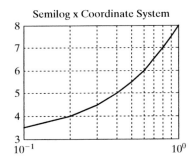

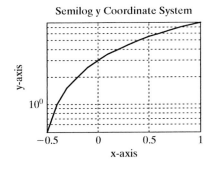

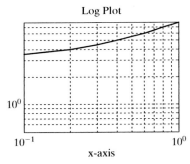

2. 
```
figure(2)
x = -1:0.1:1;
y = 3*x.^2;
subplot(2,2,1)
plot(x,y)
title('Rectangular Coordinates')
ylabel('y-axis')
grid on
subplot(2,2,2)
semilogx(x,y)
title('Semilog x Coordinate System')
grid on
subplot(2,2,3)
semilogy(x,y)
title('Semilog y Coordinate System')
```

```
ylabel('y-axis')
xlabel('x-axis')
grid on
subplot(2,2,4)
loglog(x,y)
title('Log Plot')
xlabel('x-axis')
grid on
```

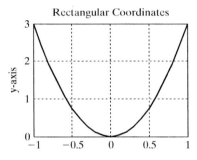

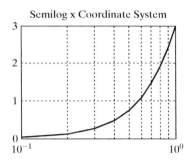

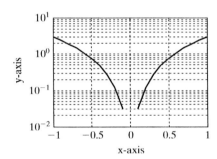

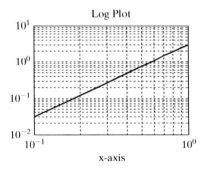

3. ```
figure(3)
x = -1:0.1:1;
y = 12*exp(x+2);
subplot(2,2,1)
plot(x,y)
title('Rectangular Coordinates')
ylabel('y-axis')
grid on
subplot(2,2,2)
semilogx(x,y)
title('Semilog x Coordinate System')
grid on
subplot(2,2,3)
semilogy(x,y)
title('Semilog y Coordinate System')
ylabel('y-axis')
xlabel('x-axis')
grid on
subplot(2,2,4)
loglog(x,y)
title('Log Plot')
xlabel('x-axis')
grid on
```
```

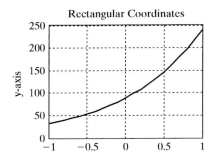

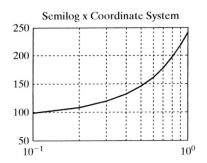

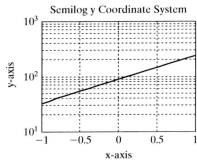

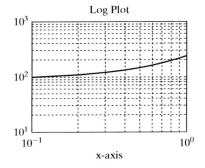

4.
```
figure(4)
x = -1:0.01:1;
y = 1./x;
subplot(2,2,1)
plot(x,y)
title('Rectangular Coordinates')
ylabel('y-axis')
grid on
subplot(2,2,2)
semilogx(x,y)
title('Semilog x Coordinate System')
grid on
subplot(2,2,3)
semilogy(x,y)
title('Semilog y Coordinate System')
ylabel('y-axis')
xlabel('x-axis')
grid on
subplot(2,2,4)
loglog(x,y)
title('Log Plot')
xlabel('x-axis')
grid on
```

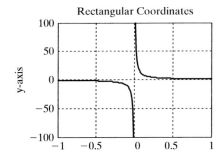

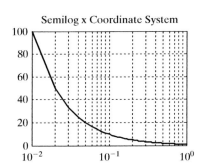

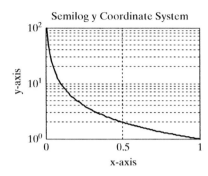

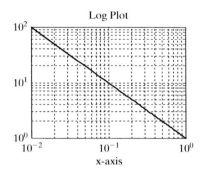

## Practice Exercises 5

1. 
```
fplot('5*t^2',[-3,+3])
title('5*t^2')
xlabel('x-axis')
ylabel('y-axis')
```

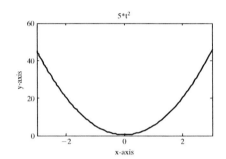

2. 
```
fplot('5*sin(t)^2 +
 t*cos(t)^2',[-2*pi,2*pi])
title('5*sin(t)^2 +
t*cos(t)^2')
xlabel('x-axis')
ylabel('y-axis')
```

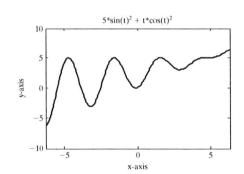

3. 
```
fplot('t*exp(t)',[0,10])
title('t*exp(t)')
xlabel('x-axis')
ylabel('y-axis')
```

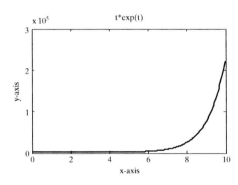

4. 
```
fplot('log(t)+ sin(t)',[0,pi])
title('log(t)+sin(t)')
xlabel('x-axis')
ylabel('y-axis')
```

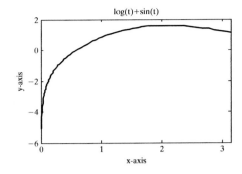

# 6

# User-Defined Functions

## Objectives

After reading this chapter, you should be able to

- create and use your own MATLAB functions with both single and multiple inputs and outputs
- store and access your own functions in toolboxes
- create and use anonymous functions
- create and use function handles
- create and use subfunctions and nested subfunctions

## INTRODUCTION

The MATLAB programming language is built around functions. A *function* is a piece of computer code that accepts an input argument from the user and provides output to the program. Functions allow us to program efficiently, enabling us to avoid rewriting the computer code for calculations that are performed frequently. For example, most computer programs contain a function that calculates the sine of a number. In MATLAB, **sin** is the function name used to call up a series of commands that perform the necessary calculations. The user needs to provide an angle, and MATLAB returns a result. It isn't necessary for the programmer to know how MATLAB calculates the value of **sin(x)**.

## 1 CREATING FUNCTION M-FILES

We have already explored many of MATLAB's built-in functions, but you may wish to define your own functions—those which are used commonly in your programming. User-defined functions are stored as M-files and can be accessed by MATLAB if they are in the current directory.

### 1.1 Syntax

Both built-in MATLAB functions and user-defined MATLAB functions have the same structure. Each consists of a name, user-provided input, and calculated output. For example, the function

```
cos(x)
```

- is named **cos**,
- takes user input inside the parentheses (in this case, **x**), and
- calculates a result.

The user does not see the calculations performed, but just accepts the answer. User-defined functions work the same way. Imagine that you have created a function called **my_function**. Using

```
my_function(x)
```

**KEY IDEA: Functions allow us to program more efficiently**

in a program or from the command window will return a result, as long as **x** is defined and the logic in the function definition works.

User-defined functions are created in M-files. Each must start with a function-definition line that contains

- the word **function**,
- a variable that defines the function output,
- a function name, and
- a variable used for the input argument.

For example,

```
function   output = my_function(x)
```

is the first line of the user-defined function called **my_function**. It requires one input argument, which the program will call **x**, and will calculate one output argument, which the program will call **output**. The function name and the names of the input and output variables are arbitrary and are selected by the programmer. Here's an example of an appropriate first line for a function called **calculation**:

```
function   result = calculation(a)
```

In this case, the function name is **calculation**, the input argument will be called **a** in any calculations performed in the function program, and the output will be called **result**. Although any valid MATLAB names can be used, it is good programming practice to use meaningful names for all variables and for function names.

**FUNCTION: a piece of computer code that accepts an input, performs a calculation, and provides an output**

**Hint**

Students are often confused about the use of the word *input* as it refers to a function. We use it here to describe the input argument—the value that goes inside the parentheses when we call a function. In MATLAB, input arguments are different from the **input** command.

Here's an example of a very simple MATLAB function that calculates the value of a particular polynomial:

```
function output = poly(x)
%This function calculates the value of a third-order
%polynomial
output = 3*x.^3 + 5*x.^2 - 2*x +1;
```

The function name is **poly**, the input argument is **x**, and the output variable is named **output**.

Before this function can be used, it must be saved into the current directory. The file name *must be the same* as the function name in order for MATLAB to find it. All of the MATLAB naming conventions we learned for naming variables apply to naming user-defined functions. In particular,

- The function name must start with a letter.
- It can consist of letters, numbers, and the underscore.
- Reserved names cannot be used.
- Any length is allowed, although long names are not good programming practice.

Once the M-file has been saved, the function is available for use from the command window, from a script M-file, or from another function. You can not execute a function M-file directly from the M-file itself. This makes sense, since the input parameters have not been defined until you call the function from the command window or a script M-file. Consider the **poly** function just created. If, in the command window, we type

```
poly(4)
```

then MATLAB responds with

```
ans =
        265
```

If we set **a** equal to 4 and use **a** as the input argument, we get the same result:

```
a = 4;
poly(a)

ans =
        265
```

If we define a vector, we get a vector of answers. Thus,

```
y = 1:5;
poly(y)
```

gives

```
ans =
     7    41   121   265   491
```

If, however, you try to execute the function by selecting the save-and-run icon from the function menu bar, the following error message is displayed:

```
???Input argument "x" is undefined.
Error in ==> poly at 3
output = 3*x.^3 + 5*x.^2 - 2*x +1;
```

The value of **x** must be passed to the function when it is used—either in the command window or from within a script M-file program.

KEY IDEA: Name functions using the standard MATLAB naming conventions for variables

---

### Hint

While you are creating a function, it may be useful to allow intermediate calculations to print to the command window. However, once you complete your "debugging," make sure that all your output is suppressed. If you don't, you'll see extraneous information in the command window.

---

### Practice Exercises 1

Create MATLAB functions to evaluate the following mathematical functions (make sure you select meaningful function names) and test them. To test your functions you'll need to call them from the command window, or use them in a script M-file program. Remember, each function requires its own M-file.

1. $y(x) = x^2$
2. $y(x) = e^{1/x}$
3. $y(x) = \sin(x^2)$

Create MATLAB functions for the following unit conversions (you many need to consult a textbook or the Internet for the appropriate conversion factors). Be sure to test your functions, either from the command window, or by using them in a script M-file program.

4. inches to feet
5. calories to joules
6. watts to BTU/hr
7. meters to miles
8. miles per hour (mph) to ft/s

## EXAMPLE 1

### Converting between Degrees and Radians

Engineers usually measure angles in degrees, yet most computer programs and many calculators require that the input to trigonometric functions be in radians. Write and test a function **DR** that changes degrees to radians and another function **RD** that changes radians to degrees. Your functions should be able to accept both scalar and matrix input.

1. State the Problem
   Create and test two functions, **DR** and **RD**, to change degrees to radians and radians to degrees (see Figure 1).

2. Describe the Input and Output

   **Input**    A vector of degree values
              A vector of radian values

   **Output**   A table converting degrees to radians
              A table converting radians to degrees

**Figure 1**
Trigonometric functions require angles to be expressed in radians. Trigonometry is regularly used in engineering drawings.

3. Develop a Hand Example

$$\text{degrees} = \text{radians} \times 180/\pi$$
$$\text{radians} = \text{degrees} \times \pi/180$$

| Degrees to Radians | |
|---|---|
| Degrees | Radians |
| 0 | 0 |
| 30 | $30(\pi/180) = \pi/6 = 0.524$ |
| 60 | $60(\pi/180) = \pi/3 = 1.047$ |
| 90 | $90(\pi/180) = \pi/2 = 1.571$ |

4. Develop a MATLAB Solution

```
%Example 1
%
clear, clc
%Define a vector of degree values
degrees = 0:15:180;
% Call the DR function, and use it to find radians
radians = DR(degrees);
```

```
%Create a table to use in the output
degrees_radians =[degrees;radians]'
%Define a vector of radian values
radians = 0:pi/12:pi;
%Call the RD function, and use it to find degrees
degrees = RD(radians);
radians_degrees = [radians;degrees]'
```

The functions called by the program are

```
function output = DR(x)
%This function changes degrees to radians
output = x*pi/180;
```

and

```
function output = RD(x)
%This function changes radians to degrees
output = x*180/pi;
```

Remember that in order for the script M-file to find the functions, they must be in the current directory and must be named **DR.m** and **RD.m**. The program generates the following results in the command window:

```
degrees_radians =
     0       0.000
    15       0.262
    30       0.524
    45       0.785
    60       1.047
    75       1.309
    90       1.571
   105       1.833
   120       2.094
   135       2.356
   150       2.618
   165       2.880
   180       3.142


radians_degrees =
   0.000         0.000
   0.262        15.000
   0.524        30.000
   0.785        45.000
   1.047        60.000
   1.309        75.000
   1.571        90.000
   1.833       105.000
   2.094       120.000
   2.356       135.000
   2.618       150.000
   2.880       165.000
   3.142       180.000
```

5. Test the Solution

Compare the MATLAB solution with the hand solution. Since the output is a table, it is easy to see that the conversions generated by MATLAB correspond to those calculated by hand.

**EXAMPLE 2**

### ASTM Grain Size

**Figure 2**
Typical microstructures of iron (400×). (From *Metals Handbook*, 9th ed., Vol. 1, American Society of Metals, Metals Park, Ohio, 1978.)

You may not be used to thinking of metals as crystals, but they are. If you look at a polished piece of metal under a microscope, the structure becomes clear, as seen in Figure 2. As you can see, every crystal (called a grain in metallurgy) is a different size and shape. The size of the grains affects the metal's strength; the finer the grains, the stronger the metal.

Because it is difficult to determine an "average" grain size, a standard technique has been developed by ASTM (formerly known as the American Society for Testing and Materials, but now known just by its initials). A sample of metal is examined under a microscope at a magnification of 100, and the number of grains in 1 square inch is counted. The parameters are related by

$$N = 2^{n-1}$$

where $n$ is the ASTM grain size and $N$ is the number of grains per square inch at 100×. The equation can be solved for $n$ to give

$$n = \frac{(\log(N) + \log(2))}{\log(2)}$$

This equation is not hard to use, but it's awkward. Instead, let's create a MATLAB function called **grain_size**.

1. State the Problem
   Create and test a function called **grain_size** to determine the ASTM grain size of a piece of metal.
2. Describe the Input and Output
   To test the function, we'll need to choose an arbitrary number of grains. For example:

   **Input**    16 grains per square inch at 100×

   **Output**   ASTM grain size

3. Develop a Hand Example

$$n = \frac{(\log(N) + \log(2))}{\log(2)}$$
$$n = \frac{(\log(16) + \log(2))}{\log(2)} = 5$$

4. Develop a MATLAB Solution
   The function, created in a separate M-file, is

```
function output = grain_size(N)
%Calculates the ASTM grain size n
output = (log10(N) + log10(2))./log10(2);
```

   which was saved as **grain_size.m** in the current directory. To use this function, we can call it from the command window:

```
grain_size(16)
ans =
   5
```

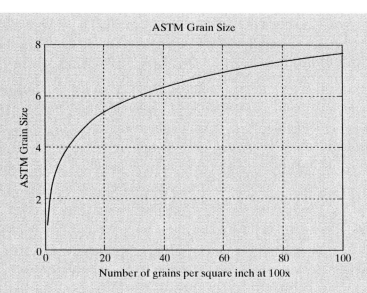

**Figure 3**
A plot of a function's behavior is a good way to help determine whether you've programmed it correctly.

5. Test the Solution

The MATLAB solution is the same as the hand solution. It might be interesting to see how the ASTM grain size varies with the number of grains per square inch. We could use the function with an array of values and plot the results in Figure 3.

```
%Example 2
%ASTM Grain Size
N = 1:100;
n = grain_size(N);
plot(N,n)
title('ASTM Grain Size')
xlabel('Number of grains per square inch at 100x')
ylabel('ASTM Grain Size')
grid
```

As expected, the grain size increases as the number of grains per square inch increases.

## 1.2 Comments

As with any computer program, you should comment your code liberally so that it is easy to follow. However, in a MATLAB function, the comments on the line immediately following the very first line serve a special role. These lines are returned when the **help** function is queried from the command window. Consider, for example, the following function:

KEY IDEA: Function comments are displayed when you use the help feature

```
function results = f(x)
%This function converts seconds to minutes
results = x./60;
```

Querying the **help** function from the command window

```
help f
```

returns

```
This function converts seconds to minutes
```

### 1.3 Functions with Multiple Inputs and Outputs

Just as the predefined MATLAB functions may require multiple inputs and may return multiple outputs, more complicated user-defined functions can be written. Recall, for example, the remainder function. This predefined function calculates the remainder in a division problem and requires the user to input the dividend and the divisor. For the problem $\frac{5}{3}$, the correct syntax is

```
rem(5,3)
```

which gives

```
ans =
      2
```

Similarly, a user-defined function could be written to multiply two vectors together:

```
function output = g(x,y)
% This function multiplies x and y together
% x and y must be the same size matrices
a = x .*y;
output = a;
```

When **x** and **y** are defined in the command window and the function **g** is called, a vector of output values is returned:

```
x = 1:5;
y = 5:9;
g(x,y)
ans =
    5    12    21    32    45
```

You can use the comment lines to let users know what kind of input is required and to describe the function. In this example, an intermediate calculation (**a**) was performed, but the only output from this function is the variable we've named **output**. This output can be a matrix containing a variety of numbers, but it's still only one variable.

You can also create functions that return more than one output variable. Many of the predefined MATLAB functions return more than one result. For example, **max** returns both the maximum value in a matrix and the element number at which the maximum occurs. To achieve the same result in a user-defined function, make the output a matrix of answers instead of a single variable, as in

```
function      [dist, vel, accel] = motion(t)
% This function calculates the distance, velocity, and
% acceleration of a car for a given value of t
accel = 0.5 .*t;
vel = accel .* t;
dist = vel.*t;
```

Once saved as **motion** in the current directory, you can use the function to find values of **distance**, **velocity**, and **acceleration** at specified times:

```
[distance, velocity, acceleration] = motion(10)

distance =
       500
velocity =
        50
acceleration =
         5
```

If you call the **motion** function without specifying all three outputs, only the first output will be returned:

```
motion(10)
ans =
     500
```

Remember, all variables in MATLAB are matrices, so it's important in the preceding example to use the .* operator, which specifies element-by-element multiplication. For example, using a vector of time values from 0 to 30 in the motion function

```
time = 0:10:30;
[distance, velocity, acceleration] = motion(time)
```

returns three vectors of answers:

```
distance =
      0    500    4000    13500
velocity =
      0     50     200      450
acceleration =
      0      5      10       15
```

It's easier to see the results if you group the vectors together, as in

```
results =[time',distance',velocity',acceleration']
```

which returns

```
results =
          0          0          0          0
         10        500         50          5
         20       4000        200         10
         30      13500        450         15
```

Because **time, distance, velocity**, and **acceleration** were row vectors, the transpose operator was used to convert them into columns.

---

### Practice Exercises 2

Assuming that the matrix dimensions agree, create and test MATLAB functions to evaluate the following simple mathematical functions with multiple input vectors and a single output vector:

1. $z(x, y) = x + y$
2. $z(a, b, c) = ab^c$
3. $z(w, x, y) = we^{(x/y)}$
4. $z(p, t) = p/\sin(t)$

Assuming that the matrix dimensions agree, create and test MATLAB functions to evaluate the following simple mathematical functions with a single input vector and multiple output vectors:

5. $f(x) = \cos(x)$
   $f(x) = \sin(x)$

6. $f(x) = 5x^2 + 2$
   $f(x) = \sqrt{5x^2 + 2}$
7. $f(x) = \exp(x)$
   $f(x) = \ln(x)$

Assuming that the matrix dimensions agree, create and test MATLAB functions to evaluate the following simple mathematical functions with multiple input vectors and multiple output vectors:

8. $f(x, y) = x + y$
   $f(x, y) = x - y$
9. $f(x, y) = ye^x$
   $f(x, y) = xe^y$

---

**EXAMPLE 3**

## How Grain Size Affects Metal Strength: A Function with Three Inputs

Metals composed of small crystals are stronger than metals composed of fewer large crystals. The metal yield strength (the amount of stress at which the metal starts to permanently deform) is related to the average grain diameter by the *Hall–Petch equation*:

$$\sigma = \sigma_0 + Kd^{-1/2}$$

where the symbols $\sigma_0$ and K represent constants that are different for every metal.
Create a function called **HallPetch** that requires three inputs—$\sigma_0$, K, and $d$—and calculates the value of yield strength. Call this function from a MATLAB program that supplies values of $\sigma_0$ and K, then plots the value of yield strength for values of $d$ from 0.1 to 10 mm.

1. State the Problem
   Create a function called **HallPetch** that determines the yield strength of a piece of metal, using the Hall–Petch equation. Use the function to create a plot of yield strength versus grain diameter.

2. Describe the Input and Output

   ***Input***    $K = 9600 \text{ psi}/\sqrt{mm}$

   $\sigma_0 = 12,000 \text{ psi}$

   $d = 0.1 \text{ to } 10 \text{ mm}$

   ***Output***   Plot of yield strength versus diameter

3. Develop a Hand Example
   The Hall–Petch equation is

   $$\sigma = \sigma_0 + Kd^{-1/2}$$

   Substituting values of 12,000 psi and 9600 psi/$\sqrt{mm}$ for $\sigma_0$ and K, respectively, then

   $$\sigma = 12,000 + 9600d^{-1/2}$$

For $d = 1$ mm,

$$\sigma = 12,000 + 9600 = 21,600$$

4. Develop a MATLAB Solution

The desired function, created in a separate M-file, is

```
function output = HallPetch(sigma0,K,d)
%Hall-Petch equation to determine the yield
%strength of metals
output = sigma0 + K*d.^(-0.5);
```

and was saved as **HallPetch.m** in the current directory:

```
%Example 3
clear,clc
format compact
s0 = 12000
K = 9600
%Define the values of grain diameter
diameter = 0.1:0.1:10;
yield = HallPetch(s0,K,d);
%Plot the results
figure(1)
plot(diameter,yield)
title('Yield strengths found with the Hall-Petch equation')
xlabel('diameter, mm')
ylabel('yield strength, psi')
```

The graph shown in Figure 4 was generated by the program.

5. Test the Solution

We can use the graph to compare the results to the hand solution.

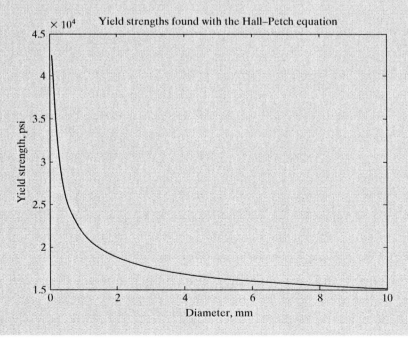

**Figure 4**
Yield strengths predicted with the Hall–Petch equation.

## EXAMPLE 4

### Kinetic Energy: A Function with Two Inputs

The kinetic energy of a moving object (Figure 5) is

$$KE = \frac{1}{2}mv^2.$$

Create and test a function called KE to find the kinetic energy of a moving car if you know the mass $m$ and the velocity $v$ of the vehicle.

1. State the Problem
   Create a function called KE to find the kinetic energy of a car.

2. Describe the Input and Output

   **Input**   Mass of the car, in kilograms
   Velocity of the car, in m/s

   **Output**   Kinetic energy, in joules

3. Develop a Hand Example
   If the mass is 1000 kg, and the velocity is 25 m/s, then

   $$KE = \frac{1}{2} \times 1000 \text{ kg} \times (25 \text{ m/s})^2 = 312{,}500 \text{ J} = 312.5 \text{ kJ}$$

4. Develop a MATLAB Solution

```
function    output = ke(mass,velocity)
output = 1/2*mass*velocity.^2;
```

5. Test the Solution

```
v = 25;
m = 1000;
ke(m,v)
ans =
        312500
```

This result matches the hand example, confirming that the function works correctly and can now be used in a larger MATLAB program.

**Figure 5**
Race cars store a significant amount of kinetic energy.
(Rick Graves/Getty Images.)

### 1.4 Functions with No Input or No Output

Although most functions need at least one input and return at least one output value, in some situations no inputs or outputs are required. For example, consider this function, which draws a star in polar coordinates:

```
function [] = star( )
theta = pi/2:0.8*pi:4.8*pi;
```

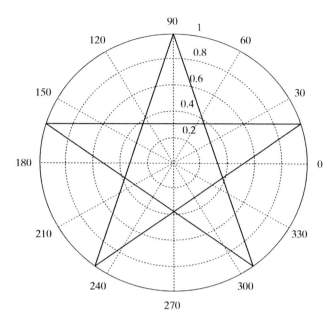

**Figure 6**
The user-defined function **star** requires no input and produces no output values, but it does draw a star in polar coordinates.

```
r=ones(1,6);
polar(theta,r)
```

The square brackets on the first line indicate that the output of the function is an empty matrix (i.e., no value is returned). The empty parentheses tell us that no input is expected. If, from the command window, you type

```
star
```

then no values are returned, but a figure window opens showing a star drawn in polar coordinates. (See Figure 6.)

---

**Hint**

You may ask yourself if the **star** function is really an example of a function that does not return an output; after all, it does draw a star. But the output of a function is defined as a *value* that is returned when you call the function. If we ask MATLAB to perform the calculation

**A = star**

an error statement is generated, because the **star** function does not return anything! Thus, there is nothing to set **A** equal to.

---

There are numerous built-in MATLAB functions that do not require any input. For example,

```
A = clock
```

returns the current time:

```
A =
  1.0e+003 *
  Columns 1 through 4
    2.0050    0.0030    0.0200    0.0150
  Columns 5 through 6
    0.0250    0.0277
```

KEY IDEA: Not all functions require an input

Also,

```
A = pi
```

returns the value of the mathematical constant $\pi$:

```
A =
    3.1416
```

However, if we try to set the MATLAB function **tic** equal to a variable name, an error statement is generated, because **tic** does not return an output value:

```
A = tic
???Error using ==> tic
Too many output arguments.
```

(The **tic** function starts a timer going for later use in the **toc** function.)

### 1.5 Determining the Number of Input and Output Arguments

There may be times when you want to know the number of input arguments or output values associated with a function. MATLAB provides two built-in functions for this purpose.

KEY IDEA: Using the **nargin** or **nargout** functions is useful in programming functions with variable inputs and outputs

The **nargin** function determines the number of input arguments in either a user-defined function or a built-in function. The name of the function must be specified as a string, as, for example, in

```
nargin('sin')
ans =
    1
```

The remainder function, **rem**, requires two inputs; thus,

```
nargin('rem')
ans =
    2
```

When **nargin** is used inside a user-defined function, it determines how many input arguments were actually entered. This allows a function to have a variable number of inputs. Recall graphing functions such as **surf**. When **surf** has a single matrix input, a graph is created, using the matrix index numbers as the $x$- and $y$-coordinates. When there are three inputs, $x$, $y$, and $z$, the graph is based on the specified $x$- and $y$-values. The **nargin** function allows the programmer to determine how to create the plot, based on the number of inputs.

The **surf** function is an example of a function with a variable number of inputs. If we use **nargin** from the command window to determine the number of declared inputs, there isn't one correct answer. The **nargin** function returns a negative number to let us know that a variable number of inputs is possible:

```
nargin('surf')
ans =
    -1
```

The **nargout** function is similar to **nargin**, but it determines the number of outputs from a function:

```
nargout('sin')
ans =
    1
```

The number of outputs is determined by how many matrices are returned, not how many values are in the matrix. We know that **size** returns the number of rows and columns in a matrix, so we might expect **nargout** to return 2 when applied to size. However,

```
nargout('size')
ans =
    1
```

returns only one matrix, which has just two elements, as for example, in

```
x = 1:10;
size(x)
ans =
    1    10
```

An example of a function with multiple outputs is **max**:

```
nargout('max')

ans =
    3
```

When used inside a user-defined function, **nargout** determines how many outputs have been requested by the user. Consider this example, in which we have rewritten the function from Section 1.4 to create a star:

```
function A = star1( )
theta = pi/2:0.8*pi:4.8*pi;
r = ones(1,6);
polar(theta,r)
if nargout==1
    A = 'Twinkle twinkle little star';
end
```

If we use **nargout** from the command window, as in

```
nargout('star1')
ans =
    1
```

MATLAB tells us that one output is specified. If we call the function simply as

```
star1
```

nothing is returned to the command window, although the plot is drawn. If we call the function by setting it equal to a variable, as in

```
x = star1
x =
Twinkle twinkle little star
```

a value for **x** is returned, based on the **if** statement embedded in the function, which used **nargout** to determine the number of output values.

## 1.6 Local Variables

The variables used in function M-files are known as *local variables*. The only way a function can communicate with the workspace is through input arguments and the output it returns. Any variables defined within the function exist only for the function to use. For example, consider the **g** function previously described:

```
function output = g(x,y)
% This function multiplies x and y together
% x and y must be the same size matrices
a = x .*y;
output = a;
```

LOCAL VARIABLE: a variable that only has meaning inside a program or function

The variables **a**, **x**, **y**, and **output** are local variables. They can be used for additional calculations inside the **g** function, but they are not stored in the workspace. To confirm this, clear the workspace and the command window and then call the **g** function:

```
clear, clc
g(10,20)
```

The function returns

```
g(10,20)
ans =
        200
```

Notice that the only variable stored in the workspace window is **ans**, which is characterized as follows:

| Name | Value | Size | Bytes | Class |
|------|-------|------|-------|-------|
| ⊞ ans | 200 | $1 \times 1$ | 8 | double array |

Just as calculations performed in the command window or from a script M-file cannot access variables defined in functions, functions cannot access the variables defined in the workspace. This means that functions must be completely self-contained: The only way they can get information from your program is through the input arguments, and the only way they can deliver information is through the function output.

Consider a function written to find the distance an object falls due to gravity:

```
function  result = distance(t)
%This function calculates the distance a falling object
%travels due to gravity
g = 9.8      %meters per second squared
result = 1/2*g*t.^2;
```

The value of **g** must be included *inside* the function. It doesn't matter whether **g** has or has not been used in the main program. How **g** is defined is hidden to the distance function unless **g** is specified inside the function.

Of course, you could also pass the value of **g** to the function as an input argument:

```
function  result = distance(g,t)
%This function calculates the distance a falling object
%travels due to gravity
result = 1/2*g*t.^2;
```

**Hint**

The same matrix names can be used in both a function and the program that references it. However, they do not *have* to be the same. Since variable names are local to either the function or the program that calls the function, the variables are completely separate. As a beginning programmer, you would be wise to use different variable names in your functions and your programs—just so you don't confuse *yourself*.

## 1.7 Global Variables

Unlike local variables, global variables are available to all parts of a computer program. In general, *it is a bad idea* to define global variables. However, MATLAB protects users from unintentionally using a global variable by requiring that it be identified both in the command-window environment (or in a script M-file) and in the function that will use it.

KEY IDEA: It is usually a bad idea to define global variables

Consider the distance function once again:

```
function  result = distance(t)
%This function calculates the distance a falling object
%travels due to gravity
global G
result = 1/2*G*t.^2;
```

GLOBAL VARIABLE: a variable that is available from multiple programs

The **global** command alerts the function to look in the workspace for the value of **G**. **G** must also have been defined in the command window (or script M-file) as a global variable:

```
global G
G = 9.8;
```

This approach allows you to change the value of **G** without needing to redefine the distance function or providing the value of **G** as an input argument to the distance function.

**Hint**

As a matter of style, always make the names of global variables uppercase. MATLAB doesn't care, but it is easier to identify global variables if you use a consistent naming convention.

**Hint**

It may seem like a good idea to use global variables because they can simplify your programs. However, consider this example of using global variables in your everyday life: It would be easier to order a book from an online bookseller if you had posted your credit card information on a site where any retailer could just look it up. Then the bookseller wouldn't have to ask you to type in the number. However, this might produce some unintended consequences (like other people using your credit card without your permission or knowledge!). When you create a global variable, it becomes available to other functions and can be changed by those functions, sometimes leading to unintended consequences.

## 1.8 Accessing M-File Code

The functions provided with MATLAB are of two types. One type is built in, and the code is not accessible for us to review. The other type consists of M-files, stored in toolboxes provided with the program. We can see these M-files (or the M-files we've written) with the **type** command. For example, the **sphere** function creates a three-dimensional representation of a sphere; thus,

```
type sphere
```

or

```
type('sphere')
```

returns the contents of the **sphere.m** file:

```
function [xx,yy,zz] = sphere(varargin)
%SPHERE Generate sphere.
%   [X,Y,Z] = SPHERE(N) generates three (N+1)-by-(N+1)
%   matrices so that SURF(X,Y,Z) produces a unit sphere.
%
%   [X,Y,Z] = SPHERE uses N = 20.
%
%   SPHERE(N) and just SPHERE graph the sphere as a SURFACE
%   and do not return anything.
%
%   SPHERE(AX,...) plots into AX instead of GCA.
%
%   See also ELLIPSOID, CYLINDER.

%   Clay M. Thompson 4-24-91, CBM 8-21-92.
%   Copyright 1984-2002 The MathWorks, Inc.
%   $Revision: 5.8.4.1 $  $Date: 2002/09/26 01:55:25 $

% Parse possible Axes input
error(nargchk(0,2,nargin));
[cax,args,nargs] = axescheck(varargin{:});

n = 20;
if nargs > 0, n = args{1}; end

% -pi <= theta <= pi is a row vector.
% -pi/2 <= phi <= pi/2 is a column vector.
theta = (-n:2:n)/n*pi;
phi = (-n:2:n)'/n*pi/2;
cosphi = cos(phi); cosphi(1) = 0; cosphi(n+1) = 0;
sintheta = sin(theta); sintheta(1) = 0; sintheta(n+1) = 0;

x = cosphi*cos(theta);
y = cosphi*sintheta;
z = sin(phi)*ones(1,n+1);

if nargout == 0
    cax = newplot(cax);
    surf(x,y,z,'parent',cax)
else
    xx = x; yy = y; zz = z;
end
```

> **Hint**
>
> Notice that the **sphere** function uses **varargin** to indicate that it will accept a variable number of input arguments. The function also makes use of the **nargin** and **nargout** functions. Studying this function may give you ideas on how to program your own function M-files. The **sphere** function also uses an if/else structure.

## 2  CREATING YOUR OWN TOOLBOX OF FUNCTIONS

When you call a function in MATLAB, the program first looks in the current directory to see if the function is defined. If it can't find the function listed there, it starts down a predefined search path, looking for a file with the function name. To view the path the program takes as it looks for files, select

KEY IDEA: Group your functions together into toolboxes

    **File** → **Set Path**

from the menu bar or type

    **pathtool**

in the command window (Figure 7).

As you create more and more functions to use in your programming, you may wish to modify the path to look in a directory where you've stored your own personal tools. For example, suppose you have stored the degrees-to-radians and radians-to-degrees functions created in Example 1 in a directory called **My_functions**.

You can add this directory (folder) to the path by selecting **Add Folder** from the list of option buttons in the Set Path dialog window, as shown in Figure 7. You'll be prompted to either supply the folder location or browse to find it, as shown in Figure 8.

MATLAB now first looks into the current directory for function definitions and then works down the modified search path, as shown in Figure 9.

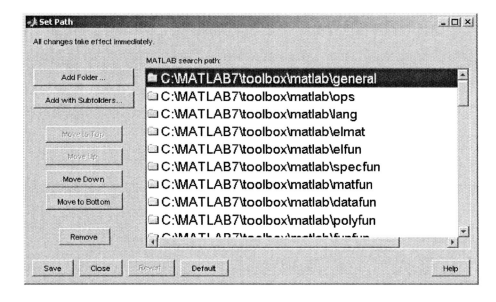

**Figure 7**
The path tool allows you to change where MATLAB looks for function definitions.

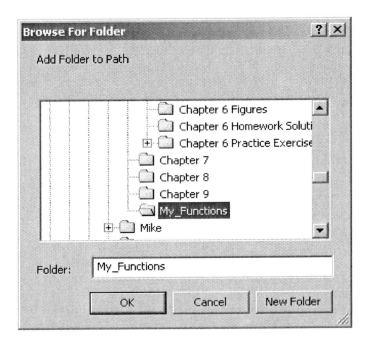

**Figure 8**
The Browse for Folder
window.

Once you've added a folder to the path, the change applies only to the current MATLAB session, unless you save your changes permanently. Clearly, you should never make permanent changes to a public computer. However, if someone else has made changes you wish to reverse, you can select the default button as shown in Figure 9 to return the search path to its original settings.

The path tool allows you to change the MATLAB search path interactively; however, the **addpath** function allows you to insert the logic to add a search path to any MATLAB program. Consult

```
help addpath
```

if you wish to modify the path in this way.

**Figure 9**
Modified MATLAB search
path.

MATLAB provides access to numerous toolboxes developed at The Math-Works or by the user community. For more information, see the firm's website, www.mathworks.com.

## 3  ANONYMOUS FUNCTIONS AND FUNCTION HANDLES

Normally, if you go to the trouble of creating a function, you will want to store it for use in other programming projects. However, MATLAB includes a simpler kind of function, called an *anonymous function*. New to MATLAB 7, anonymous functions are defined in the command window or in a script M-file and are available—much as are variable names—only until the workspace is cleared. To create an anonymous function, consider the following example:

KEY IDEA: Anonymous functions may be included in M-file programs with other commands or may be defined from the command window

```
ln = @(x) log(x)
```

- The @ symbol alerts MATLAB that **ln** is a function.
- Immediately following the @ symbol, the input to the function is listed.
- Finally, the function is defined.

The function name appears in the variable window, listed as a function_handle:

| Name | Value | Size | Bytes | Class |
|------|-------|------|-------|-------|
| @ ln | @(x) log(x) | 1x1 | 16 | function_handle |

---
**Hint**

Think of a function handle as a nickname for the function.

---

Anonymous functions can be used like any other function—for example,

```
ln(10)
ans =
      2.3026
```

Once the workspace is cleared, the anonymous function no longer exists. Anonymous functions can be saved as .mat files, just like any variable, and can be restored with the **load** command. For example to save the anonymous function **ln**, type:

```
save my_ln_function  ln
```

A file named **my_ln_function.mat** is created, which contains the anonymous **ln** function. Once the workspace is cleared, the **ln** function no longer exists, but it can be reloaded from the .mat file

```
load my_ln_function
```

It is possible to assign a function handle to any M-file function. Earlier in this chapter we created an M-file function called distance.m.

```
function  result = distance(t)
result = 1/2*9.8*t.^2;
```

The command

```
distance_handle = @(t) distance(t)
```

assigns the handle **distance_handle** to the distance function.

Anonymous functions and the related function handles are useful in functions that require other functions as input (function functions).

## 4 FUNCTION FUNCTIONS

KEY IDEA: Function functions require functions or function handles as input

One example of a MATLAB built-in function function is the function plot, **fplot**. This function requires two inputs: a function or a function handle, and a range over which to plot. We can demonstrate the use of **fplot** with the function handle **ln**, defined as

```
ln = @(x) log(x)
```

The function handle can now be used as input to the **fplot** function:

```
fplot(ln,[0.1, 10])
```

The result is shown in Figure 10. We could also use the **fplot** function without the function handle. We just need to insert the function syntax directly, as a string:

```
fplot('log(x)',[0.1, 10])
```

The advantage to using function handles isn't obvious from this example, but consider instead this anonymous function describing a particular fifth-order polynomial:

```
poly5 = @(x) -5*x.^5 + 400*x.^4 + 3*x.^3 + 20*x.^2 - x + 5;
```

Entering the equation directly into the **fplot** function would be awkward. Using the function handle is considerably simpler.

```
fplot(poly5,[-30,90])
```

The results are shown in Figure 11.

A wide variety of MATLAB functions accept function handles as input. For example, the **fzero** function finds the value of $x$ when $f(x)$ is equal to 0. It accepts a function handle and a rough guess for $x$. From Figure 11 we see that our fifth-order

**Figure 10**
Function handles can be used as input to a function function, such as **fplot**.

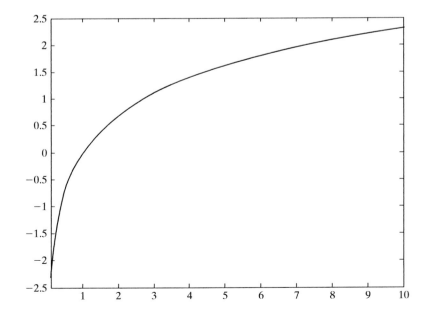

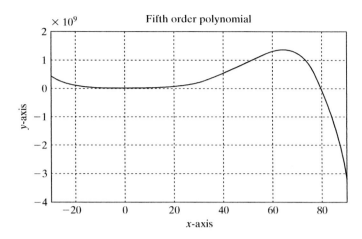

**Figure 11**
This fifth-order polynomial was plotted using the **fplot** function function, with a function handle as input.

polynomial probably has a zero between 75 and 85, so a rough guess for the zero point might be $x = 75$.

```
fzero(poly5,75)

ans =
      80.0081
```

## 5 SUBFUNCTIONS

More complicated functions can be created by grouping functions together in a single file as sub-functions. These subfunctions can be called only from the primary function, so they have limited utility. Subfunctions can be used to modularize your code and to make the primary function easier to read.

---

**Hint**

You should not attempt to create code using subfunctions until you have mastered function M-files containing a single function.

---

Each MATLAB function M-file has *one* primary function. The name of the M-file must be the same as the *primary* function name. Thus, the primary function stored in the M-file my_function.m must be named **my_function**. Subfunctions are added after the primary function, and can have any legitimate MATLAB variable name. Figure 12 shows a very simple example of a function that both adds and subtracts two vectors. The primary function is named **subfunction demo**. The file includes two subfunctions; **add** and **subtract**.

Notice in the editing window that the contents of each function are identified with a grey bracket. Each code section can be either collapsed or expanded, to make the contents easier to read, by clicking on the + or − sign included with the bracket.

When could you use subfunctions effectively? Imagine that your instructor has assigned three homework problems, each requiring you to create and test a function.

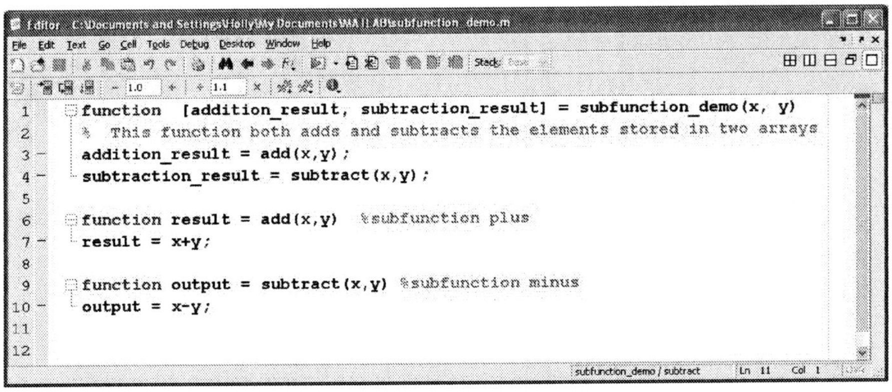

**Figure 12**
MATLAB allows the user to create subfunctions within a function M-file. This file includes the primary function, **subfunction_demo**, and two sub-functions **add** and **subtract**.

```
 1   function [addition_result, subtraction_result] = subfunction_demo(x, y)
 2   % This function both adds and subtracts the elements stored in two arrays
 3   addition_result = add(x,y);
 4   subtraction_result = subtract(x,y);
 5
 6   function result = add(x,y)    %subfunction plus
 7   result = x+y;
 8
 9   function output = subtract(x,y)  %subfunction minus
10   output = x-y;
11
12
```
```
subfunction_demo / subtract        Ln 11   Col 1
```

- Problem 1   Create and test a function called **square** to square values of $x$. Assume $x$ varies between $-3$ and $+3$.
- Problem 2   Create and test a function called **cold_work** to find the percent cold work experienced by a metallic rod, as it is drawn into a wire. Cold work is described by the following equation

$$\% \text{Cold Work} = \frac{r_i^2 - r_f^2}{r_i^2} * 100$$

where $r_i$ is the initial radius of the rod, and $r_f$ is the final radius of the rod. To test your function let $r_i = 0.5$ cm and let $r_f = 0.25$ cm.
- Problem 3   Create and test a function called **potential_energy** to determine the potential energy change of a given mass. The change in potential energy is given by

$$\Delta \text{PE} = m*g*\Delta z$$

Your function should have three inputs: $m$, $g$ and $\Delta z$. Use the following data to test your function.

$m = [1\ 2\ 3]$ kg  (The array represents three different masses.)
$g = 9.8$ m/s$^2$
$\Delta z = 5$ m

To complete the assignment you would need to create four M-files; one for each function and one to call and test the functions. We can use subfunctions to reduce the number of M-files to one.

```
function [] = sample_homework()
%  Example homework submission
%  Problem 1
x = -3:3;
disp('Problem 1')
disp('The squares of the input values are listed below')

y = square(x);
disp(y)
%  Problem 2
initial_radius = 0.5;
final_radius = 0.25;
```

```
disp('Problem 2')
disp('The percent cold work is')
cold_work(initial_radius, final_radius)
% Problem 3
m = [1,2,3];
g = 9.8;
delta_z = 5;
disp('Problem 3')
disp('The change in potential energy is ')
potential_energy(m,g,delta_z)

function result = square(x)          }   Subfunction for Problem 1
result = x.^2;

function result = cold_work(ri,rf)   }   Subfunction for Problem 2
result = (ri.^2 - rf.^2)/ri.^2;

function result = potential_energy(m,g,delta_z)  }  Subfunction for Problem 3
result = m.*g.*delta_z;
```

Note the primary function has no input and no output. To execute the primary function, type the function name at the command prompt:

```
sample_homework
```

When the primary function executes, it calls the subfunctions, and the results are displayed in the command window, as follows:

```
Problem 1
The squares of the input values are listed below
     9    4    1    0    1    4    9

Problem 2
The percent cold work is
ans =
     0.7500

Problem 3
The change in potential energy is
ans =
    49    98    147
```

In this example the four functions (primary and three subfunctions) are listed sequentially. An alternate approach is to list the subfunction *within* the primary function, usually placed near the portion of the code from which it is called. This is called *nesting*. When functions are nested, we need to indicate the end of each individual function with the **end** command.

```
function  []= sample_homework()
%  Example homework submission
% Problem 1
x = -3:3;
disp('Problem 1')
disp('The squares of the input values are listed below')
```

```
y=square(x);
disp(y)
    function result = square(x)          Nested function
    result = x.^2;
    end
% Problem 2
initial_radius = 0.5;
final_radius = 0.25;
disp('Problem 2')
disp('The percent cold work is')
cold_work(initial_radius, final_radius)
    function result = cold_work(ri,rf)    Nested function
    result = (ri.^2 - rf.^2)/ri.^2;
    end
% Problem 3
m=[1,2,3];
g = 9.8;
delta_z = 5;
disp('Problem 3')
disp('The change in potential energy is ')    Nested function
potential_energy(m,g,delta_z)
    function result = potential_energy(m,g,delta_z)
    result = m.*g.*delta_z;
    end
end
```

This end marks the
end of the primary
function

## SUMMARY

MATLAB contains a wide variety of built-in functions. However, you will often find it useful to create your own MATLAB functions. The most common type of user-defined MATLAB function is the function M-file, which must start with a function-definition line that contains

- the word **function**,
- a variable that defines the function output,
- a function name, and
- a variable used for the input argument.

For example,

```
function  output = my_function(x)
```

The function name must also be the name of the M-file in which the function is stored. Function names follow the standard MATLAB naming rules.

Like the built-in functions, user-defined functions can accept multiple inputs and can return multiple results.

Comments immediately following the function-definition line can be accessed from the command window with the **help** command.

Variables defined within a function are local to that function. They are not stored in the workspace and cannot be accessed from the command window. Global variables can be defined with the **global** command used in both the command window (or script M-file) and a MATLAB function. Good programming style suggests that you define global variables with capital letters. In general, however, it is not wise to use global variables.

Groups of user-defined functions, called "toolboxes," may be stored in a common directory and accessed by modifying the MATLAB search path. This is accomplished interactively with the path tool, either from the menu bar, as in

> **File** → **Set Path**

or from the command line, with

> **pathtool**

MATLAB provides access to numerous toolboxes developed at The Math-Works or by the user community.

Another type of function is the anonymous function, which is defined in a MATLAB session or in a script M-file and exists only during that session. Anonymous functions are especially useful for very simple mathematical expressions or as input to the more complicated function functions.

The following MATLAB summary lists and briefly describes all of the special characters, commands, and functions that were defined in this chapter:

**MATLAB SUMMARY**

| Special Characters | |
| --- | --- |
| @ | identifies a function handle, such as that used with anonymous functions |
| % | Comment |

| Commands and Functions | |
| --- | --- |
| **addpath** | adds a directory to the MATLAB search path |
| **fminbnd** | a function function that accepts a function handle or function definition as input and finds the function minimum between two bounds |
| **fplot** | a function function that accepts a function handle or function definition as input and creates the corresponding plot between two bounds |
| **fzero** | a function function that accepts a function handle or function definition as input and finds the function zero point nearest a specified value |
| **function** | identifies an M-file as a function |
| **global** | defines a variable that can be used in multiple sections of code |
| **meshgrid** | maps two input vectors onto two two-dimensional matrices |
| **nargin** | determines the number of input arguments in a function |
| **nargout** | determines the number of output arguments from a function |
| **pathtool** | opens the interactive path tool |
| **varargin** | indicates that a variable number of arguments may be input to a function |

**KEY TERMS**

anonymous
argument
comments
directory
file name
folder

function
function function
function handle
function name
global variable

in-line
input argument
local variable
M-file
toolbox

**PROBLEMS**

### Function M-Files

As you create functions in this section, be sure to comment them appropriately. Remember that, although many of these problems could be solved without a function, the objective of this chapter is to learn to write and use functions. Each of these functions (except for the anonymous functions) must be created in its own M-file and then called from the command window or a script M-file program.

1   As described in Example 2, metals are actually crystalline materials. Metal crystals are called grains. When the average grain size is small, the metal is strong; when it is large, the metal is weaker. Since every crystal in a particular sample of metal is a different size, it isn't obvious how we should describe the average crystal size. The American Society for Testing and Materials (ASTM) has developed the following correlation for standardizing grain-size measurements:

$$N = 2^{n-1}$$

The ASTM grain size ($n$) is determined by looking at a sample of a metal under a microscope at a magnification of 100× (100 power). The number of grains in a 1-square-inch area (actual dimensions of 0.01 inch × 0.01 inch) is estimated ($N$) and used in the preceding equation to find the ASTM grain size.

(a) Write a MATLAB function called **num_grains** to find the number of grains in a 1-square-inch area ($N$) at 100× magnification when the ASTM grain size is known.

(b) Use your function to find the number of grains for ASTM grain sizes $n = 10$ to 100.

(c) Create a plot of your results.

2   Perhaps the most famous equation in physics is

$$E = mc^2$$

which relates energy $E$ to mass $m$. The speed of light in a vacuum, $c$, is the property that links the two together. The speed of light in a vacuum is $2.9979 \times 10^8$ m/s.

(a) Create a function called **energy** to find the energy corresponding to a given mass in kg. Your result will be in joules, since 1 kg m²/s² = 1 joule.

(b) Use your function to find the energy corresponding to masses from 1 kg to $10^6$ kg. Use the **logspace** function (consult **help/logspace**) to create an appropriate mass vector.

(c) Create a plot of your results. Try using different logarithmic plotting approaches (e.g., **semilogy**, **semilogx**, and **loglog**) to determine the best way to graph your results.

**3** The future-value-of-money formula relates how much a current investment will be worth in the future, assuming a constant interest rate.

$$FV = PV*(1 + i)^n$$

where

*FV* is the future value

*PV* is the present value or investment

*I*  is the interest rate expressed as a fractional amount per compounding period—i.e., 5% is expressed as .05.

n  is the number of compounding periods

(a) Create a MATLAB function called **future_value** with three inputs; the investment (present value), the interest rate expressed as a fraction, and the number of compounding periods.

(b) Use your function to determine the value of a $1000 investment in 10 years, assuming the interest rate is 0.5% per month, and the interest is compounded monthly.

**4** In freshman chemistry, the relationship between moles and mass is introduced:

$$n = \frac{m}{MW}$$

where

$n$   = number of moles of a substance,

$m$   = mass of the substance, and

$MW$ = molecular weight (molar mass) of the substance.

(a) Create a function M-file called **nmoles** that requires two vector inputs— the mass and molecular weight—and returns the corresponding number of moles. Because you are providing vector input, it will be necessary to use the **meshgrid** function in your calculations.

(b) Test your function for the compounds shown in the following table, for masses from 1 to 10 g:

| Compound | Molecular Weight (Molar Mass) |
|---|---|
| Benzene | 78.115 g/mol |
| Ethyl alcohol | 46.07 g/mol |
| Refrigerant R134a (tetrafluoroethane) | 102.3 g/mol |

Your result should be a $10 \times 3$ matrix.

**5** By rearranging the preceding relationship between moles and mass, you can find the mass if you know the number of moles of a compound:

$$m = n \times MW$$

(a) Create a function M-file called **mass** that requires two vector inputs—the number of moles and the molecular weight—and returns the corresponding mass. Because you are providing vector input, it will be necessary to use the **meshgrid** function in your calculations.

**(b)** Test your function with the compounds listed in the previous problem, for values of $n$ from 1 to 10.

**6** The distance to the horizon increases as you climb a mountain (or a hill). The expression

$$d = \sqrt{2rh + h^2}$$

where

$d$ = distance to the horizon,

$r$ = radius of the earth, and

$h$ = height of the hill

can be used to calculate that distance. The distance depends on how high the hill is and on the radius of the earth (or another planetary body).

**(a)** Create a function M-file called **distance** to find the distance to the horizon. Your function should accept two vector inputs—radius and height—and should return the distance to the horizon. Don't forget that you'll need to use **meshgrid** because your inputs are vectors.

**(b)** Create a MATLAB program that uses your distance function to find the distance in miles to the horizon, both on the earth and on Mars, for hills from 0 to 10,000 feet. Remember to use consistent units in your calculations. Note that

- Earth's diameter = 7926 miles
- Mars' diameter = 4217 miles

Report your results in a table. Each column should represent a different planet, and each row a different hill height.

**7** A rocket is launched vertically. At time $t = 0$, the rocket's engine shuts down. At that time, the rocket has reached an altitude of 500 meters and is rising at a velocity of 125 meters per second. Gravity then takes over. The height of the rocket as a function of time is

$$h(t) = -\frac{9.8}{2}t^2 + 125t + 500 \quad \text{for } t > 0$$

**(a)** Create a function called **height** that accepts time as an input and returns the height of the rocket. Use your function in your solutions to parts b and c.

**(b)** Plot **height** vs. time for times from 0 to 30 seconds. Use an increment of 0.5 second in your time vector.

**(c)** Find the time when the rocket starts to fall back to the ground. (The **max** function will be helpful in this exercise.)

**8** The distance a freely falling object travels is

$$x = \frac{1}{2}gt^2$$

where

$g$ = acceleration due to gravity, 9.8 m/s$^2$

$t$ = time in seconds

$x$ = distance traveled in meters.

If you have taken calculus, you know that we can find the velocity of the object by taking the derivative of the preceding equation. That is,

$$\frac{dx}{dt} = v = gt$$

We can find the acceleration by taking the derivative again:

$$\frac{dv}{dt} = a = g$$

(a) Create a function called **free_fall** with a single input vector **t** that returns values for distance **x**, velocity **v**, and acceleration **g**.

(b) Test your function with a time vector that ranges from 0 to 20 seconds.

9   Create a function called **polygon** that draws a polygon with any number of sides. Your function should require a single input: the number of sides desired. It should not return any value to the command window but should draw the requested polygon in polar coordinates.

## Creating Your Own Toolbox

10   This problem requires you to generate temperature-conversion tables. Use the following equations, which describe the relationships between temperatures in degrees Fahrenheit ($T_F$), degrees Celsius ($T_C$), kelvins ($T_K$),and degrees Rankine ($T_R$), respectively:

$$T_F = T_R - 459.67°R$$

$$T_F = \frac{9}{5}T_C + 32°F$$

$$T_R = \frac{9}{5}T_K$$

You will need to rearrange these expressions to solve some of the problems.

(a) Create a function called **F_to_K** that converts temperatures in Fahrenheit to Kelvin. Use your function to generate a conversion table for values from 0°F to 200°F.

(b) Create a function called **C_to_R** that converts temperatures in Celsius to Rankine. Use your function to generate a conversion table from 0°C to 100°C. Print 25 lines in the table. (Use the **linspace** function to create your input vector.)

(c) Create a function called **C_to_F** that converts temperatures in Celsius to Fahrenheit. Use your function to generate a conversion table from 0°C to 100°C. Choose an appropriate spacing.

(d) Group your functions into a folder (directory) called **my_temp_conversions**. Adjust the MATLAB search path so that it finds your folder. (Don't save any changes on a public computer!)

### Anonymous Functions and Function Handles

11   Barometers have been used for almost 400 years to measure pressure changes in the atmosphere. The first known barometer was invented by Evangelista Torricelli (1608–1647), a student of Galileo during his final years in Florence, Italy. The height of a liquid in a barometer is directly proportional to the atmospheric pressure, or

$$P = \rho g h$$

where $P$ is the pressure, $\rho$ is the density of the barometer fluid, and $h$ is the height of the liquid column. For mercury barometers, the density of the fluid is 13,560 kg/m$^3$. On the surface of the earth, the acceleration due to gravity, $g$, is approximately 9.8 m/s$^2$. Thus, the only variable in the equation is the height of the fluid column, $h$, which should have the unit of meters.

(a) Create an anonymous function **P** that finds the pressure if the value of $h$ is provided. The units of your answer will be

$$\frac{\text{kg}}{\text{m}^3}\frac{\text{m}}{\text{s}^2}\text{m} = \frac{\text{kg}}{\text{m}}\frac{1}{\text{s}^2} = \text{Pa}$$

(b) Create another anonymous function to convert pressure in Pa (Pascals) to pressure in atmospheres (atm). Call the function **Pa_to_atm**. Note that

$$1 \text{ atm} = 101{,}325 \text{ Pa}$$

(c) Use your anonymous functions to find the pressure for fluid heights from 0.5 m to 1.0 m of mercury.

(d) Save your anonymous functions as **.mat** files

12   The energy required to heat water at constant pressure is approximately equal to

$$E = mC_p\,\Delta T$$

where

$m$ = mass of the water, in grams,

$C_p$ = heat capacity of water, 1 cal/g K, and

$\Delta T$ = change in temperature, K.

(a) Create an anonymous function called **heat** to find the energy required to heat 1 gram of water if the change in temperature is provided as the input.

(b) Your result will be in calories:

$$\text{g}\frac{\text{cal}}{\text{g}}\frac{1}{\text{K}}\text{K} = \text{cal}$$

Joules are the unit of energy used most often in engineering. Create another anonymous function **cal_to_J** to convert your answer from part (a) into joules. (There are 4.2 joules/cal.)

(c) Save your anonymous functions as **.mat** files.

13  (a) Create an anonymous function called **my_function**, equal to

$$-x^2 - 5x - 3 + e^x$$

(b) Use the **fplot** function to create a plot from $x = -5$ to $x = +5$. Recall that the **fplot** function can accept a function handle as input.

(c) Use the **fminbnd** function to find the minimum function value in this range. The **fminbnd** function is an example of a function function, since it requires a function or function handle as input. The syntax is

**fminbnd(function_handle, xmin, xmax)**

Three inputs are required; the function handle, the minimum value of $x$ and the maximum value of $x$. The function searches between the minimum value of $x$ and the maximum value of $x$ for the point where the function value is a minimum.

14  In Problem 7 you created an M-file function called **height** to evaluate the height of a rocket as a function of time. The relationship between time, $t$, and height, $h(t)$, is:

$$h(t) = -\frac{9.8}{2}t^2 + 125t + 500 \quad \text{for } t > 0$$

(a) Create a function handle to the **height** function called **height_handle**.

(b) Use **height_handle** as input to the **fplot** function, and create a graph from 0 to 60 seconds.

(c) Use the **fzero** function to find the time when the rocket hits the ground (i.e., when the function value is zero). The **fzero** function is an example of a function function, since it requires a function or function handle as input. The syntax is

**fzero(function_handle, x_guess)**

The **fzero** function requires two inputs—a function handle and your guess as to the time value where the function is close to zero. You can select a reasonable **x_guess** value by inspecting the graph created in part (b).

## Subfunctions

15  In Problem 10 you were asked to create and use three different temperature-conversion functions, based on the following conversion equations:

$$T_F = T_R - 459.67°R$$

$$T_F = \frac{9}{5}T_C + 32°F$$

$$T_R = \frac{9}{5}T_K$$

Recreate Problem 10 using nested subfunctions. The primary function should be called **temperature_conversions** and should include the subfunctions

```
F_to_K
C_to_R
C_to_F
```

Within the primary function use the subfunctions to:

**(a)** Generate a conversion table for values from 0°F to 200°F. Include a column for temperature in Fahrenheit and Kelvin.

**(b)** Generate a conversion table from 0°C to 100°C. Print 25 lines in the table. (Use the **linspace** function to create your input vector.) Your table should include a column for temperature in Celsius and Rankine.

**(c)** Generate a conversion table from 0°C to 100°C. Choose an appropriate spacing. Include a column for temperature in Celsius and Fahrenheit.

Recall that you will need to call your primary function from the command window or from a script M-file.

## SOLUTIONS TO PRACTICE EXERCISES

### Practice Exercises 1

Store these functions as separate M-files. The name of the function must be the same as the name of the M-file. You'll need to call these functions either from the command window or from a script M-file. You can't run a function M-file by itself.

1. ```
function output = quadratic(x)
output = x.^2;
```

2. ```
function output = one_over(x)
output = exp(1./x);
```

3. ```
function output = sin_x_squared(x)
output = sin(x.^2);
```

4. ```
function result = in_to_ft(x)
result = x./12;
```

5. ```
function result = cal_to_joules(x)
result = 4.2.*x;
```

6. ```
function output = Watts_to_Btu_per_hour(x)
output = x.*3.412;
```

7. ```
function output = meters_to_miles(x)
output = x./1000.*.6214;
```

8. ```
function output = mph_to_fps(x)
output = x.*5280/3600;
```

### Practice Exercises 2

Store these functions as separate M-files. The name of the function must be the same as the name of the M-file.

1. ```
function output = z1(x,y)
% summation of x and y
% the matrix dimensions must agree
output = x+y;
```

2. ```
function output = z2(a,b,c)
% finds a.*b.^c
% the matrix dimensions must agree
output = a.*b.^c;
```

3. 
```
function output = z3(w,x,y)
% finds w.*exp(x./y)
% the matrix dimensions must agree
output = w.*exp(x./y);
```

4. 
```
function output = z4(p,t)
% finds p./sin(t)
% the matrix dimensions must agree
output = p./sin(t);
```

5. 
```
function [a,b]=f5(x)
a = cos(x);
b = sin(x);
```

6. 
```
function [a,b] = f6(x)
a = 5.*x.^2 + 2;
b = sqrt(5.*x.^2 + 2);
```

7. 
```
function [a,b] = f7(x)
a = exp(x);
b = log(x);
```

8. 
```
function [a,b] = f8(x,y)
a = x+y;
b = x-y;
```

9. 
```
function [a,b] = f9(x,y)
a = y.*exp(x);
b = x.*exp(y);
```

# 7

# User-Controlled Input and Output

## INTRODUCTION

So far, we have explored the use of MATLAB in two modes: in the command window as a scratch pad and in the editing window to write simple programs (script M-files). The programmer has been the user. Now we move on to more complicated programs, written in the editing window, where the programmer and the user may be different people. That will make it necessary to use input and output commands to communicate with the user, instead of rewriting the actual code to solve similar problems. MATLAB offers built-in functions to allow a user to communicate with a program as it executes. The **input** command pauses the program and prompts the user for input; the **disp** and **fprintf** commands provide output to the command window.

## 1 USER-DEFINED INPUT

Although we have written programs in script M-files, we have assumed that the programmer (you) and the user are the same person. To run the program with different input values, we actually changed some of the code. We can create more general programs by allowing the user to input values of a matrix from the keyboard while the program is running. The **input** function allows us to do this. It displays a text string in the command window and then waits for the user to provide the requested input. For example,

```
z = input('Enter a value')
```

displays

```
Enter a value
```

in the command window. If the user enters a value such as

```
5
```

the program assigns the value 5 to the variable **z**. If the **input** command does not end with a semicolon, the value entered is displayed on the screen:

```
z =
     5
```

The same approach can be used to enter a one- or two-dimensional matrix. The user must provide the appropriate brackets and delimiters (commas and semicolons). For example,

```
z = input('Enter values for z in brackets')
```

KEY IDEA: The **input** function can be used to communicate with the progam user

requests the user to input a matrix such as

```
[  1,   2,   3;   4,   5,   6]
```

and responds with

```
z =
     1   2   3
     4   5   6
```

This input value of **z** can then be used in subsequent calculations by the script M-file.

Data entered with **input** does not need to be numeric information. Suppose we prompt the user with the command

```
x = input('Enter your name in single quotes')
```

and enter

```
'Holly'
```

when prompted. Because we haven't used a semicolon at the end of the **input** command, MATLAB will respond

```
x =
    Holly
```

Notice in the workspace window that **x** is listed as a $1 \times 5$ character array:

| Name | Value | Size | Bytes | Class |
|------|-------|------|-------|-------|
| abc x | 'Holly' | $1 \times 5$ | 6 | char |

If you are entering a string (in MATLAB, strings are character arrays), you must enclose the characters in single quotes. However, an alternative form of the input command alerts the function to expect character input without the single quotes by specifying string input in the second field:

```
x = input('Enter your name', 's')
```

Now you need only enter the characters, such as

```
Ralph
```

and the program responds with

```
x =
    Ralph
```

## Practice Exercises 1

1. Create an M-file to calculate the area $A$ of a triangle:

$$A = \frac{1}{2} \text{base height}$$

Prompt the user to enter the values for the base and for the height.

2. Create an M-file to find the volume $V$ of a right circular cylinder:

$$V = \pi r^2 h$$

Prompt the user to enter the values of $r$ and $h$.

3. Create a vector from 0 to $n$, allowing the user to enter the value of $n$.

4. Create a vector that starts at $a$, ends at $b$, and has a spacing of $c$. Allow the user to input all of these parameters.

**EXAMPLE 1**

### Freely Falling Objects

Consider the behavior of a freely falling object under the influence of gravity. (See Figure 1.)

The position of the object is described by

$$d = \frac{1}{2} g t^2$$

where  $d$  =  distance the object travels,
$g$  =  acceleration due to gravity, and
$t$  =  elapsed time

**Figure 1**
The Leaning Tower of Pisa.
(Courtesy of Tim Galligan.)

We shall allow the user to specify the value of $g$—the acceleration due to gravity—and a vector of time values.

1. State the Problem
   Find the distance traveled by a freely falling object and plot the results.
2. Describe the Input and Output

   **Input**  Value of $g$, the acceleration due to gravity, provided by the user
   Time, provided by the user

   **Output**  Distances
   Plot of distance versus time

3. Develop a Hand Example

$$d = \frac{1}{2}gt^2, \text{ so, on the moon at 100 seconds,}$$

$$d = \frac{1}{2} \times 1.6 \text{ m/s}^2 \times 100^2 \text{ s}^2$$

$$d = 8000 \text{ m}$$

4. Develop a MATLAB Solution

```
%Example 1
%Free fall
clear, clc
%Request input from the user
g = input('What is the value of acceleration due to
   gravity?')
start = input('What starting time would you like? ')
finish = input('What ending time would you like? ')
incr = input('What time increments would you like
   calculated? ')
time = start:incr:finish;
%Calculate the distance
distance = 1/2*g*time.^2;
%Plot the results
loglog(time,distance)
title('Distance Traveled in Free Fall')
xlabel('time, s'),ylabel('distance, m')
%Find the maximum distance traveled
final_distance = max(distance)
```

The interaction in the command window is:

```
What is the value of acceleration due to gravity? 1.6
g =
  1.6000
What starting time would you like? 0
start =
  0
What ending time would you like? 100
finish =
  100
What time increments would you like calculated? 10
```

```
incr =
   10
final_distance =
   8000
```

The results are plotted in Figure 2.

5. Test the Solution

Compare the MATLAB solution with the hand solution. Since the user can control the input, we entered the data used in the hand solution. MATLAB tells us that the final distance traveled is 8000 m, which, since we entered 100 seconds as the final time, corresponds to the distance traveled after 100 seconds.

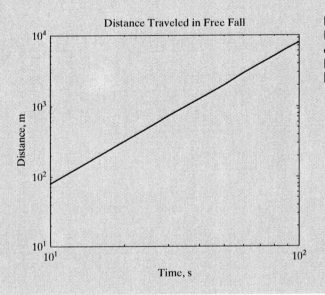

**Figure 2**
Distance traveled when the acceleration is 1.6 m/s². Notice that the figure is a loglog plot.

## 2 OUTPUT OPTIONS

There are several ways to display the contents of a matrix. The simplest is to enter the name of the matrix, without a semicolon. The name will be repeated, and the values of the matrix will be displayed, starting on the next line. For example, first define a matrix **x**:

```
x = 1:5;
```

Because there is a semicolon at the end of the assignment statement, the values in **x** are not repeated in the command window. However, if you want to display **x** later in your program, simply type in the variable name

```
x
```

which returns

```
x =
     1     2     3     4     5
```

MATLAB offers two other approaches to displaying results: the **disp** function and the **fprintf** function.

KEY IDEA: The **disp** function can display either character arrays or numeric arrays

### 2.1 Display Function

The display (**disp**) function can be used to display the contents of a matrix without printing the matrix name. It accepts a single array as input. Thus,

```
disp(x)
```

returns

```
1     2     3     4     5
```

The display command can also be used to display a string (text enclosed in single quotation marks). For example,

```
disp('The values in the x matrix are:');
```

returns

```
The values in the x matrix are:
```

When you enter a string as input into the **disp** function, you are really entering an array of character information. Try entering the following on the command line:

```
'The values in the x matrix are:'
```

MATLAB responds

```
ans =
'The values in the x matrix are:'
```

CHARACTER ARRAY: stores character information

The workspace window lists **ans** as a 1 × 32 character array.

| Name | Size | Bytes | Class |
|---|---|---|---|
| abc ans | 1 × 32 | 90 | char array |

Character arrays store character information in arrays similar to numerical arrays. Characters can be letters, numbers, punctuation, and even some nondisplayed characters. Each character, including spaces, is an element in the character array.

When we execute the two display functions

```
disp('The values in the x matrix are:');
disp(x)
```

KEY IDEA: Characters can be letters, numbers or symbols

MATLAB responds

```
The values in the x matrix are:
1   2   3   4   5
```

Notice that the two **disp** functions are displayed on separate lines. You can get around this feature by creating a combined matrix of your two outputs, using the **num2str** (number to string) function. The process is called concatenation and creates a single character array. Thus,

```
disp(['The values in the x array are: ' num2str(x)])
```

returns

```
The values in the x array are: 1 2 3 4 5
```

The **num2str** function changes an array of numbers into an array of characters. In the preceding example, we used **num2str** to transform the **x** matrix to a character array, which was then combined with the first string (by means of square brackets, [ ] ) to make a bigger character array. You can see the resulting matrix by typing

```
A = ['The values in the x array are: ' num2str(x)]
```

which returns

```
A =
      The values in the x array are: 1 2 3 4 5
```

Checking in the workspace window, we see that **A** is a $1 \times 45$ matrix. The workspace window also tells us that the matrix contains character data instead of numeric information. This is evidenced both by the icon in front of **A** and in the class column.

| Name | Size | Bytes | Class |
|------|------|-------|-------|
| abc A | $1 \times 45$ | 90 | char array |

**Hint**

If you want to include an apostrophe in a string, you need to enter the apostrophe twice. If you don't do this, MATLAB will interpret the apostrophe as terminating the string. An example of the use of two apostrophes is

```
disp('The moon"s gravity is 1/6th that of the earth')
```

You can use a combination of the **input** and **disp** functions to mimic a conversation. Try creating and running the following M-file:

```
disp('Hi There');
disp('I"m your MATLAB program');
name = input('Who are you?','s');
disp(['Hi ',name]);
answer = input('Don't you just love computers?', 's');
disp([answer,'?']);
disp('Computers are very useful');
disp('You''ll use them a lot in college!!');
disp('Good luck with your studies')
pause(2);
disp('Bye bye')
```

This interaction made use of the **pause** function. If you execute **pause** without any input, the program waits until the user hits the Enter key. If a value is used as input to the **pause** function, the program waits for the specifed number of seconds, and then continues.

## 2.2 Formatted Output— The fprintf Function

The **fprintf** function (formatted print function) gives you even more control over the output than you have with the **disp** function. In addition to displaying both text and matrix values, you can specify the format to be used in displaying the values, and you can specify when to skip to a new line. If you are a C programmer, you will be familiar with the syntax of this function. With few exceptions, the MATLAB **fprintf** function uses the same formatting specifications as the C **fprintf** function. This is hardly surprising, since MATLAB was written in C. (It was originally written in Fortran and then later rewritten in C.)

The general form of the **fprintf** command contains two arguments, one a string and the other a list of matrices:

```
fprintf(format-string, var,...)
```

Consider the following example:

```
cows = 5;
fprintf('There are %f cows in the pasture ', cows)
```

The string, which is the first argument inside the **fprintf** function, contains a placeholder (%) where the value of the variable (in this case, **cows**) will be inserted. The placeholder also contains formatting information. In this example, the **%f** tells MATLAB to display the value of **cows** in a default fixed-point format. The default format displays six places after the decimal point:

```
There are 5.000000 cows in the pasture
```

Besides defaulting to a fixed-point format, MATLAB allows you to specify an exponential format, **%e**, or lets you allow MATLAB to choose whichever is shorter, fixed point or exponential (**%g**). It also lets you display character information (**%c**) or a string of characters (**%s**). The decimal format (**%d**) is especially useful if the number you wish to display is an integer.

```
fprintf('There are %d cows in the pasture ', cows)
There are 5 cows in the pasture
```

Table 1 illustrates the various formats supported by **fprintf**, and the related **sprintf** functions.

KEY IDEA: The **fprintf** function allows you to control how numbers are displayed

MATLAB does not automatically start a new line after an **fprintf** function is executed. If you tried out the preceding **fprintf** command example, you probably noticed that the command prompt is on the same line as the output:

```
There are 5.000000 cows in the pasture >>
```

If we execute another command, the results will appear on the same line instead of moving down. Thus, if we issue the new commands

```
cows = 6;
fprintf('There are %f cows in the pasture', cows);
```

### Table 1  Type Field Format

| Type Field | Result |
|---|---|
| **%f** | fixed-point notation |
| **%e** | exponential notation |
| **%d** | decimal notation—does not include trailing zeros if the value displayed is an integer. If the number includes a fractional component, it is displayed using exponential notation. |
| **%g** | whichever is shorter, **%f** or **%e** |
| **%c** | character information (displays one character at a time) |
| **%s** | string of characters (displays the entire string) |

Additional type fields are described in the help feature.

from an M-file, MATLAB continues the command window display on the same line:

```
There are 5.000000 cows in the pasture There are 6.000000
cows in the pasture
```

To cause MATLAB to start a new line, you'll need to use **\n**, called a linefeed, at the end of the string. For example, the code

```
cows = 5;
fprintf('There are %f cows in the pasture \n', cows)
cows = 6;
fprintf('There are %f cows in the pasture \n', cows)
```

returns the following output:

```
There are 5.000000 cows in the pasture
There are 6.000000 cows in the pasture
```

KEY IDEA: The **fprintf** function allows you to display both character and numeric information with a single command

---

**Hint**

The backslash (\) and forward slash (/) are different characters. It's a common mistake to confuse them—and then the linefeed command doesn't work! Instead, the output to the command window will be

```
There are 5.000000 cows in the pasture /n
```

---

Other special format commands are listed in Table 2. The tab (**\t**) is especially useful for creating tables in which everything lines up neatly.

You can further control how the variables are displayed by using the optional **width field** and **precision field** with the format command. The **width field** controls the minimum number of characters to be printed. It must be a positive decimal integer. The **precision field** is preceded by a period (.) and specifies the number of decimal places after the decimal point for exponential and fixed-point types. For example, **%8.2f** specifies that the minimum total width available to display your result is eight digits, two of which are after the decimal point. Thus, the code

```
voltage = 3.5;
fprintf('The voltage is %8.2f millivolts \n',voltage);
```

returns

```
The voltage is     3.50 millivolts
```

Notice the empty space before the number 3.50. This occurs because we reserved six spaces (eight total, two after the decimal) for the portion of the number to the left of the decimal point.

**Table 2  Special Format Commands**

| Format Command | Resulting Action |
| --- | --- |
| **\n** | linefeed |
| **\r** | carriage return (similar to linefeed) |
| **\t** | tab |
| **\b** | backspace |

Often when you use the **fprintf** function, your variable will be a matrix—for example,

```
x = 1:5;
```

MATLAB will repeat the string in the **fprintf** command until it uses all the values in the matrix. Thus,

```
fprintf('%8.2f \n',x);
```

returns

```
1.00
2.00
3.00
4.00
5.00
```

If the variable is a two-dimensional matrix, MATLAB uses the values one *column* at a time, going down the first column, then the second, and so on. Here's a more complicated example:

```
feet = 1:3;
inches = feet.*12;
```

Combine these two matrices:

```
table = [feet;inches]
```

MATLAB then returns

```
table =
     1    2    3
    12   24   36
```

Now we can use the **fprintf** function to create a table that is easier to interpret. For instance,

```
fprintf('%4.0f %7.2f \n',table)
```

sends the following output to the command window:

```
1   12.00
2   24.00
3   36.00
```

Why don't the two outputs look the same? The **fprintf** statement we created uses two values at a time. It goes through the **table** array one *column* at a time to find the numbers it needs. Thus, the first two numbers used in the **fprintf** output are from the first column of the **table** array.

The **fprintf** function can accept a variable number of matrices after the string. It uses all of the values in each of these matrices, in order, before moving on to the next matrix. As an example, suppose we wanted to use the feet and inches matrices without combining them into the table matrix. Then we could type

```
fprintf('%4.0f %7.2f \n', feet, inches)
 1    2.00
 3   12.00
24   36.00
```

The function works through the values of **feet** first and then uses the values in **inches**. It is unlikely that this is what you really want the function to do (in this example it wasn't), so the output values are almost always grouped into a single matrix to use in **fprintf**.

The **fprintf** command gives you considerably more control over the form of your output than MATLAB's simple format commands. It does, however, require some care and forethought to use.

In addition to creating formatted output for display in the command window, the **fprintf** function can be used to send formatted output to a file. First you'll need to create and open an output file and assign it a file identifier (nickname). You do this with the **fopen** function

```
file_id = fopen('my_output_file.txt', 'wt');
```

The first field is the name of the file, and the second field makes it possible for us to write data to the file (hence the string 'wt'). Once the file has been identified and opened for writing, we use the **fprintf** function, adding the file identifier as the first field in the function input.

```
fprintf(file_id, 'Some example output is %4.2f \n', pi*1000)
```

This form of the function sends the result of the formatted string

```
Some example output is 3141.59
```

to **my_output_file.txt**. To the command window the function sends a count of the number of bytes transferred to the file.

```
ans =
    32
```

### Hint

A common mistake new programmers make when using **fprintf** is to forget to include the field type identifier, such as **f**, in the placeholder sequence. The **fprintf** function won't work, but no error message is returned either.

### Hint

If you want to include a percentage sign in an **fprintf** statement, you need to enter the % twice. If you don't, MATLAB will interpret the % as a placeholder for data. For example,

```
fprintf('The interest rate is %5.2f %% \n', 5)
```

results in

```
The interest rate is 5.00 %
```

**EXAMPLE 2**

## Free Fall: Formatted Output

Let's redo Example 1, but this time let's create a table of results instead of a plot, and let's use the **disp** and **fprintf** commands to control the appearance of the output.

1. State the Problem
   Find the distance traveled by a freely falling object.

2. Describe the Input and Output

   **Input**   Value of *g*, the acceleration due to gravity, provided by the user
   Time *t*, provided by the user

   **Output** Distances calculated for each planet and the moon

3. Develop a Hand Example

$$d = \frac{1}{2}gt^2, \text{ so, on the moon at 100 seconds,}$$

$$d = \frac{1}{2} \times 1.6 \text{ m/s}^2 \times 100^2 \text{ s}^2$$

$$d = 8000 \text{ m}$$

4. Develop a MATLAB Solution

```
%Example 2
%Free Fall
clear, clc
%Request input from the user
g = input('What is the value of acceleration due to
  gravity? ')
start = input('What starting time would you like? ')
finish = input('What ending time would you like? ')
incr = input('What time increments would you like
  calculated? ')
time = start:incr:finish;
%Calculate the distance
distance = 1/2*g*time.^2;
%Create a matrix of the output data
table = [time;distance];
%Send the output to the command window
fprintf('For an acceleration due to gravity of %5.1f
  seconds \n the following data were calculated \n', g)
disp('Distance Traveled in Free Fall')
disp('time, s distance, m')
fprintf('%8.0f %10.2f\n',table)
```

This M-file produces the following interaction in the command window:

```
What is the value of acceleration due to gravity? 1.6
g =
  1.6000

What starting time would you like? 0
start =
  0

What ending time would you like? 100
finish =
  100

What time increments would you like calculated? 10
incr =
  10

For an acceleration due to gravity of 1.6 seconds
  the following data were calculated
```

```
Distance Traveled in Free Fall
  time, s      distance, m

      0            0.00
     10           80.00
     20          320.00
     30          720.00
     40         1280.00
     50         2000.00
     60         2880.00
     70         3920.00
     80         5120.00
     90         6480.00
    100         8000.00
```

5. Test the Solution
Compare the MATLAB solution with the hand solution. Since the output is a table, it is easy to see that the distance traveled at 100 seconds is 8000 m. Try using other data as input, and compare your results with the graph produced in Example 1.

---

### Practice Exercises 2

In an M-file,

1. Use the **disp** command to create a title for a table that converts inches to feet.
2. Use the **disp** command to create column headings for your table.
3. Create an **inches** vector from 0 to 120 with an increment of 10.
   Calculate the corresponding values of **feet**.
   Group the **inch** vector and the **feet** vector together into a **table** matrix.
   Use the **fprintf** command to send your table to the command window.

---

### 2.3 Formatted Output—The sprintf Function

The **sprintf** function is similar to **fprintf**, but instead of just sending the result of the formatted string to the command window, **sprintf** assigns it a name and sends it to the command window.

KEY IDEA: The **sprintf** function is similar to **fprintf** and is useful for annotating plots

```
a = sprintf('Some example output is %4.2f \n', pi*1000)
a =
    Some example output is 3141.59
```

When would this be useful? In Example 3 the **sprintf** function is used to specify the contents of a text box, which is shown as an annotation on a graph.

---

**EXAMPLE 3**

## Projectile Motion: Annotating a Graph

Recall from earlier examples that the equation describing the range of a projectile fired from a cannon is

$$R(\theta) = \frac{v^2}{g}\sin(2\theta)$$

where

$R(\theta)$ is the range in meters
$v$ is the initial projectile velocity in m/s
$\theta$ is the launch angle
$g$ is the acceleration due to gravity, 9.9 m/s$^2$

Plot the angle on the $x$-axis versus the range on the $y$-axis and add a text box indicating the value of the maximum range.

1. State the Problem
   Find and plot the distance traveled by projectile, as a function of launch angle. Annotate a plot, indicating the maximum range.

2. Describe the Input and Output

   **Input**  Acceleration due to gravity, $g = 9.9$ m/s$^2$
   Launch angle
   Initial projectile velocity, 100 m/s

   **Output** An annotated graph indicating the maximum range.

3. Develop a Hand Example
   We know from physics and from previous examples that the maximum range occurs at a launch angle of 45 degrees. Substituting into the provided equation,

$$R(45^0) = \frac{100^2 \, m^2/s^2}{9.9 \, m/s^2} \sin(2 * 45^0)$$

   Since the angle is specified in degrees, you must either set your calculator to accept degrees into the sine function, or else convert 45 degrees to the corresponding number of radians ($\pi/4$). After you have done so, the result is

$$R(45°) = 1010 \text{ meters}$$

4. Develop a MATLAB Solution

```
% Example 5
% Find the maximum projectile range for a given set of
    conditions
% Create an annotated graph of the results
% Define the input parameters
  g=9.9;   %Acceleration due to gravity
  velocity = 100; %Initial velocity, m/s^2
  theta = [0:5:90]  %Launch angle in degrees
% Calculate the range
  range = velocity^2/g*sind(2*theta);
% Calculate the maximum range
  maximum = max(range);
% Create the input for the textbox
  text_input=sprintf('The maximum range was %4.0f
    meters \n',maximum);
% Plot the results
  plot(theta,range)
  title('Range of a Projectile')
  xlabel('Angle, degrees')
  ylabel('Range, meters')
  text(10,maximum,text_input)
```

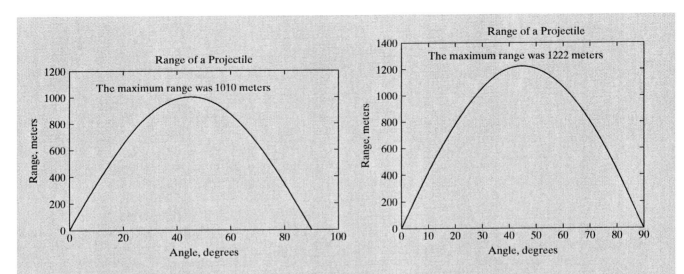

**Figure 3**
The contents of the text box change, depending on the input to the program, and are controlled by the **sprintf** function.

There are several things to notice about this program. First, we took advantage of the **sind** function to calculate the value of sine, using degrees as input. Second, the location of the text box will always start on the graph at 10 degrees (measured on the *x*-axis), but the *y* location depends on the maximum range. This M-file produces the graph shown in Figure 3a:

5. Test the Solution
   Compare the MATLAB solution with the hand solution. The text box used to annotate the graph lists the maximum range as 1010 meters, the same value calculated by hand. We could also test the program with a different initial velocity, for example 110 m/sec. The result is shown in Figure 13

## 3 GRAPHICAL INPUT

MATLAB offers a technique for entering ordered pairs of *x*- and *y*-values graphically. The **ginput** command allows the user to select points from a figure window and converts the points into the appropriate *x*- and *y*-coordinates. In the statement

```
[x,y] = ginput(n)
```

MATLAB requests the user to select *n* points from the figure window. If the value of **n** is not included, as in

```
[x,y] = ginput
```

MATLAB accepts points until the return key is entered.

This technique is useful for picking points off a graph. Consider the graph in Figure 4.

The figure was created by defining *x* from 5 to 30 and calculating *y*:

```
x = 5:30;
y = x.^2 - 40.*x + 400;
plot(x,y)
axis([5,30,-50,250])
```

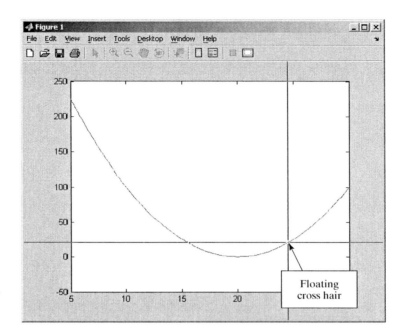

**Figure 4**
The **ginput** function allows the user to pick points off a graph.

The axis values were defined so that the graph would be easier to trace.
Once the **ginput** function has been executed, as in

```
[a,b] = ginput
```

MATLAB adds a floating cross hair to the graph, as shown in Figure 4. After this cross hair is positioned to the user's satisfaction, right- clicking and then selecting Return (Enter) sends the values of the *x*- and *y*-coordinates to the program:

```
a =
   24.4412
b =
   19.7368
```

## 4  USING CELL MODE IN MATLAB M-FILES

New to MATLAB 7 is a utility that allows the user to divide M-files into sections, or cells, that can be executed one at a time. This feature is particularly useful as you develop MATLAB programs. The cell mode also allows the user to create reports in a number of formats showing the program results.

KEY IDEA: Cell mode is new to MATLAB 7

To activate the cell mode, select

```
Cell → Enable Cell Mode
```

from the menu bar in the edit window, as shown in Figure 5. Once the cell mode has been enabled, the cell toolbar appears, as shown in Figure 6.

To divide your M-file program into cells, you can create cell dividers by using a double percentage sign followed by a space. If you want to name the cell, just add a name on the same line as the cell divider:

```
%% Cell Name
```

It's important to include the space after the double percentage sign (%%). If you don't, the line is recognized as a comment, not a cell divider.

Cell Menu

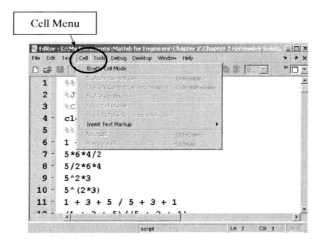

**Figure 5**
You can access the cell mode from the menu bar in the edit window.

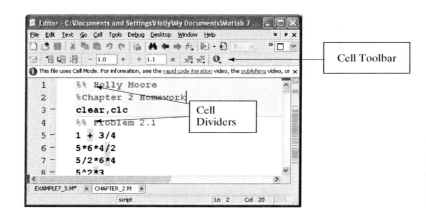

Cell Toolbar

Cell Dividers

**Figure 6**
The cell toolbar allows the user to execute one cell, or section, at a time. Notice the links to animated demonstrations below the toolbar.

Once the cell dividers are in place, if you move the cursor anywhere inside the cell, the entire cell turns pale yellow. For example, in Figure 6, the first three lines of the M-file program make up the first cell. Now we can use the evaluation icons on the cell toolbar to either evaluate a single section, evaluate the current section and move on to the next section, or evaluate the entire file. Also on the cell toolbar is an icon that lists all the cell titles in the M-file, as shown in Figure 7. Table 3 lists the icons available on the cell toolbar, together with their functions.

Figure 7 shows the first 14 lines of an M-file written to solve some homework problems. By dividing the program into cells, it was possible to work on each problem separately. Be sure to save any M-files you've developed this way by selecting **Save** or **Save As** from the file menu:

```
File → Save          or
File → Save As
```

The reason for using these commands is that in cell mode, the program is not automatically saved every time you run it.

Dividing a homework M-file into cells offers a big advantage to the person who must grade the paper. By using the **evaluate cell and advance** function, the grader can step through the program one problem at a time. Even more important,

KEY IDEA: Cell mode allows you to execute portions of the code incrementally

CELL: a section of MATLAB code located between cell dividers (% %)

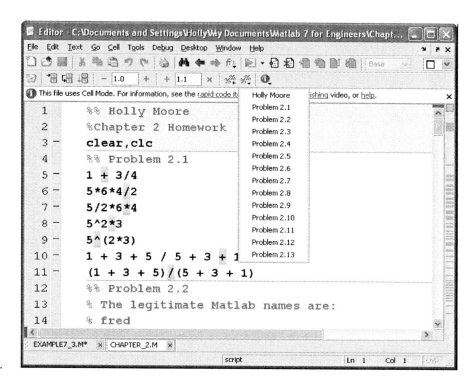

**Figure 7**
The Show Cell Titles icon lists all the cells in the M-file.

the programmer can divide a complicated project into manageable sections, and evaluate these sections independently.

The cell toolbar also allows the user to publish an M-file program to an HTML file. MATLAB runs the program and creates a report showing the code in each cell, as well as the calculational results that were sent to the command window. Any figures created are also included in the report. The first portion of the report created from the M-file of Figure 7 is shown in Figure 8. If you prefer a report in a different format, such as Word or PowerPoint, you can use the menu bar option

**KEY IDEA: Cell mode allows you to create reports in HTML, Word and PowerPoint**

**File → Publish To**

to send the results in your choice of several different formats. The publish feature does not work well if you have programmed user interactions such as prompts for data input into the file. During the publishing process the M-file program is executed,

**Table 3  Cell Toolbar**

| | |
|---|---|
| | evaluate the current cell |
| | evaluate cell and advance |
| | evaluate the entire file |
| | show cell titles |
| | save and publish to HTML |
| | links to demonstrations |

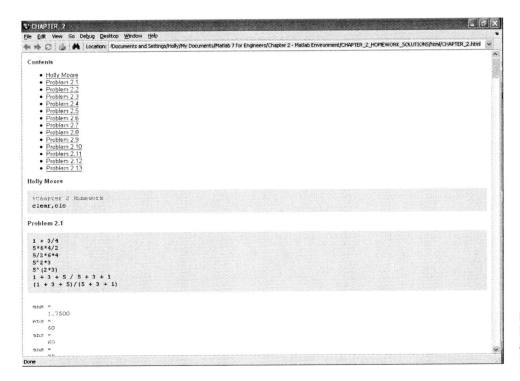

**Figure 8**
HTML report created from a MATLAB M-file using the **Publish to HTML** feature.

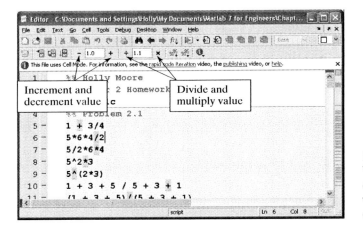

**Figure 9**
Value manipulation tools allow the user to experiment with changing values in calculations.

but no values are available for the user input. This results in an error message, which is included in the published version of the file.

The cell toolbar includes a set of value-manipulation tools, as shown in Figure 9. Whatever number is closest to the cursor (in Figure 9, it's the number 2) can be adjusted by the factor shown on the toolbar by selecting the appropriate icon ($-$, $+$, $\div$, or $\times$). When this feature is used in combination with the **evaluate cell** tool, you can repeat a set of calculations multiple times while easily adjusting a variable of interest.

**EXAMPLE 4**

## Interactively Adjusting Parameters

On the basis of an energy balance calculation, you know that the change in enthalpy of a 1-kmol (29-kg) sample of air going from state 1 to state 2 is 8900 kJ. You'd like to know the final temperature, but the equation relating the change in enthalpy to temperature, namely,

$$\Delta h = \int_1^2 C_p \, dT$$

where

$$C_p = a + bT + cT^2 + dT^3$$

is too complicated to solve for the final temperature. However, using techniques learned in calculus, we find that

$$\Delta h = a(T_2 - T_1) + \frac{b}{2}(T_2^2 - T_1^2) + \frac{c}{3}(T_2^3 - T_1^3) + \frac{d}{4}(T_2^4 - T_1^4)$$

If we know the starting temperature ($T_1$) and the values of $a$, $b$, $c$, and $d$, we can guess values of the final temperature ($T_2$) until we get the correct value of $\Delta h$. The interactive ability to modify variable values in the cell mode makes solving this problem easy.

1. State the Problem
   Find the final temperature of air when you know the starting temperature and the change in internal energy.

2. Describe the Input and Output

   *Input*   Used in the equation for $C_p$, these values of $a, b, c,$ and $d$ will give a heat capacity value in kJ/kmol K:

   $$a = 28.90$$
   $$b = 0.1967 \times 10^{-2}$$
   $$c = 0.4802 \times 10^{-5}$$
   $$d = -1.966 \times 10^{-9}$$
   $$\Delta h = 8900 \text{ kJ}$$
   $$T_1 = 300 \text{ K}$$

   *Output*   For every guessed value of the final temperature, an estimate of $\Delta h$ should print to the screen.

3. Develop a Hand Example
   If we guess a final temperature of 400 K, then

   $$\Delta h = a(T_2 - T_1) + \frac{b}{2}(T_2^2 - T_1^2) + \frac{c}{3}(T_2^3 - T_1^3) + \frac{d}{4}(T_2^4 - T_1^4)$$

   $$\Delta h = 28.9(400 - 300) + \frac{0.1967 \cdot 10^{-2}}{2}(400^2 - 300^2) + \frac{0.4802 \cdot 10^{-5}}{3}$$

   $$\times (400^3 - 300^3) + \cdots \frac{-1.966 \cdot 10^{-9}}{4}(400^4 - 300^4)$$

which gives

$$\Delta h = 3009.47$$

4. Develop a MATLAB Solution

```
%% Example 3
% Interactively Adjusting Parameters
clear,clc
a = 28.90;
b = 0.1967e-2;
c = 0.4802e-5;
d = -1.966e-9;
T1 = 300
%% guess T2 and adjust
T2 = 400
format bank
delta_h = a*(T2-T1) + b*(T2.^2 - T1.^2)/2 + c*(T2.^3-
T1.^3)/3 + d*(T2.^4-T1.^4)/4
```

Run the program once, and MATLAB returns

**T1 = 300.00**

**T2 = 400.00**

**delta_h = 3009.47**

Now position the cursor near the **T2 = 400** statement, as shown in Figure 10. (In this example, the edit window was docked with the MATLAB desktop.) By selecting the Increment Value icon, with the value set at 100, we can quickly try several different temperatures. (See Figure 11.) Once we're close, we can change the increment and zero in on the answer.

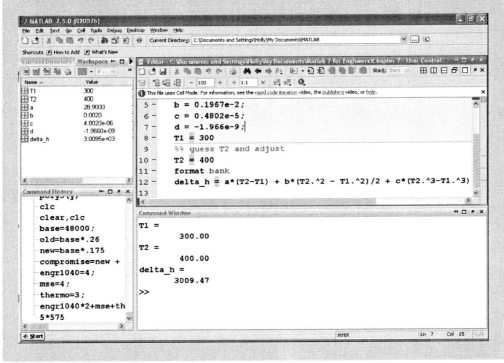

**Figure 10**
The original guess gives us an idea of how far away we are from the final answer.

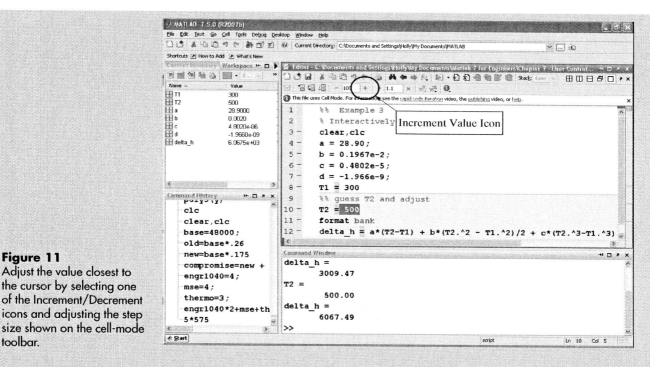

**Figure 11**
Adjust the value closest to the cursor by selecting one of the Increment/Decrement icons and adjusting the step size shown on the cell-mode toolbar.

A $T_2$ value of 592 K gave a calculated $\Delta h$ value of 8927, which is fairly close to our goal. We could get closer if we believed that the added accuracy was justified.

5. Test the Solution

Substitute the calculated value of $T_2$ into the original equation, and check the results with a calculator:

$$\Delta h = 28.9(592 - 300) + \frac{0.1967 \cdot 10^{-2}}{2}(592^2 - 300^2)$$

$$+ \frac{0.4802 \cdot 10^{-5}}{3}(592^3 - 300^3) + \frac{-1.966 \cdot 10^{-9}}{4}(592^4 - 300^4)$$

$$\Delta h = 8927.46$$

## 5  READING AND WRITING DATA FROM FILES

KEY IDEA: MATLAB can import data from files using a variety of formats

Data are stored in many different formats, depending on the devices and programs that created the data and on the application. For example, sound might be stored in a .wav file, and an image might be stored in a .jpg file. Many applications store data in Excel spreadsheets (.xls files). The most generic of these files is the ASCII file, usually stored as a .dat or a .txt file. You may want to import these data into MATLAB to analyze in a MATLAB program, or you might want to save your data in one of these formats to make the file easier to export to another application.

**Table 4  Data File Types Supported by MATLAB**

| File Type | Extension | Remark |
|-----------|-----------|--------|
| Text | .mat | MATLAB workspace |
| | .dat | ASCII data |
| | .txt | ASCII data |
| | .csv | Comma-separated values ASCII data |
| Other common scientific data formats | .cdf | common data format |
| | .fits | flexible image transport system data |
| | .hdf | hierarchical data format |
| Spreadsheet data | .xls | Excel spreadsheet |
| | .wk1 | Lotus 123 |
| Image data | .tiff | tagged image file format |
| | .bmp | bit map |
| | .jpeg or jpg | joint photographics expert group |
| | .gif | graphics interchange format |
| Audio data | .au | audio |
| | .wav | Microsoft wave file |
| Movie | .avi | audio/video interleaved file |

## 5.1  Importing Data

### *Import Wizard*

If you select a data file from the current directory and double-click on the file name, the Import Wizard launches. The Import Wizard determines what kind of data is in the file and suggests ways to represent the data in MATLAB. Table 4 is a list of some of the data types MATLAB recognizes. Not every possible data format is supported by MATLAB. You can find a complete list by typing

```
doc fileformats
```

in the command window.

The Import Wizard can be used for simple ASCII files and for Excel spreadsheet files. You can also launch the Import Wizard from the command line, using the **uiimport** function:

```
uiimport(' filename.extension ')
```

For example, to import the sound file **decision.wav**, type

```
uiimport(' decision.wav ')
```

The Import Wizard then opens, as shown in Figure 12

Either technique for launching the Import Wizard requires an interaction with the user (through the Wizard). If you want to load a data file from a MATLAB program, you'll need a different approach.

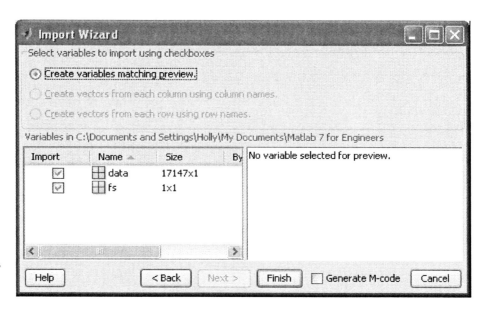

**Figure 12**
The Import Wizard launches when the **uiimport** command is executed.

### Import Commands

You can bypass the Wizard interactions by using one of the functions that are especially designed to read each of the supported file formats. For example, to read in a .wav file, use the **wavread** function:

```
[data,fs] = wavread('decision.wav')
```

Clearly, you need to understand what kind of data to expect, so that you can name the created variables appropriately. Recall that you can find a list of import functions by typing

```
doc fileformats
```

**EXAMPLE 5**

### 2001: A Space Odyssey: Sound Files

One of the most memorable characters in the movie *2001: A Space Odyssey* is the computer Hal. Sound bites from Hal's dialogue in the movie have been popular for years with computer programmers and with engineers who use computers. You can find .wav files of some of Hal's dialogue at http://www.palantir.net/2001/ and at other popular-culture websites. Insert Hal's comments into a MATLAB program. (You'll need the **sound** function—consult the **help** tutorial for details on its use.)

1. State the Problem
   Load sound files into a MATLAB program, and play them at appropriate times.

2. Describe the Input and Output

   ***Input***    Sound files downloaded from the Internet. For this example, we'll assume that you've downloaded the following three files:
   dave.wav
   error.wav
   sure.wav

   ***Output***   Play the sound files inside a MATLAB program.

3. Develop a Hand Example
Although working a hand example is not appropriate for this problem, you can listen to the sound files from the Internet before inserting them into the program.

4. Develop a MATLAB Solution
Download the sound files and save them into the current directory before you run the following program:

```
%% Example 4
% Sound Files
%% First Clip
[dave,fs_dave] = wavread('dave.wav');
disp('Hit Enter once the sound clip is finished playing')
sound(dave,fs_dave)
pause
%% Second Clip
[error,fs_error] = wavread('error.wav');
disp('Hit Enter once the sound clip is finished playing')
sound(error,fs_error)
pause
%% Third Clip
[sure,fs_sure] = wavread('sure.wav');
disp('Hit Enter once the sound clip is finished playing')
sound(sure,fs_sure)
pause
disp('That was the last clip')
```

5. Test the Solution
Many audio files are available to download from the Internet. Some are as simple as these, but others are complete pieces of music. Browse the Internet and insert a "sound byte" into another MATLAB program, perhaps as an error message for your users. Some of our favorites are from *Star Trek* (try http://services.tos.net/sounds/sound.html#tos) and *The Simpsons*.

## 5.2 Exporting Data

The easiest way to find the appropriate function for writing a file is to use the **help** tutorial to find the correct function to read it and then to follow the links to the **write** function. For example, to read an Excel spreadsheet file (.xls), we'd use **xlsread**:

```
xlsread('filename.xls')
```

At the end of the tutorial page, we are referred to the correct function for writing an Excel file, namely,

```
xlswrite('filename.xls', M)
```

where **M** is the array you want to store in the Excel spreadsheet.

**SUMMARY**

MATLAB provides functions that allow the user to interact with an M-file program and allow the programmer to control the output to the command window.

The **input** function pauses the program and sends a prompt determined by the programmer to the command window. Once the user has entered a value or values and hits the return key, program execution continues.

The display (**disp**) function allows the programmer to display the contents of a string or a matrix in the command window. Although the **disp** function is adequate for many display tasks, the **fprintf** function gives the programmer considerably more control over the way results are displayed. The programmer can combine text and calculated results on the same line and specify the number format used. The **sprintf** function behaves exactly the same way as the **fprintf** function. However, the result of **sprintf** is assigned a variable name and can be used with other functions that require strings as input. For example, the functions used to annotate graphs such as **title**, **text**, and **xlabel** all accept strings as input and therefore will accept the result of the **sprintf** function as input.

For applications in which graphical input is required, the **ginput** command allows the user to provide input to a program by selecting points from a graphics window.

The cell mode allows the programmer to group M-file code into sections and to run each section individually. The **publish to HTML** tool creates a report containing both the M-file code and results as well as any figures generated when the program executes. The Increment and Decrement icons on the cell toolbar allow the user to automatically change the value of a parameter each time the code is executed, making it easy to test the result of changing a variable.

MATLAB includes functions that allow the user to import and export data in a number of popular file formats. A complete list of these formats is available in the **help** tutorial on the File Formats page (doc fileformats). The **fprintf** function can also be used to export formatted output to a text file.

**MATLAB SUMMARY**     The following MATLAB summary lists all the special characters, commands, and functions that were defined in this chapter:

| Special Characters | |
| --- | --- |
| ' | begins and ends a string |
| % | placeholder used in the **fprintf** command |
| %f | fixed-point, or decimal, notation |
| %e | exponential notation |
| %g | either fixed-point or exponential notation |
| %s | string notation |
| %% | cell divider |
| \n | linefeed |
| \r | carriage return (similar to linefeed) |
| \t | tab |
| \b | backspace |

| Commands and Functions | |
| --- | --- |
| disp | displays a string or a matrix in the command window |
| fprintf | creates formatted output which can be sent to the command window or to a file |
| ginput | allows the user to pick values from a graph |
| input | allows the user to enter values |

| Commands and Functions (Continued) | |
| --- | --- |
| **num2str** | changes a number to a string |
| **pause** | pauses the program |
| **sound** | plays MATLAB data through the speakers |
| **sprintf** | similar to **fprintf** creates formatted output which is assigned to a variable name and stored as a character array |
| **uiimport** | launches the Import Wizard |
| **wavread** | reads wave files |
| **xlsimport** | imports Excel data files |
| **xlswrite** | exports data as an Excel file |

cell
cell mode
character array

formatted output
precision field
string

width field

## Input Function

1   Create an M-file that prompts the user to enter a value of $x$ and then calculates the value of $\sin(x)$.

2   Create an M-file that prompts the user to enter a matrix and then use the **max** function to determine the largest value entered. Use the following matrix to test your program:

$$[1, 5, 3, 8, 9, 22]$$

3   The volume of a cone is

$$V = \frac{1}{3} \times \text{area\_of\_the\_base} \times \text{height}$$

Prompt the user to enter the area of the base and the height of the cone (Figure P3). Calculate the volume of the cone.

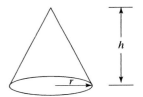

**Figure P3**
Volume of a cone.

## Disp Function

4   One of the first computer programs many students write is called "Hello, World." The only thing the program does is print this message to the computer screen. Write a "Hello, World" program in an M-file, using the **disp** function.

5   Use two separate **input** statements to prompt a user to enter his or her first and last names. Use the **disp** function to display those names on one line. (You'll need to combine the names and some spaces into an array.)

6   Prompt the user to enter his or her age. Then use the **disp** function to report the age back to the command window. If, for example, the user enters 5 when prompted for her age, your display should read

```
Your age is 5
```

This output requires combining both character data (a string) and numeric data in the **disp** function—which can be accomplished by using the **num2str** function.

**7** Prompt the user to enter an array of numbers. Use the **length** function to determine how many values were entered, and use the **disp** function to report your results to the command window.

### fprintf

**8** Repeat Problem 7, and use **fprintf** to report your results.

**9** Use **fprintf** to create the multiplication tables from 1 to 13 for the number 6. Your table should look like this.

> 1 times 6 is 6
>
> 2 times 6 is 12
>
> 3 times 6 is 18
>
> ⋮

**10** Before calculators were readily available (about 1974), students used tables to determine the values of mathematical functions like sine, cosine, and log. Create such a table for sine, using the following steps:

- Create a vector of angle values from 0 to $2\pi$ in increments of $\pi/10$.
- Calculate the sine of each of the angles, and group your results into a table that includes the angle and the sine.
- Use **disp** to create a title for the table and a second **disp** command to create column headings.
- Use the **fprintf** function to display the numbers. Display only two values past the decimal point.

**11** Very small dimensions—those on the atomic scale—are often measured in angstroms. An angstrom is represented by the symbol Å and corresponds to a length of $10^{-10}$ meter. Create an inches-to-angstroms conversion table as follows for values of inches from 1 to 10:

- Use **disp** to create a title and column headings.
- Use **fprintf** to display the numerical information.
- Because the length represented in angstroms is so big, represent your result in scientific notation, showing two values after the decimal point. This corresponds to three significant figures (one before and two after the decimal point).

**12** Use your favorite Internet search engine and World Wide Web browser to identify recent currency conversions for British pounds sterling, Japanese yen, and the European euro to U.S. dollars. Use the conversion tables to create the following tables (use the **disp** and **fprintf** commands in your solution, which should include a title, column labels, and formatted output):

**(a)** Generate a table of conversions from yen to dollars. Start the yen column at 5 and increment by 5 yen. Print 25 lines in the table.

**(b)** Generate a table of conversions from the euros to dollars. Start the euro column at 1 euro and increment by 2 euros. Print 30 lines in the table.

**(c)** Generate a table with four columns. The first should contain dollars, the second the equivalent number of euros, the third the equivalent number of pounds, and the fourth the equivalent number of yen. Let the dollar column vary from 1 to 10.

**Problems Combining the input, disp, and fprintf Commands**

13    This problem requires you to generate temperature conversion tables. Use the following equations, which describe the relationships between temperatures in degrees Fahrenheit ($T_F$), degrees Celsius ($T_C$), kelvins ($T_K$), and degrees Rankine ($T_R$), respectively:

$$T_F = T_R - 459.67°R$$

$$T_F = \frac{9}{5}T_C + 32°F$$

$$T_R = \frac{9}{5}T_K$$

You will need to rearrange these expressions to solve some of the problems.

(a) Generate a table of conversions from Fahrenheit to Kelvin for values from 0°F to 200°F. Allow the user to enter the increments in degrees F between lines. Use **disp** and **fprintf** to create a table with a title, column headings, and appropriate spacing.

(b) Generate a table of conversions from Celsius to Rankine. Allow the user to enter the starting temperature and the increment between lines. Print 25 lines in the table. Use **disp** and **fprintf** to create a table with a title, column headings, and appropriate spacing.

(c) Generate a table of conversions from Celsius to Fahrenheit. Allow the user to enter the starting temperature, the increment between lines, and the number of lines for the table. Use **disp** and **fprintf** to create a table with a title, column headings, and appropriate spacing.

14    Engineers use both English and SI (Système International d'Unités) units on a regular basis. Some fields use primarily one or the other, but many combine the two systems. For example, the rate of energy input to a steam power plant from burning fossil fuels is usually measured in Btu/hour. However, the electricity produced by the same plant is usually measured in joules/sec (watts). Automobile engines, by contrast, are often rated in horsepower or in ft lb$_f$/s. Here are some conversion factors relating these different power measurements:

$$1\ kW = 3412.14\ Btu/h = 737.56\ ft\ lb_f/s$$

$$1\ hp = 550\ ft\ lb_f/s = 2544.5\ Btu/h$$

(a) Generate a table of conversions from kW to hp. The table should start at 0 kW and end at 15 kW. Use the **input** function to let the user define the increment between table entries. Use **disp** and **fprintf** to create a table with a title, column headings, and appropriate spacing.

(b) Generate a table of conversions from ft lb$_f$/s to Btu/h. The table should start at 0 ft lb$_f$/s but let the user define the increment between table entries and the final table value. Use **disp** and **fprintf** to create a table with a title, column headings, and appropriate spacing.

(c) Generate a table that includes conversions from kW to Btu/h, hp, and ft lb$_f$/s. Let the user define the initial value of kW, the final value of kW, and the number of entries in the table. Use **disp** and **fprintf** to create a table with a title, column headings, and appropriate spacing.

**ginput**

**15** At time $t = 0$, when a rocket's engine shuts down, the rocket has reached an altitude of 500 meters and is rising at a velocity of 125 meters per second. At this point, gravity takes over. The height of the rocket as a function of time is

$$h(t) = -\frac{9.8}{2}t^2 + 125t + 500 \text{ for } t > 0$$

Plot the height of the rocket from 0 to 30 seconds, and

- Use the **ginput** function to estimate the maximum height the rocket reaches and the time when the rocket hits the ground.
- Use the **disp** command to report your results to the command window.

**16** The **ginput** function is useful for picking distances off a graph. Demonstrate this feature by doing the following:

- Create a graph of a circle by defining an array of angles from 0 to $2\pi$, with a spacing of $\pi/100$.
- Use the **ginput** function to pick two points on the circumference of the circle.
- Use **hold on** to keep the figure from refreshing, and plot a line between the two points you picked.
- Use the data from the points to calculate the length of the line between them. (*Hint*: Use the Pythagorean theorem in your calculation.)

**17** In recent years the price of gasoline has increased dramatically. Automobile companies have responded with more fuel-efficient cars, in particular hybrid models. But will you save money by purchasing to purchase a hybrid such as the Toyota Camry rather a Camry with a standard engine? The hybrid vehicles are considerably more expensive, but get better gas mileage. Consider the vehicle prices and gas efficiencies shown in Table P17

**Table P17  A Comparison of Standard and Hybrid Vehicles**

| Year | Model | Base MSRP | Gas Efficiency, in-town/highway |
|------|-------|-----------|---------------------------------|
| 2008 | Toyota Camry | $18,720 | 21/31 mpg |
| 2008 | Toyota Camry Hybrid | $25,350 | 33/34 mpg |
| 2008 | Toyota Highlander 4WD | $28,750 | 17/23 mpg |
| 2008 | Toyota Highlander 4WD Hybrid | $33,700 | 27/25 mpg (Hybrids may actually get better mileage in town than on the road) |
| 2008 | Ford Escape 2WD | $19,140 | 24/28 mpg |
| 2008 | Ford Escape 2WD Hybrid | $26,495 | 34/30 mpg |

One way to compare two vehicles is to find the "cost to own".

cost to own = purchase cost + upkeep + gasoline cost

Assume for this exercise that the upkeep costs are the same, so in our comparison we'll set them equal to zero.

**(a)** What do you think the cost of gasoline will be over the next several years? Prompt the user to enter an estimate of gasoline cost in dollars/gallon.

**(b)** Find the "cost to own" as a function of the number of miles driven for a pair of vehicles from the table, based on the fuel price estimate from part a. Plot your results on an *x–y* graph. The point where the two lines cross is the break-even point.

**(c)** Use the **ginput** function to pick the break-even point off the graph.

**(d)** Use **sprintf** to create a string identifying the break-even point, and use the result to create a text-box annotation on your graph. Position the text box using the **gtext** function.

### Cell Mode

**18** Create an M-file containing your solutions to the homework problems from this chapter. Use cell dividers (%%) to divide your program into cells (sections), and title each section with a problem number. Run your program by using the **evaluate cell and advance** feature from the cell toolbar.

**19** Publish your program and results from Problem 18 to HTML, using the **publish to HTML** feature from the cell toolbar. Unfortunately, because this chapter's assignment requires interaction with the user, the published results will include errors.

**20** Revisit Problem 17, which compares the cost-to-own for hybrids versus standard-engine vehicles.

**(a)** Instead of allowing the user to enter an estimate of fuel cost, assume that gasoline will cost $2.00 per gallon for the next several years.

**(b)** Use the incremental value adjustment tool on the cell-mode toolbar to change the value of the gasoline cost, until the break-even point occurs at less than 100,000 miles.

### Importing Data

**21** Search the Internet for some fun sound bytes to include in your programs. Two sources are http://www.wavcentral.com and http://www/wavsource.com. Import the sound byte and use it in an appropriate spot in your program. For example, end your program with Elmer Fudd singing "Kill the Wabbit."

**22** Use the **wavrecord** function to record your own voice and import it into MAT-LAB. Use the help function for details on how to use this and the related **wavplay** function.

## SOLUTIONS TO PRACTICE EXERCISES

### Practice Exercises 1

1. 
```
b = input('Enter the length of the base of the triangle: ');
h = input('Enter the height of the triangle: ');
Area = 1/2*b*h
```

When this file runs, it generates the following interaction in the command window:

```
Enter the length of the base of the triangle: 5
Enter the height of the triangle: 4
Area =
  10
```

2. 
```
r = input('Enter the radius of the cylinder: ');
h = input('Enter the height of the cylinder: ');
Volume = pi*r.^2*h
```

When this file runs, it generates the following interaction in the command window:

```
Enter the radius of the cylinder: 2
Enter the height of the cylinder: 3
Volume =
  37.6991
```

3. 
```
n = input('Enter a value of n: ')
vector = 0:n
```

When this file runs, it generates the following interaction in the command window:

```
Enter a value of n: 3
n =
   3
vector =
   0 1 2 3
```

4. 
```
a = input('Enter the starting value: ');
b = input('Enter the ending value: ');
c = input('Enter the vector spacing: ');
vector = a:c:b
```

When this file runs, it generates the following interaction in the command window:

```
Enter the starting value: 0
Enter the ending value: 6
Enter the vector spacing: 2
vector =
   0 2 4 6
```

## Practice Exercises 2

1. `disp('Inches to Feet Conversion Table')`
2. `disp('  Inches  Feet')`
3. 
```
inches = 0:10:120;
feet = inches./12;
table = [inches; feet];
fprintf(' %8.0f %8.2f \n',table)
```

The resulting display in the command window is

**Inches to Feet Conversion Table**

| Inches | Feet |
|---|---|
| 0 | 0.00 |
| 10 | 0.83 |
| 20 | 1.67 |
| ... | ... |
| ... | ... |
| ... | ... |
| 100 | 8.33 |
| 110 | 9.17 |
| 120 | 10.00 |

# 8

# Logical Functions and Control Structures

## Objectives

After reading this chapter, you should be able to

- understand how MATLAB interprets relational and logical operators
- be able to use the **find** function
- understand the appropriate uses of the **if/else** family of commands
- understand the **switch/case** structure
- be able to write and use **for** loops and **while** loops

## INTRODUCTION

One way to think of a computer program (not just MATLAB) is to consider how the statements that compose it are organized. Usually, sections of computer code can be categorized as *sequences*, *selection structures*, and *repetition structures*. (See Figure 1.) So far, we have written code that contains sequences but none of the other structures:

- A sequence is a list of commands that are executed one after another.
- A selection structure allows the programmer to execute one command (or set of commands) if some criterion is true and a second command (or set of commands) if the criterion is false. A selection statement provides the means of choosing between these paths, based on a *logical condition*. The conditions that are evaluated often contain both *relational* and *logical* operators or functions.
- A repetition structure, or loop, causes a group of statements to be executed multiple times. The number of times a loop is executed depends on either a counter or the evaluation of a logical condition.

## 1 RELATIONAL AND LOGICAL OPERATORS

The selection and repetition structures used in MATLAB depend on relational and logical operators. MATLAB has six relational operators for comparing two matrices of equal size, as shown in Table 1.

Comparisons are either true or false, and most computer programs (including MATLAB) use the number 1 for true and 0 for false. (MATLAB actually takes any number that is not 0 to be true.) If we define two scalars

```
x = 5;
y = 1;
```

and use a relational operator such as <, the result of the comparison

```
x<y
```

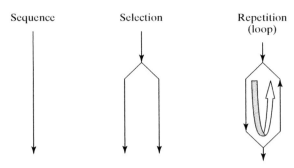

**Figure 1**
Programming structures used in MATLAB.

is either true or false. In this case, **x** is not less than **y**, so MATLAB responds

```
ans =
     0
```

indicating that the comparison is false. MATLAB uses this answer in selection statements and in repetition structures to make decisions.

Of course, variables in MATLAB usually represent entire matrices. If we redefine **x** and **y**, we can see how MATLAB handles comparisons between matrices. For example,

```
x = 1:5;
y = x -4;
x<y
```

returns

```
ans =
     0     0     0     0     0
```

MATLAB compares corresponding elements and creates an answer matrix of zeros and ones. In the preceding example, **x** was greater than **y** for every comparison of elements, so every comparison was false and the answer was a string of zeros. If, instead, we have

```
x = [ 1, 2, 3, 4, 5];
y = [-2, 0, 2, 4, 6];
x<y
```

then

```
ans =
     0     0     0     0     1
```

**Table 1  Relational Operators**

| Relational Operator | Interpretation |
|:---:|:---|
| < | less than |
| <= | less than or equal to |
| > | greater than |
| >= | greater than or equal to |
| == | equal to |
| ~= | not equal to |

KEY IDEA: Relational operators compare values

**Table 2  Logical Operators**

| Logical Operator | Interpretation |
|:---:|:---|
| & | and |
| ~ | not |
| | | or |
| xor | exclusive or |

The results tell us that the comparison was false for the first four elements, but true for the last. For a comparison to be true for an entire matrix, it must be true for *every* element in the matrix. In other words, all of the results must be ones.

MATLAB also allows us to combine comparisons with the logical operators *and*, *not*, and *or*. (See Table 2)

KEY IDEA: Logical operators are used to combine comparison statements

The code

```
x = [ 1, 2, 3, 4, 5];
y = [-2, 0, 2, 4, 6];
z = [ 8, 8, 8, 8, 8];
z>x & z>y
```

returns

```
ans =
    1    1    1    1    1
```

because z is greater than both x and y for every element. The statement

```
x>y | x>z
```

is read as "x is greater than y or x is greater than z" and returns

```
ans =
    1    1    1    0    0
```

This means that the condition is true for the first three elements and false for the last two.

These relational and logical operators are used in both selection structures and loops to determine what commands should be executed.

## 2  FLOWCHARTS AND PSEUDOCODE

With the addition of selection structures and repetition structures to your group of programming tools, it becomes even more important to plan your program before you start coding. Two common approaches are to use flowcharts and to use pseudocode. Flowcharts are a graphical approach to creating your coding plan, and pseudocode is a verbal description of your plan. You may want to use either or both for your programming projects.

KEY IDEA: Flow charts and pseudocode are used to plan programming tasks

For simple programs, pseudocode may be the best (or at least the simplest) planning approach:

- Outline a set of statements describing the steps you will take to solve a problem.
- Convert these steps into comments in an M-file.
- Insert the appropriate MATLAB code into the file between the comment lines.

Here's a really simple example: Suppose you've been asked to create a program to convert mph to ft/s. The output should be a table, complete with a title and column headings. Here's an outline of the steps you might follow:

- Define a vector of mph values.
- Convert mph to ft/s.
- Combine the mph and ft/s vectors into a matrix.
- Create a table title.
- Create column headings.
- Display the table.

Once you've identified the steps, put them into a MATLAB M-file as comments:

```
%Define a vector of mph values
%Convert mph to ft/s
%Combine the mph and ft/s vectors into a matrix
%Create a table title
%Create column headings
%Display the table
```

Now you can insert the appropriate MATLAB code into the M-file

```
%Define a vector of mph values
  mph = 0:10:100;
%Convert mph to ft/s
  fps = mph*5280/3600;
%Combine the mph and ft/s vectors into a matrix
  table = [mph;fps]
%Create a table title
  disp('Velocity Conversion Table')
%Create column headings
  disp('     mph     f/s')
%Display the table
  fprintf('%8.0f  %8.2f \n',table)
```

If you put some time into your planning, you probably won't need to change the pseudocode much, once you start programming.

Flowcharts alone or flowcharts combined with pseudocode are especially appropriate for more complicated programming tasks. You can create a "big picture" of your program graphically and then convert your project to pseudocode suitable to enter into the program as comments. Before you can start flowcharting, you'll need to be introduced to some standard flowcharting symbols. (See Table 3.)

Figure 2 is an example of a flowchart for the mph-to-ft/s problem. For a problem this simple, you would probably never actually create a flowchart. However, as problems become more complicated, flowcharts become an invaluable tool, allowing you to organize your thoughts.

Once you've created a flowchart, you should transfer the ideas into comment lines in an M-file and then add the appropriate code between the comments.

Remember, both flowcharts and pseudocode are tools intended to help you create better computer programs. They can also be used effectively to illustrate the structure of a program to nonprogrammers, since they emphasize the logical progression of ideas over programming details.

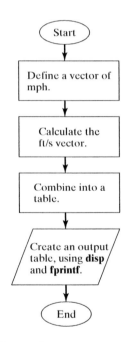

**Figure 2**
Flowcharts make it easy to visualize the structure of a program.

FLOWCHART: a pictoral representation of a computer program

**Table 3 Flowcharting for Designing Computer Programs**

An oval is used to indicate the beginning or the end of a section of code.

A parallelogram is used to indicate input or output processes.

A diamond indicates a decision point.

Calculations are placed in rectangles.

PSEUDOCODE: a list of programming tasks necessary to create a program

## 3 LOGICAL FUNCTIONS

MATLAB offers both traditional selection structures, such as the family of **if** functions, and a series of logical functions that perform much the same task. The primary logical function is **find**, which can often be used in place of both traditional selection structures and loops.

### 3.1 Find

The **find** command searches a matrix and identifies which elements in that matrix meet a given criterion. For example, the U.S. Naval Academy requires applicants to be at least 5′6″ (66″) tall. Consider this list of applicant heights:

```
height = [63,67,65,72,69,78,75]
```

You can find the index numbers of the elements that meet our criterion by using the **find** command:

```
accept = find(height>=66 )
```

This command returns

```
accept =
    2    4    5    6    7
```

KEY IDEA: Logical functions are often more efficient programming tools than traditional selection structures

The **find** function returns the index numbers from the matrix that meet the criterion. If you want to know what the actual heights are, you can call each element, using the index number:

```
height(accept)
ans =
    67    72    69    78    75
```

An alternative approach would be to nest the commands

```
height(find(height(>=66)))
```

You could also determine which applicants do *not* meet the criterion. Use

```
decline = find(height<66)
```

which gives

```
decline =
   1   3
```

To create a more readable report use the **disp** and **fprintf** functions:

```
disp('The following candidates meet the height requirement');
  fprintf('Candidate # %4.0f is %4.0f
  inches tall \n', [accept;height(accept)])
```

These commands return the following table in the command window:

```
The following candidates meet the height requirement
Candidate #    2 is    67 inches tall
Candidate #    4 is    72 inches tall
Candidate #    5 is    69 inches tall
Candidate #    6 is    78 inches tall
Candidate #    7 is    75 inches tall
```

Clearly, you could also create a table of those who do not meet the requirement:

```
disp('The following candidates do not meet the height
  requirement')
fprintf('Candidate # %4.0f is %4.0f inches tall \n',
  [decline;height(decline)])
```

Similarly to the previous code, the following table is returned in the command window:

```
The following candidates do not meet the height requirement
Candidate #    1 is    63 inches tall
Candidate #    3 is    65 inches tall
```

You can create fairly complicated search criteria that use the logical operators. For example, suppose the applicants must be at least 18 years old and less than 35 years old. Then your data might look like this:

| Height, Inches | Age, Years |
|---|---|
| 63 | 18 |
| 67 | 19 |
| 65 | 18 |
| 72 | 20 |
| 69 | 36 |
| 78 | 34 |
| 75 | 12 |

Now we define the matrix and find the index numbers of the elements in column 1 that are greater than 66. Then we find which of those elements in column 2 are also greater than or equal to 18 and less than or equal to 35. We use the commands

```
applicants = [ 63, 18; 67, 19; 65, 18; 72, 20; 69, 36; 78,
         34; 75, 12]
pass = find(applicants(:,1)>=66 & applicants(:,2)>=18
         & applicants(:,2) < 35)
```

which return

```
pass =
   2
   4
   6
```

the list of applicants that meet all the criteria. We could use **fprintf** to create a nicer output. First create a table of the data to be displayed:

```
result = [pass,applicants(pass,1),applicants(pass,2)]';
```

Then use **fprintf** to send the results to the command window:

```
fprintf('Applicant # %4.0f is %4.0f inches tall and %4.0f
   years old\n',results)
```

The resulting list is

```
Applicant #    2 is    67 inches tall and 19 years old
Applicant #    4 is    72 inches tall and 20 years old
Applicant #    6 is    78 inches tall and 34 years old
```

So far, we've used **find** only to return a single index number. If we define two outputs from **find**, as in

```
[row, col] = find( criteria)
```

it will return the appropriate row and column numbers (also called the row and column index numbers or subscripts).

Now, imagine that you have a matrix of patient temperature values measured in a clinic. The column represents the number of the station where the temperature was taken. Thus, the command

```
temp = [95.3, 100.2, 98.6; 97.4,99.2, 98.9; 100.1,99.3, 97]
```

gives

```
temp =
    95.3000   100.2000    98.6000
    97.4000    99.2000    98.9000
   100.1000    99.3000    97.0000
```

and

```
element = find(temp>98.6)
```

gives us the element number for the single-index representation:

```
element =
     3
     4
     5
     6
     8
```

When the **find** command is used with a two-dimensional matrix, it uses an element numbering scheme that works down each column one at a time. For example, consider our 3 × 3 matrix. The element index numbers are shown in Figure 3. The elements that contain values greater than 98.6 are shown in bold.

**Figure 3**
Element-numbering sequence for a matrix

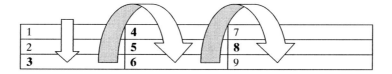

In order to determine the row and column numbers, we need the syntax

```
[row, col] = find(temp>98.6)
```

which gives us the following row and column numbers:

```
row =
   3
   1
   2
   3
   2

col =
   1
   2
   2
   2
   3
```

| 1, 1 | **1, 2** | 1, 3 |
|------|----------|------|
| 2, 1 | **2, 2** | **2, 3** |
| **3, 1** | **3, 2** | 3, 3 |

**Figure 4**
Row, element designation for a 3 × 3 matrix. The elements that meet the criterion are shown in bold.

Together, these numbers identify the elements shown in Figure 4.

Using **fprintf**, we can create a more readable report. For example,

```
fprintf('Patient%3.0f at station%3.0f had a temp of%6.1f
   \n', [row,col,temp(element)]')
```

returns

```
Patient  3 at station  1 had a temp of  100.1
Patient  1 at station  2 had a temp of  100.2
Patient  2 at station  2 had a temp of   99.2
Patient  3 at station  2 had a temp of   99.3
Patient  2 at station  3 had a temp of   98.9
```

## 3.2 Flowcharting and Pseudocode for Find Commands

The **find** command returns only one answer: a vector of the element numbers requested. For example, you might flowchart a sequence of commands as shown in Figure 5. If you use **find** multiple times to separate a matrix into categories, you may choose to employ a diamond shape, indicating the use of **find** as a selection structure.

```
%Define a vector of x-values
 x = [1,2,3; 10, 5,1; 12,3,2;8, 3,1]
%Find the index numbers of the values in x >9
 element = find(x>9)
%Use the index numbers to find the x-values
%greater than 9 by plugging them into x
 values = x(element)
% Create an output table
 disp('Elements greater than 9')
 disp('Element # Value')
 fprintf('%8.0f %3.0f \n', [element';values'])
```

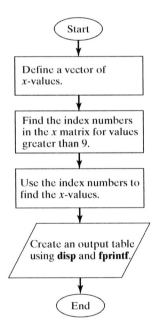

**Figure 5**
Flowchart illustrating the **find** command.

## EXAMPLE 1

**Figure 6**
Oscilloscopes are widely used in signal-processing applications. (Courtesy of Agilent Technologies Inc.)

### Signal Processing Using the Sinc Function

The sinc function is used in many engineering applications, but especially in signal processing (Figure 6). Unfortunately, this function has two widely accepted definitions:

$$f_1(x) = \frac{\sin(\pi x)}{\pi x} \quad \text{and} \quad f_2(x) = \frac{\sin x}{x}$$

Both of these functions have an indeterminate form of 0/0 when $x = 0$. In this case, l'Hôpital's theorem from calculus can be used to prove that both functions are equal to 1 when $x = $ zero. For values of $x$ not equal to zero, the two functions have a similar form. The first function, $f_1(x)$, crosses the $x$-axis when $x$ is an integer; the second function crosses the $x$-axis when $x$ is a multiple of $\pi$.

Suppose you would like to define a function called **sinc_x** that uses the second definition. Test your function by calculating values of **sinc_x** for **x** from $-5\pi$ to $+5\pi$ and plotting the results.

1. State the Problem
   Create and test a function called **sinc_x**, using the second definition:

$$f_2(x) = \frac{\sin x}{x}$$

2. Describe the Input and Output

   **Input**    Let $x$ vary from $-5\pi$ to $+5\pi$.

   **Output**    Create a plot of **sinc_x** versus **x**.

3. Develop a Hand Example
4. Develop a MATLAB Solution
   Outline your function in a flowchart, as shown in Figure 7. Then convert the flowchart to pseudocode comments, and insert the appropriate MATLAB code. Once we've created the function, we should test it in the command window:

```
sinc_x(0)
ans =
        1
sinc_x(pi/2)
ans =
        0.6366
sinc_x(pi)
ans =
        3.8982e-017
sinc_x(-pi/2)
ans =
        0.6366
```

Notice that **sinc_x(pi/2)** equals a very small number, but not zero. That is because MATLAB treats $\pi$ as a floating-point number and uses an approximation of its real value .

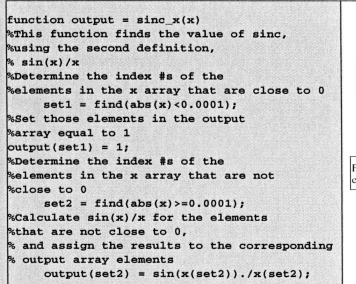

```
function output = sinc_x(x)
%This function finds the value of sinc,
%using the second definition,
% sin(x)/x
%Determine the index #s of the
%elements in the x array that are close to 0
    set1 = find(abs(x)<0.0001);
%Set those elements in the output
%array equal to 1
output(set1) = 1;
%Determine the index #s of the
%elements in the x array that are not
%close to 0
    set2 = find(abs(x)>=0.0001);
%Calculate sin(x)/x for the elements
%that are not close to 0,
% and assign the results to the corresponding
% output array elements
    output(set2) = sin(x(set2))./x(set2);
```

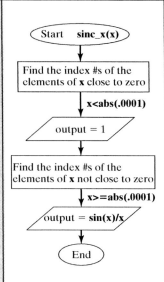

**Figure 7**
Flowchart of the sinc
function.

Table 4  Calculating the Sinc Function

| x | sin(x) | sinc_x(x) = sin(x)/x |
|---|--------|----------------------|
| 0 | 0 | 0/0 = 1 |
| $\pi/2$ | 1 | $1/(\pi/2) = 0.637$ |
| $\pi$ | 0 | 0 |
| $-\pi/2$ | $-1$ | $-1/(\pi/2) = -0.637$ |

5. Test the Solution

When we compare the results with those of the hand example, we see that the answers match. Now we can use the function confidently in our problem. We have

```
%Example 1
    clear, clc
%Define an array of angles
    x = -5*pi:pi/100:5*pi;
%Calculate sinc_x
    y = sinc_x(x);
%Create the plot
    plot(x,y)
    title('Sinc Function'), xlabel('angle,
    radians'),ylabel('sinc')
```

which generates the plot in Figure 8.

The plot also supports our belief that the function is working properly. Testing **sinc_x** with one value at a time validated its answers for a scalar input; however, the program that generated the plot sent a vector argument to the function. The plot confirms that it also performs properly with vector input.

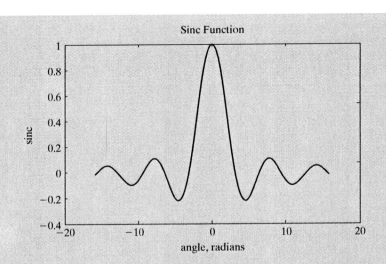

**Figure 8**
The sinc function.

If you have trouble understanding how this function works, remove the semicolons that are suppressing the output, then run the program. Understanding the output from each line will help you understand the program logic better.

In addition to **find**, MATLAB offers two other logical functions: **all** and **any**. The **all** function checks to see if a logical condition is true for *every* member of an array, and the **any** function checks to see if a logical condition is true for *any* member of an array. Consult MATLAB's built-in **help** function for more information.

**Practice Exercises 1**

Consider the following matrices:

$$x = \begin{bmatrix} 1 & 10 & 42 & 6 \\ 5 & 8 & 78 & 23 \\ 56 & 45 & 9 & 13 \\ 23 & 22 & 8 & 9 \end{bmatrix} \quad y = \begin{bmatrix} 1 & 2 & 3 \\ 4 & 10 & 12 \\ 7 & 21 & 27 \end{bmatrix} \quad z = \begin{bmatrix} 10 & 22 & 5 & 13 \end{bmatrix}$$

1. Using single-index notation, find the index numbers of the elements in each matrix that contain values greater than 10.
2. Find the row and column numbers (sometimes called subscripts) of the elements in each matrix that contain values greater than 10.
3. Find the values in each matrix that are greater than 10.
4. Using single-index notation, find the index numbers of the elements in each matrix that contain values greater than 10 and less than 40.
5. Find the row and column numbers for the elements in each matrix that contain values greater than 10 and less than 40.
6. Find the values in each matrix that are greater than 10 and less than 40.

7. Using single-index notation, find the index numbers of the elements in each matrix that contain values between 0 and 10 or between 70 and 80.

8. Use the **length** command together with results from the **find** command to determine how many values in each matrix are between 0 and 10 or between 70 and 80.

## 4 SELECTION STRUCTURES

Most of the time, the **find** command can and should be used instead of an **if** statement. In some situations, however, the **if** statement is required. This section describes the syntax used in **if** statements.

### 4.1 The Simple If

A simple **if** statement has the following form:

```
if comparison
    statements
end
```

If the comparison (a logical expression) is true, the statements between the **if** statement and the **end** statement are executed. If the comparison is false, the program jumps immediately to the statement following **end**. It is good programming practice to indent the statements within an **if** structure for readability. However, recall that MATLAB ignores white space. Your programs will run regardless of whether you do or do not indent any of your lines of code.

Here's a really simple example of an **if** statement:

```
if G<50
    disp('G is a small value equal to:')
    disp(G);
end
```

This statement (from **if** to **end**) is easy to interpret if **G** is a scalar. If **G** is less than 50, then the statements between the **if** and the **end** lines are executed. For example, if **G** has a value of 25, then

KEY IDEA: **if** statements usually work best with scalars

```
G is a small value equal to:
    25
```

is displayed on the screen. However, if **G** is not a scalar, then the **if** statement considers the comparison true **only if it is true for every element**! Thus, if **G** is defined from 0 to 80,

```
G = 0:10:80;
```

the comparison is false, and the statements inside the **if** statement are not executed! In general, **if** statements work best when dealing with scalars.

### 4.2 The If/Else Structure

The simple **if** allows us to execute a series of statements if a condition is true and to skip those steps if the condition is false. The **else** clause allows us to execute one set of statements if the comparison is true and a different set if the comparison is false.

Suppose you would like to take the logarithm of a variable $x$. You know from basic algebra classes that the input to the **log** function must be greater than 0. Here's a set of **if/else** statements that calculates the logarithm if the input is positive and sends an error message if the input to the function is 0 or negative:

```
if x >0
   y = log(x)
else
    disp('The input to the log function must be positive')
end
```

When **x** is a scalar, this is easy to interpret. However, when **x** is a matrix, the comparison is true only if it is true for every element in the matrix. So, if

```
x = 0:0.5:2;
```

then the elements in the matrix are not all greater than 0. Therefore, MATLAB skips to the **else** portion of the statement and displays the error message. The **if/else** statement is probably best confined to use with scalars, although you may find it to be of limited use with vectors.

---

**Hint**

MATLAB includes a function called **beep** that causes the computer to "beep" at the user. You can use this function to alert the user to an error. For example, in the **if/else** clause, you could add a beep to the portion of the code that includes an error statement:

```
x = input('Enter a value of x greater than 0: ');
if x >0
   y = log(x)
else
  beep
   disp('The input to the log function must be positive')
end
```

---

### 4.3 The Elseif Structure

When we nest several levels of **if/else** statements, it may be difficult to determine which logical expressions must be true (or false) in order to execute each set of statements. The **elseif** function allows you to check multiple criteria while keeping the code easy to read. Consider the following lines of code that evaluate whether to issue a driver's license, based on the applicant's age:

```
if age<16
   disp('Sorry - You'll have to wait')
elseif age<18
   disp('You may have a youth license')
elseif age<70
   disp('You may have a standard license')
else
   disp('Drivers over 70 require a special license')
end
```

In this example, MATLAB first checks to see if **age < 16.** If the comparison is true, the program executes the next line or set of lines, displays the message **Sorry – You'll**

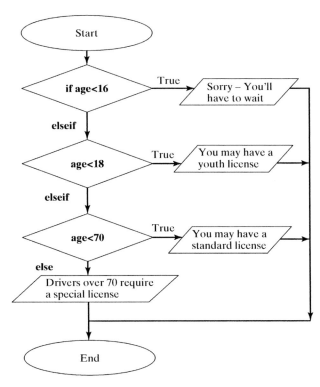

**Figure 9**
Flowchart using multiple **if** statements.

**have to wait**, and then exits the **if** structure. If the comparison is false, MATLAB moves on to the next **elseif** comparison, checking to see if **age < 18** this time. The program continues through the **if** structure until it finally finds a true comparison or until it encounters the **else**. Notice that the **else** line does not include a comparison, since it executes if the **elseif** immediately before it is false.

The flowchart for this sequence of commands (Figure 9) uses the diamond shape to indicate a selection structure.

This structure is easy to interpret if **age** is a scalar. If it is a matrix, the comparison must be true for every element in the matrix. Consider this age matrix

```
age = [15,17,25,55,75]
```

The first comparison, **if age<16**, is false, because it is not true for every element in the array. The second comparison, **elseif age<18**, is also false. The third comparison, **elseif age<70**, is false as well, since not all of the ages are below 70. The result is **Drivers over 70 require a special license**—a result that won't please the other drivers

---

**Hint**

One common mistake new programmers make when using **if** statements is to overspecify the criteria. In the preceding example, it is enough to state that **age < 18** in the second **if** clause, because age cannot be less than 16 and still reach this statement. You don't need to specify **age<18** and **age >=16**. If you overspecify the criteria, you risk defining a calculational path for which there is no correct answer. For example, in the code

```
if age<16
    disp('Sorry - You''ll have to wait')
```

```
    elseif age<18 & age>16
        disp('You may have a youth license')
    elseif age<70 & age>18
        disp('You may have a standard license')
    elseif age>70
        disp('Drivers over 70 require a special license')
    end
```

there is no correct choice for age = 16, 18, or 70.

In general, **elseif** structures work well for scalars, but **find** is probably a better choice for matrices. Here's an example that uses **find** with an array of ages and generates a table of results in each category:

```
age = [15,17,25,55,75];
set1 = find(age<16);
set2 = find(age>=16 & age<18);
set3 = find(age>=18 & age<70);
set4 = find(age>=70);

fprintf('Sorry - You''ll have to wait - you"re only %3.0f
   \n',age(set1))
fprintf('You may have a youth license because you"re %3.0f
   \n',age(set2))
fprintf('You may have a standard license because you"re
   %3.0f \n',age(set3))
fprintf('Drivers over 70 require a special license. You"re
   %3.0f \n',age(set4))
```

These commands return

```
Sorry - You'll have to wait - you're only 15
You may have a youth license because you're 17
You may have a standard license because you're 25
You may have a standard license because you're 55
Drivers over 70 require a special license. You're 75
```

Since every **find** in this sequence is evaluated, it is necessary to specify the range completely (for example, **age>=16 & age<18**).

**EXAMPLE 2**

## Assigning Grades

The **if** family of statements is used most effectively when the input is a scalar. Create a function to determine test grades based on the score and assuming a single input into the function. The grades should be based on the following criteria:

| Grade | Score |
|-------|-------|
| A | 90 to 100 |
| B | 80 to 90 |
| C | 70 to 80 |
| D | 60 to 70 |
| E | < 60 |

1. State the Problem
   Determine the grade earned on a test.
2. Describe the Input and Output

   **Input**    Single score, not an array

   **Output**    Letter grade

3. Develop a Hand Example
   85 should be a B
   But should 90 be an A or a B? We need to create more exact criteria.

| Grade | Score |
|-------|-------|
| A | $\geq$ 90 to 100 |
| B | $\geq$ 80 and < 90 |
| C | $\geq$ 70 and < 80 |
| D | $\geq$ 60 and < 70 |
| E | < 60 |

4. Develop a MATLAB Solution
   Outline the function, using the flowchart shown in Figure 10.

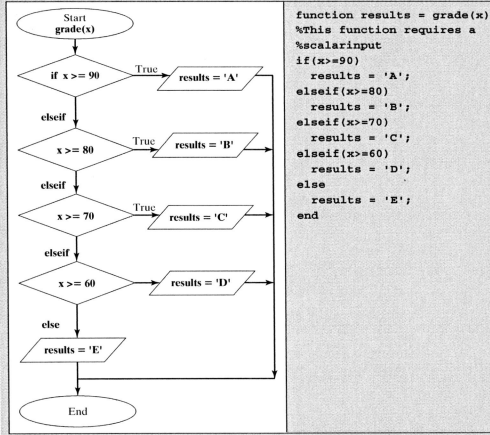

```
function results = grade(x)
%This function requires a
%scalarinput
if(x>=90)
   results = 'A';
elseif(x>=80)
   results = 'B';
elseif(x>=70)
   results = 'C';
elseif(x>=60)
   results = 'D';
else
   results = 'E';
end
```

**Figure 10**
Flowchart for a grading scheme.

5. Test the Solution

Now test the function in the command window:

```
grade(25)
ans =
E
grade(80)
ans =
B
grade(-52)
ans =
E
grade(108)
ans =
A
```

Notice that although the function seems to work properly, it returns grades for values over 100 and values less than 0. If you'd like, you can now go back and add the logic to exclude those values:

```
function results = grade(x)
%This function requires a scalar input
    if(x>=0 & x<=100)
    if(x>=90)
       results = 'A';
    elseif(x>=80)
       results = 'B';
    elseif(x>=70)
       results = 'C';
    elseif(x>=60)
       results = 'D';
    else
       results = 'E';
    end
    else
       results = 'Illegal Input';
end
```

We can test the function again in the command window:

```
grade(-10)
ans =
Illegal Input
grade(108)
ans =
Illegal Input
```

This function will work great for scalars, but if you send a vector to the function, you may get some unexpected results, such as

```
score = [95,42,83,77];
grade(score)
ans =
E
```

## Practice Exercises 2

The **if** family of functions is particularly useful in functions. Write and test a function for each of these problems, assuming that the input to the function is a scalar:

1. Suppose the legal drinking age is 21 in your state. Write and test a function to determine whether a person is old enough to drink.

2. Many rides at amusement parks require riders to be a certain minimum height. Assume that the minimum height is 48″ for a certain ride. Write and test a function to determine whether the rider is tall enough.

3. When a part is manufactured, the dimensions are usually specified with a tolerance. Assume that a certain part needs to be 5.4 cm long, plus or minus 0.1 cm (5.4 ± 0.1 cm). Write a function to determine whether a part is within these specifications.

4. Unfortunately, the United States currently uses both metric and English units. Suppose the part in Exercise 3 was inspected by measuring the length in inches instead of cm. Write and test a function that determines whether the part is within specifications and that accepts input into the function in inches.

5. Many solid-fuel rocket motors consist of three stages. Once the first stage burns out, it separates from the missile and the second stage lights. Then the second stage burns out and separates, and the third stage lights. Finally, once the third stage burns out, it also separates from the missile. Assume that the following data approximately represent the times during which each stage burns:

| | |
|---|---|
| Stage 1 | 0–100 seconds |
| Stage 2 | 100–170 seconds |
| Stage 3 | 170–260 seconds |

Write and test a function to determine whether the missile is in Stage 1 flight, Stage 2 flight, Stage 3 flight, or free flight (unpowered).

## 4.4 Switch and Case

The **switch/case** structure is often used when a series of programming path options exists for a given variable, depending on its value. The **switch/case** is similar to the **if/else/elseif**. As a matter of fact, anything you can do with **switch/case** could be done with **if/else/elseif**. However, the code is a bit easier to read with **switch/case**, a structure that allows you to choose between multiple outcomes, based on some criterion. This is an important distinction between **switch/case** and **elseif**. The criterion can be either a scalar (a number) or a string. In practice, it is used more with strings than with numbers. The structure of **switch/case** is

```
switch variable
case option1
  code to be executed if variable is equal to option 1
case option2
  code to be executed if variable is equal to option 2
     :
     :
```

```
case option_n
  code to be executed if variable is equal to option n
otherwise
  code to be executed if variable is not equal to any of
    the options
end
```

Here's an example: Suppose you want to create a function that tells the user what the airfare is to one of three different cities:

```
city = input('Enter the name of a city in single quotes: ')
switch city
  case 'Boston'
    disp('$345')
  case 'Denver'
    disp('$150')
  case 'Honolulu'
    disp('Stay home and study')
  otherwise
    disp('Not on file')
end
```

If, when you run this script, you reply **'Boston'** at the prompt, MATLAB responds

```
city =
Boston
$345
```

You can tell the **input** command to expect a string by adding 's' in a second field. This relieves the user of the awkward requirement of adding single quotes around any string input. With the added 's', the preceding code now reads as follows:

```
city = input('Enter the name of a city: ','s')
switch city
  case 'Boston'
    disp('$345')
  case 'Denver'
    disp('$150')
  case 'Honolulu'
    disp('Stay home and study')
  otherwise
    disp('Not on file')
end
```

The **otherwise** portion of the **switch/case** structure is not required for the structure to work. However, you should include it if there is any way that the user could input a value not equal to one of the cases.

**Switch/case** structures are flowcharted exactly the same as **if/else** structures.

---

### Hint

If you are a C programmer, you may have used **switch/case** in that language. One important difference in MATLAB is that once a "true" case has been found, the program does not check the other cases.

EXAMPLE 3

## Buying Gasoline

Four countries in the world do not officially use the metric system: the United States, the United Kingdom, Liberia, and Myanmar. Even in the United States, the practice is that some industries are almost completely metric and others still use the English system of units. For example, any shade-tree mechanic will tell you that although older cars have a mixture of components—some metric and others English—new cars (any car built after 1989) are almost completely metric. Wine is packaged in liters, but milk is packaged in gallons. Americans measure distance in miles, but power in watts. Confusion between metric and English units is common. American travelers to Canada are regularly confused because gasoline is sold by the liter in Canada, but by the gallon in the United States.

Imagine that you want to buy gasoline (Figure 11). Write a program that

- asks the user whether he or she wants to request the gasoline in liters or in gallons
- prompts the user to enter how many units he or she wants to buy
- calculates the total cost to the user, assuming that gasoline costs $2.89 per gallon.

Use a **switch/case** structure.

1. State the Problem
   Calculate the cost of a gasoline purchase.
2. Describe the Input and Output

   *Input*   Specify gallons or liters
             Number of gallons or liters

   *Output*  Cost in dollars, assuming $2.89 per gallon

3. Develop a Hand Example
   If the volume is specified in gallons, the cost is

$$\text{volume} \times \$2.89$$

so, for 10 gallons,

$$\text{cost} = 10 \text{ gallons} \times \$2.89/\text{gallon} = \$28.90$$

If the volume is specified in liters, we need to convert liters to gallons and then calculate the cost:

$$\text{volume} = \text{liters} \times 0.264 \text{ gallon/liter}$$

$$\text{cost} = \text{volume} \times \$2.89$$

So, for 10 liters,

$$\text{volume} = 10 \text{ liters} \times 0.264 \text{ gallon/liter} = 2.64 \text{ gallons}$$

$$\text{cost} = 2.64 \text{ gallons} \times 2.89 = \$7.63$$

**Figure 11**
Gasoline is sold in both liters and gallons.

4. Develop a MATLAB Solution

First create a flowchart (Figure 12). Then convert the flowchart into pseudocode comments. Finally, add the MATLAB code:

```
clear,clc
%Define the cost per gallon
 rate = 2.89;
%Ask the user to input gallons or liters
 unit = input('Enter gallons or liters\n ','s');
%Use a switch/case to determine the conversion factor
 switch unit
   case 'gallons'
     factor = 1;
   case 'liters'
     factor = 0.264;
   otherwise
     disp('Not available')
     factor = 0;
end

%Ask the user how much gas he/she would like to buy
 volume = input( [';Enter the volume you would like to buy
 in ',unit,': \n'] );
%Calculate the cost of the gas
if factor ~ = 0
  cost = volume * factor*rate;
%Send the results to the screen
  fprintf('That will be $ %5.2f for %5.1f %s
          \n',cost,volume,unit)
end
```

There are several things to notice about this solution. First, the variable **unit** contains an array of character information. If you check the workspace window after you run this program, you'll notice that **unit** is either a $1 \times 6$ character array (if you entered liters) or a $1 \times 7$ character array (if you entered gallons). On the line

```
unit = input('Enter gallons or liters ','s');
```

the second field, **'s'**, tells MATLAB to expect a string as input. This allows the user to enter gallons or liters without the surrounding single quotes.
On the line

```
volume = input(['Enter the volume you would like to buy in
                ',unit,': '] );
```

we created a character array out of three components:

- the string **'Enter the volume you would like to buy in'**
- the character variable **unit**
- the string **':'**

By combining these three components, we were able to make the program prompt the user with either

```
Enter the volume you would like to buy in liters:
```

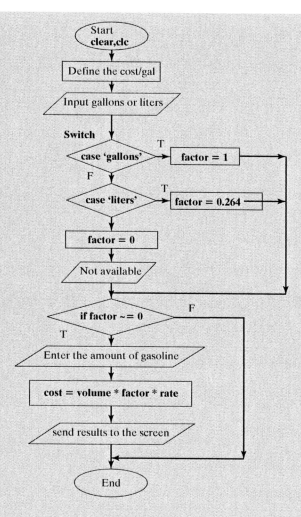

**Figure 12**
Flowchart to determine the cost of gasoline, using the **switch/case** structure.

or

**Enter the volume you would like to buy in gallons:**

In the **fprintf** statement, we included a field for string input by using the place-holder **%s**:

```
fprintf('That will be $ %5.2f for %5.1f %s
      \n',cost,volume,unit)
```

This allowed the program to tell the users that the gasoline was either measured in gallons or measured in liters.

Finally, we used an **if** statement so that if the user entered something besides gallons or liters, no calculations were performed.

5. Test the Solution

We can test the solution by running the program three separate times, once for gallons, once for liters, and once for some unit not supported. The interaction in the command window for gallons is

```
Enter gallons or liters
gallons
Enter the volume you would like to buy in gallons:
10
That will be $ 28.90 for 10.0 gallons
```

For liters, the interaction is

```
Enter gallons or liters
liters
Enter the volume you would like to buy in liters:
10
That will be $ 7.63 for 10.0 liters
```

Finally, if you enter anything besides gallons or liters, the program sends an error message to the command window:

```
Enter gallons or liters
quarts
Not available
```

Since the program results are the same as the hand calculation, it appears that the program works as planned.

## 4.5 Menu

KEY IDEA: Graphical user interfaces like the menu box reduce the opportunity for user errors, such as spelling mistakes

The **menu** function is often used in conjunction with a **switch/case** structure. This function causes a menu box to appear on the screen, with a series of buttons defined by the programmer.

```
input = menu('Message to the user','text for button
    1','text for button 2', etc.)
```

We can use the **menu** option in our previous airfare example to ensure that the user chooses only cities about which we have information. This also means that we don't need the **otherwise** syntax, since it is not possible to choose a city "not on file."

```
city = menu('Select a city from the menu:
    ','Boston','Denver','Honolulu')
switch city
    case 1
        disp('$345')
    case 2
        disp('$150')
    case 3
        disp('Stay home and study')
end
```

Notice that a case number has replaced the string in each **case** line. When the script is executed, the menu box shown in Figure 13 appears and waits for the user to select one of the buttons. If you choose Honolulu, MATLAB will respond

```
city =
    3
Stay home and study
```

Of course, you could suppress the output from the **disp** command, which was included here for clarity.

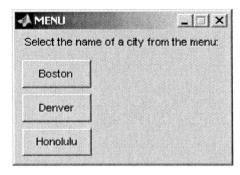

**Figure 13**
The pop-up menu window.

EXAMPLE 4

## Buying Gasoline: A Menu Approach

In Example 3, we used a **switch/case** approach to determine whether the customer wanted to buy gasoline measured in gallons or in liters. One problem with our program is that if the user can't spell, the program won't work. For example, if, when prompted for gallons or liters, the user enters

```
litters
```

The program will respond

```
Not available
```

We can get around this problem by using a menu; then the user need only press a button to make a choice. We'll still use the **switch/case** structure, but will combine it with the menu.

1. State the Problem
   Calculate the cost of a gasoline purchase.

2. Describe the Input and Output

   *Input*   Specify gallons or liters, using a menu
             Number of gallons or liters

   *Output*  Cost in dollars, assuming $2.89 per gallon

3. Develop a Hand Example
   If the volume is specified in gallons, the cost is

   $$volume \times 2.89$$

   So, for 10 gallons,

   $$cost = 10 \text{ gallons} \times \$2.89/\text{gallon} = \$28.90$$

   If the volume is specified in liters, we need to convert liters to gallons and then calculate the cost:

   $$volume = liters \times 0.264 \text{ gallon/liter}$$
   $$cost = volume \times \$2.89$$

   So, for 10 liters,

   $$volume = 10 \text{ liters} \times 0.264 \text{ gallon/liter} = 2.64 \text{ gallons}$$
   $$cost = 2.64 \text{ gallons} \times 2.89 = \$7.63$$

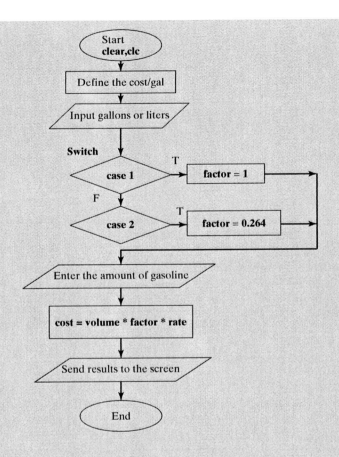

**Figure 14**
Flowchart to determine the cost of gasoline, using a menu.

4. Develop a MATLAB Solution
   First create a flowchart (Figure 14). Then convert the flowchart into pseudocode comments. Finally, add the MATLAB code:

```
%Example 4
clear,clc
%Define the cost per gallon
 rate = 2.89;
%Ask the user to input gallons or liters, using a menu
 disp('Use the menu box to make your selection ')
 choice = menu('Measure the gasoline in liters or
gallons?','gallons','liters');
%Use a switch/case to determine the conversion factor
switch choice
   case 1
      factor = 1;
      unit = 'gallons'
   case 2
      factor = 0.264;
      unit = 'liters'
end

%Ask the user how much gas he/she would like to buy
 volume = input(['Enter the volume you would like to buy
   in ',unit,': \n'] );
```

```
%Calculate the cost of the gas
  cost = volume * factor*rate;
%Send the results to the screen
  fprintf('That will be $ %5.2f for %5.1f %s
  \n',cost,volume,unit)
```

This solution is simpler than the one in Example 3 because there is no chance for bad input. There are a few things to notice, however.

When we define the choice by using the menu function, the result is a number, not a character array:

```
choice = menu('Measure the gasoline in liters or
  gallons?','gallons','liters');
```

You can check this by consulting the workspace window, in which the choice is listed as a 1 × 1 double-precision number.

Because we did not use the **input** command to define the variable **unit**, which is a string (a character array), we needed to specify the value of **unit** as part of the case calculations:

```
case 1
  factor = 1;
  unit = 'gallons'
case 2
  factor = 0.264;
  unit = 'liters'
```

Doing this allows us to use the value of **unit** in the output to the command window, both in the **disp** command and in **fprintf**.

5. Test the Solution

As in Example 3, we can test the solution by running the program, but this time we need to try it only twice—once for gallons and once for liters. The interaction in the command window for gallons is

```
Use the menu box to make your selection
```

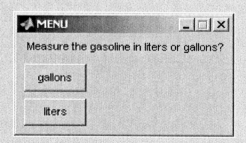

```
Enter the volume you would like to buy in gallons:
10
That will be $ 28.90 for 10.0 gallons
```

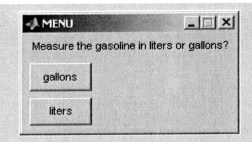

For liters, the interaction is

```
Use the menu box to make your selection
Enter the volume you would like to buy in liters:
10
That will be $ 7.63 for 10.0 liters
```

These values match those in the hand solution and have the added advantage that you can't misspell any of the input.

---

**Practice Exercises 3**

Use the **switch/case** structure to solve these problems:

1. Create a program that prompts the user to enter his or her year in school—freshman, sophomore, junior, or senior. The input will be a string. Use the **switch/case** structure to determine which day finals will be given for each group—Monday for freshmen, Tuesday for sophomores, Wednesday for juniors, and Thursday for seniors.

2. Repeat Exercise 1, but this time with a menu.

3. Create a program to prompt the user to enter the number of candy bars he or she would like to buy. The input will be a number. Use the **switch/case** structure to determine the bill, where

$$1 \text{ bar} = \$0.75$$
$$2 \text{ bars} = \$1.25$$
$$3 \text{ bars} = \$1.65$$

more than 3 bars = \$1.65 + \$0.30 (number ordered − 3)

---

## 5 REPETITION STRUCTURES: LOOPS

Loops are used when you need to repeat a set of instructions multiple times. MAT-LAB supports two different types of loops: the **for** loop and the **while** loop. **For** loops are the easiest choice when you know how many times you need to repeat the loop. **While** loops are the easiest choice when you need to keep repeating the instructions until a criterion is met. If you have previous programming experience, you may be tempted to use loops extensively. However, usually you can compose MATLAB programs that avoid loops, either by using the **find** command or by vectorizing the code. (In vectorization, we operate on entire vectors at a time instead of one element at a time.) It's a good idea to avoid loops whenever possible, because the resulting programs run faster and often require fewer programming steps.

## 5.1 For Loops

The structure of the **for** loop is simple. The first line identifies the loop and defines an index, which is a number that changes on each pass through the loop. After the identification line comes the group of commands we want to execute. Finally, the end of the loop is identified by the command **end**. In sum, we have

```
for index = [matrix]
     commands to be executed
end
```

The loop is executed once for each element of the index matrix identified in the first line. Here's a really simple example:

```
for k = [1,3,7]
  k
end
```

This code returns

```
k =
    1
k =
    3
k =
    7
```

The index in this case is **k**. Programmers often use **k** as an index variable as a matter of style. The index matrix can also be defined with the colon operator or, indeed, in a number of other ways as well. Here's an example of code that finds the value of 5 raised to powers between 1 and 3:

```
for k = 1:3
  a = 5^k
end
```

KEY IDEA: Loops allow you to repeat sequences of commands until some criterion is met

On the first line, the index, **k**, is defined as the matrix [1, 2, 3]. The first time through the loop, **k** is assigned a value of 1, and $5^1$ is calculated. Then the loop repeats, but now **k** is equal to 2 and $5^2$ is calculated. The last time through the loop, **k** is equal to 3 and $5^3$ is calculated. Because the statements in the loop are repeated three times, the value of **a** is displayed three times in the command window:

```
a =
    5
a =
    25
a =
    125
```

Although we defined **k** as a matrix in the first line of the **for** loop, because **k** is an index number when it is used in the loop, it can equal only one value at a time. After we finish executing the loop, if we call for **k**, it has only one value: the value of the index the final time through the loop. For the preceding example,

```
k
```

returns

```
k =
    3
```

Notice that **k** is listed as a $1 \times 1$ matrix in the workspace window.

A common way to use a **for** loop is in defining a new matrix. Consider, for example, the code

```
for k = 1:5
   a(k) = k^2
end
```

This loop defines a new matrix, **a**, one element at a time. Since the program repeats its set of instructions five times, a new element is added to the **a** matrix each time through the loop, with the following output in the command window:

```
a =
   1
a =
   1   4
a =
   1   4   9
a =
   1   4   9   16
a =
   1   4   9   16   25
```

### Hint

Most computer programs do not have MATLAB's ability to handle matrices so easily; therefore, they rely on loops similar to the one just presented to define arrays. It would be easier to create the vector **a** in MATLAB with the code

```
k = 1:5
a = k.^2
```

which returns

```
k =

   1   2   3   4   5

a =
   1   4   9   16   25
```

This is an example of *vectorizing* the code.

Another common use for a **for** loop is to combine it with an **if** statement and determine how many times something is true. For example, in the list of test scores shown in the first line, how many are above 90?

```
scores = [76,45,98,97];
count = 0;
for k=1:length(scores)
   if scores(k)>90
      count = count + 1;
   end
end
disp(count)
```

Each time through the loop, if the score is greater than 90, the count is incremented by 1.

Most of the time, **for** loops are created which use an index matrix that is a single row. However, if a two-dimensional matrix is defined in the index specification, MATLAB uses an entire column as the index each time through the loop. For example, suppose we define the index matrix as

$$k = \begin{bmatrix} 1 & 2 & 3 \\ 1 & 4 & 9 \\ 1 & 8 & 27 \end{bmatrix}$$

Then

```
for k = [1,2,3; 1,4,9; 1,8,27]
    a = k'
end
```

returns

```
a =
    1    1    1
a =
    2    4    8
a =
    3    9   27
```

Notice that **k** was transposed when it was set equal to **a**, so our results are rows instead of columns.

We can summarize the use of for loops with the following rules:

- The loop starts with a **for** statement and ends with the word **end**.
- The first line in the loop defines the number of times the loop will repeat, using an index matrix.
- The index of a **for** loop must be a variable. (The index is the number that changes each time through the loop.) Although **k** is often used as the symbol for the index, any variable name may be employed. The use of **k** is a matter of style.
- Any of the techniques learned to define a matrix can be used to define the index matrix. One common approach is to use the colon operator, as in

    **for index = start:inc:final**

- If the expression is a row vector, the elements are used one at a time—once for each time through the loop.
- If the expression is a two-dimensional matrix (this alternative is not common), each time through the loop the index will contain the next *column* in the matrix. This means that the index will be a column vector!
- Once you've completed a **for** loop, the index is the last value used.
- **For** loops can often be avoided by vectorizing the code.

The basic flowchart for a **for** loop includes a diamond, which reflects the fact that a **for** loop starts each pass with a check to see if there is a new value in the index matrix (Figure 15). If there isn't, the loop is terminated and the program continues with the statements after the loop.

KEY IDEA: Use **for** loops when you know how many times you need to repeat a sequence of commands

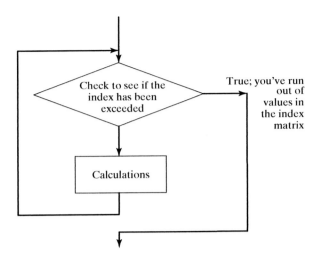

**Figure 15**
Flowchart for a **for** loop.

---

**EXAMPLE 5**

### Creating a Degrees-to-Radians Table

Although it would be much easier to use MATLAB's vector capability to create a degrees-to-radians table, we can demonstrate the use of **for** loops with this example.

1. State the Problem
   Create a table that converts angle values from degrees to radians, from 0 to 360 degrees, in increments of 10 degrees.

2. Describe the Input and Output

   *Input*  An array of angle values in degrees

   *Output*  A table of angle values in both degrees and radians

3. Develop a Hand Example
   For 10 degrees,

   $$\text{radians} = (10)\frac{\pi}{180} = 0.1745$$

4. Develop a MATLAB Solution
   First develop a flowchart (Figure 16) to help you plan your code.
   The command window displays the following results:

   ```
   Degrees to Radians
   Degrees      Radians
       10        0.17
       20        0.35
       30        0.52    etc.
   ```

5. Test the Solution
   The value for 10 degrees calculated by MATLAB is the same as the hand calculation.

   Clearly, it is much easier to use MATLAB's vector capabilities for this calculation. You get exactly the same answer, and it takes significantly less

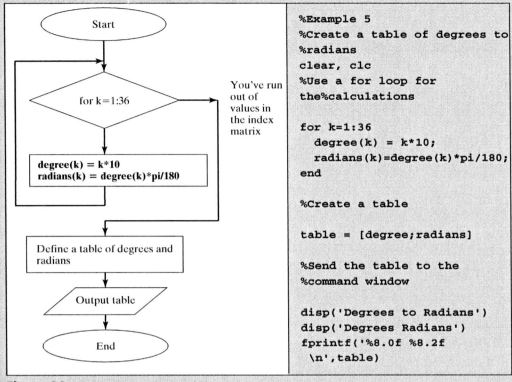

```
%Example 5
%Create a table of degrees to
%radians
clear, clc
%Use a for loop for
the%calculations

for k=1:36
    degree(k) = k*10;
    radians(k)=degree(k)*pi/180;
end

%Create a table

table = [degree;radians]

%Send the table to the
%command window

disp('Degrees to Radians')
disp('Degrees Radians')
fprintf('%8.0f %8.2f
  \n',table)
```

**Figure 16**
Flowchart for changing degrees to radians.

computing time. This approach is called vectorization of your code and is one of the strengths of MATLAB. The vectorized code is

```
degrees = 0:10:360;
radians = degrees * pi/180;
table = [degree;radians]
disp('Degrees to Radians')
disp('Degrees     Radians')
fprintf('%8.0f %8.2f \n',table)
```

**EXAMPLE 6**

## Calculating Factorials with a For Loop

A factorial is the product of all the integers from 1 to *N*. For example, 5 factorial is

$$1 \cdot 2 \cdot 3 \cdot 4 \cdot 5$$

In mathematics texts, factorial is usually indicated with an exclamation point:

$$5! \text{ is five factorial.}$$

MATLAB contains a built-in function for calculating factorials, called **factorial**. However, suppose you would like to program your own factorial function called **fact**.

1. State the Problem
   Create a function called **fact** to calculate the factorial of any number. Assume scalar input.

2. Describe the Input and Output

   **Input**    A scalar value $N$

   **Output**   The value of $N!$

3. Develop a Hand Example

   $$5! = 1 \cdot 2 \cdot 3 \cdot 4 \cdot 5 = 120$$

4. Develop a MATLAB Solution
   First develop a flowchart (Figure 17) to help you plan your code.

5. Test the Solution
   Test the function in the command window:

   ```
   fact(5)
   ans =
       120
   ```

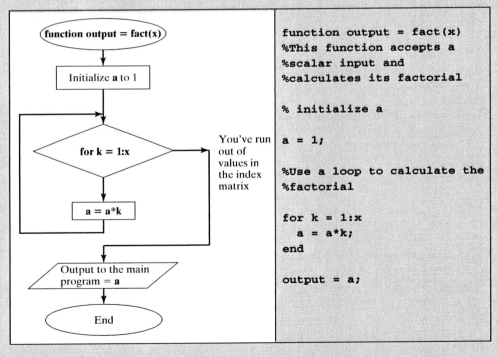

**Figure 17**
Flowchart for finding a factorial, using a **for** loop.

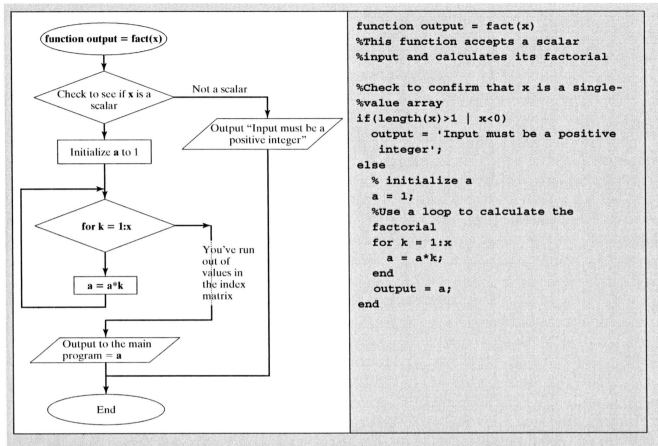

The flowchart contains:

```
function output = fact(x)
```

- Check to see if **x** is a scalar → Not a scalar → Output "Input must be a positive integer"
- Initialize **a** to 1
- for k = 1:x → You've run out of values in the index matrix
- a = a*k
- Output to the main program = **a**
- End

```
function output = fact(x)
%This function accepts a scalar
%input and calculates its factorial

%Check to confirm that x is a single-
%value array
if(length(x)>1 | x<0)
  output = 'Input must be a positive
    integer';
else
  % initialize a
  a = 1;
  %Use a loop to calculate the
  factorial
  for k = 1:x
    a = a*k;
  end
  output = a;
end
```

**Figure 18**
Flowchart for finding a factorial, including error checking.

This function works only if the input is a scalar. If an array is entered, the **for** loop does not execute, and the function returns a value of 1:

```
x=1:10;
    fact(x)
ans =
    1
```

You can add an **if** statement to confirm that the input is a positive integer and not an array, as shown in the flowchart in Figure 18 and the accompanying code. Check the new function in the command window:

```
fact(-4)
ans =
Input must be a positive integer

fact(x)
ans =
Input must be a positive integer
```

**Practice Exercises 4**

Use a **for** loop to solve the following problems:
1. Create a table that converts inches to feet.
2. Consider the following matrix of values:

$$x = [45, 23, 17, 34, 85, 33]$$

How many values are greater than 30? (Use a counter.)
3. Repeat Exercise 2, this time using the **find** command.
4. Use a **for** loop to sum the elements of the matrix in Problem 2. Check your results with the **sum** function. (Use the **help** feature if you don't know or remember how to use **sum**.)
5. Use a **for** loop to create a vector containing the first 10 elements in the harmonic series, i.e.,

1/1    1/2    1/3    1/4    1/5    . . . . . . . . . . . 1/10

6. Use a **for** loop to create a vector containing the first 10 elements in the alternating harmonic series, i.e.,

1/1    −1/2    1/3    −1/4    1/5    . . . . . . . . . . . −1/10

## 5.2 While Loops

KEY IDEA: Use **while** loops when you don't know how many times a sequence of commands will need to be repeated

**While** loops are similar to **for** loops. The big difference is the way MATLAB decides how many times to repeat the loop. **While** loops continue until some criterion is met. The format for a **while** loop is

```
while criterion
      commands to be executed
end
```

Here's an example:

```
k = 0;
while k<3
  k = k+1
end
```

In this case, we initialized a counter, **k**, before the loop. Then the loop repeated as long as **k** was less than 3. We incremented **k** by 1 every time through the loop, so the loop repeated three times, giving

```
k =
    1
k =
    2
k =
    3
```

We could use **k** as an index number to define a matrix or just as a counter. Most **for** loops can also be coded as **while** loops. Recall the **for** loop in Section 5.1

used to calculate the first three powers of 5. The following **while** loop accomplishes the same task:

```
k = 0;
while k<3
  k = k+1;
   a(k) = 5^k
end
```

The code returns

```
a =
   5
a =
   5    25
a =
   5    25    125
```

Each time through the loop, another element is added to the matrix **a**. As another example, first initialize **a**:

```
a = 0;
```

Then find the first multiple of 3 that is greater than 10:

```
while(a<10)
     a = a + 3
end;
```

KEY IDEA: Any problem that can be solved using a **while** loop could also be solved using a **for** loop

The first time through the loop, **a** is equal to 0, so the comparison is true. The next statement (**a = a + 3**) is executed, and the loop is repeated. This time **a** is equal to 3 and the condition is still true, so execution continues. In succession, we have

```
a =
   3
a =
   6
a =
   9
a =
   12
```

The last time through the loop, **a** starts out as 9 and then becomes 12 when 3 is added to 9. The comparison is made one final time, but since **a** is now equal to 12—which is greater than 10—the program skips to the end of the **while** loop and no longer repeats.

**While** loops can also be used to count how many times a condition is true by incorporating an **if** statement. Recall the test scores we counted in a **for** loop earlier. We can also count them with a **while** loop:

```
scores = [76,45,98,97];
count = 0;
k = 0;
while k<length(scores)
  k = k+1;
   if scores(k)>90
      count = count + 1;
   end
end
disp(count)
```

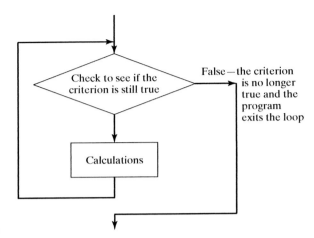

**Figure 19**
Flowchart for a **while** loop.

The variable **count** is used to count how many values are greater than 90. The variable **k** is used to count how many times the loop is executed.

The basic flow chart for a **while** loop is the same as that for a **for** loop (Figure 19).

One common use for a **while** loop is error checking of user input. Consider a program where we prompt the user to input a positive number, and then we calculate the log base 10 of that value. We can use a **while** loop to confirm that the number is positive, and if it is not, to prompt the user to enter an allowed value. The program keeps on prompting for a positive value until the user finally enters a valid number.

```
x = input('Enter a positive value of x')
while (x<=0)
  disp('log(x) is not defined for negative numbers')
  x = input('Enter a positive value of x')
end
  y = log10(x);
fprintf('The log base 10 of %4.2f is %5.2f \n',x,y)
```

If, when the code is executed, a positive value of **x** is entered, the **while** loop does not execute (since **x** is not less than 0). If, instead, a zero or negative value is entered, the **while** loop is executed, an error message is sent to the command window, and the user is prompted to re-enter the value of **x**. The **while** loop continues to execute until a positive value of **x** is finally entered.

---

**Hint**

The variable used to control the **while** loop must be updated every time through the loop. If not, you'll generate an endless loop. When a calculation is taking a long time to complete, you can confirm that the computer is really working on it by checking the lower left-hand corner for the "busy" indicator. If you want to exit the calculation manually, type **Ctrl c**. Make sure that the command window is the active window when you execute this command.

**Hint**

Many computer texts and manuals indicate the control key with the ^ symbol. This is confusing at best. The command ^c usually means to strike the Ctrl key and the c key at the same time.

EXAMPLE 7

## Creating a Table for Converting Degrees to Radians with a While Loop

Just as we used a **for** loop to create a table for converting degrees to radians in Example 5, we can use a **while** loop for the same purpose.

1. State the Problem
   Create a table that converts degrees to radians, from 0 to 360 degrees, in increments of 10 degrees.
2. Describe the Input and Output

   *Input*    An array of angle values in degrees

   *Output*   A table of angle values in both degrees and radians

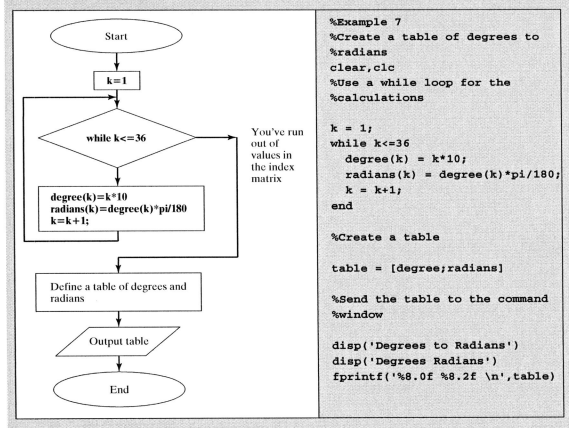

**Figure 20**
Flowchart for converting degrees to radians with a **while** loop.

3. Develop a Hand Example
For 10 degrees,

$$\text{radians} = (10)\frac{\pi}{180} = 0.1745$$

4. Develop a MATLAB Solution
First develop a flowchart (Figure 20) to help you plan your code.
The command window displays the following results:

```
Degrees to Radians
Degrees      Radians
    10        0.17
    20        0.35
    30        0.52    etc.
```

5. Test the Solution
The value for 10 degrees calculated by MATLAB is the same as the hand calculation.

---

**EXAMPLE 8**

## Calculating Factorials with a While Loop

Create a new function called **fact2** that uses a **while** loop to find $N!$. Include an **if** statement to check for negative numbers and to confirm that the input is a scalar.

1. State the Problem
Create a function called **fact2** to calculate the factorial of any number.

2. Describe the Input and Output

   *Input*    A scalar value $N$

   *Output*   The value of $N!$

3. Develop a Hand Example

$$5! = 1 \cdot 2 \cdot 3 \cdot 4 \cdot 5 = 120$$

4. Develop a MATLAB Solution
First develop a flowchart (Figure 21) to help you plan your code.

5. Test the Solution
Test the function in the command window:

```
fact2(5)
ans =
120
fact2(-10)
ans =
The input must be a positive integer
fact2([1:10])
ans =
The input must be a positive integer
```

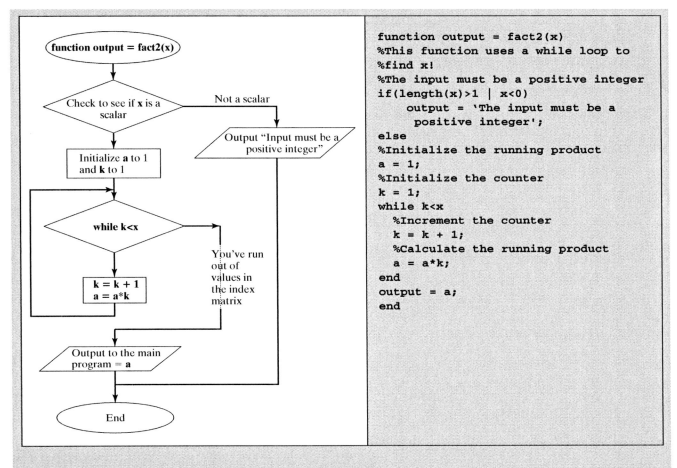

The code shown in the figure:

```
function output = fact2(x)
%This function uses a while loop to
%find x!
%The input must be a positive integer
if(length(x)>1 | x<0)
    output = 'The input must be a
        positive integer';
else
%Initialize the running product
a = 1;
%Initialize the counter
k = 1;
while k<x
  %Increment the counter
  k = k + 1;
  %Calculate the running product
  a = a*k;
end
output = a;
end
```

**Figure 21**
Flowchart for finding a factorial with a **while** loop.

---

**EXAMPLE 9**

## The Alternating Harmonic Series

The *alternating harmonic series* converges to the natural log of 2:

$$\sum_{k=1}^{\infty} \frac{(-1)^{k+1}}{k} = 1 - \frac{1}{2} + \frac{1}{3} - \frac{1}{4} + \frac{1}{5} - \cdots = \ln(2) = 0.6931471806$$

Because of this, we can use the alternating harmonic series to approximate the ln(2). But how far out do you have to take the series to get a good approximation of the final answer? We can use a **while** loop to solve this problem.

1. State the Problem

Use a **while** loop to calculate the members of the alternating harmonic sequence and the value of the series until it converges to values that vary by less than .001. Compare the result to the natural log of 2.

2. Describe the Input and Output

*Input*    The description of the alternating harmonic series

$$\sum_{k=1}^{\infty} \frac{(-1)^{k+1}}{k} = 1 - \frac{1}{2} + \frac{1}{3} - \frac{1}{4} + \frac{1}{5} - \cdots \frac{1}{\infty}$$

*Output*    The value of the truncated series, once the convergence criterion is met. Plot the cumulative sum of the series elements, up to the point where the convergence criterion is met.

3. Develop a Hand Example

Let's calculate the value of the alternating harmonic series for 1 to 5 terms. First find the value for each of the first five terms in the sequence

    1.0000    −0.5000    0.3333    −0.2500    0.2000

Now calculate the sum of the series assuming 1 to 5 terms

    1.0000    0.5000    0.8333    0.5833    0.7833

The calculated sums are getting closer together, as we can see if we find the difference between adjacent pairs

    −0.5000    0.3333    −0.2500    0.2000

4. Develop a MATLAB Solution

First develop a flowchart (Figure 22) to help you plan your code, then convert it to a MATLAB program. When we run the program, the following results are displayed in the command window.

```
The sequence converges when the final element is equal
  to    0.001
At which point the value of the series is 0.6936
This compares to the value of the ln(2), 0.6931
The sequence took 1002 terms to converge
```

The series is pretty close to the ln(2), but perhaps we could get closer with more terms. If we change the convergence criterion to 0.0001 and run the program, we get the following results

```
The sequence converges when the final element is equal
  to   -0.000
At which point the value of the series is 0.6931
This compares to the value of the ln(2), 0.6931
The sequence took 10001 terms to converge
```

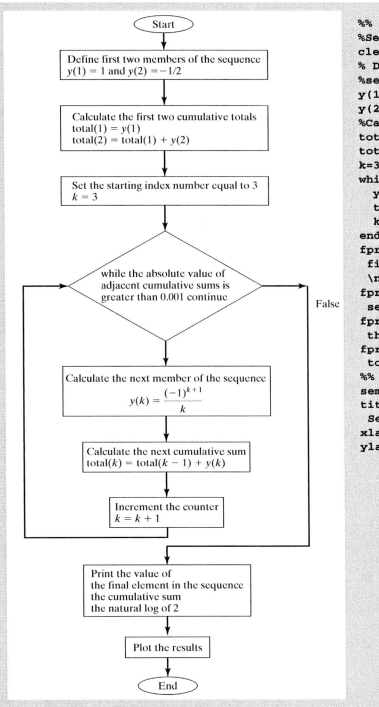

```
%% Calculating the Alternating Harmonic
%Series
clear,clc
% Define the first two elements in the
%series
y(1)=1;
y(2)=-1/2;
%Calculate the first two cumulative sums
total(1)=y(1);
total(2)=total(1) + y(2);
k=3;
while  (abs(total(k-1)-total(k-2))>.001)
  y(k)=(-1)^(k+1)/k;
  total(k) = total(k-1) + y(k);
  k = k+1;
end
fprintf('The sequence converges when the
  final element is equal to %8.3f
  \n',y(k-1))
fprintf('At which point the value of the
  series is %5.4f \n',total(k-1))
fprintf('This compares to the value of
  the ln(2), %5.4f \n',log(2))
fprintf('The sequence took %3.0f terms
  to converge \n',k)
%% Plot the results
semilogx(total)
title('Value of the Alternating Harmonic
  Series')
xlabel('Number of terms')
ylabel('Sum of the terms')
```

**Figure 22**
Flowchart to evaluate the alternating harmonic series until it
converges.

5. Test the Solution

Compare the result of the hand solution to the MATLAB solution, by examining the graph (Figure 23). The first five values for the series match those displayed in the graph. We can also see that the series seems to be converging to approximately 0.69, which is approximately the natural log of 2.

**Figure 23**
The alternating harmonic series converges to the ln(2)

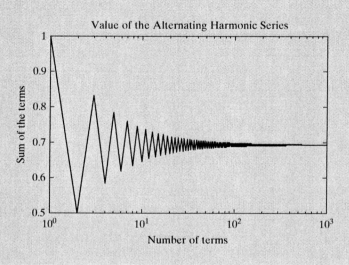

**Practice Exercises 5**

Use a **while** loop to solve the following problems:
1. Create a conversion table of inches to feet.
2. Consider the following matrix of values:

$$x = [45, 23, 17, 34, 85, 33]$$

How many values are greater than 30? (Use a counter.)
3. Repeat Exercise 2, this time using the **find** command.
4. Use a **while** loop to sum the elements of the matrix in Exercise 2. Check your results with the **sum** function. (Use the **help** feature if you don't know or remember how to use **sum**.)
5. Use a **while** loop to create a vector containing the first 10 elements in the harmonic series—, i.e.,

$$1/1 \quad 1/2 \quad 1/3 \quad 1/4 \quad 1/5 \dots \dots \dots \dots 1/10$$

6. Use a **while** loop to create a vector containing the first 10 elements in the alternating harmonic series—i.e.,

$$1/1 \quad -1/2 \quad 1/3 \quad -1/4 \quad 1/5 \dots \dots \dots \dots -1/10$$

## 5.3 Break and Continue

The **break** command can be used to terminate a loop prematurely (while the comparison in the first line is still true). A **break** statement will cause termination of the smallest enclosing **while** or **for** loop. Here's an example:

```
n = 0;
while(n<10)
      n = n+1;
      a = input('Enter a value greater than 0:');
      if(a<=0)
          disp('You must enter a positive number')
          disp('This program will terminate')
          break
      end
      disp('The natural log of that number is')
      disp(log(a))
end
```

In this program, the value of **n** is initialized outside the loop. Each time through, the input command is used to ask for a positive number. The number is checked, and if it is zero or negative, an error message is sent to the command window and the program jumps out of the loop. If the value of **a** is positive, the program continues and another pass through the loop occurs, until **n** is finally greater than 10.

INITIALIZE: define a starting value for a variable that will be changed later

The **continue** command is similar to **break**; however, instead of terminating the loop, the program just skips to the next pass:

```
n=0;
while(n<10)
      n=n+1;
      a=input('Enter a value greater than 0:');
      if(a<=0)
          disp('You must enter a positive number')
          disp('Try again')
          continue
      end
      disp('The natural log of that number is')
      disp(log(a))
end
```

In this example, if you enter a negative number, the program lets you try again—until the value of **n** is finally greater than 10.

## 5.4 Improving the Efficiency of Loops

In general, using a **for** loop (or a **while** loop) is less efficient in MATLAB than using array operations. We can test this assertion by timing the multiplication of the elements in a long array. First we create a matrix **A** containing 40,000 ones. The **ones** command creates an $n \times n$ matrix of ones:

KEY IDEA: Loops are generally less efficient than vectorized calculations

```
ones(200);
```

The result is a $200 \times 200$ matrix of ones (40,000 total values). Now we can compare the results of multiplying each element by $\pi$, using array multiplication first and then a **for** loop. You can time the results by using the **clock** function and the function **etime**, which measures elapsed time. If you have a fast computer, you may need to use a larger array. The structure of the clocking code is

```
t0 = clock;
code to be timed
etime (clock, t0)
```

The clock function polls the computer clock for the current time. The **etime** function compares the current time with the initial time and subtracts the two values to give the elapsed time.

For our problem,

```
clear, clc
A = ones(200);     %Creates a 200 x 200 matrix of ones
t0 = clock;
    B = A*pi;
time = etime(clock, t0)
```

gives a result of

```
time =
        0
```

The array calculation took 0 seconds, simply meaning that it happened very quickly. Every time you run these lines of code, you should get a different answer. The **clock** and **etime** functions used here measure how long the CPU worked between receiving the original and final timing requests. However, the CPU is doing other things besides our problem: At a minimum, it is performing system tasks, and it may be running other programs in the background.

To measure the time required to perform the same calculation with a loop, we need to clear the memory and re-create the array of ones:

```
clear
A = ones(200);
```

This ensures that we are comparing calculations from the same starting point. Now we code

```
t0 = clock;
    for k = 1:length(A(:))
        B(k) = A(k)*pi;
    end
time = etime(clock, t0)
```

which gives the result

```
time =
        69.6200
```

It took almost 70 seconds to perform the same calculation! (This was on an older computer—your result will depend on the machine you use.) The number of iterations through the **for** loop was determined by finding how many elements are in **A**. This was accomplished with the **length** command. Recall that **length** returns the largest array dimension, which is 200 for our array and isn't what we want. To find the total number of elements, we used the colon operator (:) to represent **A** as a single list, 40,000 elements long, and then used **length**, which returned 40,000. Each time through the **for** loop, a new element was added to the **B** matrix. This is the step that took all the time. We can reduce the time required for this calculation by creating the **B** matrix first and then replacing the values one at a time. The code is

```
clear
A = ones(200);
t0 = clock;
%Create a B matrix of ones
   B = A;
   for k = 1:length(A(:))
    B(k) = A(k)*pi;
   end
time = etime(clock, t0)
```

which gives the result

```
time =
      0.0200
```

This is obviously a huge improvement. You could see an even bigger difference between the first example, a simple multiplication of the elements of an array, and the last example if you created a bigger matrix. By contrast, the intermediate example, in which we did not initialize **B**, would take a prohibitive amount of time to execute.

MATLAB also includes a set of commands called **tic** and **toc** that can be used in a manner similar to the **clock** and **etime** functions to time a piece of code. Thus, the code

```
clear
A = ones(200);
tic
    B = A;
    for k = 1:length(A(:))
       B(k) = A(k)*pi;
    end
toc
```

returns

```
Elapsed time is 0.140000 seconds.
```

The difference in execution time is expected, since the computer is busy doing different background tasks each time the program is executed. As with **clock/etime**, the **tic/toc** commands measure elapsed time, not the time devoted to just this program's execution.

### Hint

Be sure to suppress intermediate calculations when you use a loop. Printing those values to the screen will greatly increase the amount of execution time. If you are brave, repeat the preceding example, but delete the semicolons inside the loop just to check out this claim. Don't forget that you can stop the execution of the program with **Ctrl c**. Be sure the command window is the active window when you execute **Ctrl c**.

## SUMMARY

Sections of computer code can be categorized as sequences, selection structures, and repetition structures. Sequences are lists of instructions that are executed in order. Selection structures allow the programmer to define criteria (conditional statements) that the program uses to choose execution paths. Repetition structures define loops in which a sequence of instructions is repeated until some criterion is met (also defined by conditional statements).

MATLAB uses the standard mathematical relational operators, such as greater than (>) and less than (<). The not-equal-to (~=) operator's form is not usually seen in mathematics texts. MATLAB also includes logical operators such as *and* (&) and *or* (|). These operators are used in conditional statements, allowing MATLAB to make decisions regarding which portions of the code to execute.

The **find** command is unique to MATLAB and should be the primary conditional function used in your programming. This command allows the user to specify a condition by using both logical and relational operators. The command is then used to identify elements of a matrix that meet the condition.

Although the **if**, **else**, and **elseif** commands can be used for both scalars and matrix variables, they are useful primarily for scalars. These commands allow the programmer to identify alternative computing paths on the basis of the results of conditional statements.

**For** loops are used mainly when the programmer knows how many times a sequence of commands should be executed. **While** loops are used when the commands should be executed until a condition is met. Most problems can be structured so that either **for** or **while** loops are appropriate.

The **break** and **continue** statements are used to exit a loop prematurely. They are usually used in conjunction with **if** statements. The **break** command causes a jump out of a loop and execution of the remainder of the program. The **continue** command skips execution of the current pass through a loop, but allows the loop to continue until the completion criterion is met.

Vectorization of MATLAB code allows it to execute much more efficiently and therefore more quickly. Loops in particular should be avoided in MATLAB. When loops are unavoidable, they can be improved by defining "dummy" variables with placeholder values, such as ones or zeros. These placeholders can then be replaced in the loop. Doing this will result in significant improvements in execution time, a fact that can be confirmed with timing experiments.

The **clock** and **etime** functions are used to poll the computer clock and then determine the time required to execute pieces of code. The time calculated is the "elapsed" time. During this time, the computer not only has been running MATLAB code, but also has been executing background jobs and housekeeping functions. The **tic** and **toc** functions perform a similar task. Either **tic/toc** or **clock/etime** functions can be used to compare execution time for different code options.

The following MATLAB summary lists and briefly describes all of the special characters, commands, and functions that were defined in this chapter:

| Special Characters | |
|---|---|
| < | less than |
| <= | less than or equal to |
| > | greater than |
| >= | greater than or equal to |
| == | equal to |
| ~= | not equal to |
| & | and |
| \| | or |
| ~ | not |

| Commands and Functions | |
|---|---|
| all | checks to see if a criterion is met by all the elements in an array |
| any | checks to see if a criterion is met by any of the elements in an array |
| break | causes the execution of a loop to be terminated |
| case | sorts responses |
| clock | determines the current time on the CPU clock |
| continue | terminates the current pass through a loop, but proceeds to the next pass |
| else | defines the path if the result of an **if** statement is false |
| elseif | defines the path if the result of an **if** statement is false, and specifies a new logical test |
| end | identifies the end of a control structure |
| etime | finds elapsed time |
| find | determines which elements in a matrix meet the input criterion |
| for | generates a loop structure |
| if | checks a condition, resulting in either true or false |
| menu | creates a menu to use as an input vehicle |
| ones | creates a matrix of ones |
| otherwise | part of the case selection structure |
| switch | part of the case selection structure |
| tic | starts a timing sequence |
| toc | stops a timing sequence |
| while | generates a loop structure |

**KEY TERMS**

control structure
index
local variable
logical condition

logical operator
loop
relational operator
repetition

selection
sequence
subscript

**PROBLEMS**

### Logical Operators: Find

1.  A sensor that monitors the temperature of a backyard hot tub records the data shown in Table 5.

    **(a)** The temperature should never exceed 105°F. Use the **find** function to find the index numbers of the temperatures that exceed the maximum allowable temperature.

    **(b)** Use the **length** function with the results from part (a) to determine how many times the maximum allowable temperature was exceeded.

    **(c)** Determine at what times the temperature exceeded the maximum allowable temperature, using the index numbers found in part (a).

    **(d)** The temperature should never be lower than 102°F. Use the **find** function together with the **length** function to determine how many times the temperature was less than the minimum allowable temperature.

    **(e)** Determine at what times the temperature was less than the minimum allowable temperature.

    **(f)** Determine at what times the temperature was within the allowable limits (i.e., between 102°F and 105°F, inclusive).

    **(g)** Use the **max** function to determine the maximum temperature reached and the time at which it occurred.

2.  The height of a rocket (in meters) can be represented by the following equation:

$$\text{height} = 2.13t^2 - 0.0013t^4 + 0.000034t^{4.751}$$

Create a vector of time ($t$) values from 0 to 100 at 2-second intervals.

**Table 5 Hot-Tub Temperature Data**

| Time of Day | Temperature, °F | Time of Day | Temperature, °F |
|---|---|---|---|
| 0:00 A.M. | 100 | 1:00 P.M. | 103 |
| 1:00 A.M. | 101 | 2:00 P.M. | 101 |
| 2:00 A.M. | 102 | 3:00 P.M. | 100 |
| 3:00 A.M. | 103 | 4:00 P.M. | 99 |
| 4:00 A.M. | 103 | 5:00 P.M. | 100 |
| 5:00 A.M. | 104 | 6:00 P.M. | 102 |
| 6:00 A.M. | 104 | 7:00 P.M. | 104 |
| 7:00 A.M. | 105 | 8:00 P.M. | 106 |
| 8:00 A.M. | 106 | 9:00 P.M. | 107 |
| 9:00 A.M. | 106 | 10:00 P.M. | 105 |
| 10:00 A.M. | 106 | 11:00 P.M. | 104 |
| 11:00 A.M. | 105 | 12:00 A.M. | 104 |
| 12:00 P.M. | 104 | | |

**(a)** Use the **find** function to determine when the rocket hits the ground to within 2 seconds. (*Hint:* The value of **height** will be positive for all values until the rocket hits the ground.)

**(b)** Use the **max** function to determine the maximum height of the rocket and the corresponding time.

**(c)** Create a plot with $t$ on the horizontal axis and height on the vertical axis for times until the rocket hits the ground. Be sure to add a title and axis labels.[*]

**3**    Solid-fuel rocket motors are used as boosters for the space shuttle, in satellite launch vehicles, and in weapons systems (see Figure P3). The propellant is a solid combination of fuel and oxidizer, about the consistency of an eraser. For the space shuttle, the fuel component is aluminum and the oxidizer is ammonium perchlorate, held together with an epoxy resin "glue." The propellant mixture is poured into a motor case, and the resin is allowed to cure under controlled conditions. Because the motors are extremely large, they are cast in segments, each requiring several "batches" of propellant to fill. (Each motor contains over 1.1 million pounds of propellant!) This casting–curing process is sensitive to temperature, humidity, and pressure. If the conditions aren't just right, the fuel could ignite or the properties of the propellant grain (which means its shape; the term *grain* is borrowed from artillery) might be degraded. Solid-fuel rocket motors are extremely expensive as well as dangerous and clearly must work right every time, or the results will be disastrous. Failures can cause loss of human life and irreplaceable scientific data and equipment. Highly public failures can destroy a company. Actual processes are tightly monitored and controlled. However, for our purposes, consider these general criteria:

**Figure P3**
Solid-fuel rocket booster to a Titan missile. (Courtesy of NASA.)

The temperature should remain between 115°F and 125°F.

The humidity should remain between 40% and 60%.

The pressure should remain between 100 and 200 torr.

Imagine that the data in Table 6 were collected during a casting–curing process.

**(a)** Use the **find** command to determine which batches did and did not meet the criterion for temperature.

**(b)** Use the **find** command to determine which batches did and did not meet the criterion for humidity.

**(c)** Use the **find** command to determine which batches did and did not meet the criterion for pressure.

**Table 6  Casting–Curing Data**

| Batch Number | Temperature, °F | Humidity, % | Pressure, torr |
|:---:|:---:|:---:|:---:|
| 1 | 116 | 45 | 110 |
| 2 | 114 | 42 | 115 |
| 3 | 118 | 41 | 120 |
| 4 | 124 | 38 | 95 |
| 5 | 126 | 61 | 118 |

---

[*]From Etter, Kancicky, and Moore, *Introduction to Matlab 7* (Upper Saddle River, NJ: Pearson/Prentice Hall, 2005).

**Table 7  Gymnastics Scores**

| Event | Gymnast 1 | Gymnast 2 |
|-------|-----------|-----------|
| Pommel horse | 9.821 | 9.700 |
| Vault | 9.923 | 9.925 |
| Floor | 9.624 | 9.83 |
| Rings | 9.432 | 9.987 |
| High bar | 9.534 | 9.354 |
| Parallel bars | 9.203 | 9.879 |

    **(d)** Use the **find** command to determine which batches failed for any reason and which passed.

    **(e)** Use your results from the previous questions, along with the **length** command, to determine what percentage of motors passed or failed on the basis of each criterion and to determine the total passing rate.

**4** Two gymnasts are competing with each other. Their scores are shown in Table 7.

    **(a)** Write a program that uses **find** to determine how many events each gymnast won.

    **(b)** Use the **mean** function to determine each gymnast's average score.

**5** Create a function called **f** that satisfies the following criteria:

$$\text{For values of } x > 2, f(x) = x^2$$
$$\text{For values of } x \leq 2, f(x) = 2x$$

Plot your results for values of $x$ from $-3$ to 5. Choose your spacing to create a smooth curve. You should notice a break in the curve at $x = 2$.

**6** Create a function called **g** that satisfies the following criteria:

$$\text{For } x < -\pi, \qquad g(x) = -1$$
$$\text{For } x \geq -\pi \text{ and } x \leq \pi, \qquad g(x) = \cos(x)$$
$$\text{For } x > \pi, \qquad g(x) = -1$$

Plot your results for values of $x$ from $-2\pi$ to $+2\pi$. Choose your spacing to create a smooth curve.

**7** A file named **temp.dat** contains information collected from a set of thermocouples. The data in the file are shown in Table 8. The first column consists of time measurements (one for each hour of the day), and the remaining columns correspond to temperature measurements at different points in a process.

    **(a)** Write a program that prints the index numbers (rows and columns) of temperature data values greater than 85.0. (*Hint*: You'll need to use the **find** command.)

    **(b)** Find the index numbers (rows and columns) of temperature data values less than 65.0.

    **(c)** Find the maximum temperature in the file and the corresponding hour value and thermocouple number.

**Table 8  Temperature Data**

| Hour | Temp1 | Temp2 | Temp3 |
|------|-------|-------|-------|
| 1 | 68.70 | 58.11 | 87.81 |
| 2 | 65.00 | 58.52 | 85.69 |
| 3 | 70.38 | 52.62 | 71.78 |
| 4 | 70.86 | 58.83 | 77.34 |
| 5 | 66.56 | 60.59 | 68.12 |
| 6 | 73.57 | 61.57 | 57.98 |
| 7 | 73.57 | 67.22 | 89.86 |
| 8 | 69.89 | 58.25 | 74.81 |
| 9 | 70.98 | 63.12 | 83.27 |
| 10 | 70.52 | 64.00 | 82.34 |
| 11 | 69.44 | 64.70 | 80.21 |
| 12 | 72.18 | 55.04 | 69.96 |
| 13 | 68.24 | 61.06 | 70.53 |
| 14 | 76.55 | 61.19 | 76.26 |
| 15 | 69.59 | 54.96 | 68.14 |
| 16 | 70.34 | 56.29 | 69.44 |
| 17 | 73.20 | 65.41 | 94.72 |
| 18 | 70.18 | 59.34 | 80.56 |
| 19 | 69.71 | 61.95 | 67.83 |
| 20 | 67.50 | 60.44 | 79.59 |
| 21 | 70.88 | 56.82 | 68.72 |
| 22 | 65.99 | 57.20 | 66.51 |
| 23 | 72.14 | 62.22 | 77.39 |
| 24 | 74.87 | 55.25 | 89.53 |

**8**  The Colorado River Drainage Basin covers parts of seven western states. A series of dams has been constructed on the Colorado River and its tributaries to store runoff water and to generate low-cost hydroelectric power. (See Figure P8.) The ability to regulate the flow of water has made the growth of agriculture and population in these arid desert states possible. Even during periods of extended drought, a steady, reliable source of water and electricity has been available to the basin states. Lake Powell is one of these reservoirs.

**Figure P8**
Glen Canyon Dam at Lake Powell. (Courtesy of Getty Images, Inc.)

**Table 9 Water-Level Data for Lake Powell, Measured in Feet above Sea Level**

|           | 2000    | 2001    | 2002    | 2003    | 2004    | 2005    | 2006    | 2007    |
|-----------|---------|---------|---------|---------|---------|---------|---------|---------|
| January   | 3680.12 | 3668.05 | 3654.25 | 3617.61 | 3594.38 | 3563.41 | 3596.26 | 3601.41 |
| February  | 3678.48 | 3665.02 | 3651.01 | 3613    | 3589.11 | 3560.35 | 3591.94 | 3598.63 |
| March     | 3677.23 | 3663.35 | 3648.63 | 3608.95 | 3584.49 | 3557.42 | 3589.22 | 3597.85 |
| April     | 3676.44 | 3662.56 | 3646.79 | 3605.92 | 3583.02 | 3557.52 | 3589.94 | 3599.75 |
| May       | 3676.76 | 3665.27 | 3644.88 | 3606.11 | 3584.7  | 3571.60 | 3598.27 | 3604.68 |
| June      | 3682.19 | 3672.19 | 3642.98 | 3615.39 | 3587.01 | 3598.06 | 3609.36 | 3610.94 |
| July      | 3682.86 | 3671.37 | 3637.53 | 3613.64 | 3583.07 | 3607.73 | 3608.79 | 3609.47 |
| August    | 3681.12 | 3667.81 | 3630.83 | 3607.32 | 3575.85 | 3604.96 | 3604.93 | 3605.56 |
| September | 3678.7  | 3665.45 | 3627.1  | 3604.11 | 3571.07 | 3602.20 | 3602.08 | 3602.27 |
| October   | 3676.96 | 3663.47 | 3625.59 | 3602.92 | 3570.7  | 3602.31 | 3606.12 | 3601.27 |
| November  | 3674.93 | 3661.25 | 3623.98 | 3601.24 | 3569.69 | 3602.65 | 3607.46 | 3599.71 |
| December  | 3671.59 | 3658.07 | 3621.65 | 3598.82 | 3565.73 | 3600.14 | 3604.96 | 3596.79 |

The file **lake_powell.dat** contains data on the water level in the reservoir for the eight years from 2000 to 2007. These data are shown in Table 9. Use the data in the file to answer the following questions:

**(a)** Determine the average elevation of the water level for each year and for the eight-year period over which the data were collected.

**(b)** Determine how many months each year exceed the overall average for the eight-year period.

**(c)** Create a report that lists the month and the year for each of the months that exceed the overall average.

**(d)** Determine the average elevation of the water for each month for the eight-year period.

**If Structures**

**9** Create a program that prompts the user to enter a scalar value of temperature. If the temperature is greater than 98.6°F, send a message to the command window telling the user that he or she has a fever.

**10** Create a program that first prompts the user to enter a value for **x** and then prompts the user to enter a value for **y**. If the value of **x** is greater than the value of **y**, send a message to the command window telling the user that **x > y**. If **x** is less than or equal to **y**, send a message to the command window telling the user that **y >= x**.

**11** The inverse sine (**asin**) and inverse cosine (**acos**) functions are valid only for inputs between −1 and +1, because both the sine and the cosine have values only between −1 and +1 (Figure P11). MATLAB interprets the result of **asin** or **acos** for a value outside the range as a complex number. For example, we might have

```
acos(-2)
ans =
   3.1416 - 1.3170i
```

which is a questionable mathematical result. Create a function called **my_asin** that accepts a single value of **x** and checks to see if it is between −1 and +1 (−**1 <= x <= 1**), If **x** is outside the range, send an error message to the screen. If it is inside the allowable range, return the value of **asin**.

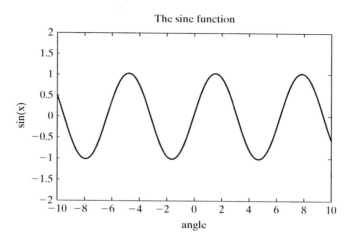

**Figure P11**
The sine function varies between −1 and +1. Thus, the inverse sine **(asin)** is not defined for values greater than 1 and values less than −1.

**12** Create a program that prompts the user to enter a scalar value for the outside air temperature. If the temperature is equal to or above 80°F, send a message to the command window telling the user to wear shorts. If the temperature is between 60°F and 80°F send a message to the command window telling the user that it is a beautiful day. If the temperature is equal to or below 60°F, send a message to the command window telling the user to wear a jacket or coat.

**13** Suppose the following matrix represents the number of saws ordered from your company each month over the last year.

```
saws = [1,4,5,3,7,5,3,10,12,8, 7, 4]
```

All the numbers should be zero or positive.

**(a)** Use an **if** statement to check whether any of the values in the matrix are invalid. (Evaluate the whole matrix at once in a single **if** statement.) Send the message "All valid" or else "Invalid number found" to the screen, depending on the results of your analysis.

**(b)** Change the **saws** matrix to include at least one negative number, and check your program to make sure that it works for both cases.

**14** Most large companies encourage employees to save by matching their contributions to a 401(k) plan. The government limits how much you can save in these plans, because they shelter income from taxes until the money is withdrawn during your retirement. The amount you can save is tied to your income, as is the amount your employer can contribute. The government will allow you to save additional amounts without the tax benefit. These plans change from year to year, so this example is just a made-up "what if."

Suppose the Quality Widget Company has the savings plan described in Table 10. Create a function that finds the total yearly contribution to your savings plan, based on your salary and the percentage you contribute. Remember, the total contribution consists of the employee contribution and the company contribution.

## Switch/Case

**15** In order to have a closed geometric figure composed of straight lines (Figure P15), the angles in the figure must add to

$$(n - 2)(180 \text{ degrees})$$

where $n$ is the number of sides.

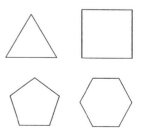

**Figure P15**
Regular polygons.

**Table 10  Quality Widget Company Savings Plan**

| Income | Maximum You Can Save Tax Free | Maximum the Company Will Match |
|---|---|---|
| Up to $30,000 | 10% | 10% |
| Between $30,000 and $60,000 | 10% | 10% of the first $30,000 and 5% of the amount above $30,000 |
| Between $60,000 and $100,000 | 10% of the first $60,000 and 8% of the amount above $60,000 | 10% of the first $30,000 and 5% of the amount between $30,000 and $60,000; nothing for the remainder above $60,000 |
| Above $100,000 | 10% of the first $60,000 and 8% of the amount between $60,000 and $100,000; nothing on the amount above $100,000 | Nothing—highly compensated employees are exempt from this plan and participate in stock options instead |

**(a)** Prove this statement to yourself by creating a vector called $n$ from 3 to 6 and calculating the angle sum from the formula. Compare what you know about geometry with your answer.

**(b)** Write a program that prompts the user to enter one of the following:

triangle
square
pentagon
hexagon

Use the input to define the value of $n$ via a **switch/case** structure; then use $n$ to calculate the sum of the interior angles in the figure.

**(c)** Reformulate your program from part (b) so that it uses a menu.

**16** At the University of Utah, each engineering major requires a different number of credits for graduation. For example, in 2005 the requirements for some of the departments were as follows:

| | |
|---|---|
| Civil Engineering | 130 |
| Chemical Engineering | 130 |
| Computer Engineering | 122 |
| Electrical Engineering | 126.5 |
| Mechanical Engineering | 129 |

Prompt the user to select an engineering program from a menu. Use a **switch/case** structure to send the minimum number of credits required for graduation back to the command window.

**17** The easiest way to draw a star in MATLAB is to use polar coordinates. You simply need to identify points on the circumference of a circle and draw lines between those points. For example, to draw a five-pointed star, start at the top of the circle ($\theta = \pi/2, r = 1$) and work counterclockwise (Figure P17).

Prompt the user to specify either a five-pointed or a six-pointed star, using a menu. Then create the star in a MATLAB figure window. Note that a six-pointed

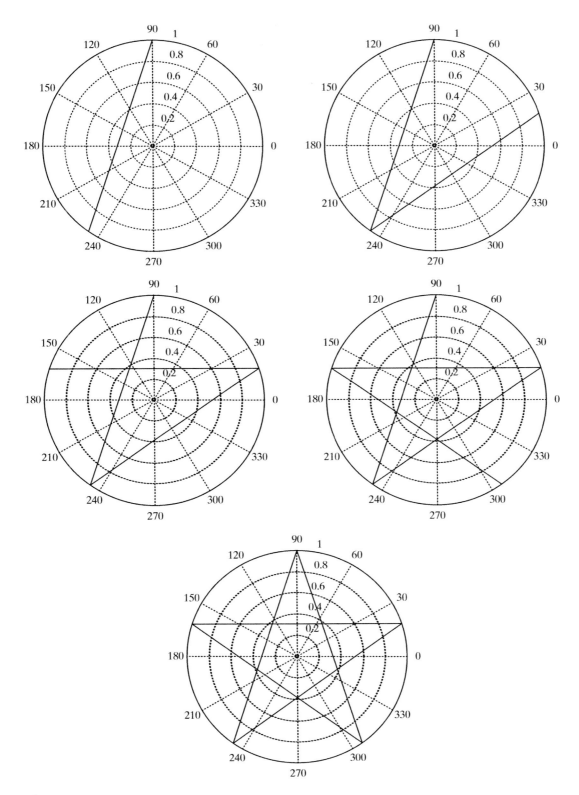

**Figure P17**
Steps required to draw a five-pointed star in polar coordinates.

star is made of three triangles and requires a strategy different from that used to create a five-pointed star.

**Repetition Structures: Loops**

18  Use a **for** loop to sum the elements in the following vector:

$$x = [\,1, 23, 43, 72, 87, 56, 98, 33\,]$$

Check your answer with the **sum** function.
19  Repeat the previous problem, this time using a **while** loop.
20  Use a **for** loop to create a vector of the squares of the numbers 1 through 5.
21  Use a while loop to create a vector of the squares of the numbers 1 through 5.
22  Use the **primes** function to create a list of all the primes below 100. Now use a **for** loop to multiply adjacent values together. For example the first 4 prime numbers are

2   3   5   7

Your calculation would be

2*3   3*5   5*7

which gives

6     15     35

23  A Fibonacci sequence is composed of elements created by adding the two previous elements. The simplest Fibonacci sequence starts with 1, 1 and proceeds as follows:

1, 1, 2, 3, 5, 8, 13, …

**Figure P23**
Chambered nautilus. (Colin Keates © Dorling Kindersley, Courtesy of the Natural History Museum, London.)

However, a Fibonacci sequence can be created with any two starting numbers. Fibonacci sequences appear regularly in nature. For example, the shell of the chambered nautilus (Figure P23) grows in accordance with a Fibonacci sequence.

Prompt the user to enter the first two numbers in a Fibonacci sequence and the total number of elements requested for the sequence. Find the sequence and store it in an array by using a **for** loop. Now plot your results on a **polar** graph. Use the element number for the angle and the value of the element in the sequence for the radius.

24  Repeat the preceding problem, this time using a **while** loop.
25  One interesting property of a Fibonacci sequence is that the ratio of the values of adjacent members of the sequence approaches a number called "the golden ratio" or Φ (phi). Create a program that accepts the first two numbers of a Fibonacci sequence as user input and then calculates additional values in the sequence until the ratio of adjacent values converges to within 0.001. You can do this in a **while** loop by comparing the ratio of element **k** to element **k – 1** and the ratio of element **k – 1** to element **k – 2**. If you call your sequence **x**, then the code for the **while** statement is

```
while abs(x(k)/x(k-1) - x(k-1)/x(k-2))>0.001
```

26  Recall from trigonometry that the tangent of both $\pi/2$ and $-\pi/2$ is infinity. This may be seen from the fact that

$$\tan(\theta) = \sin(\theta)/\cos(\theta)$$

and since

$$\sin(\pi/2) = 1$$

and

$$\cos(\pi/2) = 0$$

it follows that

$$\tan(\pi/2) = \text{infinity}$$

Because MATLAB uses a floating-point approximation of $\pi$, it calculates the tangent of $\pi/2$ as a very large number, but not infinity.

Prompt the user to enter an angle $\theta$ between $\pi/2$ and $-\pi/2$, inclusive. If it is between $\pi/2$ and $-\pi/2$, but not equal to either of those values, calculate $\tan(\theta)$ and display the result in the command window. If it is equal to $\pi/2$ or $-\pi/2$, set the result equal to **Inf** and display the result in the command window. If it is outside the specified range, send the user an error message in the command window and prompt the user to enter another value. Continue prompting the user for a new value of theta until he or she enters a valid number.

27  Imagine that you are a proud new parent. You decide to start a college savings plan now for your child, hoping to have enough in 18 years to pay the sharply rising cost of an education. Suppose that your folks give you $1000 to get started and that each month you can contribute $100. Suppose also that the interest rate is 6% per year compounded monthly, which is equivalent to 0.5% each month.

Because of interest payments and your contribution, each month your balance will increase in accordance with the formula

New Balance = Old Balance + interest + your contribution

Use a **for** loop to find the amount in the savings account each month for the next 18 years. (Create a vector of values.) Plot the amount in the account as a function of time. (Plot time on the horizontal axis and dollars on the vertical axis.)

28  Imagine that you have a crystal ball and can predict the percentage increases in tuition for the next 22 years. The following vector **increase** shows your predictions, in percent, for each year:

```
increase = [10, 8, 10, 16, 15, 4, 6, 7, 8, 10, 8, 12, 14,
    15, 8, 7, 6, 5, 7, 8, 9, 8]
```

Use a **for** loop to determine the cost of a four-year education, assuming that the current cost for one year at a state school is $5000.

29  Use an **if** statement to compare your results from the previous two problems. Are you saving enough? Send an appropriate message to the command window.

30  **Faster Loops.** Whenever possible, it is better to avoid using **for** loops, because they are slow to execute.

(a) Generate a 100,000-item vector of random digits called **x**; square each element in this vector and name the result **y**; use the commands **tic** and **toc** to time the operation.

(b) Next, perform the same operation element by element in a **for** loop. Before you start, clear the values in your variables with

```
clear x y
```

Use **tic** and **toc** to time the operation.

Depending on how fast your computer runs, you may need to stop the calculations by issuing the **Ctrl c** command in the command window.

**(c)** Now convince yourself that suppressing the printing of intermediate answers will speed execution of the code by allowing these same operations to run and print the answers as they are calculated. You will almost undoubtedly need to cancel the execution of this loop because of the large amount of time it will take. ***Recall that Ctrl c terminates the program.***

**(d)** If you are going to be using a constant value several times in a **for** loop, calculate it once and store it, rather than calculating it each time through the loop. Demonstrate the increase in speed of this process by adding **(sin(0.3) + cos(pi/3))\*5!** to every value in the long vector in a **for** loop. (Recall that ! means factorial, which can be calculated with the MATLAB function **factorial**.)

**(e)** As discussed in this chapter, if MATLAB must increase the size of a vector every time through a loop, the process will take more time than if the vector were already the appropriate size. Demonstrate this fact by repeating part (b) of this problem. Create the following vector of **y**-values, in which every element is equal to zero before you enter the **for** loop:

```
y = zeros(1,100000);
```

You will be replacing the zeros one at a time as you repeat the calculations in the loop.

**Challenge Problems**

**31**  **(a)** Create a function called **polygon** that draws a polygon in a polar plot. Your function should have a single input parameter—the number of sides.

**(b)** Use a **for** loop to create a figure with four subplots, showing a triangle in the first subplot, a square in the second subplot, a pentagon in the third subplot and a hexagon in the fourth subplot. You should use the function you created in part (a) to draw each polygon. Use the index parameter from the **for** loop to specify the subplot in which each polygon is drawn, and in an expression to determine the number of sides used as input to the **polygon** function.

**32**  Most major airports have separate lots for long-term and short-term parking. The cost to park depends on the lot you select, and how long you stay. Consider this rate structure from the Salt Lake International Airport during the summer of 2008.

- Long-Term (Economy) Parking
  - The first hour is $1.00, and each additional hour or fraction thereof is $1.00
  - Daily maximum $6.00
  - Weekly maximum $42.00
- Short-Term Parking
  - The first 30 minutes are free and each additional 20 minutes or fraction thereof is $1.00
  - Daily maximum $25.00

Write a program that asks the user the following:

- Which lot are you using?
- How many weeks, hours, days and minutes did you park?

Your program should then calculate the parking bill.

## SOLUTIONS TO PRACTICE EXERCISES

### Practice Exercises 1

Use these arrays in the exercises.

```
x = [1 10 42 6
     5 8 78 23
     56 45 9 13
     23 22 8 9];

y = [1 2 3; 4 10 12; 7 21 27];

z = [10 22 5 13];
```

1. ```
   elements_x = find(x>10)
   elements_y = find(y>10)
   elements_z = find(z>10)
   ```

2. ```
   [rows_x, cols_x] = find(x>10)
   [rows_y, cols_y] = find(y>10)
   [rows_z, cols_z] = find(z>10)
   ```

3. ```
   x(elements_x)
   y(elements_y)
   z(elements_z)
   ```

4. ```
   elements_x = find(x>10 & x< 40)
   elements_y = find(y>10 & y< 40)
   elements_z = find(z>10 & z< 40)
   ```

5. ```
   [rows_x, cols_x] = find(x>10 & x<40)
   [rows_y, cols_y] = find(y>10 & y<40)
   [rows_z, cols_z] = find(z>10 & z<40)
   ```

6. ```
   x(elements_x)
   y(elements_y)
   z(elements_z)
   ```

7. ```
   elements_x = find((x>0 & x<10) | (x>70 & x<80))
   elements_y = find((y>0 & y<10) | (y>70 & y<80))
   elements_z = find((z>0 & z<10) | (z>70 & z<80))
   ```

8. ```
   length_x = length(find((x>0 & x<10) | (x>70 & x<80)))
   length_y = length(find((y>0 & y<10) | (y>70 & y<80)))
   length_z = length(find((z>0 & z<10) | (z>70 & z<80)))
   ```

### Practice Exercises 2

1. ```
   function output = drink(x)
   if x> = 21
      output = 'You can drink';
   else
      output = 'Wait ''till you"re older';
   end
   ```

   Test your function with the following from the command window or a script M-file:
   ```
   drink(22)
   drink(18)
   ```

2. ```
   function output = tall(x)
   if x> = 48
      output = 'You may ride';
   else
      output = 'You''re too short';
   end
   ```

   Test your function with the following:
   ```
   tall(50)
   tall(46)
   ```

3. 
```
function output = spec(x)
if x> = 5.3 & x< = 5.5
   output = ' in spec';
else
   output = ' out of spec';
end
```

Test your function with the following
```
spec(5.6)
spec(5.45)
spec(5.2)
```

4. 
```
function output = metric_spec(x)
if x> = 5.3/2.54 & x< = 5.5/2.54
   output = ' in spec';
else
   output = ' out of spec';
end
```

Test your function with the following:
```
metric_spec(2)
metric_spec(2.2)
metric_spec(2.4)
```

5. 
```
function output = flight(x)
if x> = 0 & x< = 100
   output = 'first stage';
elseif x< = 170
   output = 'second stage';
elseif x<260
   output = 'third stage';
else
   output = 'free flight';
end
```

Test your function with the following:
```
flight(50)
flight(110)
flight(200)
flight(300)
```

## Practice Exercises 3

1. 
```
year = input('Enter the name of your year in school: ','s');
switch year
  case 'freshman'
    day = 'Monday';
  case 'sophomore'
    day = 'Tuesday';
  case 'junior'
    day = 'Wednesday';
  case 'senior'
    day = 'Thursday';
  otherwise
    day = 'I don''t know that year';
end
disp(['Your finals are on ',day])
```

2. 
```
disp('What year are you in school?')
disp('Use the menu box to make your selection ')
```

```
          choice = menu('Year in School','freshman','sophomore',
                        'junior', 'senior');
       switch choice
         case 1
           day = 'Monday';
         case 2
           day = 'Tuesday';
         case 3
           day = 'Wednesday';
         case 4
           day = 'Thursday';
         end
         disp(['Your finals are on ',day])
```

3. 
```
num = input('How many candy bars would you like? ');
switch num
  case 1
    bill = 0.75;
  case 2
    bill = 1.25;
  case 3
    bill = 1.65;
  otherwise
    bill = 1.65 + (num-3)*0.30;
end
fprintf('Your bill is %5.2f \n',bill)
```

## Practice Exercises 4

1. 
```
inches = 0:3:24;
for k = 1:length(inches)
  feet(k) = inches(k)/12;
end
table = [inches',feet']
```

2. 
```
x = [ 45,23,17,34,85,33];
count = 0;
for k = 1:length(x)
  if x(k)>30
      count = count+1;
  end
end
fprintf('There are %4.0f values greater than 30 \n',count)
```

3. 
```
num = length(find(x>30));
fprintf('There are %4.0f values greater than 30 \n',num)
```

4. 
```
total = 0;
for k = 1:length(x)
    total = total + x(k);
end
disp('The total is: ')
disp(total)
sum(x)
```

5. 
```
for k = 1:10
  x(k) = 1/k
end
```

6. 
```
for k = 1:10
  x(k)=(-1)^(k+1)/k
end
```

## Practice Exercises 5

1.
```
inches = 0:3:24;
k = 1;
while k<=length(inches)
    feet(k) = inches(k)/12;
    k = k+1;
end
disp(' Inches Feet');
fprintf(' %8.0f %8.2f \n',[inches;feet])
```

2.
```
x = [ 45,23,17,34,85,33];
k = 1;
count = 0;
while k< = length(x)
 if x(k)> = 30;
    count = count +1;
  end
    k=k+1;
end
fprintf('There are %4.0f values greater than 30 \n',count)
```

3.
```
count = length(find(x>30))
```

4.
```
k = 1;
total = 0;
while k< = length(x)
    total = total + x(k);
    k = k+1;
end
disp(total)
sum(x)
```

5.
```
k = 1;
while(k< = 10)
    x(k) = 1/k;
    k = k+1;
end
x
```

6.
```
k = 1;
while(k< = 10)
    x(k)=(-1)^(k+1)/k
    k = k+1;
end
x
```

# Special Characters, Commands, and Functions

| Special Characters | Matrix Definition |
| --- | --- |
| [ ] | forms matrices |
| ( ) | used in statements to group operations; used with a matrix name to identify specific elements |
| , | separates subscripts or matrix elements |
| ; | separates rows in a matrix definition; suppresses output when used in commands |
| : | used to generate matrices; indicates all rows or all columns |

| Special Characters | Operators Used in MATLAB Calculations (Scalar and Array) |
|---|---|
| = | assignment operator: assigns a value to a memory location; not the same as an equality |
| % | indicates a comment in an M-file |
| + | scalar and array addition |
| – | scalar and array subtraction |
| * | scalar multiplication and multiplication in matrix algebra |
| .* | array multiplication (dot multiply or dot star) |
| / | scalar division and division in matrix algebra |
| ./ | array division (dot divide or dot slash) |
| ^ | scalar exponentiation and matrix exponentiation in matrix algebra |
| .^ | array exponentiation (dot power or dot carat) |
| … | ellipsis: continued on the next line |
| [] | empty matrix |

| Commands | Formatting |
|---|---|
| format + | sets format to plus and minus signs only |
| format compact | sets format to compact form |
| format long | sets format to 14 decimal places |
| format long e | sets format to 14 exponential places |
| format long eng | sets format to engineering notation with 14 decimal places |
| format long g | allows MATLAB to select the best format (either fixed point or floating point), using 14 decimal digits |
| format loose | sets format back to default, noncompact form |
| format short | sets format back to default, 4 decimal places |
| format short e | sets format to 4 exponential places |
| format short eng | sets format to engineering notation with 4 decimal places |
| format short g | allows MATLAB to select the best format (either fixed point or floating point), using 4 decimal digits |
| format rat | sets format to rational (fractional) display |

| Commands | Basic Workspace Commands |
|---|---|
| **ans** | default variable name for results of MATLAB calculations |
| **clc** | clears command screen |
| **clear** | clears workspace |
| **diary** | saves both commands issued in the workspace and the results to a file |
| **exit** | terminates MATLAB |
| **help** | invokes help utility |
| **load** | loads matrices from a file |
| **quit** | terminates MATLAB |
| **save** | saves variables in a file |
| **who** | lists variables in memory |
| **whos** | lists variables and their sizes |
| **doc** | invokes the windowed **help** utility |
| **helpwin** | opens the windowed **help** function |
| **clock** | returns the time |
| **date** | returns the date |
| **intmax** | returns the largest possible integer number used in MATLAB |
| **intmin** | returns the smallest possible integer number used in MATLAB |
| **realmax** | returns the largest possible floating-point number used in MATLAB |
| **realmin** | returns the smallest possible floating-point number used in MATLAB |
| **ascii** | indicates that data should be saved in a standard ASCII format |
| **pause** | pauses the execution of a program until any key is hit |

| Special Functions | Functions with Special Meaning That Do Not Require an Input |
|---|---|
| **pi** | numeric approximation of the value of $\pi$ |
| **eps** | smallest difference recognized |
| **i** | imaginary number |
| **Inf** | infinity |
| **j** | imaginary number |
| **NaN** | not a number |

| Functions | Elementary Math |
|---|---|
| **abs** | computes the absolute value of a real number or the magnitude of a complex number |
| **exp** | computes the value of $e^x$ |
| **factor** | finds the prime factors |
| **factorial** | calculates the factorial |
| **gcd** | finds the greatest common denominator |
| **isprime** | determines whether a value is prime |
| **isreal** | determines whether a value is real or complex |
| **lcn** | finds the least common denominator |
| **log** | computes the natural logarithm, or log base $e(\log_e)$ |
| **log10** | computes the common logarithm, or log base $10(\log_{10})$ |
| **log2** | computes the log base $2(\log_2)$ |
| **nthroot** | finds the real $n$th root of the input matrix |
| **primes** | finds the prime numbers less than the input value |
| **prod** | multiplies the values in an array |
| **rats** | converts the input to a rational representation (i.e., a fraction) |
| **rem** | calculates the remainder in a division problem |
| **sign** | determines the sign (positive or negative) |
| **sqrt** | calculates the square root of a number |

| Functions | Trigonometry |
|---|---|
| **asin** | computes the inverse sine (arcsine) |
| **asind** | computes the inverse sine and reports the result in degrees |
| **asinh** | computes the inverse hyperbolic sine |
| **cos** | computes the cosine |
| **sin** | computes the sine, using radians as input |
| **sind** | computes the sine, using angles in degrees as input |
| **sinh** | computes the hyperbolic sine |
| **tan** | computes the tangent, using radians as input |

MATLAB includes all of the trigonometric functions; only those specifically discussed in the text are included here.

| Functions | Complex Numbers |
|-----------|-----------------|
| **abs** | computes the absolute value of a real number or the magnitude of a complex number |
| **angle** | computes the angle when complex numbers are represented with polar coordinates |
| **complex** | creates a complex number |
| **conj** | creates the complex conjugate of a complex number |
| **imag** | extracts the imaginary component of a complex number |
| **isreal** | determines whether a value is real or complex |
| **real** | extracts the real component of a complex number |

| Functions | Rounding |
|-----------|----------|
| **ceil** | rounds to the nearest integer toward positive infinity |
| **fix** | rounds to the nearest integer toward zero |
| **floor** | rounds to the nearest integer toward minus infinity |
| **round** | rounds to the nearest integer |

| Functions | Data Analysis |
|-----------|---------------|
| **cumprod** | computes the cumulative product of the values in an array |
| **cumsum** | computes the cumulative sum of the values in an array |
| **length** | determines the largest dimension of an array |
| **max** | finds the maximum value in an array and determines which element stores the maximum value |
| **mean** | computes the average of the elements in an array |
| **median** | finds the median of the elements in an array |
| **min** | finds the minimum value in an array and determines which element stores the minimum value |
| **mode** | finds the most common number in an array |
| **nchoosek** | finds the number of possible combinations when a subgroup of $k$ values is chosen from a group of $n$ values |
| **size** | determines the number of rows and columns in an array |
| **sort** | sorts the elements of a vector |
| **sortrows** | sorts the rows of a vector on the basis of the values in the first column |
| **prod** | multiplies the values in an array |
| **sum** | sums the values in an array |
| **std** | determines the standard deviation |
| **var** | computes the variance |

| Functions | Random Numbers |
|---|---|
| **rand** | calculates evenly distributed random numbers |
| **randn** | calculates normally distributed (Gaussian) random numbers |

| Functions | Matrix Formulation, Manipulation, and Analysis |
|---|---|
| **meshgrid** | maps vectors into a two-dimensional array |
| **diag** | extracts the diagonal from a matrix |
| **fliplr** | flips a matrix into its mirror image from left to right |
| **flipud** | flips a matrix vertically |
| **linspace** | linearly spaced vector function |
| **logspace** | logarithmically spaced vector function |
| **cross** | computes the cross product |
| **det** | computes the determinant of a matrix |
| **dot** | computes the dot product |
| **inv** | computes the inverse of a matrix |
| **rref** | uses the reduced row echelon format scheme for solving a series of linear equations |

| Functions | Two-Dimensional Plots |
|---|---|
| **bar** | generates a bar graph |
| **barh** | generates a horizontal bar graph |
| **contour** | generates a contour map of a three-dimensional surface |
| **comet** | draws an $x$–$y$ plot in a pseudo animation sequence |
| **fplot** | creates an $x$–$y$ plot on the basis of a function |
| **hist** | generates a histogram |
| **loglog** | generates an $x$–$y$ plot with both axes scaled logarithmically |
| **pcolor** | creates a pseudo color plot similar to a contour map |
| **pie** | generates a pie chart |
| **plot** | creates an $x$–$y$ plot |
| **plotyy** | creates a plot with two $y$-axes |
| **polar** | creates a polar plot |
| **semilogx** | generates an $x$–$y$ plot with the $x$-axis scaled logarithmically |
| **semilogy** | generates an $x$–$y$ plot with the y-axis scaled logarithmically |

| Functions | Three-Dimensional Plots |
|-----------|------------------------|
| **bar3** | generates a three-dimensional bar graph |
| **bar3h** | generates a horizontal three-dimensional bar graph |
| **comet3** | draws a three-dimensional line plot in a pseudo animation sequence |
| **mesh** | generates a mesh plot of a surface |
| **peaks** | creates a sample three-dimensional matrix used to demonstrate graphing functions |
| **pie3** | generates a three-dimensional pie chart |
| **plot3** | generates a three-dimensional line plot |
| **sphere** | sample function used to demonstrate graphing |
| **surf** | generates a surface plot |
| **surfc** | generates a combination surface and contour plot |

| Special Characters | Control of Plot Appearance |
|---|---|
| **Indicator** | **Line Type** |
| - | solid |
| : | dotted |
| -. | dash-dot |
| — | dashed |
| **Indicator** | **Point Type** |
| . | point |
| o | circle |
| x | x-mark |
| + | plus |
| * | star |
| s | square |
| d | diamond |
| v | triangle down |
| ^ | triangle up |
| < | triangle left |
| > | triangle right |
| p | pentagram |
| h | hexagram |
| **Indicator** | **Color** |
| b | blue |
| g | green |
| r | red |
| c | cyan |
| m | magenta |
| y | yellow |
| k | black |
| w | white |

| Functions | Figure Control and Annotation |
| --- | --- |
| axis | freezes the current axis scaling for subsequent plots or specifies the axis dimensions |
| axis equal | forces the same scale spacing for each axis |
| colormap | color scheme used in surface plots |
| figure | opens a new figure window |
| gtext | similar to text; the box is placed at a location determined interactively by the user by clicking in the figure window |
| grid | adds a grid to the current plot only |
| grid off | turns the grid off |
| grid on | adds a grid to the current and all subsequent graphs in the current figure |
| hold off | instructs MATLAB to erase figure contents before adding new information |
| hold on | instructs MATLAB not to erase figure contents before adding new information |
| legend | adds a legend to a graph |
| shading flat | shades a surface plot with one color per grid section |
| shading interp | shades a surface plot by interpolation |
| subplot | divides the graphics window up into sections available for plotting |
| text | adds a text box to a graph |
| title | adds a title to a plot |
| xlabel | adds a label to the $x$-axis |
| ylabel | adds a label to the $y$-axis |
| zlabel | adds a label to the z-axis |

| Functions | Figure Color Schemes |
|---|---|
| **autumn** | optional colormap used in surface plots |
| **bone** | optional colormap used in surface plots |
| **colorcube** | optional colormap used in surface plots |
| **cool** | optional colormap used in surface plots |
| **copper** | optional colormap used in surface plots |
| **flag** | optional colormap used in surface plots |
| **hot** | optional colormap used in surface plots |
| **hsv** | optional colormap used in surface plots |
| **jet** | default colormap used in surface plots |
| **pink** | optional colormap used in surface plots |
| **prism** | optional colormap used in surface plots |
| **spring** | optional colormap used in surface plots |
| **summer** | optional colormap used in surface plots |
| **white** | optional colormap used in surface plots |
| **winter** | optional colormap used in surface plots |

| Functions and Special Characters | Function Creation and Use |
|---|---|
| **addpath** | adds a directory to the MATLAB search path |
| **function** | identifies an M-file as a function |
| **nargin** | determines the number of input arguments in a function |
| **nargout** | determines the number of output arguments from a function |
| **pathtool** | opens the interactive path tool |
| **varargin** | indicates that a variable number of arguments may be input to a function |
| **@** | identifies a function handle, such as any of those used with in-line functions |
| **%** | comment |

| Special Characters | Format Control |
|---|---|
| ' | begins and ends a string |
| % | placeholder used in the **fprintf** command |
| **%f** | fixed-point, or decimal, notation |
| **%d** | decimal notation |
| **%e** | exponential notation |
| **%g** | either fixed-point or exponential notation |
| **%c** | character information |
| **%s** | string notation |
| **%%** | cell divider |
| **\n** | linefeed |
| **\r** | carriage return (similar to linefeed) |
| **\t** | tab |
| **\b** | backspace |

| Functions | Input/Output (I/O) Control |
|---|---|
| **disp** | displays a string or a matrix in the command window |
| **fprintf** | creates formatted output which can be sent to the command window or to a file |
| **ginput** | allows the user to pick values from a graph |
| **input** | allow the user to enter values |
| **pause** | pauses the program |
| **sprintf** | similar to **fprintf**<br>creates formatted output which is assigned to a variable name and stored as a character array |
| **uiimport** | launches the Import Wizard |
| **wavread** | reads wave files |
| **xlsread** | reads Excel files |
| **xlsimport** | imports Excel data files |
| **xlswrite** | exports data as an Excel file |
| **load** | loads matrices from a file |
| **save** | saves variables in a file |
| **celldisp** | displays the contents of a cell array |
| **imfinfo** | reads a standard graphics file and determines what type of data it contains |
| **imread** | reads a graphics file |
| **imwrite** | writes a graphics file |

| Functions | Comparison Operators |
|:---:|:---|
| < | less than |
| <= | less than or equal to |
| > | greater than |
| >= | greater than or equal to |
| == | equal to |
| ~= | not equal to |

| Special Characters | Logical Operators |
|:---:|:---|
| & | and |
| \| | or |
| ~ | not |
| **xor** | exclusive or |

| Functions | Control Structures |
|:---|:---|
| **break** | causes the execution of a loop to be terminated |
| **case** | sorts responses |
| **continue** | terminates the current pass through a loop, but proceeds to the next pass |
| **else** | defines the path if the result of an **if** statement is false |
| **elseif** | defines the path if the result of an **if** statement is false, and specifies a new logical test |
| **end** | identifies the end of a control structure |
| **for** | generates a loop structure |
| **if** | checks a condition resulting in either true or false |
| **menu** | creates a menu to use as an input vehicle |
| **otherwise** | part of the case selection structure |
| **switch** | part of the case selection structure |
| **while** | generates a loop structure |

| Functions | Logical Functions |
|:---|:---|
| **all** | checks to see if a criterion is met by all the elements in an array |
| **any** | checks to see if a criterion is met by any of the elements in an array |
| **find** | determines which elements in a matrix meet the input criterion |
| **isprime** | determines whether a value is prime |
| **isreal** | determines whether a value is real or complex |

| Functions | Timing |
|---|---|
| clock | determines the current time on the CPU clock |
| etime | finds elapsed time |
| tic | starts a timing sequence |
| toc | stops a timing sequence |
| date | returns the date |

| Functions | Special Matrices |
|---|---|
| eye | generates an identity matrix |
| magic | creates a "magic" matrix |
| ones | creates a matrix containing all ones |
| rosser | Eigenvalue test matrix |
| pascal | creates a Pascal matrix |
| zeros | creates a matrix containing all zeros |
| gallery | contains example matrices |

| Special Characters | Data Types |
|---|---|
| { } | cell array constructor |
| „ | string data (character information) |
| abc | character array |
| ⊞ | numeric array |
| ▣ | symbolic array |
| ☑ | logical array |
| ▨ | sparse array |
| {} | cell array |
| ⊞ | structure array |

| Functions | Data Type Manipulation |
|---|---|
| **celldisp** | displays the contents of a cell array |
| **cellplot** | creates a graphical representation of a cell array |
| **char** | creates a padded character array |
| **double** | changes an array to a double-precision array |
| **int16** | 16-bit signed integer |
| **int32** | 32-bit signed integer |
| **int64** | 64-bit signed integer |
| **int8** | 8-bit signed integer |
| **num2str** | converts a numeric array to a character array |
| **single** | changes an array to a single-precision array |
| **sparse** | converts a full-format matrix to a sparse-format matrix |
| **str2num** | converts a character array to a numeric array |
| **uint16** | 16-bit unsigned integer |
| **uint32** | 32-bit unsigned integer |
| **uint64** | 64-bit unsigned integer |
| **uint8** | 8-bit unsigned integer |

| Functions | Manipulation of Symbolic Expressions |
|-----------|--------------------------------------|
| **collect** | collects like terms |
| **diff** | finds the symbolic derivative of a symbolic expression |
| **dsolve** | differential equation solver |
| **expand** | expands an expression or equation |
| **factor** | factors an expression or equation |
| **findsym** | indentifies symbolic variables |
| **int** | finds the symbolic integral of a symbolic expression |
| **numden** | extracts the numerator and denominator from an expression or an equation |
| **poly2sym** | converts a vector to a symbolic polynomial |
| **simple** | tries and reports all the simplification functions, and selects the shortest answer |
| **simplify** | simplifies using Maple's built-in simplification rules |
| **solve** | solves a symbolic expression or equation |
| **subs** | substitutes into a symbolic expression or equation |
| **sym** | creates a symbolic variable, expression, or equation |
| **sym2poly** | converts a symbolic polynomial to a vector |
| **syms** | creates symbolic variables |

| Functions | Symbolic Plotting |
|-----------|-------------------|
| **ezcontour** | creates a contour plot |
| **ezcontourf** | creates a filled contour plot |
| **ezmesh** | creates a mesh plot from a symbolic expression |
| **ezmeshc** | plots both a mesh and contour plot created from a symbolic expression |
| **ezplot** | creates an $x$–$y$ plot of a symbolic expression |
| **ezplot3** | creates a three-dimensional line plot |
| **ezpolar** | creates a plot in polar coordinates |
| **ezsurf** | creates a surface plot from a symbolic expression |
| **ezsurfc** | plots both a mesh and contour plot created from a symbolic expression |

| Functions | Numerical Techniques |
|---|---|
| **cftool** | opens the curve-fitting graphical user interface |
| **diff** | computes the differences between adjacent values in an array if the input is an array; finds the symbolic derivative if the input is a symbolic expression |
| **fminbnd** | a function function that accepts a function handle or function definition as input and numerically finds the function minimum between two bounds |
| **fzero** | a function function that accepts a function handle or function definition as input and finds the zero point nearest a specified value |
| **interp1** | approximates intermediate data, using either the default linear interpolation technique or a specified higher order approach |
| **interp2** | two-dimensional interpolation function |
| **interp3** | three-dimensional interpolation function |
| **interpn** | multidimensional interpolation function |
| **ode45** | ordinary differential equation solver |
| **ode23** | ordinary differential equation solver |
| **ode113** | ordinary differential equation solver |
| **ode15s** | ordinary differential equation solver |
| **ode23s** | ordinary differential equation solver |
| **ode23t** | ordinary differential equation solver |
| **ode23tb** | ordinary differential equation solver |
| **ode15i** | ordinary differential equation solver |
| **polyfit** | computes the coefficients of a least-squares polynomial |
| **polyval** | evaluates a polynomial at a specified value of $x$ |
| **quad** | computes the integral under a curve (Simpson) |
| **quadl** | computes the integral under a curve (Lobatto) |

| Functions | Sample Data Sets and Images |
|---|---|
| **cape** | sample MATLAB image file of a cape |
| **clown** | sample MATLAB image file of a clown |
| **detail** | sample MATLAB image file of a section of a Dürer wood carving |
| **durer** | sample MATLAB image file of a Dürer wood carving |
| **earth** | sample MATLAB image file of the earth |
| **flujet** | sample MATLAB image file showing fluid behavior |
| **gatlin** | sample MATLAB image file of a photograph |
| **mandrill** | sample MATLAB image file of a mandrill |
| **mri** | sample MRI data set |
| **peaks** | creates a sample plot |
| **spine** | sample MATLAB image file of a spine X-ray |
| **wind** | sample MATLAB data file of wind-velocity information |
| **sphere** | sample function used to demonstrate graphing |
| **census** | a built-in data set used to demonstrate numerical techniques |
| **handel** | a built-in data set used to demonstrate the sound function |

| Functions | Advanced Visualization |
|---|---|
| **alpha** | sets the transparency of the current plot object |
| **camlight** | turns the camera light on |
| **coneplot** | creates a plot with markers indicating the direction of input vectors |
| **contourslice** | creates a contour plot from a slice of data |
| **drawnow** | forces MATLAB to draw a plot immediately |
| **gca** | gets current axis handle |
| **gcf** | gets current figure handle |
| **get** | returns the properties of a specified object |
| **getframe** | gets the current figure and saves it as a movie frame in a structure array |
| **image** | creates a two-dimensional image |
| **imagesc** | creates a two-dimensional image by scaling the data |
| **imfinfo** | reads a standard graphics file and determines what type of data it contains |
| **imread** | reads a graphics file |
| **imwrite** | writes a graphics file |
| **isosurface** | creates surface connecting volume data of the same magnitude |
| **movie** | plays a movie stored as a MATLAB structure array |
| **set** | establishes the properties assigned to a specified object |
| **shading** | determines the shading technique used in surface plots and pseudo color plots |

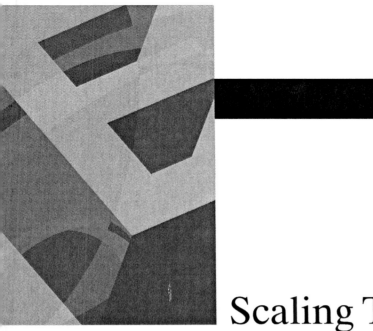

# Scaling Techniques

Plotting data using different scaling techniques is a useful way to try to determine how $y$-values change with $x$. This approach is illustrated in the following sections.

## LINEAR RELATIONSHIPS

If $x$ and $y$ are related by a linear relationship, a standard $x$–$y$ plot will be a straight line. Thus for

$$y = ax + b$$

an $x$–$y$ plot is a straight line with slope $a$ and $y$-intercept $b$.

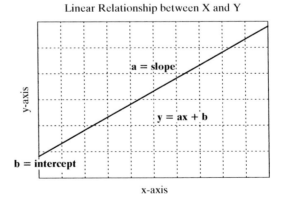

## LOGARITHMIC RELATIONSHIP

If $x$ and $y$ are related logarithmically

$$y = a \log_{10}(x) + b$$

a standard plot on an evenly spaced grid is curved. However, a plot scaled evenly on the $y$-axis but logarithmically on the $x$-axis is a straight line of slope $a$. The $y$-intercept doesn't exist, since $\log_{10}(0)$ is undefined. However when $x = 1$, the value of $\log_{10}(1)$ is zero and $y$ is equal to $b$.

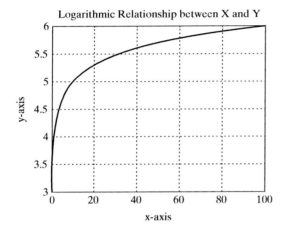

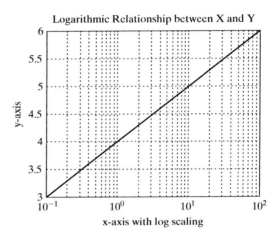

## EXPONENTIAL RELATIONSHIP

When $x$ and $y$ are related by an exponential relationship such as

$$y = b * a^x$$

a plot of $\log_{10}(y)$ vs. $x$ gives a straight line because

$$\log_{10}(y) = \log_{10}(a) * x + \log_{10}(b)$$

In this case the slope of the plot is $\log_{10}(a)$.

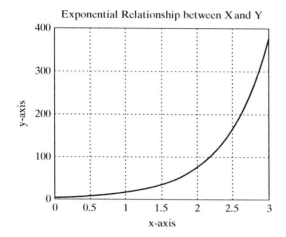

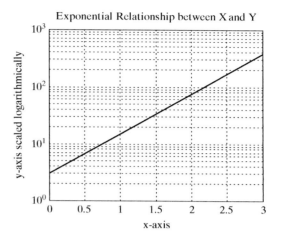

## POWER RELATIONSHIP

Finally if $x$ and $y$ are related by a power relationship such as

$$y = bx^a$$

a plot scaled logarithmically on both axes produces a straight line with a slope of $a$. When $x$ is equal to 1, the $\log_{10}(1)$ is zero, and the value of $\log_{10}(y)$ is $\log_{10}(b)$.

$$\log_{10}(y) = a * \log_{10}(x) + \log_{10}(b)$$

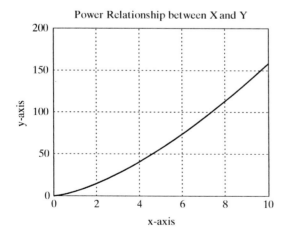

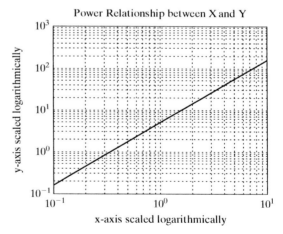

# Index